Woman of Nobility

Woman of Nobility

The Story of Sophronia Emeline Cobb Dryer

NINA BISSETT

RESOURCE *Publications* • Eugene, Oregon

WOMAN OF NOBILITY
The Story of Sophronia Emeline Cobb Dryer

Copyright © 2016 Nina Bissett. All rights reserved. Except for brief quotations in critical publications or reviews, no part of this book may be reproduced in any manner without prior written permission from the publisher. Write: Permissions, Wipf and Stock Publishers, 199 W. 8th Ave., Suite 3, Eugene, OR 97401.

Resource Publications
An Imprint of Wipf and Stock Publishers
199 W. 8th Ave., Suite 3
Eugene, OR 97401

www.wipfandstock.com

PAPERBACK ISBN: 978-1-4982-8364-9
HARDCOVER ISBN: 978-1-4982-8366-3

Manufactured in the U.S.A.

All Scripture quotations, unless otherwise indicated, are taken from the King James Version (public domain). Scriptures marked AMP are from the Amplified Version, Copyright @ 1955, 1958, 1962, 1964, 1965, 1987 by the Lockman Foundation; GWT from God's Word Translation, Copyright @ 1995 by God's Word to the Nations; NIV from the New International Version, Copyright @ 1973, 1978, 1984, 2011 by Biblica, Inc.; WEY from the Weymouth New Testament in Modern Speech Copyright @ 1913; NKJV from the New King James Version, Copyright @ 1982 by Thomas Nelson, Inc.; MSG from The Message, Copyright @1993, 1994, 1995, 1996, 2000, 2001, 2002 by Eugene H. Peterson.

Reprinted by permission from the Wisconsin Historical Society, 816 State Street, Madison, Wisconsin; *Emma Dryer* circa 1895–1901 (Figure 14, Image ID 121936) and *Emma Dryer* circa 1922 (Figure 15, Image ID 121837).

Reprinted by permission from The Newberry Library, 1321 W. Arcade Place, Chicago: Newberry Call Number D93.16; *Bible Workers, Miss Emma Dryer* (Figure 12) and *Bible Workers Home of the Chicago Bible Society* (Figure 13).

Reprinted with permission and courtesy of The Moody Bible Institute Archives, 820 N. LaSalle Blvd, Chicago; archival photo of *Emma Dryer* circa 1870 (Figure 11).

Reprinted by permission from Woodward Memorial Library, 7 Wolcott Street, LeRoy, New York; *Ingham University* web site photo (Figure 7).

Reprinted by permission from the Victor Historical Society, Town of Victor, New York Archives; *Victor Schoolhouse* 1842 (Figure 2) and *Fishers Cobblestone Pump House* 1845 (Figure 3).

Public Domain Pictures: *Union School in Palmyra, New York* (Figure 6) from Palmyra County, New York, 33; *Emma Dryer as Teacher and Preceptress* (Figure 9) and *ISNU The Main Building, Spring 1860* (Figure 10) from *Grandest of Enterprises*, 50–51 picture inserts; *Knoxville Female University* (Figure 8), Chapman, 587.

All other pictures are the author's original photographs.

This book is dedicated to a brave and noble woman of God—Emma Dryer—and to all the noble Christian men and women throughout the centuries who have spread the good news of the gospel, who have pioneered and maintained the value of Christian education, and who have held steadfast to the eternal truth of God's Word.

. . . until Christ returns . . .

Contents

List of Illustrations | xi
Acknowledgments | xiii
List of Abbreviations | xv
Introduction | xvii

1 Emma's Birth on Missionary Terrain, 1835 | 1
    Housatonic Indian Missionary Efforts in Stockbridge, Massachusetts · 1
    Seneca Indian Missionary Soil of Victor, New York · 5

2 Emma's Early Years in New York, 1838–58 | 7
    Community Life in Victor with Future Implications · 7
    Church Life in Victor as a Prelude to Missions · 9
    Schooling in Victor and Beyond · 14
    Palmyra's Union School: Circa 1850–54 · 15
    Victor Park School District 10: 1854–55 · 16
    Allen Female Seminary: 1855–56 · 17
    Ingham University: 1856–58 · 25

3 Education Positions, 1858–70 | 28
    Ingham University: 1858–60 · 28
    Knoxville Ewing Female University: 1860–64 · 29
    Illinois State Normal University: 1864–70 · 32
    Prestigious Faculty Position · 35
    ISNU Model School and Curriculum Development · 37
    Involvement in Student Life · 41
    Campus Housing · 42
    Campus Societies and Activities · 44
    Classroom and Campus Discipline · 44
    Religion and Politics · 46
    Typhoid Fever and Resignation · 47

Contents

4 Chicago Calling, 1870–73 | 49
    Divine Connection: Introduction to D. L. Moody · 51
    Seeking Guidance · 52
    Illinois Street Church: Reverend William J. Erdman and Premillennialism · 53
    Chicago Fire · 55
    Life Changing Event · 56
    Relief Work and Ministry Sacrifices · 58
    Chicago Avenue Church · 60
    Chicago Activities 1871–73 · 61
    Chicago Relief and Aide Society · 61
    Women's Auxiliary of the YMCA · 63
    Swedish School and Bible Studies · 64

5 Emma's Friendships and Acquaintances | 66
    Colonel George and Sarah Clarke: Co-Founders of Pacific Garden Mission · 66
    The Cyrus McCormick Family: McCormick Harvesting Machine Company · 68
    Glowing Flames of Friendship · 71
    Training in Business Affairs · 74
    Common Missionary Ventures · 75
    McCormick Family Association with Mr. Moody · 77
    Closing Friendship · 80
    Josiah and Lucy Rider Meyer: Co-Founders of the Chicago Training School
       for City, Home and Foreign Missions · 82
    Temperance and Holiness Associations · 82
    D. L. Moody Influence · 84
    Chicago Training School · 85
    Changing Roles of Evangelical Women · 88

6 Emma and Moody: Complementary Leadership Roles | 91
    Moody Family Support and Ties · 91
    Mutual Scripture Emphasis and Bible Teaching Leadership Roles · 96
    Leadership Roles in Prayer · 98
    Leadership Likenesses and Differences By Design · 99
    Visionary Leaders · 99
    Servant Leader Assessment · 102
    Organizational Skills · 104
    Listening and Communication Skills · 107
    Leadership Burnout · 109
    Leaders in Evangelism and Education · 111
    Education Background and Learning Styles · 113
    Educational Compensation and Impulsivity · 117
    Outlook on Education · 119
    Leaders Void of Prejudice and Bias · 121
    Persuasive Leaders · 124
    Leaders of Morality, Character, and Integrity · 126
    Leaders in Doctrinal Issues · 129
    Stewardship Leaders · 131

Contents

7   Bible Work of Chicago, 1873–86 | 134
    Initiation of a Vision · 134
    Specific Objectives and Activities of the Bible Work · 136
    Structure and Operation of the Bible Training School · 143
    Citywide Locations · 145
    Financial and Personal Support · 147
    Spafford Support · 151
    Support from Charles Blanchard · 153
    Connection with Evangelistic Meetings and Conferences · 158
    May Institute 1883–89 · 161
    Haymarket Riot: May 4, 1886 · 167
    Bible Work Testimonies · 168
    John L. Morrison · 169
    Reverend J. C. Crawford · 169
    Mr. Fredrickson and Others · 170

8   Emma's Spiritual Walk and Inspirations | 172
    Power of the Holy Spirit · 173
    Divine Healing · 175
    Inspiration of Andrew Bonar 1810–92: Free Church of Scotland · 178
    Inspiration of George Müller 1805–98: Evangelist and Missionary to Orphans · 178
    Inspiration of Andrew Murray 1828–1917: Educator and South African Minister · 180
    Inspiration of Hudson Taylor 1832–1905: Founder of China Inland Mission · 181
    Inspiration of Henry Drummond 1851–97: Scottish Professor and Author · 183

9   Chicago Evangelization Society and Bible Institute, 1885–89 | 186
    The $250,000 Challenge of 1885 · 188
    Turbulent Years 1885 to 1889 · 190
    Board Tensions and Expectations 1886 · 192
    Divergence in Vision and Objectives · 194
    Chicago Evangelization Society and Bible Work Merger 1887 · 196
    Board Organization Conflict 1887 · 199
    Women's Bible Institute and May Institute of 1888 · 206
    Harvey Dispute 1887–88 · 208
    Bouton Resignation 1888 · 210
    Further Internal Board Conflict 1888 · 212
    Board and Leadership Struggles and Conflict Resolution · 222
    Time of Transition 1889 · 224
    Sarah B. Capron and Reuben Archer Torrey · 229

10   Chicago Bible Society and Retirement, 1889–1925 | 232
    Expanded Mission Opportunities · 232
    Chicago Bible Society Affiliation · 234
    Retirement · 239
    Anita McCormick Blaine Correspondence · 241

CONTENTS

11 With Christ Our Soon Coming Lord, 1925 Throughout Eternity | 245

    Emma's Homecoming · 246

    Memorial Service · 249

    Hymns and Prayers: Reverend E. Augusta Shulls and Miss Maby · 249

    Extracts from Emma's Paper or Journal by Dr. Gray · 250

    Written Tributes from Friends · 250

    Charles Blanchard's Message and Prayer · 251

    Emma's Legacy as a Great and Noble Bible Teacher · 252

    Emma's Bible Studies · 254

    Study of Christ's Second Coming · 254

    Study of the Family and Women in the Church · 256

    Study of Jewish Roots · 257

    Study of Prayer and Faith · 258

    Study of the Glory of God and His Image · 259

    Bible Inserts · 260

    A Noble Poetic Tale That Is Told · 261

Bibliography | 265

Index | 275

Illustrations

Figure 01: 1925 Wheaton Cemetery Grave Marker for Emma Dryer, April 16, 1925 | xviii

Figure 02: Victor, NY, 1842 Cobblestone School House, Victor, New York | 6

Figure 03: Fishers Cobblestone Pump House 1845, Victor, New York | 8

Figure 04: Victor First Presbyterian Church built in 1838; a Western New York Landmark | 11

Figure 05: Victor Methodist Church built in 1832 | 13

Figure 06: Union School in Palmyra, New York | 15

Figure 07: Ingham University in LeRoy, New York | 25

Figure 08: Knoxville Female University in Knoxville, Illinois | 29

Figure 09: Emma Dryer as Teacher and Preceptress at ISNU 1863–70 | 32

Figure 10: Illinois State Normal University, *The Main Building*, Spring of 1860 | 33

Figure 11: Emma Dryer, Chicago after 1870 | 49

Figure 12: Emma Dryer and Bible Workers, Chicago Bible Society, 1899 | 235

Figure 13: Bible Workers Home, 1899 | 238

Figure 14: Emma Dryer, CBS Retirement Picture, Circa 1895–1901 | 239

Figure 15: Emma Dryer, 1922 in her Garden at 4124 West Jackson Street Residence | 245

Figure 16: Emma Dryer's Grave Marker in Victor, New York | 248

Figure 17: Emma Dryer's Bible at Moody Bible Institute Archives | 253

Figure 18: Emma Dryer's Engraved Bible at Moody Bible Institute Archives | 253

Acknowledgments

I GRATEFULLY ACKNOWLEDGE THE initial and primary encouragement of Dr. Louis Gallien and Dr. Lyle Dorsett who set me on the pathway to exploring the life of Emma Dryer. And special thanks to Dr. Jerry Root from Wheaton College who perceived and prayed God's destiny for me as a writer.

During my journey with this nineteenth and early twentieth century woman, five historical archival institutions contributed valuable information that could not have been found elsewhere: Moody Bible Institute Archives (MBI), the Wisconsin Historical Society (WHS), the Wheaton College/Billy Graham Archives (BGA), the Newberry Library, and the Victor Historical Society (VHS). The archival staff from each of these valuable institutions unfailingly extended a generous welcome and assistance. Special thanks to MBI Archival Assistants Nikki Tochalauski and Corie Zylstra; WHS Reference Archivist Harry Miller and McCormick Collection Archivist Lee Grady along with Image Reproduction and Licensing Manager Lisa Marine and Sheri Dolfen; BGC Archive Director Robert Shuster; and The Newberry Library Digital Imaging Services Manager John Powell, Digitization Technician Katie McMahon and Lauren VanNest. Babette Huber and Bonnie Waters from the VHS also pieced together some important parts of Emma Dryer's life by contributing a newspaper obituary, pictures of Emma's parents' head markers, Emma's Victor grave marker, pictures of Emma's cobblestone school house, and a photo of the Victor landmark pump house.

This exploration of Emma's life led to the contribution of others in unexpected ways. When I discovered at the Billy Graham Center Archives a stenographer's notebook holding a non-transcribed shorthand record of Emma's Memorial Service in 1925, Diana Zielinski faithfully deciphered the hand-written pages. In addition, Diana ventured with me to downtown Chicago to interview Allan Winters at the Chicago Bible Society and to visit the Newberry Library and Pacific Garden Mission. After visiting the Wisconsin Historical Society I labored to interpret Emma Dryer's unique handwriting on multiple pages of letters she had written. Pam Hapner, a teacher of young students, patiently assisted me. In addition, with her hair fashioning experience, Pam contributed valuable information regarding Emma's nineteenth and early twentieth-century hairstyles. When visiting MBI, a nurse friend and Salvation Army missionary, Diana Winters, spent hours copying documents from the Chicago Evangelization Society and the Emma Dryer Biographical Files. Another teacher, Terry Scudamore, made the lengthy trip with me to Madison, Wisconsin, to the Historical Society where she patiently copied McCormick financial records and letters from Emma Dryer written to Anita McCormick Blaine. And as if that was not enough, when she ventured through Victor, New York, she took pictures of the two landmark churches that played an integral part of Emma's spiritual life. I acknowledge all these friends, family, and more who spent long hours listening as I shared each new amazing and unexpected discovery in Emma Dryer's life.

And lastly, I acknowledge the noble life of Emma Dryer herself used by the Lord Jesus to bring about this book for his honor . . . *Until His Soon Coming Return.*

Abbreviations

ABS	American Bible Society
BGC	Billy Graham Center
CAC	Chicago Avenue Church
CBS	Chicago Bible Society
CES	Chicago Evangelization Society
CIM	China Inland Mission
CRAS	Chicago Relief and Aid Society
CTS	Chicago Training School
DISC	Dominance/Influence/Steadiness/Conscientiousness
EQ	Emotional Intelligence
ISNU	Illinois State Normal University
JISHS	Journal of the Illinois State Historical Society
JVL	Journal of Virtues and Leadership
MBI	Moody Bible Institute
PGM	Pacific Garden Mission
VHS	Victor Historical Society
WCTU	Woman's Christian Temperance Union
WHS	Wisconsin Historical Society
YMCA	Young Men's Christian Association
YWCA	Young Women's Christian Association

Introduction

"The noble make noble plans, and by noble deeds they stand."

~ISAIAH 32:8 NIV~

SEVERAL HIGHLY RESPECTED COLLEGIATE scholars presented to me the challenge of compiling the life narrative of a quite obscure woman named Emeline Dryer (1835–1925). Due to the persistent yet often unrecognized impact of her life on the well-known nineteenth-century evangelist Dwight Lyman Moody (1837–99), they concluded that she should have a book of her own. They believed that her story would most likely be limited based on an apparent lack of documentation. *Emma*, as she was prominently known, lost her library and other possessions in the 1871 Chicago Fire. She personally decided to eliminate her journals in the early 1900s and retained only a few personal items during the ending chapter of her life. However, just as increments of one's life can still be pieced together based on documentation of concurrent and extraneous events, so also relevant information regarding Emma's life was obtained by following the time line of the era during which she lived.

As with Emma Dryer, the light of one's faith is interrupted when earthly fellowship dissipates through death (1 John 1:6); however, the lives and incidents of even great and *noble* Bible men and women of faith continue, though dead, still to speak through the monuments and memories left behind (Hebrews 11:4). Emma's greatest monument to faith contained her vision and *noble plans* for a Bible training school. Her *noble* and *self-sacrificing deeds* continue to *stand* as the faithful precursor to Moody Bible Institute in Chicago, Illinois—a living legacy for Emma Dryer and Dwight L. Moody that honorably speaks even to this day.

While researching Emma's life, minor yet significant data would unexpectedly emerge. This information, with intertwining meaningful connections, instrumentally montaged her story. I discovered reminiscent experiences that drew me into a vicarious understanding of her life which otherwise could have been by-passed without notice and with untold insight. For instance, I first chanced upon *Emma* while conducting research at Wheaton College in Wheaton, Illinois. After exploring the lives of that institution's first presidents, Jonathan Blanchard (1811–92) and his son Charles Blanchard (1848–1925), my investigation led to Wheaton Cemetery where the Blanchard family members were laid to rest. I experienced an epiphany moment when standing at both men's grave sites. I pondered the greatness of these remarkable men who were used of God to establish a highly respectable Christian college in the Midwest which continues to blaze the trail for Christ and His Kingdom.

While reminiscing, I noticed a smaller head stone inconspicuously placed at an angle behind Charles's family marker. Assuming that it could belong to a younger family relative, I examined the grave site more closely and found to my delight that it belonged to Emma Dryer. Engraved on her head stone were these words: *IS NOW WITH CHRIST OUR SOON COMING LORD*. I knew of her mutual friendship with Charles Blanchard and her impact on his theological views regarding the doctrine of premillennialism. However, I remained puzzled as to why she had been laid to rest at Wheaton Cemetery rather than with her deceased adoptive parents, John Milton and Lucinda Dryer, in Victor, New York. When I reported my interest and findings to Dr. Louis Gallien and Dr. Lyle Dorsett, both former professors at Wheaton College, they challenged me to pursue the course of her life—an act of honor on her behalf. Thus, the idea and longing to explore her life began.

As I journeyed into the heart and mind of Emma Dryer, I admit that my own personal education background and experiences closely emulated her own and at times perhaps clouded a complete objectivity. However, it also lent credence due to comparable life situations mixed with a companion understanding. Emma's educational background paralleled that of my own from her beginning career in education as a teacher to that of a school principal—or the nineteenth-century term *preceptress*—accompanied by the challenge of church mission and ministry programs, and non-profit boards with committee dynamics. Likewise, Emma's Presbyterian, Congregational,

Introduction

Methodist, and Baptist backgrounds resembled my own ecumenical journey and echoed her passion for teaching young people in the academic realm while spiritually guiding students in their relationship with Jesus Christ.

Through the telling of Emma's story many readers, including kindred educators, school administrators, non-profit organizations, historians, ministers, and mission-focused individuals will have opportunity to vicariously experience and champion her life. Furthermore, the coinciding lives of those from past decades, including D. L. Moody,—who rose above the limitations and cultural expectations of church and society—will be heralded as predecessors and incumbents of a *noble* and virtuous Proverbs 31 woman who dedicated her life to serve and honor Christ until His ultimate return.

"Reward her for what she has done and let her achievements praise her . . . "
~Proverbs 31:31 GWT~

1

Emma's Birth on Missionary Terrain, 1835

"I hope that we may, within a few years, see our city filled with live missions, doing a great work for Christ and hastening the Coming of His dear Kingdom."

~1873 WRITTEN IN CHICAGO BY EMMA DRYER~

"We all, have long observed with gratitude to God the consecrated thoroughness by which, under her direction, the Bible Work has been conducted in our city; and we rejoice that its influence has extended to foreign missionary fields."

~1902 TRIBUTE TO EMMA DRYER FROM THE CHICAGO BIBLE SOCIETY~

Housatonic Indian Missionary Efforts in Stockbridge, Massachusetts

APPROXIMATELY ONE HUNDRED YEARS before Sophronia Emeline ("Emma") Cobb Dryer's birth in Stockbridge, Massachusetts, well-known missionaries such as David Brainerd (1718–47) relentlessly labored among the Indians in the Berkshire Hills on the fertile missionary soil where Emma was destined to be born. Examining the efforts of these early Stockbridge missionaries helps us to understand more clearly the missionary roots and the divine intervention extended on behalf of this honorable and self-sacrificing nineteenth-century woman of nobility.

At the age of twenty-one David Brainerd experienced a spiritual renewal in which he described being swallowed up with unspeakable joy while beholding the glory of the Divine Being: "As I was walking in a dark thick grove, unspeakable glory seemed to open to the view and apprehension of my soul . . . so captivated and delighted with the excellency, loveliness, greatness, and other perfections of God."[1] Following this experience, Brainerd, as a student at Yale College, witnessed the spiritual awakening fanned

---

1. Brainerd and Edwards, *The Life and Diary*, 12.

by the preaching of George Whitefield and Jonathan Edwards. His heart throbbed for the gospel of Jesus Christ to be spread. Despite his shattered and unfulfilled dream of becoming a minister, this longing compelled him, as it did a century later with Emma Dryer, to sacrifice health and material well-being for the spiritual security of the lost.

From 1743 to 1744 David Brainerd received the opportunity to preach and to learn the Indian language from missionary John Sergeant (1710–49). In 1734 Mr. Sergeant accepted the commission offered him by the New England Company to serve among the Housatonic or Stockbridge Indians. In the early 1700s the Mohawks had driven them out of the Hudson River Valley to Massachusetts and Connecticut. These Indians, who lived in Stockbridge and neighboring Sheffield, originated from the Mohican tribes—competing rivals of the Mohawks.[2] From this appointed location John Sergeant, a Congregational minister and Yale graduate, spent fourteen years at Stockbridge preaching and translating parts of the Bible.

Sergeant successfully witnessed the baptisms of 129 Native American Indians. He also launched a mission school and church with approval from Stockbridge Chiefs Konkapot and Umpachene. Two young Indian boys assisted Sergeant by teaching him their Indian dialect. This served as a basis for further training of the American-Indian children in the English language. Within the next century Emma would appreciate, as these early missionaries did, the enduring value of education for effectively instructing others to carry on the work of spreading the gospel of Jesus Christ.

Unquestionably, Sergeant's training contributed to David Brainerd's legendary success as a missionary to the Indians. They kindly received Brainerd and seriously attended to his words. Theologian and revivalist Jonathan Edwards (1703–58) heard of Brainerd's accomplishments and greatly admired him. He invited this young missionary to stay at his home during Brainerd's last stages of apparent tuberculosis. Edwards received permission to publish a large part of Brainerd's diaries detailing his work among the Indian tribes. This book, entitled *The Life and Diary of David Brainerd*, describes his grueling horseback travels to Stockbridge during harsh winters accompanied by his meditations and an intense personal scrutiny of his soul.

Close to a hundred years before Emma's birth on this missionary terrain, Brainerd set out on March 31, 1743, to visit John Sergeant at Stockbridge. Jonathan Edwards documented Brainerd's sense of inadequacy mixed with missionary fervor: "He was . . . dejected and very disconsolate, through the main of his journey from New Jersey to Stockbridge . . . On Saturday and [on the] Lord's day, his melancholy again prevailed; he complained of his ignorance, stupidity, and senselessness; while yet he seems to have spent the time with the utmost diligence, in study, in prayer, in instructing and counseling the Indians."[3]

On one trip into the woods in June of 1743 Brainerd found himself completely disoriented. Nevertheless, divinely shielded from fear, he peacefully camped in the

---

2. Drede, "Who Are the Mohican Indians?" para. 3.
3. Brainerd and Edwards, *The Life and Diary*, 59, 63.

outdoors. He continued his journey the next day to Stockbridge. While there, he preached and received inspiration from the Lord that he had not felt since beginning his work among the Indians. He journaled on December 5, 1743: "Rode to Stockbridge. Was almost outdone with the extreme cold. Had some refreshing meditations by the way; but was barren, wandering, and lifeless, much of the day. Thus my days roll away, with but little done for God; and this is my burden."[4] Heading into the winter months Brainerd continued his journeys to Stockbridge. He experienced weariness after undue exposure to the elements and at one point fell into a river. Following such an experience, he lamented that for him the day and evening contained little awareness of divine and heavenly things.

Edwards captured yet another one of Brainerd's Stockbridge undertakings dated January 16, 1744: "On Monday he rode down to Stockbridge, when he was distressed with the extreme cold; but notwithstanding, his mind was in a devout and solemn frame in his journey. The four next days he was very ill . . . yet he spent the time in a solemn manner."[5] In contrast, Emma would never physically suffer in her missionary endeavors to the extreme of David Brainerd. However, in her full time mission outreach, which began at the time of the 1871 Chicago Fire, she would likewise experience discouragement as she faced the mental and physical challenges of educating and ministering to prostitutes, prisoners, the sick, and the homeless.

Ultimately, after Brainerd's death in 1747 and Sergeant's death in 1749, Jonathan Edwards continued the mission effort to the Housatonic Indians while pastoring a church in Stockbridge. He found these Indians amiable and obliging in their support of the colonists during the French and Indian Wars (1754–63). Moreover, in the following years they opposed the British during the Revolutionary War (1775–83). For their heroism they received commendation from George Washington in 1778 after a tremendous loss of warriors against a British ambush.[6]

On this rich missionary soil, Emma was born on Wednesday, January 28, 1835, amid the rolling Berkshire Hills of West Stockbridge, Massachusetts.[7] Emma's English and Dutch ancestors from the Cobb side of her family were descendants of the first pilgrims who landed at Plymouth Rock on the Mayflower in 1620.[8] Emma often boasted

---

4. Ibid., 83.

5. Ibid., 88.

6. Miles, "Stockbridge Mohican," para. 4.

7. Town of Victor, New York, Archives, 8 May 1925, *Victor Herald* Newspaper Obituary. The *Victor Herald* newspaper obituary column reported: "Sophronia Emeline Cobb, daughter of Hiram and Emeline (Wilson) Cobb, was born at West Stockbridge, Mass., January 28, 1835." This writer concurs with home town information regarding Emma's birth over the records of West Stockbridge, Massachusetts, in which the compilers explain that errors may occur. Their records were obtained through church entries, Bibles, private records, and/or gravestones. In those records *Hiram and Emmeline Cobb* had a daughter on March 3, 1832, named Sophrona Elenor. The possibility exists that this was a daughter born before Emma with no record of Emma's actual birth on January 28, 1835. See http://archive.org/stream/vitalrecordsofwe02wests#page/16/mode/2up/search/Cobb.

8. Emma kept a handwritten note in her Bible, currently located in the Moody Archives in

of her pilgrim heritage. Her descendants survived the first cruel winter with the aid of the Native American Indians from the Wampanoag Nation and Chief Massasoit of Pokanoket. Although aware of this history, she regretfully explained years later how additional important records of her genealogy had been significantly burned during the 1871 Chicago Fire with sparse fragments remaining.[9]

Even so, Emma recognized and acknowledged this early Stockbridge Indian connection. In 1724, over one hundred years after the landing of the Mayflower, the Stockbridge Indian leader, the sachem Konkapot, sold a huge territory—including West Stockbridge and a half dozen more communities—to European settlers. Stockbridge, approximately 160 miles west of Boston, became incorporated as a town in 1739. Thirty-five years later on March 9, 1774, the town sectioned off an area of land designated as West Stockbridge with an official founding date of August 23, 1775. The year before this redistribution, approximately forty families inhabited the town. As the population increased, churches began to flourish with the Congregational Church becoming the town's first organized church in 1789.

By 1830 Stockbridge had been altered from John Sergeant's Indian mission to a quiet village with 1,209 inhabitants. During this time Emma's Christian parents, Hiram Cobb (1797–?) and Emeline C. Wilson Cobb (1806–36), resided in Stockbridge. Little is known of the Cobb family; however, Hiram's sister, Lucinda Cobb (1799–1876), resided in Victor, New York. She married John Milton Dryer (1798–1876) who was originally from West Stockbridge. Both Lucinda and John would within a few years greatly impact Emma's life.

Meanwhile, Hiram and Emeline birthed a son, George Hiram Cobb, on June 26, 1828. Just a few weeks after his sister Emma was born, young George died on February 13, 1835, at six years of age. Within thirteen months of Emma's birth, her mother died of unknown causes on February 27, 1836, at thirty years of age according to church records. No documentation exists of her father Hiram's death. However, it can be assumed that he most likely left his infant daughter less than two years later in 1838 when Emma was three. Her newly adopted parents, John and Lucinda Dryer, lovingly escorted her two hundred and fifty miles westward to Victor, New York.

Quite ironically, in God's providence, less than two years after Emma's birth and less than fifty miles northwest of the hilly town of West Stockbridge in western Massachusetts, another missionary destined individual was born who would dynamically impact Emma's life—evangelist Dwight L. Moody from Northfield. Within thirty-five years the distinct paths of Emma and Dwight, as divinely appointed by God, would converge in the mission laden city of Chicago, Illinois, where they would share their missionary burden for the souls of the lost.

Chicago, Illinois, where she penned: "My ancestors came over in the Mayflower." She also kept a news article dated Wednesday, September 2 in her Bible: "Descendants on Mayflower List on the Increase: Plymouth, Mass." Emma Dryer Bibles, Historical Collection.

9. Emma Dryer to Caroline E. Waite, 18 July 1924, Biographical File of Emma Dryer.

Emma's Birth on Missionary Terrain, 1835
Seneca Indian Missionary Soil of Victor, New York

Over thirty years prior to a Chicago 1870 encounter with Mr. Moody, Emma grew up in the midst of the undulating hills of the peaceful village of Victor, New York, nestled in the northwest corner of Ontario County. She trod on soil previously inhabited by a member of the Six Nations Confederacy (1700s) in western New York State known as the Seneca Indians. During her early years in Victor she listened with deep interest to the stories from her Dryer relatives about these Indians and the first white missionary, Jesuit priest Father Chaumonot, who visited this tribe in 1656.

The Senecas, known as the *Keepers of the Western Door*, fiercely guarded their village of Gandagaro from invasion. On July 13, 1687, Marquis Denonville, the French governor of New France, shattered this door when he initiated an expedition against the Seneca tribe. He destroyed their village in a battle fought near the present day city of Victor. This property would later be owned by the Dryer family and would become the site for the Presbyterian Church, the fifth oldest church in western New York. This invasion successfully depopulated the Seneca tribe. Yet at the same time, the assault opened up the territory for further missionary endeavors including that of Presbyterian and Congregational minister Reverend Samuel Kirkland (1741–1808)—the first missionary among the Seneca and Oneida tribes in Victor and Ontario County.[10]

As Emma attended the Victor school during her early years she was exposed to the history of her small town as well as the past details of an expanding country. She learned that during the Revolutionary War in 1788 land speculator and United States House Representative Oliver Phelps with Nathaniel Gorham, President of the Continental Congress, purchased over two million acres of land from the Indians. This transaction secured the future location for the town of Victor. Settlers soon followed from New England and from Emma's place of birth—West Stockbridge, Massachusetts. In 1789, under the name of Bloomfield, a town was planned which included acreage for a cemetery, school, and village square. By 1812 the town of Victor was sectioned off from Bloomfield and named in honor of Claudius Victor Boughton, a hero in the progressing War of 1812.

Enos and Jared Boughton from Stockbridge first settled in Bloomfield with four families and twenty other people in July 1790. They purchased the land from Phelps and Gorham for twenty cents an acre. Other farming settlers from New England followed, and agriculture soon became the town's most important industry. Jared Boughton and other early settlers identified with the Victor Presbyterian Church, the church Emma and her family would attend approximately forty years later.[11]

Victor was organizationally structured as a town at a meeting on April 6, 1813, in the Proprietors' Meeting House. This building stood on the hill behind William

---

10. Backus, *Historical Sketch*, 14.
11. Ibid., 13.

Gallup's post office and general store built in 1835 by Thomas Embry. Reportedly, the store, to Emma's childhood delight, sold everything from *toothpicks to elephants*.[12]

In 1838, on this missionary soil, Emma's newly formed family resided for one year in a log house on the Daniel Dryer farm. They later moved to a farm at the edge of Mendon afterwards owned by banker William Strong. During this time, as a young child, Emma began her formal education in a log schoolhouse built in 1816 across from the homestead of long-time Victor resident and relative Otis Dryer. When Emma was seven years old, the school was replaced by a small cobblestone schoolhouse which still exists today. After this time, her family moved to a farm half a mile west of Powell's Corner which became her adoptive parents' home until their death in 1876.[13]

Although her destiny might have followed that of other orphans during the mid-1800 era of *orphan trains*, Emma divinely escaped the uncertainty of approximately 250,000 homeless children. Parental death, abandonment, or neglect scattered orphans from New York by train to prearranged foster families across the country. The Dryer family ties had been closely knit and established through many decades and continued on Emma's behalf as she settled into her new home with her aunt and uncle in Victor, New York.

"She is not afraid . . . her whole family is clothed with scarlet."

~PROVERBS 31:21 GWT~

---

12. Ibid., 11.; Ontario County New York Genweb, para. 10.
13. Town of Victor, New York, Archives, 8 May 1925, *Victor Herald* Newspaper Obituary.

2

Emma's Early Years in New York, 1838–58

"She was devoted to her family and friends, especially to her foster parents with whom she spent several weeks every year as long as they lived."

~Victor Herald, Obituary, April 1925~

Community Life in Victor with Future Implications

Few details of Emma's early childhood in the Victor community are known. She most likely spent some time during the summer frolicking around the countryside and exploring the Mud and Fish Creeks with her friends as she satisfied her scientific curiosity. She also followed the country dirt roads from the farm where she lived to small village operations such as the saw and gristmills situated in the northwest section of Victor.

Emma would have been intrigued by *The Old Stone General Store* with operator Albert Simonds, the local F. E. Cobb druggist shop, the shoe maker stores, William B. Gallop's merchant store and post office, and the wagon and harness maker shops. Perhaps she watched with captivated interest as the town Walling and Brace tailors worked with material which the fulling and carding mill had processed from the wool of the local sheep flocks.[1] Unknown to Emma during these early years, her familiarity with the coordinated work of the home town tailors and the carding mill would equip her with the indispensable background to train young women in Chicago to work with fabric in her sewing classes to provide clothing for the poor and homeless.

Emma's relatives were actively involved in the town. Victor Hotel, with its grand opening on Christmas Day in 1819, became a landmark for ninety-five years. Rufus Dryer (1780–1820), who came to Victor in 1798 as part of the Stockbridge Dryer clan, built and ran the hotel with its brick Colonial style architecture and a hand fashioned iron latch on the front door. In 1804 he married Lydia Cobb (1775–1855) from

---

1. See "Ontario County New York GenWeb."

Conway, Massachusetts. They had five children who also gained recognition in the area. Rufus took over James Hawley's tavern and became a prominent landlord and town proprietor.[2] Emma most certainly was warned by her prohibitionist church going parents to stay away from every local tavern and distillery. More than likely this directive set the initial stage for Emma's prospective temperance position.

In 1840 as a young girl of five Emma excitedly witnessed the completed construction of the Auburn and Rochester Railroad. In 1845 she watched the railroad crew build the Victor cobblestone pump house which supplied water for the steam trains passing outside the town. The Victor station, about half a mile from the center of the village, contributed to the accessibility of passengers to and from Rochester with trains traveling at an average speed of fourteen miles an hour. Emma found that this expanding mode of transportation would prove significant to her courageous traversal into the educational world beyond Victor.

Although the first town newspaper, *The Victor Herald*, did not begin official publication until 1881 with its circulation to northwestern Ontario County, it would nevertheless be the instrument through which Victor would proudly keep a record

2. Ibid.

of the life and activities of Emma Dryer who they considered to be one of their own endearing residents. In 1893 historian George S. Conover promoted its distribution: "The paper is in all respects a worthy and enterprising publication, and deservedly enjoys its large circulation and a good advertising patronage."[3] Perhaps Emma's small town acquaintance with *The Victor Herald* served to stir and enhance her subsequent enthusiasm for Christian publications. Her emerging relationship with Dwight Moody from 1870 to 1899 in Chicago forged a mutual interest in the publication of Christian literature. By 1894 the Bible Institute Colportage Association was successfully established to provide reasonable and accessible Christian materials and books for both believers and nonbelievers.[4] Emma's love for books and learning would motivate her to take every opportunity to advertise conferences and to procure and distribute printed materials for her own Chicago mission outreaches from publishing enterprises beyond her small Victor community newspaper.

Church Life in Victor as a Prelude to Missions

Emma fondly cherished her adventures as a young girl. While she inquisitively scouted out the small town of Victor with its railroad and surrounding farmland, her parents focused on actively providing their adopted daughter a solid Bible background through religious training in their Christian home. They were devoted to God's word and gave her sound biblical instruction supplemented by their attendance at the First Presbyterian Church. Emma's mother, Lucinda Dryer, was regularly listed on the church roll during Reverend Kay's residence from January 24, 1833, to July 3, 1836.[5]

Emma attended the Presbyterian Sabbath School, organized in 1814, which influenced her decision to follow Christ at an early age.[6] Her personal knowledge and understanding of the importance of the Sabbath or Sunday school in a young child's life prompted her later involvement in teaching adult classes at D. L. Moody's church. Before moving to Chicago in 1870 she had heard the reports of *Crazy Moody's* Sabbath School teaching methods to recruit children from the poor and unruly *Chicago Sands* district. She would become steadily intrigued with this man who grew up in Northfield, Massachusetts, not far from her own birthplace in Stockbridge—a man who lacked the quality of education that she would obtain, yet a man who would nevertheless change his world for Christ.

From this Presbyterian Church and Sabbath School, members were sent worldwide to serve the Lord as missionaries. Reverend Clarence W. Backus made special mention in his 1888 *Historical Sketch of the First Presbyterian Church* of his belief that

---

3. Conover, *History of Ontario County*, 373.
4. By 1941 the Bible Institute Colportage Association became Moody Press or Publishers.
5. Backus, *Historical Sketch*, 89.
6. Ruelas, *Women and the Landscape*, 8.

the Sabbath School contributed to the outpouring of missionary efforts including that of their *Emma*. He wrote: "These were all members of this Sabbath School . . . and most of them members of the church while they lived in Victor. I should also mention Miss Emeline Dryer and Miss Mary Jane Moore, both of whom are now engaged in the Bible work at Chicago, Ill."[7]

Emma acquired her burning desire for mission work as she heard the Sabbath School narrative accounts of earlier missionaries such as John Sergeant, David Brainerd, Jonathan Edwards, and Samuel Kirkland. Inspiration also came from Richard Kay, the minister of the Presbyterian Church at the time of Emma's birth. He regularly presented updates to his congregation regarding Miss Marietta Rawson whom the church sent into the missionary field of Bombay, India, on April 19, 1834.[8] Years later, recalling these spiritually nurturing times, Emma reflectively wrote in January of 1916 to her friend Charles Albert Blanchard, second president of the Chicago area's Wheaton College: "My own interest in Christian work began in my childhood, and followed the lines of our Sunday-School and church work, giving me some acquaintance with home and foreign missions, and the Bible and Tract Societies."

Emma heard stories from the older church members about early preachers and pioneer day revivals in Bloomfield—before its Victor land redistribution—which contributed to a sustained unity of the church. The founders of Victor, dedicated to the spiritual nurturing of their community, provided religious training for their families. At their request Reverend Reuben Parmele was installed in September 1798 with the charge to preach the gospel of Jesus Christ. The next year after Reverend Seth Williston officiated at the installation, Williston became instrumental in bringing about the *Great Revival* of 1799 which impacted Bloomfield and the whole county with religious fervor. The First Presbyterian Church of Victor became the outgrowth of Parmele's work as he led the church during the 1799 revival.

Early Victor settler Jared Boughton continued to be active as a member of the original board of trustees for the First Presbyterian Church at its incorporation on September 13, 1798. The church initially met in houses, barns, or in the open air until a more permanent structure could be built. The religious preferences of the early settlers, which they brought with them from New England, were primarily Congregational and Presbyterian. These members loyally supported the structure or makeup of the church they founded. In 1804 the town owners purchased land on which to build a meeting place known as the *Proprietors' Church* since they all took part in the building project. Officers were elected including Nathaniel Boughton as town assessor and Emma's relative Rufus Dryer as an overseer of the poor.[9]

As the town grew, various denominational preferences emerged which resulted in a withdrawal of some groups to establish their own meeting locations. However,

---

7. Backus, *Historical Sketch*, 43.
8. Ibid., 42–43.
9. Ibid., 13, 21.

Emma's Early Years in New York, 1838–58

by January 1828 a major division within the Proprietors' Church took place due to disagreement regarding church government. With their prior background training and doctrinal awareness regarding spiritual warfare, the involved parties settled their disputes by peacefully forming a newly organized and independent Congregational church which lasted until 1858 when replaced by a formal Presbyterian governance.[10] Years later Emma would also be involved in a church struggle in Chicago trying to understand the dynamics of church organizational conflict and stability.

Before Emma became a resident of Victor at the age of three, the First Presbyterian Church edifice was constructed at a cost of $3,500. At the age of nine she saw this future western New York landmark substantially enlarged and repaired in both 1844 and 1860. Also during this time frame, Emma sat under the instruction of five different ministers. Before she came to Victor, Reverend Kay—born in Dublin, Ireland, and a 1799 graduate of Auburn Theological Seminary—served at the Victor church beginning in 1833. Reverend Jairus Wilcox (1836–38) followed Reverend Kay as their next minister.

After Emma's arrival, Reverend Charles E. Furman resided in Victor in March 1838 and was formally installed on June 15, 1840. He had married Harriet Emeline Johnson of Rochester, New York, with revivalist Charles G. Finney (1792–1875)

---

10. Conover, *History of Ontario County,* 41.

presiding. As a former agent of the American Tract Society in Ohio from 1828 to 1829, Reverend Furman brought with him to the Victor church the importance of this society's publication ministry in spreading the gospel. After he left Victor in April of 1846 when Emma was eleven years old, he relocated to Medina, New York, for eight years. In May of 1854 to 1859 he resided in Rochester, New York, where he worked for the American Bible Society.[11] During this time Emma would attend the Allen Female Seminary in Rochester where, quite providentially, Reverend Furman had further positive influence on Emma's imminent participation in the distribution of Bibles in connection with the Chicago Bible Work and the Chicago Bible Society.

Emma's impending strong opposition to slavery developed in part from the teaching she received while under Reverend Furman. He and his congregation openly opposed slavery with this church declaration made in December 1843: "Slavery as it exists in this country, is a moral, social, and political evil. An evil that results in oppression, ignorance, licentiousness, and heathenism; and hence in the ruin of immortal souls; and therefore ought to be abolished immediately."[12] Future pastors of Emma's home church, such as Calvin Waterbury, similarly added their support to this abolition issue.

For the following three years, until Emma turned fourteen years old, her church commissioned two new pastors—Reverend Charles M. Meruin (1846–49) as an 1840 Auburn Theological Seminary graduate and Reverend A. Van H. Powell until 1851. Reverend Calvin Waterbury, who for one year attended Lane Theological Seminary with its abolition controversy,[13] greatly impacted Emma during her teenage years. He graduated from Auburn Seminary in 1836 and served as Emma's pastor from 1851 to 1855. He was known as a person of principled conviction: "Whatever he felt was duty, in that he engaged with all his might. Believing that education was the true handmaid of religion, he was found, where he went, an ardent and zealous worker in that cause. He was a man of indomitable will; difficulties never deterred him. He had a very strong and abiding faith in the promises and truth of God."[14] Waterbury greatly empowered Emma's faith with his preaching of God's word, his challenge for her to work with all her might as unto the Lord, and the solidification of her belief in the partnership of education and religion.

During the time in which Emma would attend the Allen Female Seminary in Rochester, New York, Reverend Charles C. Carr, an interim minister and 1841 graduate from Auburn Theological Seminary, served at the Presbyterian Church in Victor for ten months followed by Reverend Job Pierson (1856–63). Pierson earned a degree from Williams College in 1842 and graduated from Auburn Theological Seminary

---

11. Backus, *Historical Sketch*, 45.

12. Ibid., 47.

13. *See* Donald Dayton's (1976) historical work, *Discovering An Evangelical Heritage,* for an extensive account of the Lane Rebellion with its regulations forbidding antislavery involvement of students.

14. Backus, *Historical Sketch*, 51.

in 1847. By the time Emma would attend Ingham University from 1856 to 1858, the membership of her home church had reached one hundred under the leadership of Reverend Pierson.

Reverend Ennis was the First Presbyterian minister when Emma lost her mother on February 12, 1876, followed nine days later by the death of her father. Interestingly, and almost as a divine tribute to their lives, on April 24, 1876, the hand of God ignited the fires of revival in this church for an unforgettable season of divine outpouring that continued until August 1877.

Emma's parents had faithfully instructed her with the powerful *Faith Statement* of the First Presbyterian Church of Victor: "The success of a church is not dependent upon any one man, but upon the piety and devotion of its people, and in that favor of God which is their life. It is not enough to be satisfied with a past, the future beckons on to grander achievement and more enduring success."[15] Years later, while learning the importance of embracing a church's vision, Emma would be thrust into urban ministries developing in Chicago. Even in that setting, she would always welcome the news from her parents and friends from the Victor First Presbyterian Church conveying their continued mission emphasis. Emma heartily commended them for strong mission and ministry outreaches such as the *Ladies Missionary Society* organized in 1874 and the 1885 *Children's Lend a Hand Missionary Band*.

15. Ibid., 66.

Conceivably, while in her small home town of Victor Emma was also introduced to the Methodists who flourished right behind the Presbyterians. As part of the riding circuit, Reverend Joseph Jewell visited Victor until an official organization was established in 1807 with services held in the town's schoolhouse or in the Proprietors' meeting house. By 1821, they secured their own meeting place which expanded in 1832 right before Emma arrived in Victor as a young child. After Emma left the village, a larger facility in 1870 replaced the 1821 structure with which she was so familiar.[16]

Evidence of the Methodist influence on Emma's life can still be seen in the denomination's present day *claim* on Emma. Dr. Abraham Ruelas, who wrote the 2010 book *Women and the Landscape of American Higher Education: Wesleyan Holiness and Pentecostal Founders,* documents Emma as a Wesleyan-Holiness founder of a Bible training school later named Moody Bible Institute. After Emma made her home in Chicago she began attending Reverend William H. Daniels's First Methodist Episcopal Church and later became acquainted with D. L. Moody's faithful music associate, Ira Sankey (1840–1908), who possessed a Methodist Episcopal background. Ruelas also includes a chapter regarding Lucy Rider Meyer, a Methodist Episcopal deaconess trainer closely associated with Emma during her years in Chicago.

Emma grew up in a town with several other religious affiliations—the Universalist Society structured in 1834 with organizational completion in 1844; St. Patrick's Catholic Church founded around 1852 after Emma left the area for further schooling; and the Episcopalians established in 1871.[17] Thus, Emma's early exposure to a wide variety of denominations prepared her for the ecumenical nature of ministry awaiting her ultimate destiny in Chicago.

Schooling in Victor and Beyond

Few accounts exist regarding Emma's early school years. However, based on her later teaching assignments she would have held primary interest in math, astronomy, grammar, and drawing. She was *ambitious for education*[18] and apparently discovered a passion for teaching at some stage in her educational journey which began in Victor. Emma excelled as a student while attending school in both the one room log and cobblestone Victor schoolhouses.[19] From approximately 1840 to 1858 she studied diligently and would surpass the education of most rural middle-class young ladies.

With rapid industrialization and urbanization men received high paying wages which opened up education opportunities for women to cultivate their own intellectual roles and enter the field of education. Following the introduction of female seminaries in the early 1800s, advancement for women in education accelerated with

16. Ibid.
17. Ibid., 16–17.
18. Town of Victor, New York, Archives, 8 May 1925, *Victor Herald* Newspaper Obituary.
19. Huber, "A Brief History: A Driving Tour of Historic Victor," 13.

the establishment of women's colleges, normal schools, and ultimately schools with co-educational training. Emma resolutely followed this progressive pattern of education for women after leaving her school in Victor.

Palmyra's Union School: Circa 1850–54

Around 1850 Emma continued her education at *Union School* established in Palmyra, New York.[20] With guidance from Principal Justus H. French, she became one of over five hundred students who attended this coeducational high school located approximately twelve miles southeast of Rochester and twelve miles northeast of Victor.[21] During her high school training Emma retained her permanent residence in Victor according to the 1850 federal census. Despite the distance from her Victor home, she quickly transitioned from the quiet rustic village of three hundred and eleven residents to the hustle and bustle of a thriving town of four to five thousand Palmyra residents.

While attending high school, Emma most likely boarded with friends or relatives in Palmyra due to the rugged twenty-four mile round trip journey. Although Emma could have traveled by stagecoach, the Auburn and Rochester Railroad provided the opportunity for her to commute from Victor to Rochester. She would have continued

---

20. Town of Victor, New York, Archives, 8 May 1925, *Victor Herald* Newspaper Obituary.
21. French, "Profile of Palmyra."; Women's Society of the Western Presbyterian Church, *Palmyra*, 31–32.

by boat to the canal town of Palmyra through the Erie Canal finished in 1825 or by train on the New York Central Railroad built in 1853.

Historically, in 1793 two log schoolhouses had been constructed in Palmyra—one on land donated by General John Swift, founder of Palmyra, and the other designated as Hopkins School located in East Palmyra. Politics later entered into the educational arena resulting in two new separate frame school buildings—one constructed by the Federalists and the other by the Democratic party. Palmyra Academy, a two story school built before 1835, housed the first school bell in Palmyra and boldly stood on the ridge of a hill. Three stone schoolhouses were built in 1835 but consolidated in 1846 with a new name—*Union School No. 1 of Palmyra.*

Emma attended this new three story, eleven room brick facility around the fall of 1850 to the spring of 1854. As part of her curriculum, she was introduced to instrumental and vocal music by instructors E. Lusk, C. D. Foster, and J. H. French. She developed further interest for various aspects of biology through DeWitt McIntyre's lectures on physiology. Four years after Emma graduated from the Palmyra Union School the school name was changed to the *Palmyra Classical Union School* until 1889 with the construction of a larger facility.[22]

During Emma's high school years she continued to be introduced to various religious ministries and to faithful Christians being sent to the mission field. Palmyra claimed four different religious institutions. More than likely, Emma attended the Congregational Church, established in 1797, which had adopted the government of the Presbyterian Church in 1793. Horace Eaton (1848–79) pastored the church during Emma's attendance at Union School. Emma would also have known of another prominent church, the Methodist Episcopal Church of Palmyra, which began its circuits in 1811. The Zion Episcopal Church could possibly have introduced Emma to noted Indian missionary Davenport Phelps. The First Baptist Church of Palmyra, organized in 1800, would have expanded Emma's rich knowledge of missions with their commissioning of Dr. and Mrs. James Haswell to the Burma mission field from 1835 to 1884.[23]

Victor Park School District 10: 1854–55

Following graduation from Palmyra's *Union School* Emma spent a short season at the *Victor Park School District 10* where she taught at the cobblestone elementary school located at 7728 Dryer Road—the school she attended as a child. She also served as preceptress in 1854.[24] Little else is known about her experiences at the Victor School.

Meanwhile, D. L. Moody left Northfield, Massachusetts, for Boston in 1854 to work at the S. S. Holton shoe store and assist at the Young Men's Christian Association

---

22. Women's Society of the Western Presbyterian Church, *Palmyra,* 32.
23. Ibid., 48.
24. Town of Victor, New York, Archives, 8 May 1925, *Victor Herald* Newspaper Obituary.

(YMCA). During his God-directed transition to Boston, Emma felt and responded to a divergent nudging of the Lord. Her divinely inspired decision, combined with encouragement from her parents, led to her departure from Victor to pursue a higher level of education at a prominent female seminary in Rochester, New York.

Allen Female Seminary: 1855–56

Mary B. Allen's *Female Seminary* was established in 1847 during the 1820–50 era of female seminary popularity. At the age of twenty Emma registered for the 1855–56 school year at the Allen Female Seminary located at 14 Allen Street in Rochester, New York.[25] Her name was recorded in the city directory as Miss E. S. Dryer, a boarding student at the school.[26] More than likely, throughout her school term Emma would periodically return by train or stagecoach to her home in Victor. The 1855 census for Victor listed her as *Sophronia Dryer* living at the residence of John M. and Lucinda Dryer. However, with the arrival of further educational opportunities, Emma would no longer be included in the Victor census.

At the Allen Female Seminary Emma took advantage of studying math, language, history, science, music, and art at a school attended by notable young ladies such as Emily Ketcham (1838–1907).[27] Miss Ketcham became a teacher at the age of fifteen and around 1862 attended the seminary. While enrolled, Emily became acquainted with famous suffragist Susan B. Anthony (1820–1906) and later joined the ranks as a tenacious advocate for women's suffrage.

Although not acquainted at that time with Emily Ketcham, Emma undoubtedly participated in spirited debates with her fellow seminary classmates regarding the right of women to vote. These discussions would have been led by preceptress Mary B. Allen (1800?–1870), known for her strict Christian beliefs regarding abolition and women's rights. Miss Allen wrote a book entitled *Looking Backward or Memories of the Past* (1870) in which she documented her social views and personal reflections as an educator. Looking into Miss Allen's memoirs one can gain insights into her social and spiritual impact on young ladies such as Emily Ketcham and Emma Dryer.

Emma identified with this ambitious woman who had several comparable family losses—her father when she was two years old and her infant sister. In remembering the death of her father, Mary Allen wrote:

> Young children feel troubles and disappointments as severely as they do at any time in after life . . . As I looked up into his pale face, he said that I must be a good girl and love God and my mother, and when I was old enough to go to school, study well and get a good education. It is astonishing how deep and

---

25. Ibid.
26. *Dewey's Rochester City Directory*, 146.
27. Ketcham Family Papers, Grand Rapids History and Special Collection Archives and Public Library, Collection 293.

lasting the impressions are which are received in early childhood . . . The little one sits in his mother's arms with eyes and ears open, and with the first dawning of an intellect which his living soul compels him to use for his own benefit, gathers knowledge from everything that occurs around him.[28]

Miss Allen's mother also died not long after her daughter opened the seminary in 1847 leaving her with no close family relatives. With God-given assurance she recalled: "I had no . . . near relative on whom I could rely for counsel or support; but as the arm of the flesh failed me, I was enabled to cling the closer to the Everlasting Arm, and to rely on the promise, 'When thy father and mother forsake thee, the Lord will take thee up.'"[29] During Emma's year spent at the seminary she most certainly received consolation from Miss Allen who could personally identify with Emma's own family losses.

Emma admired the sharp intellect of her seminary preceptress and would have been fascinated and challenged by Miss Allen's illustrative stories. As a child prodigy Mary Allen had been told that she could talk months before she could walk and at ten months could actually recite the alphabet. She began reading through the Bible at three years of age and recalled finishing before she turned five. Subsequently, Mary started school at five with proficient reading skills.

Miss Allen relayed the story of her first school reading experience. Because she did not want to trouble her teacher or make her feel badly, out of courtesy she did not tell her teacher that she could read. She obediently recited the ABC's followed by one syllable, then two syllable, and then three syllable words to the triumphant praise of the teacher. When her mother heard what she had done, she assured Mary that she should respectfully tell the teacher about her current reading ability. Her teacher immediately placed her in a higher class. Not surprisingly, at the age of nine Mary had mastered grammar and at ten commenced with the instruction of other students in English grammar.

Mary admitted to being quite outspoken as a child. When radically converted at a revival at ten years of age she non-reluctantly shared her testimony at school. Even after personally contracting spotted fever, she proceeded to quickly offer sound counsel and instruction to her concerned mother on how to pray with another sick woman for her salvation. Her new boldness in Christ laid the foundation for her non-reticent instruction to seminary students regarding theological and contemporary social issues of the day.

As Miss Allen shared her early learning experiences with her seminary students, Emma would have been intrigued with her story of a Dartmouth College professor who visited and lectured on meteor stones and the earth's composition—information not yet published in books. Miss Allen's education advanced even further when she and her mother boarded in a house where the town library was kept. Mary devoured

---

28. King, *Looking Backward*, 6–8.
29. Ibid., 176.

literature and avidly perused the works of Milton, Josephus, and Lutheran historian Johann Lorenz Mosheim's (1693–1755) book, *Church History*. When Mary turned twelve years of age a town trustee approached her mother about possibly engaging Mary as a teacher in the school. Her mother promptly refused by stating that Mary was far too young.

Miss Allen influenced her students' philosophy and values concerning parental discipline. She stated a resolute educational ideology regarding the importance of training children. Recalling a spanking she herself received as a child, she wrote:

> Although I was then but a year and a half old, I can still remember it. I think the foundation of a long and happy life was then laid. The parent is the only God the young child knows, and if he does not bring him early under subjection to his authority he will grow up impatient of restraint, disobedient to law, and though he may in after life, through much chastisement, be brought to yield himself to God, yet he will seldom make a submissive and trusting Christian . . . I think it possible for every child to be so well governed before three years of age that he will never afterward need correction; but in order to do this, parents need much grace and great consistency of character . . . He must be brought right when you please, *not* in his own time . . . While I would advocate great kindness in the government of a child, I am sure I have seen many children ruined by being subjected to 'moral suasion' instead of a firm, healthy compulsion to do right.[30]

As Emma listened to her educational and spiritual mentor she must have reflected on the truth of these words knowing that her own devoted parents had nurtured and trained her to be respectful and submissive to those in authority. Throughout her life Emma faithfully honored her parents and returned to Victor every year to visit them until their deaths in 1876.

Miss Allen firmly believed in the use of God's word to develop the intellect. She reflected, "I have always noticed that children are better satisfied with stories about the Bible characters than with any other, and that by their influence a solid and truthful foundation is laid for intellectual greatness."[31] She realized the importance of a child's early corrective training regarding character flaws. She wrote: "A child, when young, has in embryo, all the unlovely traits of character that will trouble him in after life. These traits become stronger as the objects upon which they are exercised are of more importance."[32]

Miss Allen wisely instructed youth and their parents concerning sin and the importance of accepting God's word: "Never speak of sin in his hearing as a light thing. Trifles in the eyes of an older person are weighty matters in the mind of a child who

---

30. Ibid., 4–5.
31. Ibid., 9.
32. Ibid., 13.

is busy with his play-things on the floor beside you . . . Don't reject the Bible or grieve the Holy Spirit when you are young—else your life may be a preparation for misery instead of happiness hereafter."[33] Emma's year at Miss Allen's seminary validated the sacred blend of God's word, and her faith and Christ-like character with a genuine passion for learning—moral leadership qualities that would follow her throughout her subsequent years of ministry.

Emma would have attentively listened to Miss Allen share stories with her students of historical events such as the War of 1812. As a fourteen year old Mary Allen witnessed soldiers marching to the battle of Plattsburg. She recalled: "We all rushed out of the house, and . . . there was the appearance of two armies in combat. Whether this was mirage, or the aurora to which our imagination gave this appearance, I know not; but the figures were there, and twenty-four hours after news was received of the battle of Lake Champlain, or battle of Plattsburg, which was in progress at that time. Few people knew, or nothing was said in our school books, of the mirage at that time, and many thought this appearance in the heavens supernatural."[34]

Similarly, she would have shared the 1814 death of her grandmother, Mary Winslow, a direct descendant of the Winslow family who sailed to America on the Mayflower. The grandmother would have told her stories of the Pilgrims and their harrowing experiences. Perhaps Miss Allen's account of her grandmother's Plymouth ordeals inspired a deeper awareness and appreciation within Emma for her own Mayflower descendant heritage.

In her instruction to students at the seminary Miss Allen conceivably shared the value and contribution of her own Sunday school experiences which attributed to the success of her first year of teaching in 1816. Emma could have unconsciously hidden these noteworthy stories in her heart as preparation for future involvement in the Sunday school work in Chicago.

Emma would have also listened eagerly to Miss Allen's account of missionaries such as William Goodell (1792–1896) who provided practical training to young aspiring scholars in the winter of 1816. While a student at Dartmouth College Mr. Goodell boarded at Miss Allen's cousin's house. Miss Allen wrote about his proverbial cheerfulness and easy conversational style. As a young girl she showed him her sketch of two saints with beams of glory over their heads. He laughed quite jovially as others joined him. He began instructing his eager learners on the glory of God that could only faintly be realized here on earth. Miss Allen concluded: "He had the heart of a missionary then and the whole district felt his influence."[35]

On another occasion Emma would have been stirred with a passionate longing mixed with an uncertain knowing while sitting under Miss Allen's instruction. Mary Allen described an innovative 1834 program for women in Rochester which

33. Ibid., 19, 24.
34. Ibid., 42.
35. Ibid., 56.

sent missionary *infant-school teachers* to the west. One young lady named Miss Kirby traveled to Chicago to teach a group of twenty-five or thirty young people from ages five to twenty-five. Likewise, Miss Allen shared about other Allen Female Seminary students who became missionaries to the Indians and ministers of the gospel including Henry Everard Peck, later appointed as a professor at Charles Finney's Oberlin College—a school established in 1833 with an open door admission policy for students of all races and gender.

While listening to Miss Allen's stories, Emma's heart perhaps unconsciously began to embrace or reaffirm her own future calling to work in missions. Reflecting on her earlier education opportunities, she wrote in 1916 to President Charles Blanchard of Wheaton College, "As a student and teacher . . . I was much interested in foreign missions, and in Christian work among women in our own country."[36]

Miss Allen quite possibly conversed with Emma and her classmates about the 1830 revival at Rochester High School where she taught until 1837. Emma previously heard of Charles Finney and the 1830 Rochester revival from her former Victor Presbyterian pastor, Charles E. Furman, who resided at that time in Rochester. Now she was hearing first hand not only from Reverend Furman but also from Miss Allen about the remarkable events that had transpired.

Miss Allen had been burdened with the spiritual condition of her fellow teachers and students with only two boys out of sixty from Professor Benedict's class professing to be religious.[37] In view of the Rochester revival during Miss Allen's educational oversight, one revival observer noticed a substantial increase of godly behavior in the lives of the young people and neighboring towns.[38] In support of the lasting steadfastness of Finney's converts Miss Allen wrote: "I have not known one who has been drawn away by the many errors which have since been introduced into our city."[39] She estimated that the revivals led by Charles Finney brought about the conversion of almost 800 people which served to strengthen the school and the Rochester area churches.

Miss Allen, after leaving Rochester High School, traveled by boat in 1838 to Barhamville, South Carolina, to assist at a ladies school. In 1839 she rode by stagecoach to Augusta, Georgia, and returned thereafter to New York to teach at the Monroe Academy in Henrietta. While there, her heart was again burdened when hearing the report that none of the students professed to be Christians. As Emma sat under this well seasoned teacher, she undoubtedly acquired a similar heaviness for the souls of those without Christ—a spiritual state that would further be nourished under the pastoral care of evangelist D. L. Moody.

By 1847 Miss Allen received an offer from over eighty Rochester residents to establish a seminary for women. With land purchased on Allen Street, she opened up

---

36. Emma Dryer to Charles Blanchard, 1916, Biographical File of Emma Dryer.
37. Truesdale, *The Younger Generation*, 7.
38. Ibid.
39. King, *Looking Backward*, 141.

the institution in three months with 125 students and seven teachers. Her seminary advanced as a distinguished institution with an outstanding curriculum and gifted graduates some of whom studied painting abroad. The 1855 Rochester city directory listed, along with Emma, eight other seminary boarding students: Sarah J. Allen; Elizabeth Bennett; Gertrude Donaldson; Henrietta Donaldson; Francis A. Hawks; Harriet E. Osborn; Miss Elizabeth Sutton; and Cornelia A. Wilkinson.[40] Emma's experience in boarding with these scholarly associates prepared her for a future ministry with young adults.

The Rochester city directory also listed the school's personnel and instructors—those who influenced Emma's own teaching methodology. In 1855 the directory included the following: Miss Mary B. Allen, Principal; Harriet Freeman, Assistant; Daton F. Merrill, Latin and Greek; Mrs. Caroline M. Brockway, Drawing; Caroline R. Wilkinson, Oil Painting; Horace H. Allen, Vocal Music; professor Benjamin F. Hill, Music teacher and Piano Forte (Englishman); Julia A. Hill, Music; and Miss Margaret Hoffman, domestic. Miss Allen spoke highly of her faithfully committed teachers, yet she did not hesitate to share their struggles as well. Music professor Benjamin F. Hill, who would have taught Emma an appreciation for the rudiments of music, invited the school's clientele to hear the great English opera tenor, John Braham (1774–1856), in concert:

> Mr. H. was very anxious that the people should hear him. Concerts were not very common at that time in Rochester. He sang one evening at a hall in the city, and the next evening, Saturday, he was to sing portions of Handel's Messiah in the Third church. I went in after he had commenced. In the vestibule I met one of our gentlemen going out. Some one said to him, 'Are you going away, sir?' 'Yes,' he replied; 'he sings just like Hill, and it is not worth spending your time to hear.' If Braham was now alive, and could sing to us in Rochester, we should have thousands who would not only gladly spend one night but many, in listening to his wonderful performance.[41]

Miss Allen relayed this story to indicate that "judgment is frequently given not because of knowledge but because of ignorance."[42] Miss Allen regularly extended advice for every aspiring teacher "to place himself in advance of the times and to draw up his pupils; otherwise, when they are ready for action in the world, they will find themselves falling below the advance which science has made during the time."[43] Emma would have learned from Miss Allen the art of successfully motivating her own pupils and how to carefully curtail one's judgments of others.

---

40. *Central Library of Rochester and Monroe County*, 1855 Rochester City Directory, 146.
41. King, *Looking Backward*, 179.
42. Ibid.
43. Ibid., 180.

Emma's Early Years in New York, 1838–58

With great affection Miss Allen presented the following story of one of her greatly admired like-minded seminary teachers who served as a godly role model to students such as Emma:

> Miss E. Stella Randall... is remembered with respect and affection by hundreds of our pupils. She never obtruded herself or her own opinions on others. Her manners were lady-like and attractive. She had respect for the judgment of others, but no amount of argument or persuasion could induce her to swerve in the least from what her conscience told her to be right. When I was away from home, and had left the school in her charge, I felt just as sure that my rules would be carried out, even to the letter, as though I had been present... It seemed to be easy with her to do by others as she would that they should do by her... I thought she did more for me than she would desire me to do for her.[44]

When a fire broke out at the seminary Miss Allen commended Miss Randall's quick action on behalf of the students. Furthermore, Miss Randall sacrificially neglected her own possessions for the recovery of others. Emma could not have foreseen that she herself, as a teacher and preceptress, would one day be faced with a similar situation yet on a much larger scale while in Chicago at the time of the 1871 fire.

Emma would have listened attentively to Miss Allen's unrelenting instruction to her seminary students regarding the social issues of the times. In 1837 Miss Allen witnessed slavery first hand during her trip to South Carolina. She distressingly wrote: "My blood boiled as I saw the poor creature standing with streaming eyes ready to be struck off to the highest bidder."[45] In addition, with strong passion she opposed the use and sell of alcohol: "It is disreputable not only to drink, but to make or sell liquor."[46]

In 1850 Miss Allen spoke out against the use of necromancy and spiritualism. Rochester history recorded the rise of spiritualism in Wayne County where the famous Fox sisters lived. The story was told of knocking sounds being heard in a house where a peddler had supposedly been murdered. The two daughters of a blacksmith, Margaret and Katherine (Katy), reportedly heard coded rappings from the slain peddler, Charles B. Rosna, referred to as Mr. Splitfoot. In 1849 the family moved to Rochester where Katy attended the Allen Female Seminary. Miss Allen had also instructed Katy when she attended elementary school.

On November 14, 1849, staged public demonstrations of the Fox sisters' psychic powers, used to contact spirits from the grave, gained nationwide attention in the city of Rochester. One attendee, President Augustus H. Strong of the Rochester Theological Seminary, recalled that many spectators found the sisters' performance to be genuine. However, he mentioned that Miss Mary Allen was not one of them. He recalled that Katy Fox officiated the open question and answer session. Miss Allen

---

44. Ibid., 181.
45. Ibid., 146.
46. Ibid., 38.

challenged her to inquire of Katy's own dead grandmother regarding the spelling of the word scissors. When Katy responded *s-i-s-s-e-r-s*, Miss Allen shrewdly pointed out that when Katy was her student, she spelled scissors the exact same way.[47]

Mary Allen distinctively recalled her observations of Katherine Fox when teaching her at approximately seven years of age:

> Her parents frequently allowed her to be taken out in the evening to amuse a public audience. The child became so affected by it, that if I looked at her steadily a moment or two at any time in school, she would go into what they call a mesmeric state, and it would be very difficult to awaken her. I sent word to her parents that they were ruining their child. I thought that I would watch the effect of this when she became older. They moved out of the city for a while, and when she was about fourteen, I again had her as a pupil. I found her to possess much imagination and a fine taste for music, but she was nervous, and could not easily control herself. I think parents often unconsciously lay the foundation for either morbid sensibilities, or over-excited nervous action in their children, which might have been avoided by a different training in their earliest years.[48]

Miss Allen's prophetic words to the Fox sisters' parents were realized when, after years of drinking problems and a recantation, the sisters died tragic deaths as paupers.[49] These illustrations from Miss Allen would have prepared Emma as she faced the temperance, abolitionist, and biblical inerrancy issues of her generation.

Emma conceivably recalled Miss Allen's faith in the healing power of God years later when confronted with her own physical infirmities. Miss Allen, well acquainted with the power of prayer, recovered from cholera in 1832, bronchitis in 1837, and other prevalent sicknesses. She recognized the close association of physical well-being and rigorous employment of the mind: "For eighteen years we never had the services of a physician for any one pupil three times in succession, and did not call a doctor to average once a year. We never had one dangerous case among our boarders, and in the three or four thousand scholars that attended my school while I taught in the city, I recollect but four who were removed by death while members of my school. I mention these things to show that well-regulated study does not injure the health, but rather prolongs life."[50]

Although we have no further record of Emma's association with Miss Allen after 1856, Emma would surely have known during her residency at the school that Mary Allen faced the reality of blindness. In 1853 Miss Allen realized her failing eyesight. Within fifteen years she completely lost sight in both eyes. In spite of this loss, doors

---

47. Merrill, *Rochester Sketchbook*, Section 3.
48. King, *Looking Backward*, 170–71.
49. *See* Davenport, *The Death-Blow to Spiritualism* for further information.
50. King, *Looking Backward*, 177–78.

opened for her to travel to Europe from May 25, 1859, to July 1860 during which time she attended a conference in Bolton, England, featuring Charles Finney and his wife Elizabeth Ford Atkinson (1799–1863). She had the privilege of attending a ladies' supper hosted by Mrs. Finney. Her return trip aboard the *Persia* ocean liner was highlighted by her introduction to famous stage actress Miss Charlotte Cushman (1816–76) who was returning after a performance in Rome.

By 1863 Miss Allen retired from the seminary. Three years later she married Mr. Moses King and with his encouragement dictated her memoirs to him for publication. We do not know if Emma ever received the opportunity to read Miss Allen's 1870 autobiography. Regardless, this remarkable mentor of aspiring young women elevated Emma's intellectual and spiritual insight to a higher level and contributed to her future prominence in education.

Ingham University at LeRoy, New York: 1856–58

Just before Emma began attending the Allen Female Seminary, her forthcoming mentor, D. L. Moody, at eighteen years of age, experienced a spiritual conversion in Boston. The following year in September of 1856 he impetuously, yet ambitiously, left to travel by train to Chicago where he would be torn between the business world and his newfound Christian devotion.

Meanwhile, Emma left Rochester and forged ahead with her calling in education by entering the Presbyterian affiliated women's college—LeRoy Female Seminary at LeRoy, New York, which became Ingham University in 1857.[51] Located approximately thirty miles west of Victor, LeRoy had been developed in the late 1700s by land owner

---

51. Town of Victor, New York, Archives, 8 May 1925, *Victor Herald* Newspaper Obituary.

Herman LeRoy from New York City. His son, Jacob LeRoy, managed the 86,000 acres of land. The seasonal Oatka Creek and the impressive Buttermilk Falls, where the Seneca Indians first established settlements, provided the essential water power for the town's milling industry.[52] Emma eagerly viewed this scenic landscape of LeRoy with its 1860 population of 4,227 residents in anticipation of her three years of teacher training at Ingham University.[53]

Emma would likely have attended the LeRoy Presbyterian Church due to her own Presbyterian background and the church affiliation of Ingham University. The Presbyterians organized the first church in LeRoy on February 7, 1812, followed by the Baptist Church in 1819 and the Methodist Episcopal Church in 1828. Many itinerant missionaries and preachers, including Reverend Davenport Phelps of the Episcopal Church, had visited this small town.[54] In 1822 Jacob LeRoy and his father financially supported the building of the Episcopal church completed in 1826. Jacob also built a three story home which he used to secure the Underground Railroad journey for slaves before the Civil War. Upon making the decision to return to upper state New York, he sold the house to A. F. Bartow who turned it over in 1856 to abolitionist Dr. Samuel Hanson Cox.

The Ingham sisters, Marietta and Emily, lived in a mansion across the street from the LeRoy house. They invited Cox, known for his fluency in Latin and Greek, to be the chancellor of the school that they founded in 1837 as the LeRoy Female Seminary. Originally from Connecticut, they arrived at LeRoy in 1837 as educators and missionaries to the *West*. They began their first summer with forty-one students in the primary grades and seventy-six in the upper grades. Thereafter, students attended the school from many sections of the country, and before long the school ranked with other outstanding women's schools.[55]

Accomplished teachers at Ingham University taught courses in art, literature, math, and astronomy. Emma received excellent training in the arts from one professor who became a noted landscape painter—Professor Lemuel M. Wiles (1826-1905).[56] Colonel Phineas Staunton, another gifted painter, married Emily Ingham in 1847 and became vice-chancellor of Ingham. Regrettably, in 1867 he died unexpectedly in Quito, South America on a science expedition in which he was commissioned to sketch the landscape of the Andes.[57]

Just before Emma graduated in 1858, Ingham University became the first chartered women's university to grant a four year degree. During the time that Emma

---

52. *First Presbyterian Church: LeRoy, New York.*

53. Emma would have possibly attended Ingham University as a three year school bringing with her a year of seminary training from the Allen School.

54. Child, *The Gazetteer and Business Directory*, 98.

55. Mount Holyoke, "Schools in the United States."

56. Southold Historical Society, "Wiles Family Papers," 3.

57. See Parsons, *Reminiscences of the Life and Character of Colonel Phineas Staunton*, 1867.

attended the school, an 1846 Ingham graduate named Marilla (Houghton) Gallup (1825–94) served as co-principal from 1855 to 1859 and principal from 1859 to 1860.[58] The school produced other successful alumni such as American physicist and astronomer Sarah Frances Whiting (1846–1927) who graduated from Ingham University in 1864.[59] Years later Emma would have disappointedly read the editorial in the December 18, 1906, *New York Times* regarding the final foreclosure of her former school known for having "exercised an uplifting influence upon the community and upon the lives of . . . generations of young women to whom LeRoy will be remembered . . . as the seat of their beloved alma mater."[60] After several years of financial difficulties, the school declined and closed in 1892 having trained approximately eight thousand young ladies.

Before that unfortunate closure, Emma, an exceptional student since her early school education in Victor, graduated from Ingham University in 1858 with high academic honors.[61] In fact, the administration highly valued and recognized her abilities and appropriately offered her a teaching position. For the next two years she trained students in astronomy and mathematics before accepting a principal position at Ewing Female University in Knoxville, Illinois.[62]

While Emma rose in educational distinction, D. L. Moody, actively involved in the Chicago YMCA, gradually began to abandon his business aspirations. In the process he met Emma C. Revell (1843–1903], the sister of publisher Fleming Hewitt Revell (1849–1931). Within two years Miss Revell became Moody's wife on August 28, 1862, and would also become a future God-chosen friend to another notable woman, Sophronia Emeline Cobb Dryer.

"She dresses with strength and nobility, and she smiles at the future."

~Proverbs 31:25 GWT~

---

58. Mount Holyoke, "Schools in the United States."
59. CWP at UCLA, "Some Important Contributions," Section on Education.
60. Ball, "Sale of Ingham University," para. 3.
61. Dorsett, *Passion For Souls,* 165.
62. Ogorek, "Dryer, Emma," 230 para. 1.

3

Education Positions, 1858–70

"Do your best to present yourself to God as a tried-and-true worker who isn't ashamed to teach the word of truth correctly."

~2 Timothy 2:15 GWT~

Ingham University: 1858–60

After graduation from Ingham University in 1858, Emma began her new position as a member of the Ingham faculty. She resided with twelve other faculty members at this Christian school located at 123 Wolcott Street in LeRoy, New York. The 1860 LeRoy census listed her as Emeline Dryer, math teacher at the *Female College*. The census included three Ingham music teachers as well as instructors for drawing, painting, Greek, and Latin with most of her colleagues close in age to Emma.[1] The survey disclosed no real estate, personal valuables, or savings for most of these industrious women.[2] Perhaps these details, mixed with the Lord's divine guidance and some premonition of the school's future foreclosure, freed Emma to make the momentous decision to move eight hundred miles further west in 1860 to Knoxville, Illinois, to become the principal of an 1859 state chartered school.

---

1. This census taken on June 1, 1860, listed Emma as twenty-three years old. This information has perhaps added some confusion as to her birth date since this census would have made Emma's birth in the year 1837 instead of 1835. Due to the early death of her parents, the assumption can be made that her adopted parents and relatives would have been most familiar with her actual birthday and therefore the documentation from her home town newspaper, *The Victor Herald*, has been used throughout this book as a basis for her time line events.
2. New York GenWeb Project, Census Records.

EDUCATION POSITIONS, 1858–70

Knoxville Ewing Female University: 1860–64

After Emma's extended journey to Knoxville, she quickly became acquainted with yet another small town. Knoxville, located approximately two hundred miles southwest of Chicago, displayed its patriotism by naming the town and county after General Henry Knox (1750–1806) who served under General George Washington (1732–99) during the Revolutionary War of 1775. Knoxville followed the example of many other cities and counties named after military heroes.[3] Emma may have been drawn to this *western* town after hearing about the seven statewide 1858 Illinois Senate debates between Abraham Lincoln (1809–65) and Stephen A. Douglas (1813–61). Their fifth debate was held in Galesburg, approximately ten miles northwest of Knoxville.

In any event, this self-motivated twenty-five year old discovered that she was now in a village much smaller in population than either Palmyra or LeRoy. The country side was lined with abundant fruit trees spread out over level agricultural land—a contrast to the rolling hills of New York.

---

3. Campbell, "Knox Township History, Educational Institutions," para. 11.

Emma scouted out the neighboring Methodist Episcopal Church founded in 1831, St. John's Episcopal Church in 1843, and the Swedish Lutheran Church in 1853.[4] Although she discovered no officially organized Presbyterian denomination in Knoxville, she more than likely heard of the Presbyterian Church in nearby Galesburg and its association with Knox College. Little could Emma have imagined that within the next two decades she would secure the loyal support of Knox College's former president, Jonathan Blanchard and his son Charles Blanchard. As a Congregationalist-Presbyterian minister and president of Knox College, Jonathan Blanchard resigned in 1857 and departed with his family to meet the new challenges waiting for them at Wheaton College not far from Chicago.

Meanwhile, Emma presented herself as an adventurous and dynamic young lady in vogue with her impressive nineteenth-century stylish flaxen-colored *banana curls* or *ringlets*. Her light colored eyes sparkled with adventure as she enthusiastically commenced her Knoxville principal position. She maintained oversight of one hundred and five admiring young female students at the newly built, sizeable school facility pointed out by some as an accommodating but unattractive building. At this fledgling school, purportedly named in honor of an elderly city resident,[5] Emma taught some of the younger students while at the same time maintaining her role as principal.

During Emma's first year at Ewing University, Dwight Moody continued his work in nearby Chicago. He had the privilege of receiving an unexpected visitor who offered encouragement for his Sunday school effort—a mission to youth which Emma and he clearly valued. President-elect Abraham Lincoln in November 1860 heard of Moody's street-mission work with Chicago's youth and his involvement with the local YMCA. Lincoln took notice and visited this Sunday school child recruiter who rode his missionary pony loaded down with scruffy-looking neglected, but elated, children throughout a city that he considered his parish.[6]

Emma heard these secondhand stories of this Chicago missionary and stories of Moody's assistance in the war effort. He systematically reached out to Civil War soldiers by establishing camp chapels for prayer and for ministering the love and comfort of Christ to weary and wounded soldiers. At this time he also deepened his relationship with Emma C. Revell through their covenant of marriage. With her support they established the Illinois Street Independent Church in 1864 with the vision of forming a body of redeemed sinners with Christ as head over all. This was a church calling for which it was said: "Mr. Moody never received any other ordination than that of providence and the spirit of God."[7]

---

4. Campbell, "Knox Township," 856.

5. Leffingwell, "St. Mary's School," para. 4; Chapman, *History of Knox County, Illinois,* 585.

6. Daniels, 1875/1876, *D. L. Moody and His Work*, 66; Williams, *Life and Work of Dwight L. Moody*, 52–53.

7. Williams, *Life and Work of Dwight L. Moody*, 98.

Education Positions, 1858–70

During this ministry time in Moody's life, Emma patriotically supported the Civil War effort through her active involvement in the semi-annual Knox County Teacher's Institute. In the second 1863 meeting she added to a resolution committee report by citing the need for educators and students to maintain a solid allegiance to the country, strong support for President Lincoln, and religious involvement. The final report stated: "That to our country in this hour of strife we swear anew our allegiance, pledging ourselves to assist her, if need be with our lives, praying God to continue to give wisdom to her rulers, courage to her soldiers and victory to her arms."[8]

A year before the final days of the Civil War and before the tragic assassination of President Lincoln on April 14, 1865, Emma resigned from Ewing University at the end of the 1863–64 term. Indeed, four years after assuming this position Emma, at the age of twenty-nine, left the institution during a time of national unrest and before the college could achieve its goal of prominence. The school purportedly did not meet the wants of the people and in the process did not fulfill public expectations. Knoxville Ewing Female University later closed in 1867.

Those financially responsible desired to continue using the facility for the education of young ladies. They agreed to turn it over to the Protestant Episcopal Church. Dr. Charles Wesley Leffingwell (1840–1928) managed the new school renamed St. Mary's School as it reopened on April 12, 1868.[9] In a letter written by Emma in 1916 she noted this ongoing educational institution: "You ask me where I was occupied before working with Mr. Moody. I had been a teacher in some way in common schools, High Schools, and Ingham College, where I graduated, and in Western Illinois. The last mentioned School is still working in the hands of Episcopalians."[10]

Miss Antionette Proseus replaced Emma as principal of Ewing University assuming leadership of the following 1865 faculty: Miss M. Hester, Miss Gabriella Taylor, Miss S. M. Gray, and Miss S. A. Hill.[11] While Emma began preparation for her elevated new role at Illinois State Normal University (ISNU), Dwight Moody sought to deepen his own knowledge and understanding of God's word. Through discipleship from businessman and evangelist J. B. Stillson, Moody transitioned into a *Man of One Book*[12]—the Bible—while Emma honed her talents and positioned herself to become a noble woman of further educational influence.

---

8. Perry, *History of Knox County*, 500.
9. Leffingwell, "St. Mary's School," para. 5.
10. Emma Dryer to Caroline Waite, 24 June 1886, Biographical File of Emma Dryer.
11. Chapman, *History of Knox County*, 586.
12. Williams, *Life and Work of Dwight L. Moody*, 122.

Illinois State Normal University: 1864–70

In the fall of 1864 Emma traveled eighty miles southeast from Galesburg to Bloomington-Normal, Illinois, most likely on the Chicago and Alton Railroad. Seven years earlier while traveling on this railroad line from Galesburg to Bloomington, another school teacher known as P. Atkinson recorded memoirs of his railroad excursion which cost $1.50 for the five hour trip. Four years earlier he had taken the lengthy ten hour trip by stagecoach.[13] Whether Emma traveled by stagecoach or train is uncertain. Either way, she viewed the flat country landscape with growing anticipation of furthering her career in the prominent and escalating teacher education movement.

During her journey she plausibly reflected on the school's history. She would have envisioned farmers cultivating the land on which Illinois State Normal University had been built. On February 18, 1857, the Illinois legislature approved the establishment of ISNU. Republican Illinois governor William H. Bissell (1811–60) signed the bill followed by Attorney Abraham Lincoln's commission to draw up the legal work regarding the school's funding.[14] This made Illinois's first public university available to all aspiring young people who held at least an eighth grade education.

Atypically, the town of Normal was established after the approval for the school's location and was designated by the State of Illinois as North Bloomington. Now Emma found herself travelling to ISNU through a sparse and quiet prairie land interrupted by the occasional sound of distant railroad trains. With an inner educational passion

---

13. Atkinson, "Notes of Travel," 2.
14. Harper, *Development of the Teacher College*, 28.

she eagerly arrived at a town which had officially become known on April 6, 1858, as Normal, Illinois.[15]

Emma discovered that this legislative action for the town of Normal supported the 1857 vision of businessman Jessie W. Fell (1808–87) for the establishment of an institution of higher learning in Illinois. Mr. Fell possessed a fascinating interest in a tree-planting initiative for the new territory. With this in mind he planted thousands of trees which significantly influenced the State Board of Education's choice for the location of the new university. As Emma beheld Normal's strikingly beautiful landscape, she undoubtedly appreciated the creative aesthetic direction of Mr. Fell. He stipulated that the university streets be given the names of his planted trees to serve as a distinctive trademark for the school.

Emma surely approved of Mr. Fell's goal to develop a town with enviable citizens. They would be granted land deeds only upon agreement to not sell liquor or procure a license to sell it. He obtained the support of 1,800 residents who agreed to "sobriety, morality, good society, and all the elements for an educational center."[16] A significant number of Normal families openly expressed their primary reason for coming to this quiet university town. They desired that their children be raised "in the most moral and best behaved community they could find with first-class educational advantages."[17] They were not disappointed as they joined Mr. Fell with his vision for a school which he characterized as a *grand university*. He actively solicited the support of educator Horace Mann (1796–1859),[18] the well-known *Father of American Education* who campaigned for tax supported free education for all.

15. Burnham, *History of Bloomington and Normal*, 115.
16. Ibid., 116.
17. Ibid., 136.
18. Ibid., 116.

Mr. Fell, instrumental in securing the Bloomington-Normal railroad crossings, knew that such an endeavor would enhance the town's development. The school opened in 1860 with most students gaining train access across the state to Bloomington. They roomed at thirty some residencies, but within two years the need arose for more boarding places. In 1864 with the increase of railroad connections, Emma arrived at this flourishing town where its accelerated population of one thousand residents provided necessary accommodations for ISNU students.

Emma would most likely have been unacquainted with Charles E. Hovey (1827–97), the school's first principal (1857–62). His title was a term loosely used until after the 1860s for the modern day designation of *president*. Mr. Hovey attended the first annual 1859 convention for the American Normal School Association. He was questioned as to why his *normal* school had the title of *university*. He explained that the school did not initially meet the qualifications for such a designation. Nevertheless, the State of Illinois wisely looked beyond the critical need of teachers to provide a compromising mandate and to discover future leaders in the universal fields of science, agriculture, and physiology.[19]

Emma had many questions regarding the background, function, activities, and responsibilities awaiting her at a *normal* school. The concept of normal schools continued to be fairly new in the Midwest with the state of Illinois breaking new ground.[20] In 1794 the first short-lived normal school was established in France. The school instructed prospective teachers in basic pedagogical methodology, in morals, and practical virtues.[21] After 1819 a normal school with over forty teacher seminars successfully trained the sons of peasants who thereafter taught at schools in the rural areas of Prussia. In October of 1839 John S. Wright headed up a similar movement in Illinois to inaugurate the state to this new European movement.[22] Unlike the Eastern normal schools with their elementary grade emphasis, ISNU—the second normal school in the West and earliest university—expanded teacher training to include all grade levels.[23]

As Emma tried to comprehend the vastness of this new education venture, she would once again include as a priority her search for a new church in the Bloomington-Normal area. She had learned that the university held the village's first church services in 1860 with the rotation of area pastors until more settlers arrived. The Congregationalists and Methodists led the way followed by the organization of the First Baptist Church on July 13, 1866. Emma would have most certainly welcomed the construction of the first Congregational and Presbyterian Church building on June 23,

---

19. Freed, *Journal of the Illinois State Historical Society*, 12–13.
20. Burnham, *History of Bloomington and Normal*, 117.
21. Freed, *Journal of the Illinois State Historical Society*, 4.
22. Ibid., 5.
23. Harper, *A Century of Public Teacher Education*, 80.

1867.[24] It was not long before she gratifyingly adjusted to the exquisite view of church spires surrounded by the delicate fragrance and beauty of Mr. Fell's flowering trees.

Prestigious Faculty Position

In a written copy of a historical address presented by school president, Dr. Richard Edwards (1822–1908), Emma was listed as Emmeline [sic] Dryer in the Normal Department.[25] She joined at least twenty-nine other Illinois State Normal University Model School teachers. Emma quickly settled into her new boarding room at the home of Thomas Loer. She shared her enthusiasm with housekeeper Mary Thomas while preparing for her first fifteen week term beginning on Monday, September 5, 1864, at an annual salary of $800.[26]

With an enrollment of 304 students, she noted that the war efforts had noticeably lowered the male student population.[27] Yet that did not dampen her enthusiasm. Emma's educational background and training at Ingham University and Allen Seminary equipped her to teach her assigned grammar and drawing classes.[28] With her impressive education credentials, sharp intellect, and excellent administrative skills, Emma quickly advanced to the position of principal, or preceptress and dean of the women's female faculty.

After Emma's first year she replaced the preceptress, Miss Margaret E. Osband, who resigned in order to marry Professor Albert Stetson.[29] According to ISNU's second president, Dr. Edwards, Miss Osband "was a faithful and capable teacher, and her discontinuance was altogether owing to her unaccountable preference for another position."[30] At the same time, Dr. Edwards presented to the ISNU Board the following report: "The Faculty . . . continues as heretofore, except that Miss Emeline Dryer has taken the place vacated by Mrs. Stetson. Miss Dryer's services bid fair to be in the highest degree valuable to the institution, and I can not help regarding it as a fortunate circumstance that we are able to secure them. Her place was temporarily filled by Miss Fanny L. D. Strong during the first term and a part of the second."[31]

---

24. Marshall, *Grandest of Enterprises*, 116.

25. Cook and McHugh, *A History of the Illinois State Normal University*, 204.

26. The U.S. Census 1870 for "Emaline Dryer" registers her as living in the household of Thomas Loer, Illinois. Listed with Loer was Mary Thomas (48 years old) as the Express Agent or housekeeper with all Caucasian residents in five dwellings with the ages of the residents noted. Emma was listed as a 35 year old school teacher born in Massachusetts living in Normal Township in Illinois on July 26, 1870. Assuming this information is correct, Emma would have been ninety years old at the time of her death in 1925 which confirms the report from her home town newspaper, the *Victor Herald*.

27. Harper, *Development of the Teacher College*, 90.

28. *Catalogue of the State Normal University*, June 28, 1866, 4.

29. Felmley, *Semi-Centennial History of the Illinois State Normal University*, 101.

30. Edwards, *Decennial Address*, 18.

31. *Proceedings*, 27–28 June 1865, Illinois State Board of Education.

In this demanding position Emma not only provided oversight for the teachers and students, but kept a full time teaching schedule. She was to become one of the distinguished educators in the West, a status enhanced by her association with President Edwards.

Dr. Edwards consistently raised the standards for his staff while affirming them as professional educators. He contended that the credentials and standards for teacher colleges were comparable to that of medical colleges.[32] He ornately declared before Emma and her fellow teachers: "Education of the children . . . is the grandest of enterprises."[33]

More than likely unknown to Emma at the time of her initial employment, financial difficulties regarding state funding for the school existed. However, Dr. Edwards and the board intervened on behalf of ISNU and its staff. At the June 27 and 28, 1866, Board proceedings Dr. Edwards reported the repercussion of delayed payments from the State Treasurer over the past several years: "The consequence has been an entire derangement of the finances of the Institution. Great delay becomes unavoidable in the payment of bills which ought to be settled at once. Members of the Faculty find it necessary to resort to perplexing expedients for want of money justly due them. The evil is a very serious one; and if additional legislation is necessary to correct it . . . I sincerely hope that the attention of the legislature may be early and effectually called to the matter."[34] Dr. Edwards stated emphatically that the Illinois State School and its faculty had incurred considerable loss.

At a time when women were receiving higher academic acclaim, Dr. Edwards and his school board assiduously prioritized the raising of salaries. The Board recorded their financial commitments and commendations regarding Emma which coincided with their increased admiration of her educational expertise. After her first year, the Board recommendations from the June 27 and 28, 1866, meetings stipulated that "the salary of Miss Emaline [sic] Dryer, Preceptress of the Normal Department, be placed at $900. It is now $800. Miss Dryer's services in guiding the minds, and improving the habits and tastes of the young ladies, have been very valuable."[35] Likewise, the Board issued new teachers a beginning salary of $550 with the principal of the primary school, Miss Edith T. Johnson, having a salary increase from $550 to $650.[36]

Although men still received higher incomes, Dr. Edwards continued to press for increased wages for the women staff. In December of 1867 the board granted four male professors a $500 increase from $1,500 and a $200 raise for Emma. They recognized the reasonableness of the request and resolved: "We will proceed with as little delay as possible to make efforts to have the salaries of the Professors of the University

32. Borrowman, *Teacher Education in America,* 80.
33. Marshall, *Grandest of Enterprises,* 328.
34. *Proceedings,* 27–28 June 1866, Illinois State Board of Education.
35. Ibid.
36. Ibid.

increased to amounts commensurate with their very valuable labors, and we express great confidence that our efforts will be successful . . . And that we further express the purpose of the Board . . . to increase the salary of Miss Emaline [sic], Preceptress in the Normal University, to the sum of $1,100."[37] The Board followed with another $100 increase on June 23, 1869. They recommended that $400 be added to Grammar School instructor Joseph Carter's annual salary and that Miss Dryer from the Normal Department should also have a salary increase of $100 per year.[38]

The 1864–65 ISNU catalog listed Emma's initial position as *Instructress in Grammar and Drawing*. She had the privilege of working beside an exceptional faculty—Edwin C. Hewett instructor in Geography and History; Joseph A. Sewall, Instructor in Natural Science; Thomas Metcalf, Math Instructor; and Albert Stetson, Instructor in Language. This strong educational group was depicted as being "full of determination to make the school worthy of regard, and to compel regard for it."[39] Along with Emma, they were known as an enthusiastic faculty who made quite a stir.

With this team of educators Dr. Edwards initiated in 1863 an annual state teacher conference or institute to be held in September for two to four weeks. The conference utilized the Normal faculty and other prominent educators to further train teachers in the state of Illinois. With Emma's arrival in 1864 she willingly participated in the institute along with 128 state wide teachers. They instructed workshops in the art of education, mental arithmetic, gymnastics, derivation of words, intuitive instruction for children, and geology of Illinois. Emma joined other educators in publishing a 140 page thorough report of the conference. They were known as forerunners in educational journalism in Illinois from 1857 to 1890.[40]

Emma participated in the faculty publications and conferences which continued in popularity in conjunction with three school terms of fifteen weeks, thirteen weeks, and twelve weeks. However, in one instance she sent a letter along with other attendees such as Senators Logan and Davis, Governor Cullom, Professor E. W. Coy, and Professor Burrington expressing regrets for an unavoidable absence.[41] After twenty-six years the conferences that registered over 349 institutes and 503 addresses, were finally discontinued due to the lack of compensation and Normal instructor burnout.

ISNU Model School and Curriculum Development

Emma qualified as a skilled educational practitioner of the ISNU Model or Practice School under the supervision of the High School principal for the primary grades

37. *Proceedings,* 17–18 December 1867, Illinois State Board of Education.
38. *Proceedings,* 1869, Paper 57, Illinois State Board of Education.
39. Harper, *Development of the Teacher College,* 52.
40. Ibid., 157.
41. Cook and McHugh, *A History of the Illinois State Normal University,* 233.

through high school. She functioned as an integral part of the Normal School training for teachers involving three years or nine school terms. The Model School exposed potential ISNU teachers to both clinical observations and practicum with teaching assistance. This method for teacher training provided ample opportunity for the ISNU students to put their teaching knowledge into practice.[42] In the first year of the institution (1857) children from the area school district were all enrolled in the *Model School*. Public funds were directed for the expenses of the new school. Six years later the Model School enrolled around 170 students occupying six classrooms.

Emma arrived at ISNU during this time of growth for the Model School. As the village increased, the number of children multiplied, and the rooms at the University became too small for their accommodation. Accordingly, a schoolhouse was built by the school district. In April of 1867 Emma assisted in the move of the Model School grammar and intermediate grades to the new building. By 1868 the Illinois State Board of Education voted to terminate the ISNU control of the school. A local village school, established in 1868 with a local school district, received school revenues instead of the university. While in her fourth year at ISNU Emma realized the results of this action as Model School enrollment dropped from 630 students to 318.

In the Normal School, President Edwards supervised the student teachers. He was a well known "prominent, able, and, in every respect, blessing-working man [who] . . . understands the dangers of slavish obedience of the text-book, and emphasizes properly the advantages of oral instruction."[43] Dr. Edwards encouraged Professor Metcalf and his assistants, including preceptress Emma Dryer, to model for these student teachers "the theoretical, practical and disciplinary work of teaching."[44]

Emma's prospective student teachers would take charge of the primary classes at the Model School during their third year of course work in order to put into practice what they had observed from Miss Dryer's demonstrations. Her students trained in the four recitation rooms occupied by the grammar school, high school, and primary department. The second floor provided assembly rooms with desks for 270 pupils, eight additional recitation rooms, a 1,200 volume reference library, and reading rooms furnished with leading publications. The third floor contained a museum with collections valued around $100,000. A library with a piano provided a weekly meeting place for the two literary societies—the Philadelphian and Wrightonian.[45]

When Emma arrived at ISNU in 1864 two hundred ladies and one hundred and four young men were eagerly awaiting their new teaching assignments in order to enter the field of public school instruction. The Model School exposed these aspiring teachers to a full range of subject matter, elementary to high school, including science and the art of teaching all ages. Emma taught Dr. Edwards's integrated pedagogical

42. Ibid., 197.
43. Ibid., 255.
44. Ibid., 27.
45. Burnham, *History of Bloomington and Normal*, 126.

techniques throughout the curriculum using these methods: "By exercises in conducting the regular class of the Normal Schools; by classes of normal pupils assuming for the time the character of children, and receiving instruction and answering questions as they think children would; and by a separate school of children in which the novice is intrusted with the charge of a class, either permanently or for a stated period."[46] Edwards considered the Model School to be an indisputable necessity for fulfilling the purpose and design of a normal school.[47]

Throughout Emma's appointment at ISNU her course assignments remained basically unchanged. Teaching only first and third year students, her grammar and drawing classes were listed along with the following courses:

1. Grammar: 1st year students 13 weeks for 2nd semester and 12 weeks for third semester in addition to arithmetic, geography, history, reading, spelling, history and method of education, and English literature.

2. Drawing: 3rd year for 26 weeks along with natural philosophy, physiology, astronomy, bookkeeping, school law of Illinois, the constitution, history and method of education, and writing.[48]

In addition, since 1862 students had been required to participate in music embellished gymnastics in which "the musical accompaniment gave the double advantage of precision to the movements and of adding vastly to the interest and enjoyment of the exercises."[49] This course was enhanced by Dr. Leo Lewis in 1866 who made it adaptable to light exercise in the regular classroom.[50]

During the early curriculum development days of ISNU educators proposed innovative methods of teaching. Edwards and Hewitt constructed their own courses including *Theory and Art of Teaching* from their lecture notes with materials from David P. Page's *Theory and Practice of Teaching,* Karl Rosencranz's *A Treatise on Pedagogics as a System,* Barnard's *Journal,* and Samuel R. Hall's *Lectures on School Keeping*. When developing her grammar curriculum Emma was keenly aware of the requirements for student admission which consisted of student recall of all parts of speech along with their relationship and function.[51] President Edwards additionally clarified: "Explanation is not at all needed for the purpose at hand which is to accustom the pupil to the proper use of speech. Language, as practically used, is a matter of habit and not a matter of philosophy. Children learn to speak correctly and elegantly by speaking correctly and elegantly and not by studying philosophy. The study of philology is . . . useful for explaining what is, and not for creating what is not—namely good habits

46. Edwards, *Decennial Address,* 81.
47. Ibid.
48. Harper, *Development of the Teacher College,* 125.
49. Ibid., 126.
50. Ibid.
51. Ibid., 122.

of speech in persons addicted to bad ones."[52] When instructing her students, Emma carefully modeled and applied Edwards's directives regarding the proper teaching of grammar and speech.

Emma observed President Edwards's conservative investigation of all new educational trends including the *Oswego Training Method* developed by E. A. Sheldon (1823–97). Although ISNU was the first among normal schools in the Midwest, Sheldon pronounced his New York school as the first teacher on-site training school based on the Pestalozzi method.[53] On December 2, 1861, the School of the Home and Colonial School Society of London extended an invitation to ISNU to attend training for the Oswego Method at Oswego, New York, scheduled for February of 1862. This invitation was sent to distinguished educators including W. H. Wells as Superintendent of the Chicago schools and Miss L. E. Ketcham, Principal or Superintendent of the ISNU Experimental Department or School of Practice.[54]

Livonia Ketcham, paying for her own expenses to Oswego, New York, accepted the invitation to personally observe and receive instruction from London's Oswego Model School representative, Miss Jones. However, little is known about the degree to which the Pestalozzi method infiltrated Normal University's Model School due to Miss Ketcham's resignation in the spring.[55] Nevertheless, after her return from New York in 1862 the ISNU societies kept the debate alive with this resolution: "Resolved, that the labors of Pestalozzi in the educational field have been of more value to mankind than those of Horace Mann. Affirmative, L. Kellogg and A. McClure, Wrightonians; negative, E.F. Bacon and J. I. Thompson, Philadelphians (Williston, John)."[56]

As an established educator Emma would have been acquainted with the Pestalozzi method and its emphasis on object teaching and hands-on curriculum. It is unknown to what extent it would have influenced her teaching especially with its prominent emphasis on the inclusion of drawing techniques. She could have encouraged other drawing methods for learning similar to those propagated by Norman Allison Calkins (1822–95) in his popular 1861 book titled *Primary Object Lessons*.

Nonetheless, she observed Dr. Edwards's tremendous influence on curriculum development. She recognized that he was an admirer of Pestalozzi, but was also outspoken regarding his methods. Edwards participated as a member of an 1864

---

52. Ibid., 133.

53. Swiss philanthropist and educational reformer Johann Heinrich Pestalozzi (1746-1827) developed an educational method of learning whereby knowledge is obtained through the perception of the senses. The goal was to cultivate the mind for further self-learning rather than communicating technical knowledge. The Pestalozzian method of teacher training dealt with establishing concrete memory of information through the use of observation and hands-on practice accomplished through such resources as Model Schools. See Sheldon's autobiography for a history of the Pestalozzi movement developed in America by Edward Sheldon.

54. Sheldon, *Autobiography*, 148–49.

55. Marshall, *Grandest of Enterprises*, 94.

56. Cook and McHugh, *A History of the Illinois State Normal University*, 142.

committee regarding the effectiveness of the Oswego method. He was minimally opposed to a methodical process such as object teaching and lectured about its defects: "Object teaching tends to be mechanical, develops verbalism, and makes the work of making a teacher too easy a task."[57] Ultimately, ISNU's staff circumvented the issue by substituting the term *methods* which was ultimately the same as Pestalozzi's object teaching.[58]

Joining the ISNU spirit of debate regarding the Pestalozzi method, Emma would have observed how her associate, Professor Edwin C. Hewett, in 1866 disparagingly critiqued the Oswego method in his lecture to the school's Philadelphian Society:

> The strangest of all strange things in respect to Pestalozzi is that he, after his full/and clear enunciation of educational principles as enduring as the eternal hills, should have fallen into just this mistake and should have taken for granted that, when his pupils made his statements after him, they comprehended all the ideas that those statements covered; and . . . that he could write down correct processes of teaching in a book in such a way, that, by its aid, the most stupid could teach as well as the most intelligent . . . I query if Pestalozzi's mistake died with him.[59]

Even with Hewett's objections, the school endorsed the purpose of this instruction in their school catalogue: "To awaken the perceptive faculties, and to form a habit of accurate observation. Children thus trained make not only more thorough scholars, but also more practical men and women."[60] Despite faculty disagreement, Emma conscientiously followed the catalogue guidelines by directing the use of object lessons from the Oswego Method which were prepared and used in the Model School.

Involvement in Student Life

In the fall of 1860 ISNU students enthusiastically trekked along the newly built town sidewalks. Within a few years they would continue their walk to check the mail at the new local post office operated by Postmaster Robert E. Bower. They purchased items from Mr. Phillips's store on the corner of Linden Street next to the Chicago and Alton Railroad. By 1865 Emma had adapted to this new education setting. She joined the students who were admitted according to ISNU requirements mandating that males be at least seventeen and females sixteen. Students were required to submit adult references to certify their high moral character. They signed a pledge indicating their goal to teach in the state of Illinois.

---

57. Harper, *Development of the Teacher College*, 130.
58. Ibid., 129.
59. Ibid., 130–31. A full copy of Edwin C. Hewett's lecture can be found at https://archive.org/details/pestalozzilecturoohewe.
60. Ibid., 131.

Emma realized that most of the Normal students were from rural areas like herself. Although without a high school education, most of them had prior teaching experience. She believed from personal experience that even rural kids could succeed educationally if they applied themselves and displayed the moral character ISNU required.

Emma's own parents financially assisted in her education and made significant sacrifices as rural New York farmers. Emma deeply appreciated their support and understood the sacrifices being made by families for these rural ISNU students. She would have been encouraged to see that tuition was free for those who pledged to teach in Illinois schools. Otherwise, tuition at $30 a year remained the same for both ISNU and Model High School students.[61] Later, Edwin Hewett, as the third ISNU President, initially charged $25 for high school tuition and $15 for grammar school. Emma would also have understandably and agreeably supported the *no charge* offer for faculty children and extended families.

Campus Housing

The Normal institution opened a new building for housing in the fall of 1860. However, with a subsequent rise in enrollment there were still not enough rooms in the village boarding houses for all the students. Many obtained rooms in nearby Bloomington. Although Emma did not live on campus at the time of her 1864 arrival, she became actively concerned about the housing conditions for her students. In her association with President Edwards she identified with his mission to improve student housing. In 1864 he unsuccessfully invited several industrialists to contribute $50,000 for building an elaborate dormitory to be supervised by ISNU faculty.

Edwards stimulated further interest and support for his delayed housing proposal by enlisting Miss Dryer's assistance. He most likely shared with her the story of his first year endeavor at ISNU to determine why some female students were not attending class. He discovered that during the rainy season, due to the absence of sidewalks to *The Main Building*, students were forced to spend time washing and drying their garments and feet. Edwards immediately found a remedy with the construction of new sidewalks. He conveyed his other ongoing cares: "I regard the question of how to lighten the burden of those persons of worthy character but limited means, who, with a few dollars more than they actually possess, would fit themselves for high usefulness as teachers—I regard this question as *the one* which bears most emphatically upon the success of our institution."[62]

Sharing President Edwards's disquieting concerns, Emma surveyed student living conditions and submitted an innovative and original heartfelt account which the Board adopted as part of its legislative report. She empathically contested:

61. Cook and McHugh, *A History of the Illinois State Normal University*, 280.
62. Harper, *Development of the Teacher College*, 105.

> Sometimes three or four persons occupy one room, but oftener two live in a small room. I have found cases like this: two ladies in one room, paying six or seven dollars a month; the furniture being bought by them or secured by extra rent; no closet, no cellar privileges, a bare floor; uncurtained windows . . . a rickety coal stove; a couple of wooden chairs; some trunks and boxes containing food and clothes; a rough table on which to study and eat; a small open cupboard for dishes, made of rough boards and sticks of wood; and under the table a few cooking utensils, an oil can, dish pan, etc. Add to this an abundance of coal dust and bad air, and you have a picture of the visible home life led by most of the young women who board themselves.[63]

While reporting on the ladies' rooming situation, she also advocated for the men. She viewed them as having even more dire conditions due to their cooking and cleaning inexperience.

Furthermore, in her report Emma pointed out Normal's high living costs which added to the distressing financial and physical needs of the students. They were becoming ill from improperly cooked food in their rooms. They also experienced medical problems due to the physical burden of hauling heating supplies, water, and trash up and down multiple flights of stairs. Emma described their "rickety bedsteads with straw ticks, soiled bedding, inadequate lighting, ventilation, and closet space for clothing" all of which represented a drab dormitory picture that would continue beyond the end of the nineteenth century.[64]

Despite these housing conditions, students continued with determined commitment to finish their course work as Emma continued her strong support of President Edwards's dormitory proposal. She compellingly opposed the "hard hearted legislature which refused the President's request for a 'boarding hall' to be erected at a cost of but $25,000" and upheld his "plan for accommodating approximately one hundred and fifty students [with] . . . cooking apparatus, sleeping, bathing and study rooms, parlors for guests, and a gymnasium."[65]

Edwards's dormitory requests injudiciously produced an alternative state legislative vote in 1867 to fund $3,000 for landscaping, $500 for campus repairs, and $2,500 toward the school's Natural History Museum.[66] Despite the loss of dormitory funding, the ISNU Board remained deeply grateful for Emma's keen insights and work on behalf of the school. On December 16, 1868, they notably motioned: "Mr. Bateman moved that the thanks of the Board be tendered Miss Dryer, for her very forcible, interesting and impressive address, and the motion was unanimously adopted."

---

63. Ibid., 105–6.
64. Marshall, *Grandest of Enterprises*, 112.
65. Harper, *Development of the Teacher College*, 106.
66. Marshall, *Grandest of Enterprises*, 118.

Campus Societies and Activities

Beyond her involvement in campus housing issues, Emma observed the activities and customs of the Wrightonian and Philadelphian Societies. With Emma's past training regarding social issues, she would have avidly attended, read, or listened to the society's regular debates which included topics such as the following:

- 1866 Debate: Ought the election franchise to be restricted to such persons as can read and write understandingly?
- 1867 Debate: Should the congress of the United States regulate suffrage in the States?
- 1868 Debate: Resolved, That Maximillians' career in connection with Mexican affairs shows that he possessed a noble character as a man and high abilities as a statesman.
- 1869 Debate: Free Trade[67]

After the winter semester they held society exhibitions followed in the spring by a series of lectures. The societies celebrated the end of the term with a picnic in the blooming Jessie Fell flower and tree groves.[68]

Emma realized that even in the midst of such exhilarating debates, students still needed time to simply be students and to enjoy their new residential campus experience. She discovered a well-intentioned summer Wrightonian student tradition involving the serenading of the ISNU faculty. Students looked forward to hiring a band from Bloomington to accompany them in their circuit from one teacher's house to another. Emma most certainly wondered, with the initiation of the Civil War and hard economic times, how the students could afford to pay the band forty dollars. She quickly found out as the days went by without a serenade. The student committee went from cancelling the band, to suggesting that a wagon pick up the faculty for less expense, to finally cancelling the whole event.[69] Experiences such as these served as a training ground for Emma's interaction with young adults in her future Chicago ministry.

Classroom and Campus Discipline

Just as President Edwards held students to a strict and high level of achievement, he was also known as a stringent disciplinarian for rules. He asserted, "A regulation . . . should never be announced until consideration was given all circumstances bearing upon it, and once made, obedience should be inexorably and impartially insisted

---

67. Cook and McHugh, *A History of the Illinois State Normal University*, 143–44.
68. Ibid., 113.
69. Ibid.

upon; but always a student should be approached in a kind and courteous manner."[70] While perhaps reflecting on the instructions of her mentor Mary B. Allen regarding discipline, Emma conscientiously followed President Edwards's example. She encouraged her students to develop successful classroom management skills for instruction including his conservative use of a bell rather than a ruler to call the class to order. Edwards instructed his teachers to teach and manage their students "with vigor, precision and efficiency with no unnecessary bustle, noise or display."[71]

Faculty members were instructed to aggressively address classroom discipline. However, it appeared that the need was diminished for restrictions regarding the extra-curricular social life of students at this early formative coeducational institution. Emma and her colleagues recognized that idle hands work mischief, but the hand of the diligent, especially those without financial means, produced maturity and less time for misconduct.[72]

President Edwards advocated not only for men but for women's active roles in both academic and campus events. Citing society minded and educationally astute women such as Harriet Beecher Stowe and Elizabeth Barrett Browning, he said, "In view of what these and a hundred other women have done, is it not the acme of absurdity for you and me, because we happen to grow beards, to step forward, with our little measuring strings, and attempt to fix, before hand, the scope of women's investigation of truth?"[73] At the same time Edwards assured the parents of his students that both sexes would be held to elevated academic and social standards. He implemented a 10:00 Saturday night curfew with the assurance of proper supervision of distinct entryways, bathrooms, and stairways.[74]

In the office of preceptress Emma carefully enforced these guidelines as noted by Professor G. W. Hoss in *The Indianan School Journal* in 1868 after a campus visit. He wrote: "It is just to state that we have never seen a body of pupils so unremittingly and in some cases so severely diligent. If there be a fault at all in this particular, it is the fault of overwork."[75] With President Edwards's example of rigorous discipline as a guide, Emma would ultimately carry these high academic and disciplinary standards with her when she arrived in Chicago in 1870—at the expense of overwork.

Emma and her staff held their students, who had minimal cultural experience and exposure to higher education, in high regard. Students reciprocated this respect toward Miss Dryer and her colleagues. One student reflected his admiration: "It [ISNU] impressed us with the dignity and value of our profession by bringing us into contact with men and women whose characters were earnest, genuine, inspiring, and

70. Marshall, *Grandest of Enterprises*, 94.
71. Harper, *Development of the Teacher College*, 133.
72. Ibid., 110.
73. Ibid., 107.
74. Ibid.
75. Ibid., 110.

evoked the cause of education. These teachers of ours were themselves students. They knew all that was known at the time about the best methods of teaching, and passed that knowledge on to us."[76] Emma's students viewed their ISNU training as a job to be taken seriously. She considered it a tremendous privilege to teach and instill upright character in her students—noble qualities faithfully exemplified and demonstrated firsthand by their preceptress, Miss Dryer.

Religion and Politics

Emma, known on campus as a skilled teacher who morally influenced her students, served as God's instrument in the conversion of many individuals.[77] Along with her staff she modeled high standards of integrity for these prospective teachers and Model School students. President Edwards likewise modeled moral, religious, and sociopolitical responses. He advocated for abolition and Negro equality. In 1867 Emma approvingly observed his response to the first black child enrolled at the Model School. The *Chicago Republican* newspaper reported in the May 11, 1867, edition: "The other morning a little girl of color was found sitting in her right mind in the Model School . . . Topsy stuck to her seat. The teachers taught her; the president treated her as he thought the Savior would have treated her if she had come to Him to be taught. All is now quiet at Normal."[78]

However, much controversy continued regarding President Edwards's abolition stance. The *Chicago Times* on Feb. 22, 1868, disparagingly reported: "Here is an institution supported at great expense by the taxpayers of Illinois, and run in the interest of nigger-radicals and radical niggers. Our hope is that if ever white people have a voice in controlling the affairs of Illinois again, they will blot out of existence this, and all similar institutions, that are carried on for the benefit of the radical party and niggers, at the expense of the people. They are of no benefit, save only as miscegenation and money-squandering establishments."[79] Despite these negatively charged accusations, Emma knew that the ISNU Board backed their school president. They affirmed that in their judgment all the young people in the state of Illinois had an equal right to participate in the public education system and especially in education at Normal University which was founded and established to guarantee these rights as assured by the laws of Illinois.[80]

President Edwards, with his Calvinistic Methodist Church background, openly supported religious advancement. To Emma's complete satisfaction he encouraged the presence of Christian associations including the YMCA that were rapidly developing

76. Ibid.
77. Memorial Service for Miss Emma Dryer, 31 May 1925, Moody Church Collection.
78. Harper, *Development of the Teacher College*, 111.
79. Ibid.
80. Ibid.

around the country and positively contributing to the religious atmosphere on college campuses.[81] In 1866 Emma's future associate, Dwight L. Moody, dynamically engaged in the YMCA as the elected president of the Chicago branch. Moody would discover within a few years that throughout Emma's teaching career she displayed a deep commitment to Christ. She was actively involved in Christian work at ISNU and other localities during her vacations and summer months as a teacher, volunteer relief worker, evangelist, and discipleship trainer.[82] While developing relationships with various YMCA missionaries she had also begun to network with Chicago Protestant missions and Moody associates such as Reverend and Mrs. W. H. Daniels who would prove instrumental in Moody's future introduction to Emma Dryer.

Typhoid Fever and Resignation

By 1870 ISNU exceeded the enrollment, vision, and annual expenditures of any other normal school in the nation. The school reported an enrollment of 158 men and 157 ladies in 1869 and 208 men and 206 ladies at the end of the following year.[83] For five of the past six years Emma faithfully served as head of the women faculty at ISNU. She was known as a gifted and skilled educator who significantly inspired and shaped the historical practices of ISNU.[84]

President Edwards valued and esteemed Emma as a leading teacher and efficient administrator. As her faithful mentor he modeled curriculum development, teacher training, and pedagogical techniques in a Model School setting with community and statewide education networking.[85] As an active participant in the normal school movement Emma experienced first-hand what a training school should be. ISNU prepared her for future work in a Bible based educational setting where she would train lower class and rural students for educational and spiritual leadership roles.

At the height of a successful and well paid career at this prestigious university Emma chose to put aside her respectful position and submit her resignation. The December 1870 ISNU Board proceedings stated: "Miss Emaline [sic] Dryer has resigned her place on the Faculty. She had been in your service six years, and I believe it is the unanimous opinion of all who were acquainted with her work that her influence upon the students was in a remarkable degree efficient and improving. Her resignation was generally and sincerely regretted." The Board most certainly understood this decision. They were aware of Miss Dryer's recent setback with typhoid fever. It is unclear how Emma contracted this disease known to occur in unsanitary environments through contaminated food or water. The fatality rate for typhoid during the nineteenth

---

81. Ibid., 115.
82. Dorsett, *A Passion For Souls*, 166.
83. Harper, *Development of the Teacher College*, 90.
84. Foster, et al., *Educating Clergy*, 199.
85. Ibid.

century, especially around the Civil War times, registered around sixty deaths per one hundred thousand. In Philadelphia alone more Civil War soldiers in 1864 were killed due to typhoid and dysentery than on the confederate battlefield.

The fear of this disease would have been utmost in Emma's mind as it became a reality to her. The date for the onset of her illness with an initial four to six week recovery time is unknown. However, at the end of the spring school term of 1870 Emma travelled to Chicago to regain her health. She referred to this season in which she contracted this dreaded sickness as a time from which neither she nor her doctor expected her to recover.

While in Chicago Emma stayed with a friend, Mrs. Lucy Helmer, originally from Chicopee, Massachusetts, forty miles east of her birthplace in Stockbridge. W. H. Daniels, pastor of the First Methodist Episcopal Church of Chicago and a friend of D. L. Moody, had performed the wedding ceremony for Lucy and her husband, Joshua Stark Helmer. They later moved to a home near Lincoln Park in Chicago and graciously invited Emma to join them for this time of healing and recovery.

Now, providentially, during this summer of 1870 the *past* circumstances and experiences of both Emma Dryer and Dwight L. Moody divinely collided with their *present* to forge a God-destined *future*—a future that would miraculously and unfalteringly birth a religious training school that would continue to spread the gospel even into the twenty-first century.

> *"She sees that she is making a good profit. Her lamp burns late at night.*
> *She puts on strength like a belt and goes to work with energy."*
>
> Proverbs 31:17–18 GWT

4

Chicago Calling, 1870–73

"I have heard how you left your father and mother and your own land to live here among complete strangers. May the Lord, the God of Israel, under whose wings you have come to take refuge, reward you fully for what you have done."

~Ruth 2:11b–12 New Living Translation~

WHILE AT ISNU, EMMA networked with various Chicago area mission organizations and education professionals. Consequently, Chicago was not a total unknown to her. In 1870 she ventured to this Midwest metropolis, known as the *Muddy City*, at a serious juncture in her life to acquire much needed rest. She was still a country girl at heart. Nevertheless, coming to this big city of approximately 300,000 residents would have been quite exhilarating even under less than normal healthy circumstances.

One evening in 1870 Emma dined at the 100 Warren Avenue home of her Lincoln Park friends, Mr. and Mrs. Joshua Helmer in Chicago with Reverend and Mrs. W. H. Daniels. They conveyed that D. L. Moody had been asking about her. This came as a total surprise to Emma. To be inquired of by a well-known evangelist whom she had never personally met must have added to her sense of wonderment regarding God's future for her despite her recent illness.

Reverend Daniels explained that Moody was always looking for Christian workers. As president of the YMCA and organizer of the Chicago Relief Aid Society, Moody had been asking for additional help especially from women to work among women. He was unable to give the necessary time to make all the calls to the poor of the city. Reverend Daniels spoke to Emma regarding Moody: "He knows everybody; he has been to a S.S. [Sunday School] or a prayer meeting, and heard you. He wants to see you: he is an excellent man." Despite Daniels's glowing commendation, he protectively guarded Emma in her recovery from typhoid fever by advising her: "But don't you have anything to do with him. He is full of work, and in a little while you will work yourself sick."[1]

Not long after this conversation John F. Eberhart (1829–73), a fellow educator and friend of Emma, reaffirmed Moody's inquiry. In the fall of 1859 when Emma was on staff at Ingham University, Eberhart was appointed to the position of superintendent of Chicago's Cook County Schools. Superintendent Eberhart and his wife Matilda Charity, both trained teachers, later become friends with Emma through ISNU. Eberhart, also a close friend of Jesse Fell, played an instrumental role in the approval of the ISNU site at Normal, Illinois, in 1859. He likewise assisted in 1867 in the founding of Chicago State University. A deeply religious man, John Eberhart could identify with Emma's recent fears regarding her illness. He had himself been diagnosed in 1853 with consumption or tuberculosis and given only a few months to live.[2] Concerned with her health at this time and acquainted with Moody's energetic personality, he forewarned Emma: "I wish we had a regiment like Moody, and I do all I can to keep him going, but don't you go near him, you'll see just as he does, and in a little while, you will work yourself to death."[3]

Along with this additional word of caution, Emma could have pondered her childhood stories of missionary David Brainerd. He was guardedly warned by Jonathan Edwards to avoid excessive work in his ministry "taking due care to proportion his fatigues to his strength."[4] Emma must have also considered the tremendous sacrificial work that could be awaiting her.

1. Emma Dryer to Caroline Waite, 13 July 1924, Biographical File of Emma Dryer.
2. *Album of Genealogy and Biography,* 151–54.
3. Emma Dryer to Caroline Waite, 13 July 1924, Biographical File of Emma Dryer.
4. Brainerd and Edwards, *The Life and Diary,* 9.

Chicago Calling, 1870–73
Divine Connection: Introduction to D. L. Moody

Emma discovered that two of her close Chicago missionary friends who were members of the YMCA—Mrs. Sarah G. Cleveland and Miss Alice Miller—were unaware of Daniels's and Eberhart's conversations with Emma. They shared that they had recently spoken with Mr. Moody. Miss Miller worked at the YMCA located at 150 Madison Street three blocks from where Moody and his wife lived. He asked them if Miss Dryer ever visited them, and if so, could he be informed of her next visit. These friends were instrumentally used to arrange a divinely destined connection for Emma Dryer and Dwight Moody.

Before long Emma received an invitation to attend one of Moody's noon prayer meetings. Upon meeting him, she first spoke to him about his church and his work at the YMCA. Then with sudden abruptness, this thirty-three year old man, two years younger than Emma, quickly escorted her to a parlor room. He presented her a chair in which to be seated and pointedly asked about her understanding of the return of Jesus and his Kingdom. She admitted that she did not have complete clarification on the issue but firmly believed in the Lord's return. After he asked her where she obtained that information, Emma quickly stated that she had found it in the Bible. Pleased with her response, he affirmed that with her knowledge of Christ's return she possessed the key to understanding the Scriptures. Moody encouraged her to find further clarification through the instruction of Mrs. Nellie Goodwin, the wife of Reverend Dr. Edward Payson Goodwin (1832–1901), pastor of the west side First Congregational Church where Moody held numerous meetings. Later that day Moody optimistically shared with Mrs. Goodwin his amiable meeting and conversation with Emma.

After their initial meeting Dwight Moody communicated his awareness of Emma's sincere enthusiasm for education and for God's word. She impressed Moody as "a woman of high intelligence, with superb teaching skills and a deep, practical knowledge of Scripture."[5] While Mr. Moody admired Emma's profound faith, he perceived even more. Having begun his own family, he understood the special gift that women possessed in nurturing and training young mothers and their children. Learning more of her background as a teacher he found that she was superbly qualified. She quite capably understood and trained young children and young adults—a passion which he likewise shared.

Inspired by Moody's earnestness and directness regarding premillennialism—a subject which deeply interested Emma and which she considered to be a fundamental truth—she corresponded with a friend in New York City: "Deeply impressed by [Moody's] earnest consideration to the will and work of God."[6] Years later, reflecting on these early events, Emma wrote:

---

5. History's Women, "Emeline Dryer: Christian Educator and Administrator," para. 6.
6. Beatty, "The City to Come: Emma Dryer," para. 12.

> I had recently recovered from a dreadful sickness, during which time, reading my Bible, I had clearly seen the Coming of Christ. But a *Millerite* was the only name we knew for one believing in the Second Coming. I answered Mr. Moody, 'I would not like to say I understand it all, for it is such a great subject, but I believe it all.' Harry Moorehouse had been teaching him for a week. Mr. Moody added, 'Do you know Mr. and Mrs. Goodwin?' I said, "I have not met them yet, they have just come to town.' He replied, 'Mrs. Goodwin understands.' (Dr. Erdman had been teaching the Goodwins.) He added, 'Now there is Mrs. Goodwin, myself, and yourself, and that makes three in Chicago who understand the Coming and Kingdom of Christ.' There are hundreds and thousands that understand it now.[7]

This brief introduction to D. L. Moody set the stage for Emma's subsequent discovery of God's plan for her life in Chicago.

Seeking Guidance

During this time of physical recovery Emma spiritually reflected on her illness and personally pondered her future. In later years she admitted that she had prepared to die. Perhaps she recalled the stories from her former mentor, Mary B. Allen, regarding Miss Allen's grandmother's experience with heavenly music when consumed with congestion of the lungs or Miss Allen's own healing from cholera and bronchitis. Regardless, as the summer months of 1870 passed, Emma affirmed in a letter to a friend her sincere belief that God had healed her.[8] She believed that her healing would deepen her understanding regarding the needs of the world around her without Christ. With renewed hope and assurance of Christ's return, she wrote: "In my earnest, prayerful meditation, God gave me new light from the Scriptures, and taught me the coming of Christ."[9]

All those who knew Emma witnessed with astonishment her authentic and complete recovery. At this time she received another call to return to ISNU for the term. Emma began a heart searching inquiry as to whether she should resume her prestigious position in Normal, Illinois, or remain in Chicago. She wrote regarding this struggle:

> I saw that the question must be [do I have] a conscientious conviction, from God. I earnestly sought His guidance; and tried to reach a decision; I set apart a day for united prayer, asking selected friends, near and far, to join me, that I might understand God's will, and that they might understand God's will... Their answers began to come... Each believed that I should remain in Christian work; and so I understood. Dear old Mrs. Pithy, who sat in her chair and

---

7. Emma Dryer to Caroline Waite, 18 July 1924, Biographical File of Emma Dryer.
8. Howat, *Ten Girls Who Made History*, 27.
9. Emma Dryer to Charles Blanchard, 1916, Biographical File of Emma Dryer.

prayed for her food, and lived by faith, and from whom Dr. Shipman said he learned so much, said, 'My dear, I understand the Lord wants you to remain in Chicago.'[10]

During this time Moody continued to urge Emma to move permanently to Chicago. Referring to ISNU he said, "That is good work for its kind; but there are teachers enough, who want to teach school, and schools enough that want them; but there aint enough to do *this* work, and this is the best work."[11] Emma recognized from her conversations with him that presenting the gospel to all people was truly God's chosen plan to bring redemption to men.[12] Moved by what Moody referred to as *the best work*, she longed to be involved in such a mission-inspired calling.

This would have been a difficult choice for Emma if not for the prayers of friends and the sanctioned assurance of the Lord's guidance. It is unknown to what degree she reflected on her Stockbridge, Massachusetts, and Victor, New York, missionary heritage. Nonetheless, at this point Emma decisively dedicated her life to full time inner city mission work. With an affirmed confidence from the Lord, she resigned her position as head of the women faculty at ISNU. Emma chose to walk by faith and trust in God's provision and direction as she ascended a consecrated mountain of service to a new and unknown educational pinnacle.

Illinois Street Church: Reverend William J. Erdman and Premillennialism

After being convinced of God's direction for her life, this thirty-five year old educator left her job at ISNU in December of 1870 to join the urban inner-city work of the YMCA in Chicago. Obviously, Emma was drawn to this ministry not by money or status but by Moody's appealing gospel challenge. She wrote of her concern for "the needs of this dying world . . . and especially the fallen, wretched condition of the masses around me" and understood that even "the heathen in foreign lands were in a far worse condition than the masses in our cities, and in our own country."[13] She carefully meditated on Scriptures regarding the second coming from which she acknowledged that the Lord had given her understanding. She admitted that she still had much to learn but was cautious as to what she learned and from whom:

---

10. Ibid. It is uncertain whether Dr. George Elias Shipman (1820–1893) was Emma's doctor. He was a prominent New York physician who promoted homeopathy in his medical practice. Emma would have been drawn to his compassion for neglected and adoptive children for whom he started the Chicago Foundling Home in 1871 based on his own declaration of obedience to the leading of the Lord.

11. Ibid.

12. Ibid.

13. Ibid.

> I was aware that I had miss-learned much generally approved religious doctrine. Through Mrs. E. P. Goodwin, I became acquainted with Reverend Dr. Wm. J. Erdman, of Jamestown, New York;—the man whom Mr. Moody said knew his Bible better than any other man, he ever met before. I praise God for Dr. Erdman's ever-to-be remembered friendship and ministry. Instructed by him, I began a systematic study of that doctrine, and found it, as others do, 'the key to the Scriptures.' The Bible became a new Book. God's plans were not experiments, His Word never failed. Faith, that belief in *God* that trusts His Word, cannot fail, because *God*, and God only, is the author and finisher of faith. And so, the Spirit of God opened anew the Holy Scriptures to me, and filled me with new desires for His blessed service.[14]

While Emma boarded with Reverend Daniels's family she also began her new acquaintance with Mr. Moody. Great admiration existed between them and extended as Emma forged a close friendship with Moody's wife and their children.

As in her college and career transition years, Emma's continued priority was to become established in a church home. Immediately, she began attending the First Methodist Episcopal Church with Reverend Daniels's family. Reverend Erdman spoke at the church and instrumentally influenced her conclusions regarding the second coming of Christ with the doctrine of premillennialism. This view claimed a literal coming of Christ followed by his thousand year reign on the earth opposing the more prevalent view of postmillennialism. Postmillennialism espoused that Christ would come after Christians set up the kingdom of God on earth—a view advocated among American evangelicals between the Revolution and the Civil War.

Both Emma and Moody embraced premillennialism. Moody would often include nuances of this teaching in his messages. He later gave opportunities for premillennialists such as W. E. Blackstone, A. T. Pierson, A. J. Gordon, G. F. Pentecost, Reuben A. Torrey, and James W. Gray to champion its cause at his Northfield, Massachusetts, conferences—meetings which Emma eagerly attended.[15] Although Moody's evangelism promoted this belief, his primary message continued to be that of God's love and the souls of men rather than theological issues. He held to a basic theology in an attempt to avoid controversy especially among those holding to the fundamentalist and premillennial beliefs.

Moody faced the challenge of providing organized discipleship to an unorganized group of converts. They found it difficult to blend in with the unfamiliar ways of the organized church. To the satisfaction of these converts Moody decided in 1863 to organize a new church stemming from his own mission outreach. He invited area pastors and lay people to the Illinois Street Chapel to discuss its organization. Although diversified denominational clergy shared their support, they could not agree on the polity of the church. The Congregationalists stayed to the end of the meeting and

---

14. Ibid.
15. Gustafson, *Moody and Swedes*, 180.

consented to assist in organizing the *Illinois Street Church*—a non-denominational church that became *a company of saved sinners* with Mr. Moody as the pastor and Jesus Christ as *head over all*.[16]

At the Illinois Street Church—renamed the North Side Tabernacle after the 1871 Chicago Fire and changed to the Chicago Avenue Church in May of 1873—Moody inspired Emma's acceptance and appreciation of premillennialism's convergence of evangelism and missions. When she joined his church, Emma wrote brief notes of his sermons and noon prayer meetings in her Bible such as the one opposite the Isaiah 50:7 passage: "Mr. Moody's text in 1873" which stated "For the Lord God will help me, therefore shall I not be confounded; therefore have I set my face like a flint, and I know that I shall not be ashamed." Emma unashamedly utilized her own solid educational background. She advocated the centrality of an education that corresponded to a new believer's spiritual development and scripturally supported social change.

Throughout this transitional process Emma found herself driven by a deep missionary fervor to see the souls of people saved. Like her Massachusetts missionary predecessor, David Brainerd, her heart reflected his passion. He displayed her sense of fervor in one diary entry on April 1, 1743, when riding to Kaunaumeek twenty miles from Stockbridge: "Of late I have thought much of having the kingdom of Christ advanced in the world" and on October 17, 1743: "My heart is indeed refreshed, when I have any prevailing hopes of Zion's prosperity. O that I may see the glorious day, when Zion shall become the joy of the whole earth! Truly there is nothing that I greatly value in this lower world."[17] Emma now joyfully echoed Brainerd's heart's desire.

Emma, no longer clinging to material security, had left Normal, Illinois, and ISNU behind her. With a renewed missionary zeal she set out on a benevolent pathway to educate and evangelize the poor and homeless, the prisoners, the hospitalized, prostitutes and wayward women—a calling to Chicago where she unflinchingly and laboriously dedicated her life.

Chicago Fire

Three years prior to Moody's introduction to Emma Dryer he journeyed to England where he made numerous new acquaintances including evangelists Charles H. Spurgeon (1834–92) and George Müller (1805–98). This trip broadened Moody's circle of influence internationally and opened up further opportunities back in the states. In 1870 he met singer and song writer Ira Sankey[18] at an International Convention of the

---

16. Williams, *Life and Work of Dwight L. Moody*, 97–98.
17. Brainerd and Edwards, *The Life and Diary*, 82.
18. According to Daniels (1875) Sankey possessed a Methodist Episcopal background claiming a baptism in the Holy Spirit which he needed in order to use his singing as a tool for the gospel. Although there is no record of Emma mentioning Ira Sankey, she would have known him in association with the Chicago Avenue Church, Northfield conferences, and various campaigns. Her music background would have drawn forth her support for this man so closely associated with Moody during

YMCA. He would later enlist Sankey's services for his 1873 campaign in Great Britain. However, before that campaign and approximately a year after Emma and Moody's introduction, they experienced with other Chicagoans an unexpected loss of dynamic proportions.

Life Changing Event

On Sunday evening, October 8, 1871, Moody had concluded his message at Farwell Hall when the city bells unrelentingly signaled the onset of the Great Chicago Fire. The city burned until Tuesday morning consuming both Moody's house and the Illinois Street Church. At this time Emma was not among those attending his Sunday service but was visiting her friends, John and Matilda Eberhart in Chicago. Watching in anxious disbelief Emma recalled the following: "A recurring attack of typhoid fever detained me in their home, where we watched the veering wind, fearing that the fire might be blown one more point westward, and so destroy the entire city. The wind held its northward course, and the West Side was spared."[19]

Nine years later Emma reflected on this life changing event in a letter written on Bible Work Room stationary to Anita McCormick, the daughter of philanthropists Cyrus and Nettie McCormick. Emma had just opened a package forwarded to her by Anita from Anita's own delicately slender and vibrant mother. In her letter to Anita Emma recalled her own early fondness for decorative and lacey party dresses. That desire changed with her calling to Chicago. She wrote:

> My dear friend—Miss Anita. The package which you kindly sent from your mother was duly rec'd. I shall promptly put the dress into wear enlarging it sufficiently to fit me & shall rejoice that so much of your dear Mother's mantle falls on me. The dress is very pretty; & shall I tell you what recollections it awakened? . . . At the time of the Chicago Fire I was planning to sell a blue silk & with the money received repair a brown one. 'For,' I said to a friend, 'what but parties is it good for & I shall not go into society anymore.' The Lord had then opened my eyes to see what sin is doing to mankind & what Christ is waiting to do for their salvation. But the fire came & settled all . . . leaving only the common black one which I was wearing. I lost a good wardrobe, but no regret has ever passed its shade over me. The Lord who fed & clothed & kept & cared for me from infancy has proved Himself to me over & over again, 'the same speaks day & today & forever,' & it is inexpressibly blessed to trust Him.[20]

Although Emma left those worldly yearnings behind, she could appreciatively delight in the material blessings of her friends. At the time of the Chicago Fire Nettie

---

his campaigns.

19. Emma Dryer to Charles Blanchard, 1916, Biographical File of Emma Dryer.

20. Emma Dryer to Anita McCormick Blaine, 23 December 1880, Anita Blaine McCormick Correspondence and Papers.

McCormick, wife of the reaper inventor Cyrus McCormick, possessed a *colorful inventory* of personal items. Her treasures, stored at the railroad station to escape the fire, were ultimately destroyed: "More than forty separate dresses, wraps, waists, mantles, bonnets, and headdresses . . . looking down that list one gains charming impressions of Mr. McCormick's young wife in the clothing and garments he had bought to adore her beauty [with a] . . . pearl fan, inlaid with silver, richly carved . . . a white velvet with ostrich feather and lace (bonnet), headdresses of green silk velvet, of crimson velvet, and black . . . fabrics from Tibet and India . . . Etruscan necklace set with carbuncles and pearls."[21] During Nettie's later years Anita ordered clothing for her deeply appreciated mother made of "the daintiest embroidered muslins, in white, gray, mauve for summer, an abundance of warm things for winter; including the type of bonnet with ties, sometimes trimmed with ostrich tips, that she habitually wore."[22] Certainly unforeseeable to Emma at the time of the fire, Anita and her family's generosity to Emma would bountifully continue for years to come.

After the fire Emma's instinctive compassion immediately caused her to reach out to those in need. She witnessed firsthand that the disadvantaged and underprivileged were deprived not only of physical necessities but, even more, they were removed from the word of God needed to nourish their souls.[23] She faithfully ministered alongside D. L. Moody and thousands of others. A twelve column article from the *Chicago Times* published on October 11 captured the camaraderie of the Chicago community and the American spirit: "The Christian world is coming to our relief. The worst is already over. In a few days more, all of the dangers will be past, and we can resume the battle of life with Christian faith and western grit. Let us all cheer up!"[24]

Moody once again took a leadership role as he secured financial, spiritual, and physical help for the needy. He unhesitatingly secured Emma's commitment to head up the Chicago Women's Aid Society. She also taught Bible classes at Moody's church and served as superintendent of the Women's Auxiliary of the YMCA. Meanwhile, Moody traveled east to procure funds for rebuilding.

Just as Emma had experienced her own soul-searching crisis regarding God's will, Moody was likewise in an unsettling phase in his own spiritual life. Vision and initiative were his strengths. However, they became his weakness as he relied on his own ingenious plans rather than seeking God's direction. Reverend Augustus Warner Williams (1844–1920), writing one of the first biographies of Moody in 1900, recorded Moody's words regarding his spiritual struggle surrounding the months of the Chicago Fire:

---

21. Roderick, *Nettie Fowler McCormick*, 77.

22. Ibid., 306.

23. *Sixty-Second Annual Report of the Chicago Bible Society*, 1902, Biographical File of Emma Dryer.

24. Williams, *Life and Work of Dwight L. Moody*, 142.

> I got into a cold state. It did not seem as if there was any unction resting upon my ministry. For four long months God seemed to be just showing me myself . . . I was not preaching for Christ; I was preaching for ambition; I found everything in my heart that ought not to be there, and I was a miserable man. But after four months the anointing came . . . as I was walking in the streets of New York . . . At last I had returned to God again, and I was wretched no longer. I almost prayed in my joy, 'O stay Thy hand!' I thought this earthen vessel would break. He filled me so full of the Spirit . . . preceded by a wrestling and hard struggle![25]

Williams continued with a comparison of Moody's spiritual condition to that of the Chicago ruins. He wrote: "The baptism of fire which had swept over Chicago had also passed over his soul. Everything for which he had been ambitious had been completely destroyed . . . this fire had, as it were, swept him back, beaten, to the feet of Christ. He must begin again at the bottom, literally humbled into dust and ashes. There the Lord met him . . . and under a glorious baptism of the Holy Spirit he had returned to his ministry among the poor and the lowly."[26]

The Chicago Fire kindled a new endowment of power within Moody to preach God's word accompanied by a similar anointing on Mr. Sankey who led music with his harmonium. Moody returned to Chicago now aflame with a new passion for the Lord. Emma watched in amazement as waves of revival began to sweep over the desperate and disheartened crowds. Reverend Daniels wrote: "Mr. Moody . . . went out to bear their sorrows, and struggle through their toils, with a stronger and more hopeful heart . . . The fire had taken away everything else, but it had left them Christ, and one another."[27]

As Moody embraced a deeper spiritual walk, Emma's own fires of infirmity expanded the depths of the spiritual riches of God in her life. The Chicago Fire refined and called forth an eager and learned woman of God. Emma was ready and equipped for the challenging task of providing relief work to the suffering Chicago residents. Five years after the fire, Reverend Daniels graciously painted the following portrait of this noble and self-sacrificing woman of God: "It was a picture fit for angels to gaze upon: a learned and honored Christian woman, stepping down from her high position to become a teacher and evangelist."[28]

Relief Work and Ministry Sacrifices

Relief work after the Chicago Fire was immediate as churches rallied around the homeless, sick, and suffering. Emma wrote of those days:

25. Ibid., 146–47.
26. Ibid., 147.
27. Daniels, *D. L. Moody and His Work*, 205.
28. Ibid., 187.

> The YMCA accepted the offer of Reverend Dr. Patterson's church, and organized their forces there; and the YWCA, took a part of the church with them, and organized their Employment Bureau. And rooms were quickly arranged for the distribution of clothing, sent from many parts of our country. I was unexpectedly forced into the work of various kinds, which crowded us. Churches, Sunday-Schools, day schools . . . The hungry were to be fed, the naked clothed, the sick cared for. I was accustomed to organize and conduct schools, and not all willing hearts and hands around me, could organize as quickly as I could . . . I saw clearly, that I must remain for a time and learn much while teaching and helping others.[29]

While Moody conducted numerous daily services for the homeless and needy, Emma held meetings for the poor mothers and women who traveled miles through the burned ashes in search of aide. She assisted in the relief efforts by organizing a sewing school for girls to make new garments. She realized that they needed more than just clothing, food, and shelter. Emma led them in singing, prayer, and Scripture recitation as she praised God for the skilled training he had given her since her early days in Victor, New York.

Emma also participated in the Protestant operated *Erring Women's Refuge* located at that time at 3111 South Indiana. The refuge had been established specifically for rescuing and reforming prostitutes from the sex industry which had been so rampant before the fire.[30] In the process of ministering to the needs of thousands at the refuge, Emma developed a curriculum for Bible study and guidelines in home visitation for young ladies. As Emma's presence and work in Chicago spread, she became known as a heroic woman whose "mercies were called into requisition in a wider sphere."[31]

As an educator her heart went out to the youth who no longer had a school facility in which to keep up their studies. Moody would gather the young people of Chicago, and Emma would devotedly instruct them in their academic studies and in her Bible Study classes. Moody was intrigued by her leadership and teaching ability. He encouragingly walked beside Emma as well as many others in the reestablishment of their city. His interest in education continued to be sparked by Emma's educational innovations to meet the needs of the people. He began discussing with her a broader vision for educating and training individuals in missions and evangelistic work. As Moody witnessed the educational transformation that Emma brought to the ministry, he was convinced that she should pilot this program under the covering of his church. So it was that Emma began developing an educational program designated as the *Bible Work* for members of the Illinois Street Church.

To assist in meeting her own financial needs during this time she wrote for the New York weekly periodical *Christian Union Magazine* edited by clergyman Henry

29. Emma Dryer to Charles Blanchard, 1916, Biographical File of Emma Dryer.
30. Linehan, "Erring Women's Refuge."
31. Daniels, *D. L. Moody and His Work*, 187.

Ward Beecher (1813–87), the brother of Harriet Beecher Stowe (1811–96).[32] She used her writing skills to report the events of the YMCA and to contribute to the Religious News section. Her educational and writing expertise had burgeoned since leaving Victor with its *Victor Herald* publication. These new efforts broadened her connection to other evangelical urban ministries as well.

Chicago Avenue Church

The Chicago Avenue Church, formerly the Illinois Street Church, had been partially rebuilt after the fire as a nondenominational evangelical church. The sign over the door read: "Welcome to this House of God are strangers and the poor."[33] Less than two years after the Chicago Fire, the newly named church officially hired Emma to direct the Bible Work of Chicago. She served as its Bible teacher and superintendent. She trained urban workers to lead in prayer and Bible studies while distributing Bibles provided by the Chicago Bible Society. Emma would be instrumental in sending students from her Bible classes to enroll in Moody's Northfield and Mt. Hermon schools in Massachusetts established in 1879 and 1881.[34]

Moody showed his support for Emma by writing various potential donors asking their financial assistance in this work. In May, 1873, he wrote the following influential letter to Mrs. Nettie McCormick:

> Dear Friend . . . Since the fire we have had only a few at work, and now want to get them into all parts of the city if you would like to support one for a month or longer, I should be very glad if you would designate some month in 1873 in which you would be willing to pay the salary of a good worker. I know of three or four whose services can be secured. Hoping to hear from you. I remain Yours in Christ. D. L. Moody[35]

Knowing that the Bible Work was now in Emma's capable hands, Moody set out for a return visit to England on June 7, 1873. On this trip he conducted numerous evangelistic crusades for over two years in Ireland and Scotland.

During these early transitional years the Chicago Avenue Church began struggling financially and spiritually without a pastor. Upon hearing of this situation Moody instructed his friends, Major D. W. Whittle (1840–1901)[36] and Reverend Goodwin, to locate a minister who would teach "the radical truths of the Bible, in unquestioned orthodoxy, . . . be a competent interpreter of the Holy Scriptures, and the leading teacher

---

32. See Ogorek, "Dryer, Emma," 230.
33. Chapman, *The Life and Work of Dwight Lyman Moody*, 108.
34. Emma Dryer to Charles Blanchard, 1916, Biographical File of Emma Dryer.
35. D. L. Moody, May 1873, Biographical File of Emma Dryer.
36. Daniels describes Major Whittle as Moody's comrade who resigned from a lucrative manager position with the Elgin Watch Company to fulfill Moody's belief in him as "a chosen instrument for the great work of God." Daniels, *D. L. Moody and His Work*, 22.

in the Bible-Work."[37] Already familiar with the Chicago area, Reverend Erdman, a Presbyterian Church pastor, accepted the position to minister at this highly ecumenical church beginning on April 14, 1875. As a great supporter of Dr. Erdman, Emma would warmly write of him years later: "He was highly esteemed, as a harmonizer of the church and instructor of the studious, a co-operating friend, in all evangelistic and gospel work. The Bible-Work rejoiced in his Bible function, and in all his counsel; and many Christian workers came to be with us."[38]

The leaders of the Chicago Avenue Church held Moody in high esteem. They valued the financial support that came to the church through Sankey and Moody's hymnal and book royalties. However, Moody's extensive travel schedule and absences placed additional pressure on the congregation and especially on the pastors. Lyle Dorsett, in *A Passion For Souls: The Life of D. L. Moody*, affirmed that it was difficult for the pastors to be dominated by a traveling evangelist disconnected from their own community. Matters were complicated when "for better or worse, D. L. Moody was incapable of letting go and delegating responsibilities for the Chicago Avenue Church that he no longer felt led to pastor."[39]

Meanwhile, during Moody's prolonged absence abroad from 1873 to 1875, Emma directed her highly developed educational and administrative skills toward establishing the Bible training school which she and Moody envisioned. After the Chicago Fire she began to historically document this work. Years later on March 15, 1888, she would articulately and memorably read this historical account to a board of managers who were laying out the blueprint for the official establishment of the Moody Bible Institute.

Chicago Activities 1871–73

As Emma established herself within the numerous mission outreaches of Chicago she brought with her a strong Bible and education background. She eagerly began implementing her educational expertise in programs such as the Chicago Relief and Aid Society, the Women's Auxiliary of the YMCA, and the Chicago Swedish community.

Chicago Relief and Aid Society

During the first year after the Chicago Fire the YWCA joined with other minor societies operating from local churches. They united in the relief effort under the auspices of the Chicago Relief and Aid Society (CRAS). At the time of the fire Mayor Roswell B. Mason made the Relief and Aid Society the official agent for distributing funds for

---

37. Emma Dryer to Charles Blanchard, 1916, Biographical File of Emma Dryer.
38. Ibid.
39. Dorsett, *A Passion For Souls*, 272.

the fire relief effort.⁴⁰ This social work group with a soul-saving emphasis existed in order to bring a connecting relationship between the workers and the recipients.⁴¹ Relief was only for the *worthy poor* who were destitute through no fault of their own. This assistance provided temporary relief and encouraged self-sufficiency instead of habitual dependency. Exemplifying Christian social work efforts the society provided food, clothing, and health care to the working poor of Chicago. At Moody's encouragement, Emma joined this relief effort. She headed up the Women's Aid Society, one of the charities that secured a relief voucher from CRAS in the amount of $207.⁴²

Emma viewed her relief work as a societal opportunity to share the gospel. She assisted with victim relief by organizing the Children's Sewing and Industrial Schools in churches and missions with Bible classes. Her leadership goal as head of the Women's Aid Society was to assist young ladies in becoming self-sufficient. She opened rooms for women to manufacture both women's and children's garments. After her successful relief work, the society reorganized as the YWCA with Emma serving as the superintendent.⁴³ She boldly, yet sensibly, visited the poor, the unfortunate, and the degraded in slums, hospitals, and prisons while ministering to their physical and spiritual needs. With caution, yet no fear of her surroundings, Emma assured her parents in New York that "her escort in the worst quarters of Chicago was a better safeguard than that of a policeman."⁴⁴

By 1873, Emma, well established in her various mission roles, became better acquainted with the man God used to place her into the heart of Chicago. Emma shared about one unforgettable Sunday after New Year's in 1873 when seated around the table with Moody and many other common acquaintances:

> He asked us to recite our texts which we had selected for the year, and to explain what they meant to us. His text peculiarly interested me, because I saw its application and contemplated (but not openly announced) evangelistic work in England; and, when his remarkable experience in that country followed, I believe that God gave that text to him. He read his text: Isaiah 50:7 ... And he remarked that in a convention in England, a Christian brother [British revivalist Henry Varley] said that this world had yet to see what God would do with a man wholly consecrated to the Lord; and Mr. Moody added, 'I just said in my heart, 'I'll try to be that man.' And he read and re-read the text, commenting on it. How appropriate it was, to the great revival which began

---

40. Sawislak, "Chicago Relief and Aid Society," para. 2.

41. Ibid., para. 3.

42. The Chicago Relief and Aid Society annually submitted a fund distribution report to the city mayor. On October 31, 1871, the report was submitted to Mayor Mason in which the Women's Aid Society was listed as receiving voucher 1179 for $207. This report may be found at http://quod.lib.umich.edu/m/moa/AAW4226.0001.001/12?rgn=main;view=image.

43. Emma Dryer to Charles Blanchard, 1916, Biographical File of Emma Dryer.

44. Town of Victor, New York, Archives, *Victor Herald* Newspaper Obituary.

in Scotland, that year, and continued through his life, and the results of which we still rejoicingly trace.[45]

Six months following this prophetic New Year's gathering Emma began expansion of her noble and magnanimous plans for the Bible Work. Meanwhile, Moody and his family left for England in June of 1873. What was to be an eight to ten month crusade was providentially extended to August 14, 1875.

Women's Auxiliary of the YWCA

When Moody first arrived in Chicago in 1856 he immediately volunteered at the YMCA as a janitor and enthusiastically served in whatever capacity he was needed. Before long the revival of 1857 or the Businessman's Revival with its noon meetings increased Moody's enthusiasm for the souls of men.[46] He became chairman of a committee for visiting strangers and the afflicted. By 1860 Moody left the business world and expended more of his time at the YMCA where he was appointed as the city missionary. Due to the Civil War and the changing political scene in the country, Moody expanded his YMCA connections as a powerful tool for ministry among the northern soldier camps.

By the end of the war Moody, elected YMCA president, immediately pursued the construction of a new YMCA building. Prior to this, the YMCA rooms had been extended to Reverend Daniels's Methodist Church facility, so the need for a new building was great. A new YMCA structure on Madison Street was erected. It contained a large 3,000 seat hall and a noon prayer meeting room. The hall was dedicated September 29, 1867, and christened *Farwell Hall* in honor of Moody's faithful entrepreneur friend and leading dry goods merchant, Mr. John Villiers Farwell (1825–1908). The services were described as "cosmopolitan, catholic, and free."[47] And as a man of God's word, Moody insisted on Scripture covering the entire building. Mr. Moody became identified with the YMCA work throughout the United States and Canada. His services were in frequent demand for conventions and revival meetings. To Moody's dismay, four months after its dedication, Farwell Hall burned to the ground, and by October of 1871 the second Farwell Hall also went down in the Chicago Fire.

At this time the Chicago Relief and Aid Society teamed with the Women's Auxiliary of the YWCA. In November 1871 as superintendent of the YWCA Emma, like Moody, began corresponding with groups and individuals all over the country. She was significantly involved in fundraising and often wrote personal thank-you notes to her supporters. In 1889 one of those faithful supporters, railroad industrialist John Crerar (1827–89), awarded Emma a life-long YWCA membership from this organization

---

45. Emma Dryer to Charles Blanchard, 1916, Biographical File of Emma Dryer.
46. Chapman, *The Life and Work of Dwight Lyman Moody*, 100.
47. Daniels, *D. L. Moody and His Work*, 120.

that he so faithfully supported.[48] Many of her lengthy donor letters contained a clear outline of the gospel. Emma wanted to take every opportunity to share the gospel with everyone she encountered. At the top of her stationary she inscribed both a Bible verse and a short quote: "Philippians 2:16, 'Holding forth the Word of Life' and 'Unlike all other books, the Bible is its own interpreter.'" Emma wanted God's word to be the basis for all that would issue forth from her life on behalf of others.

Swedish School and Bible Studies

In 1873 Emma was introduced to Reverend John F. Okerstein (1837–1920), a Swedish immigrant, successful evangelist, and city missionary for the Chicago Avenue Church (CAC). He worked with Emma in coordinating Swedish meetings and teaching Swedish Sunday school. He also served as Superintendent for the Scandinavian Christian Work for the Minnesota Congregational Church and assisted Emma at the Bible Work during the 1876 Moody meetings. She portrayed Okerstein as "a man remarkably used of God, first in this city, and later among his Swede countrymen in Minnesota . . . He walked with God and led many others to do the same."[49]

Moody's preaching and conferences attracted the Swedes to his ministry and provided access to his books which were published by Fleming H. Revell and translated into Swedish by the Bible Institute Colportage Association.[50] E. A. Skogsbergh, who earned the title of *The Swedish Moody,* published the Swedish newspaper—the *Chicago-Bladet*—which featured Moody's sermons and evangelization events.[51] Emma wholeheartedly joined hundreds of Swedes attending the morning CAC service as they sang Lydia O. Baxter's (1809–74) hymn *There is a Gate That Stands Ajar* in their native tongue—*Jag vet en port som öppen står.* The Swedish meetings at the CAC were limited to bimonthly worship services on Sunday afternoons with Sunday school classes and Wednesday night meetings—as long as the CAC had no pressing schedule conflicts.[52] These revival-like meetings were described as being high-spirited and vivacious as Christians were encouraged to lead fruitful lives and unbelievers were brought to the Lord.[53]

Emma's teaching and administration instincts emerged as she quickly initiated plans for Bible studies, home visitations, music instruction, and literacy among the Swedish population. She zealously conducted a Swedish School held on Wednesday evenings. Emma taught Scandinavians to read in English as they studied Bible texts and were introduced to commonly used religious terms. The average attendance was

---

48. Emma Dryer to Caroline Waite, 18 July 1924, Biographical File of Emma Dryer.
49. Emma Dryer to Charles Blanchard, 1916, Biographical File of Emma Dryer.
50. Gustafson, *Moody and Swedes,* 238.
51. Ibid., 243, 263, 297–98.
52. Ibid., 160.
53. Ibid.

reported to be around eighty-three.[54] Emma's deep desire to teach others to read the Bible drew her in part to this rich ethnic group. She also had contact with them through the Chicago Swedish YMCA and the Swedish Lutheran Church from her teaching years at Knoxville Ewing Female University.

The Swedish fellowship adopted the title of *Swedish Free Mission* patterning the Chicago Avenue Church's non-sectarian, ecumenical nature. As it grew in size, the CAC's own church facility experienced an increased demand for its own ministries. Within ten years tensions mounted regarding the Swedish influence on the church, the nature of their meetings, and other church requests for use of the facility. After a CAC Board review, they moved Emma's Swedish school to the lecture room and her Wednesday Swedish meetings to the library. When a request for conference use in October 1883 was denied, the Swedish ministry moved the conference to Bush Hall on Chicago Avenue with its seating capacity of 750.

Despite these inconveniences, Emma continued to nurture a positive friendship with Reverend Okerstein and the Swedish brethren. Together they sought good will between the Chicago Avenue Church and the Swedish Mission patterning Moody's ideal for unity and church cooperation.

> *"She opens her hands to oppressed people and stretches them out to needy people."*
>
> ~Proverbs 31:20 GWT~

---

54. Bible Work Report, 17 February 1882, Biographical File of Emma Dryer.

5

Emma's Friendships and Acquaintances

"Nothing reveals a man's heart better than his friendships."
~James Russell Miller (1840–1912)~

Although little is known of Emma's friendships from her early years, her ministry in Chicago produced a golden treasure-trove of friends. Their endorsement and inspiration served to replenish and reinvigorate her in service to others. The Reverend Daniels, who had welcomed Emma to Chicago in 1870, verified her character: "Thoroughly educated, she also possesses a most winning address and gentle manners, which every-where surround her with loving and appreciative friends."[1]

In later years at her 4124 West Jackson Boulevard residence, Emma would reminiscently remove from a specially designated basket many valued letters received from friends. These devoted supporters were used in the Lord's eternal plan to encourage her life as he fashioned her heart into his likeness.

Colonel George and Sarah Clarke: Co-Founders of Pacific Garden Mission

In the aftermath of the Chicago Fire, Christian mission outreaches were rapidly established. Many of them provided continued relief to the poor and also addressed the negative influence of saloons, houses of prostitution, and gambling halls. In 1869 a New York state teacher named Sarah Dunn (1835–1918), born less than 100 miles southeast of Emma's childhood town of Victor, moved to Chicago with an intense desire to rescue souls. Sarah formed a Sunday school mission at State and Twenty-Third Street for the poor and needy. In 1872 another New York native by the name of George R. Clarke (1827–92)—a former school principal, newspaper editor, lawyer, Civil War officer, and real estate businessman—became acquainted with Miss Dunn. In 1873, a

---

1. Daniels, *Moody: His Words, Work, and Workers*, 505–6.

few years after the Chicago Fire, they were married. With kindred hearts they began a rescue mission on September 15, 1877, in the interior of the crime-ridden city.[2]

During the time Emma served in her supervisory position at the YMCA, she became acquainted with the Clarkes. She quickly bonded with this couple in a mutual friendship shared by their common New York roots and strong educational backgrounds. During the 1870s and 1880s Emma and Sarah undauntedly partnered together to evangelize prostitutes and read the Bible to men in the local jails.[3] Emma ministered with Sarah as they visited inmates such as John Callahan, a west side gang member who was awaiting trial. As Sarah entered his cell he begged her to pray for God's mercy upon him. After serving in Joliet prison he later became the superintendent of Hadley Rescue Hall in New York.[4]

Prisons became familiar ministry territory not only for Emma and the Clarkes, but also for D. L. Moody. After his arrival in Chicago he frequently visited war and convict prisons. He ministered to more than 600 black Methodist prisoners, a large group of black Baptists, and around a thousand black Presbyterians.[5] Emma and Sarah understood his early burden to provide inexpensive tracts for the prisoners made possible by Fleming Revell's publishing company established in 1869. Consequently, Moody considered the Clarkes' ministry as the finest of works and frequently visited the mission with his gospel message.[6]

In 1880 the mission relocated to 100 East Van Buren Street at the former location of the infamous Pacific Beer Garden. Upon Moody's return from evangelistic meetings, he wholeheartedly endorsed the new location. He suggested that the name be embellished by removing the word *Beer* and changing it to the *Pacific Garden Mission* (PGM).[7] With a mutual prohibitionist stance, Emma also joined Moody and the Clarkes as they enthusiastically agreed to the mission's new name. Little did any of them realize at that time the domino gospel effect their ministries would futuristically activate. D. L. Moody influenced the deeper Christian life of Baptist minister Frederick Brotherton Meyer (1847–1929) who influenced evangelist John Wilbur Chapman (1859–1918). Chapman became willing to be made willing and influenced the life and initial ministry of Billy Sunday (1862–1935), a baseball player turned evangelist. Billy, converted under the Clarke's ministry, secured Baptist preacher Mordecai Ham (1877–1961) to preach in North Carolina where Ham in 1934 influenced Billy Graham (1918–) for salvation[8]—a world changed through the initial obedient expression of *one*.

2. Henry, *The Pacific Garden Mission*, 27.
3. Joiner, *Sin in the City*, 51.
4. Henry, *The Pacific Garden Mission*, 31.
5. Powell, *Heavenly Destiny*, 120.
6. Henry, *The Pacific Garden Mission*, 29.
7. Ibid.
8. "Who Led Billy Graham to Christ," Billy Graham Center Archives.

Upon attending the Pacific Garden Mission services, Emma heard the simple and tearful salvation messages expounded by Colonel Clarke. She caringly witnessed the unshackling of gangsters, alcoholics, gamblers, and prostitutes. She received inspiration with many others from viewing the clearly posted signs bearing the Scriptures "*GOD IS LOVE*" and "*THOU GOD SEEST ME.*" At the PGM's new location Emma was thrilled to hear Sarah's testimony regarding the privilege of leading the Chicago White Stockings baseball player Billy Sunday to the Lord. In 1886 Billy heard the gospel from the horse drawn mission Gospel Wagon and came to the meeting.[9] Emma was touched by the gentleness with which her friends ministered to Billy as well as to disruptive alcoholics.

As she did for her own ministry, Emma also mingled her faith with Sarah's to pray and believe that God could provide for the financial needs of the mission. She rejoiced with George and Sarah when they discovered mushrooms mysteriously covering the front yard of their home—enough to sell, pay their rent, and meet the mission expenses.[10]

With their benevolent ministries Emma and Sarah projected a multi-faceted female side to evangelism.[11] Despite Sarah's small stature and eighty-five pound frame, neither she nor, for that part, Emma lurked away from sharing the gospel with the destitute and needy. Even Moody himself was quick to promote the tenacity of these women when he stated, "Give me a woman every time . . . Women have more tact and offend less; if we had more of them as city missionaries we would have less anarchism and communism."[12]

As Emma heard the news of Sarah's departure from this earth in 1918 she surely recalled the deeds of this kindred woman of God. They shared a friendship fashioned from the depths of God's love as they witnessed the power of his word to convert the souls of men.

The Cyrus McCormick Family: McCormick Harvesting Machine Company

Before his June trip to England in 1873 Moody commissioned Emma to put down her roots in Chicago. He encouraged her to also join his church and make Chicago her place for a life-long ministry.[13] From the onset of this work Emma realized the need to secure funding. With earnest endeavor she placed her faith in the Lord to provide for the Bible Work ministry. Emma experienced great comfort and consolation knowing that the Lord had provided for her throughout the Chicago Fire crisis and had also

---

9. Henry, *The Pacific Garden Mission,* 41–46.
10. Ibid., 32.
11. Joiner, *Sin in the City,* 51.
12. *Record of Christian Work*, May 1888, 7.
13. Moody Bible Institute, "Emma Dryer."

guided her to this needy city. She knew that he would continue to meet her needs for both finances and friendships. She would not be disappointed.

On one occasion a friend, Mrs. William B. Shute, asked Emma if she was acquainted with the wife of industrialist Cyrus H. McCormick (1809–84). Emma admitted that she had heard of the prestigious McCormick family but had not personally met them. Mrs. Shute explained that she met Mrs. McCormick at the church of Reverend Dr. Kitrige and spoke to her of Emma's Bible Work in Chicago. Mrs. Nancy "Nettie" Fowler McCormick (1835–1923) quickly responded with interest and asked if perhaps Emma could visit her home at 62 North Sheldon Street. Emma later recalled how thrilled she was to visit with Nettie and to share with her the objectives and activities that she envisioned for the Bible Work. Nettie took an immediate heart-warming interest in Emma's plans for house prayer meetings, Sunday schools, visitations of the sick, and those in jail.[14] After her presentation, Emma was surprisingly delighted to receive a generous monetary gift from Nettie followed by a sincere invitation for her to visit again.[15]

Years later, Emma voiced her appreciation for Nettie's $500 gift and her continued support: "That was the first large contribution, I had received . . . It led to *many other* important ones. God gave her [Nettie] a *ceaseless watchfulness*, for important helpfulness in Christ's service; and it still continues. Mine is no single testimony! A multitude of Christian workers praise God for her devoted Christian ministry, in home and in foreign lands."[16] In virtue of on-going promised assistance, Nettie would faithfully keep her word.

Emma recalled her first visit with Mrs. McCormick's husband. She had received the Lord's provision to travel east to visit her parents in Victor, New York, and extended her trip to New York City. She wrote: "I had no visible means for my journey. I was in a new field, learning new lessons of trusting the Lord for guidance. He sent me by friends, unasked, all I needed!"[17] While in New York she visited with hymn writer and evangelist Major Daniel Webster Whittle who was working with composer and singer P. P. Bliss (1838–76) at Moody's church. He contacted Emma with a request from Moody that she visit his friend, Cyrus McCormick, to gain assistance with his work at the YMCA.

The McCormick family was resting at the *Sanitarium*, a health institution founded by Dr. James C. Jackson at Danville, New York. They enjoyed the luxury of resting at this resort, also known as *Our Home on the Hillside*. Nettie reported that along with Dr. Jackson's vegetarian and health oriented regime, he included spiritual nourishment with inspirational messages on the power and authority of God's Spirit.[18] Emma

14. Roderick, *Nettie Fowler McCormick*, 90.
15. Emma Dryer to Charles Blanchard, 1916, Biographical File of Emma Dryer.
16. Ibid.
17. Ibid.
18. Roderick, *Nettie Fowler McCormick*, 111.

also enjoyed these health-oriented surroundings as she documented her brief layover: "I enjoyed my visit with Mr. McCormick. That great and good Christian man was much interested in our Bible-work, related as it was to Christian life in the homes visited. He was always interested in the home, and in the school education of children, and his life was early devoted to the preaching of the Gospel of Jesus Christ, and to multiplied industrial and educational blessings, among his fellow men. His numerous abiding works are his fitting monument."[19]

When Emma finished speaking with Mr. McCormick, Nettie entered the room with their young daughters, Virginia and Anita. Emma thought they were twins and remarked that they were the most beautiful little girls she had ever seen.[20] She often reflected on Cyrus McCormick and his family's *great welcome* and how he and Nettie endeavored to present effectively and comprehensively the remarkable truth of God's word.[21]

As Emma became more closely acquainted with this family she learned that Cyrus Hall McCormick had been born in Virginia as the son of a strict Presbyterian farmer and inventor. Although he did not possess a formal education, this did not prevent him from pragmatically patenting in 1834 a farm implement called a reaper that separated harvested grain. This resourceful invention combated hunger and poverty world-wide with increased food productivity. By 1847 Cyrus moved to the agricultural Midwest where the McCormick Harvesting Machine Company prospered despite numerous legal disputes over invention rights.

Emma observed that Cyrus worked fourteen hours a day as a shrewd organizer in production, advertising, and sales. She heard that this industrialist and entrepreneur friend claimed the sale of 5,000 reapers in 1856 alone. Although still a bachelor at the age of forty-seven, he noticed beyond his masterful inventions a young twenty-one year old northwestern New York philanthropist, Nancy Maria Fowler. Cyrus recognized the hand of the Lord in bringing her into his life.

Nettie and Emma, born only a few weeks apart, shared not only close birthdays, but also a common experience as orphans. Nettie was orphaned at the age of seven along with two older siblings. Emma could relate to this separation crisis from Nettie's past. After the death of her mother and father Nettie recalled her loneliness when preparing to go to sleep. She missed their good night wishes and their kneeling with her in prayer. Emma would have supportively agreed as Nettie lamented: "Oh, it was the first taste of the bitter cup which every orphan drinks!"[22]

Nettie shared the story of her New York Methodist upbringing by her wealthy grandmother and uncle. In turn, Emma told about her own Victor, New York, church

19. Emma Dryer to Charles Blanchard, 1916, Biographical File of Emma Dryer.

20. Emma Dryer to Anita McCormick Blaine, 1 July 1924, Anita Blaine McCormick Correspondence and Papers.

21. Ibid.

22. Roderick, *Nettie Fowler McCormick*, 21.

Emma's Friendships and Acquaintances

attendance with her adopted Presbyterian parents. Emma also delighted in hearing about Nettie's short-term teaching experience at the school she had attended as a youth. Nettie recounted: "Teaching is something I have, from childhood, loved to think of. I always loved children and to preside over a body of youth . . . was once the ambition of my life. I think the children seemed pleased with me."[23] They both collaboratively mused as Nettie shared her fledgling attempt to manage a classroom of particularly unruly students.

Nettie and Emma exchanged stories of their higher level education experiences which for Nettie included her attendance at the Troy Female Seminary. In 1853 she attended the Genesee Wesleyan Seminary where from 1866 to 1867 temperance leader Frances E. Willard (1839–98) would later teach. Emma and Nettie compared their common passionate longing for aiding and assisting others. Nettie perhaps read to Emma her journal entry in 1862 where she wrote her philanthropic aspirations: "*Usefulness* is the *great thing* in life, after all. To do something for others leaves a sweeter odor than a life of pleasure."[24]

Emma learned that despite the twenty-six year age gap between Cyrus and Nettie, they lovingly agreed on God's guidance as they entered marriage on January 26, 1858. Cyrus found that Nettie possessed a valuable "comprehension of business affairs . . . [in which] the precision of her memory and the grasp of her mind upon the multifarious details of human nature and manufacturing, made her an ideal wife . . . and . . . most influential factor in the industrial and philanthropic development of the United States."[25] The McCormicks warmly welcomed Emma into their family of seven children, two of whom died before the initiation of Emma's friendship. The children included their oldest son Cyrus Hall McCormick Jr. (1859–1932) and Harold (1872–1941) who married Edith Rockefeller (1872–1932) of Rockefeller acclaim.

Emma became especially close to their second daughter Anita (1866–1954). In 1889 Anita married Emmons Blaine, son of Senator and statesman James G. Blaine. Emmons died unexpectedly from appendicitis in 1892.[26] Emma kept a life time correspondence with Anita encouraging her throughout difficult times as they also shared their common interest in missions and educational reform.

Glowing Flames of Friendship

Although unacquainted with the McCormick family at the time of the Chicago Fire, Emma surely discussed that tragic event with them. In Chicago on business, Cyrus heard the alarming news of the fire. He telegraphed Nettie in New York requesting her to come immediately. As Emma relayed her story of the fire, so also Nettie conveyed

23. Ibid., 30.
24. Ibid., 135.
25. Casson, *Cyrus Hall McCormick*, 182–83.
26. Roderick, *Nettie Fowler McCormick*, 183.

the tragic view of Chicago with its "desolation—smoking debris, charred skeletons of buildings, towering piles of burning wheat and of coal, stifling smoke and dust everywhere—and already men picking their way among the ruins on their way to rebuild Chicago."[27] After arriving in Chicago Nettie's first glimpse of Cyrus was that of a man "weary and haggard, in a partly burned coat . . . [who] received them . . . with a spirit unbroken and a courage unspent."[28] She would have mentioned how she and Cyrus, like Emma, rushed forward with assistance at the Chicago Relief and Aid Society. They organized and distributed aid for homeless Chicagoans in spite of the personal loss of Cyrus's reaper factory.

Emma witnessed a mutually honoring relationship between Nettie and Cyrus as they united in prayer regarding the undefined future of the McCormick Harvesting Machine Company. In 1921 Emma wrote the following post-fire account to Anita regarding a major decision Cyrus had posed to her mother at the time of the Chicago Fire. Mr. McCormick said, "Nettie, I have come to my conclusion. You will outlive me, & have the children to care for. You must decide it."[29] Nettie carefully examined the Lord's *providential leadings* based on their well established Chicago church ties and Cyrus's industrious plans for a Chicago theological seminary. With assuring confidence she energetically began to rebuild the factory and establish Chicago as their permanent home. By February 1, 1873, the new McCormick reaper factory was reopened.[30]

The fire destroyed the McCormick's first Chicago home built in 1860 at 230 Dearborn Street. After the fire they moved in April 1872 to a furnished house at 62 North Sheldon where Emma had first met Mrs. McCormick.[31] By the spring of 1875 they moved into a magnificent three story house built at 135 (later 675) Rush Street. Cyrus had purchased the lot during the 1850s. As a frequent visitor, Emma was astonished as she viewed the centralized ballroom on the third floor of her friends' house. She wrote about one of her visits. With evident love for the children, she shared her impressions upon seeing young Anita preparing for a party. She maternally observed that Anita "was very sweet & lovely in her white dress . . . pink flowers & ribbons! She seems to be moving things beautifully—dear little girl . . . I loved—who did not? —a sweet little girl whose great innocent eyes used to look up into mine . . . there is so much of her."[32]

In later years Emma recounted to Anita her memories of time spent with the family: "Cyrus was in High School. Many Saturday nights I stayed at your home, & your mother showed me his accts [accounts] for the week. Nothing was foolishly

27. Ibid., 97.
28. Ibid.
29. Ibid., 99.
30. Ibid., 53.
31. Ibid.
32. Letter to Nettie McCormick from Emma Dryer, 12 March 1888, Biographical File of Emma Dryer.

spent!"[33] The next day Emma would leave the family to attend her own services at Moody's church. Afterward she would return to the four story Bible Work home located on Warren Avenue.

Emma heard about Cyrus and Nettie's traveling adventures to England and Europe to promote and demonstrate the reaper. In 1862 Nettie and Cyrus travelled to London for the International Exhibition of Arts and Manufacturers. During this trip Cyrus wanted her to hear the famous Charles H. Spurgeon whom he had heard on his 1851 trip. Nettie observed that Mr. Spurgeon delivered his messages without having any notes as his listeners concentrated on his every word. Nettie shared with Emma her impression of a man who spoke with a forcefulness comparable to his notoriety.[34] While visiting in Scotland for business, Nettie and Cyrus celebrated an official honeymoon they had never had. And Emma eagerly listened as Nettie shared their adventures in France while attending the 1867 Universal Exposition.

On another occasion in 1878 Nettie traveled throughout Europe with her family. Emma daily reviewed the newspaper for reports of their return. She faithfully prayed for her friends: "May our Lord give you rest and a health-giving voyage . . . Let us pray that you be preserved from their [ocean] perils. What a restless, unsatisfying world this is! But our Lord has brought His salvation into it and for His dear sake, we can well afford to work on, with *bright hopes*. We shall soon see His dear face, & be forever with Him . . . In the sweet hopes which Christ gives us, I am with daily prayers & love. Your friend. E. Dryer."[35]

On November 24, 1878, Nettie wrote her prayer partner requesting that Emma remember Cyrus during his time of recovery from surgery. Emma sympathetically responded: "My dear friend: According to your kind request about Mr. McCormick's sickness. I am very glad to be permitted to know this, that I may pray with you for his recovery according to the will of our Lord. How dreadful have been his sufferings! And the operation was dreadful! Your own anxiety must have been the greatest which you can well bear. I am praying that you have health through this severe trial."[36] Emma remained faithful in prayer on behalf of the McCormick family. They also served as a surrogate family for her especially after the death of her own foster parents.

In the summer of 1881 the McCormicks built a country home at Clayton Lodge in Richfield Springs, New York. Until the middle 1890s Nettie spent much of her time caring for her invalid daughter, Virginia, in the Adirondacks at her apartment on Madison Avenue and later in California. At times Emma accompanied Nettie on visits to the California ranch. Although she and Emma met less frequently during

---

33. Letter to Anita McCormick Blaine from Emma Dryer, 1 October 1923, Anita Blaine McCormick Correspondence and Papers.

34. Roderick, *Nettie Fowler McCormick,* 79.

35. Letter to Nettie McCormick from Emma Dryer, 24 November 1878, Biographical File of Emma Dryer.

36. Ibid.

these times, Emma continued her correspondence with Nettie and her family as they enjoyed the scenic beauty of the Adirondacks and their rest at the lodge.

Training in Business Affairs

Emma carefully observed the business tenacity of her friends as Nettie worked closely with Cyrus. As with so many others, Emma noted Nettie's consistent pattern of wisdom mixed with kindness and generosity. Nettie possessed a deep love for people along with a high degree of diplomacy in her position as both a wife and a mediator. Nettie would honorably address Cyrus as *Mr. McCormick* in public deferring to him as the great businessman that she knew he was. Nettie took seriously his concerns and held a remarkable fascination for the business side of his work.[37] By 1884 Nettie had become a respected businesswoman well-equipped to handle Cyrus's company responsibilities.

On May 13, 1884, her business prowess was put to the test when Cyrus left behind his dedicated wife of twenty-six years. Emma wrote Nettie's son, Cyrus McCormick Jr., a letter in which she reflected on his father who had so graciously welcomed her and her Bible Work ministry. She referred to Cyrus as "your great & good Father . . . interested in your Mother's cooperation because it was *Bible*-work."[38]

Emma remembered her own Christmas gift to Cyrus in 1883—a yearly Scripture wall hanging which he enjoyed reading every morning while the nurse tended to him. She compassionately recalled: "The morning of his Home-going, the nurse hung it on the wall at the foot of his bed in his room upstairs. It read, 'finally brethren, farewell. Be perfected, be comforted; be of one mind; live in peace; & the God of love & peace shall be with you. Salute one another with a holy kiss.' His heart ceased to beat & his watch by his head stopped . . . Your mother sat in her room where his body waited. She said, 'Must one die to be appreciated?' So Christ died & she & he have so revealed Him to a multitude."[39] Years later in Emma's Bible, now located in the Moody Bible Institute Archival case below the bound volumes of *Moody Monthly*, she wrote by hand the following: "II Cor. 13:11 Last message of Cyrus H. McCormick as he died. His heart stopped beating and so did his watch . . . Finally Brethren farewell."

After Cyrus's death in 1884 Nettie continued to proficiently manage her husband's affairs. She met the challenge of their first company strike in the spring of 1885. The strike, due to a fifteen percent wage cut of molders, preceded the crisis a year later known as the *Haymarket Riot*.[40] Emma witnessed her friend's proficient communication with lawyers and corporate agents. These included world famous financier J.

---

37. Roderick, *Nettie Fowler McCormick*, 72.

38. Emma Dryer to Cyrus H. McCormick Jr., 24 July 1924, Anita Blaine McCormick Correspondence and Papers.

39. Ibid.

40. Roderick, *Nettie Fowler McCormick*, 146.

Emma's Friendships and Acquaintances

Pierpont Morgan (1837–1913) and businessman Charles Deering (1852–1927) whose company merged with the McCormick Reapers in 1902 to form the International Harvester Company.

In the summer of 1885 Nettie also found herself in the position of dealing with family tensions. Her greatest desire was to see her family living in cooperation and serenity. However, reoccurring arguments centered on which family member rightfully invented the reaper. Nettie, committed to the memory of her husband, determined to settle this and other disputes within her family to the satisfaction of all, regardless of money.[41] Through this crisis Emma observed the loyalty and conflict management effectiveness in which her friend unwaveringly held her ground.

Common Missionary Ventures

As a leading philanthropist and constant friend, Nettie faithfully advocated on Emma's behalf. Despite her active social and business life, she always scheduled time for Emma especially when it involved their common interests in charities and missions. They would often slip away to the garden or to one of the beautifully designed rooms in Nettie's house to pray for the Bible Work and other ministries. They coordinated literature reviews to discuss books they had in common such as premillennialist William E. Blackstone's (1841–1935) book *Jesus is Coming*, first published in 1878.

Over the years Emma watched Nettie open her home to more than 700 missionaries.[42] Nettie and Cyrus believed patriotism, business, and religious faith could not be separated.[43] Consequently, they faithfully distributed their wealth among numerous missions in Siam or Thailand, to a leper asylum, and other medical missions. In 1889 Nettie contributed to the Hebrew Mission with which Emma was associated. Emma communicated her gratitude and ministry struggles in a letter dated September 3, 1889: "My dear Mrs. McCormick: I find a receipt for your contribution to the Hebrew Mission. It had lain here while I was away. Mrs. Rounds who is the Treasurer wished me to thank you & to say that they would be glad to have you come some time to see the Mission . . . We plod on making a little progress in our work; but our movements are necessarily slow."[44]

Nettie's passionate urgency regarding mission outreaches increased after Cyrus's death. She had originally questioned her zeal for missions and whether she still possessed the strong drive she had when Cyrus was alive.[45] Yet time revealed that Nettie's *works* effectually continued on his behalf and included contributions to the

---

41. Ibid., 153.
42. Ibid., 110.
43. Hutchinson, *Cyrus Hall McCormick*, 595.
44. Letter to Nettie McCormick from Emma Dryer, 3 September 1889, Biographical File of Emma Dryer.
45. Roderick, *Nettie Fowler McCormick*, 157.

McCormick Theological Seminary and many other schools of higher education. She supported an orphanage headed by Dr. William Palmer Jacobs in South Carolina. The orphanage, of interest to Emma as well, was for Nettie a reflection of her special affection toward children which brought back memories of her own past as an orphan.[46]

Nettie likewise gave support to Emma's circle of friends including George and Sarah Clarke of the Pacific Garden Mission. When she had guests at her home, they would eagerly make a request to go to the PGM to witness firsthand the marvelous work of Colonel George and Sarah Clarke.[47] Mrs. McCormick also assisted Emma in the jail ministry along with Sarah Clarke. Emma started a day school at the jail which opened on June 1, 1882. Previously, Emma conducted Sunday school classes at the facility. She quickly discerned the need among the boys for instruction in reading and writing. Without Nettie's generous support and that of other donors, the school could not have been established.

Nettie also volunteered her assistance to the Woman's Christian Temperance Union's (WCTU) rescue missions with Matilda B. Carse who succeeded Frances Willard (1839–98) in 1878. Emma realized that Nettie held a neutral stance regarding the suffrage movement without actually opposing it. Her son Cyrus's wife Harriet hosted a 1916 suffrage meeting and parade for around one hundred suffrage leaders. Harriet's mother-in-law admiringly supported Harriet by attending as a guest.[48] Although Mrs. McCormick helped intermittently with the Union's rescue missions, her finance papers disclose no gifts given to the organization.[49]

Emma and Nettie bonded their friendship with a mutual spiritual connection. Emma held an overpowering sense of God's greatness. On September 20, 1888, she communicated to Nettie her worshipful reflections on God's creation and redemption:

> My dear Mrs. McCormick: Your charming letter . . . came duly . . . I am glad that you [love] the beautiful country . . . Oh what will this redeemed earth be, when Christ brings His glory to brighten every color & to beautify every hue! Come Lord Jesus, come quickly . . . thy death & resurrection have overcome! Let us hasten the gospel to every creature that earth's long-spoken benediction becomes living blessing to old & to young. As the beasts of the field & the trees of the forests! Lord, come make thy mountains break forth into singing & all the trees of the forests clap their hands![50]

Likewise, Emma added her joy regarding Nettie's family trip to D. L. Moody's schools in Massachusetts: "God sent you to Northfield! I am glad! God did it!"

---

46. Ibid., 164.
47. Ibid., 195.
48. Ibid.
49. Financial File of Nettie Fowler McCormick, 1843–1923, McCormick Collection.
50. Emma Dryer to Nettie McCormick, 20 September 1888, Biographical File of Emma Dryer.

Emma's Friendships and Acquaintances

Nettie also financially supported Emma's Bible Reader staff in response to personal donation requests written by Emma:

> Dear Mrs. McCormick. I wish to place two perhaps three new Bible Readers in the work. If you know of ladies who would like to support them or to contribute to their support will you please inform me? I hope that our Lord will multiply greatly the number of workers. Oh how much we need . . . workers in all parts of this city . . . I always feel that it is a pleasure to see you & therefore shall be glad at any time to call. Affectionately E. Dryer.[51]

Like Emma, Nettie's missionary spirit contained the qualities of meticulousness and self-sacrifice in which she gave whole-heartedly of her time, ideas, prayers, and love. They both creatively contributed their own personal interests and abilities to each ministry in which they became involved. With intricate unity Emma and Nettie mutually agreed on the value of the Chicago Bible Work which Moody encouraged in 1873—a ministry that would not have continued without Emma's uncommon determination and the financial support of the McCormicks.

McCormick Family Association With Mr. Moody

The specific circumstances regarding the initial meeting of Cyrus McCormick and D. L. Moody are unclear. Cyrus's business background and benevolent generosity would surely have paved the way for their introduction and continued amiable association. Moody quickly found himself as a popular guest and friend of the McCormicks. These business-minded visionaries frequently met in Cyrus's Rush Street home study. They expressed their strong views regarding what they believed to be most advantageous for the economic growth of Chicago as well as the most reliable and Christ-ordained methods for evangelization. Emma, as well as family members who were keenly aware of Moody and Cyrus's relationship, noted the commonality of these two indomitable and impetuous personalities. Yet even when they providentially met elsewhere, both men continued to hold a common respect and high regard for one another.[52]

Moody quickly found that Cyrus held a deep interest not only in the work of the Presbyterian Church and the McCormick Theological Seminary, but also in the YMCA.[53] When presenting his visionary plan for a new YMCA facility, Moody successfully convinced Cyrus to invest in a building that would be larger than the 1865 lavishly designed Crosby Opera House in Chicago.[54] Cyrus was likewise impressed with the efficacy of Moody's ministry among the underprivileged and the positive results of his expanding Sunday school.

---

51. Ibid., June 12, 1916.
52. Ibid.
53. Hutchinson, *Cyrus Hall McCormick*, 302–3.
54. Ibid., 303.

Moody's spirited personality won him the financial backing of other Chicago businessmen such as J. V. Farwell and Philip Danford Armour (1832–1901), a developer of a leading meat packing company. Chicago businessmen, including Cyrus McCormick, quickly noted Moody's contagious energy for accomplishing mammoth tasks. In recruiting funds for the YMCA Moody implemented an attractive business investment incentive. Investors would receive stock in the organization with assurance of a financial return accrued from the building's occupant rental fees. Any accumulated income would be donated to local charities.[55]

To encourage Mr. McCormick's participation in the YMCA project, Moody tenaciously informed Cyrus in April 1866 that his name held the power of swaying the public to embrace a successful endeavor.[56] McCormick responded with a $10,000 pledge. Tragically, the building burned on January 7, 1868. Moody relentlessly conducted another fundraiser for reconstruction costs of $135,000. McCormick once again gave $10,000 for the new hall which was completed by January 19, 1869, but followed by the Chicago Fire on October 8, 1871.

Within three years another YMCA was under construction. At this time Cyrus McCormick was a potential candidate for governor of Illinois, a United States senator, or possibly vice-president. Although giving the appearance of political motivation, John Farwell shared Moody's belief that a five thousand dollar gift from Cyrus to Moody's work would receive wide Associated Press coverage. This action could promote his possible bid for the vice-presidency. Moody encouraged Cyrus that his donation would be worth more than any amount he could donate to manipulating politicians.[57]

After the Chicago Fire, Cyrus McCormick continued to support Moody's future endeavors as a financier of Moody's on-going harvest for souls. When Moody initiated plans for the Chicago Bible Work in 1873, entrusting the leadership of this new work to Emma, she accepted the task of raising money for the work. Cyrus's steadfast commitment to Moody, plus Nettie's own prominent evangelical faith, invoked their continued backing of Emma's Bible Work.

With their critical support and that of other businessmen and philanthropists, Emma forged ahead with the administration of the program. From a distance Moody wrote letters to potential donors asking for support. In a letter to Mr. McCormick similar in style to Emma's own donation letters, he requested funds of $50 a month for each lady Bible reader to minister to the poor and needy in Chicago and to share the gospel of Jesus in homes where darkness had prevailed.[58] He also suggested that

---

55. Ibid.
56. Ibid.
57. Ibid., 337n104.
58. D. L. Moody to Cyrus McCormick, 24 February 1873, Chicago Evangelization Society File.

Cyrus's donation of $600 would adequately support one of their well-qualified lady workers for a full year.[59]

In another letter sent in 1887 to the McCormick Harvesting Machine Company, Moody stipulated the need of donations for the following reasons: Sabbath desecration, intemperance, crime, arrests with more than 40,000 inmates filling the jails, correction houses to overflowing, a shortage of Bible readers and workers, and funds for filling the Bible Work Institute's immediate need of thirty more workers. With his usual forceful persuasion Moody added: "We will keep up this aggressive effort all the year around if the business men of Chicago will sustain us."[60]

The McCormicks recognized Moody's passion for evangelization. They held vivid memories of his Chicago meetings. For the winter meeting of 1876–77 Nettie recalled Cyrus's intense interest in attending. The night before the morning service he would make preparations for a 7:00 a.m. gas light breakfast with a departing time of 9:00. Cyrus and Nettie with their three older children would arrive in their carriage at the church and find seats close to the front in the soon to be crowded hall. Cyrus desired to absorb every word proclaimed in worship and every word of Moody's sermon. Nettie recalled how her husband graciously provided a carriage at the end of the meetings to escort Moody to his home.[61]

Nettie continued to affirm her husband's faithful friendship and support of D. L. Moody even after Cyrus's death. During the 1893 World's Columbian Exposition or Chicago World's Fair Moody invited multiple speakers worldwide for the six months of evangelistic meetings including renowned German anti-Semitic preacher Reverend Dr. Adolf Stoecker (1835–1909).[62] Both Emma and Nettie were among thousands gathered to hear the gospel message being presented to their Chicago German believers and unbelievers by this speaker in spite of the media's negative reports and the reservations of friends.

Nettie had previously proposed that an area be allocated on the Chicago World's Fairgrounds to hold Moody's evangelistic meetings. Although the fair committee turned down her request, Moody was not stopped. He secured circus tents with a ten thousand seat capacity, local movie theaters and hotels, and over 125 other meeting places. His final acquisition was the prestigious Central Music Hall (1879–1900) for the last two months of the fair.[63]

This campaign so moved Nettie that she generously gave an additional $2,500 for the expenses. She provided for Moody's stay in her home along with his request to escort Adolf Stoecker to Central Music Hall. She thoroughly enjoyed hearing this pastor

---

59. Dorsett, *A Passion For Souls*, 169.

60. D. L. Moody on behalf of the Chicago Evangelization Society to the McCormick Harvesting Company, 17 June 1887, Chicago Evangelization Society File.

61. Roderick, *Nettie Fowler McCormick*, 107.

62. Hartzler, *Moody in Chicago*, 120–25.

63. Roderick, *Nettie Fowler McCormick*, 187–88.

give his message in German with Reverend Niclaus Boldt from the German church in St. Paul serving as interpreter. Undoubtedly, Emma attended this world fair evangelism event with her friend and eagerly shared the excitement of the international service. Sadly, on the last day of the campaign Carter Harrison, the mayor of Chicago, was assassinated. Nettie shared her conflicted feelings: "What a great and awful calamity . . . How we pause in our rave statements about the glory and magnificence of this great city which has made the Fair!"[64]

Seven years after the Chicago World's Fair Nettie wrote an article in the widely circulated Presbyterian religious journal called *The Chicago Interior* in which she reviewed the rewarding friendship that existed between Moody and her family. Cyrus had bailed out the journal years earlier and had faithfully seen the paper used to promote his seminary and church. Now Nettie not only continued to edit the journal, but she also contributed information to assure that their friendship with Mr. Moody would be steadfastly recorded for eternity.[65]

Closing Friendship

In October 1916 Nettie moved to a new country house in Lake Forest, Illinois, referenced by her son Harold as *The House of Peace* and appropriately named by her daughter Anita as the *House-in-the-Woods*. Anita described it as "a lovely house, artistically designed, arranged for perfect comfort as well as charm and set in a forest of its own."[66] Nettie and Emma dined in the tea-house with its walled garden and walked the trails through the woods. Although Nettie appreciated her new exquisite *House of Peace*, she continued to return to her beloved home on Rush Street. At other times when traveling to her California home in late winter and early spring, she would continue her voluminous correspondence with Emma and numerous friends.

On February 8, 1915, at 675 Rush Street, family and friends celebrated Nettie's eightieth birthday. Anita sensed her mother's depression and loneliness during this wintery Chicago season. She sent invitations to relatives, business associates from the International Harvester Company, school and college faculties, missions, the YMCA, and to others worldwide. And of course, Emma received an invitation to which she responded: "Thanks for your invitation which I gladly accept to dine with your Mother next Monday evening, February the eighth."[67] Seated next to Anita's son during the gathering, Emma delighted to see the stereopticon presentation with years of visual memories and achievements. She understandably noted her friend's sudden humble

---

64. Ibid., 188.
65. Hutchinson, *Cyrus Hall McCormick*, 305, Footnote 116.
66. Roderick, *Nettie Fowler McCormick*, 300.
67. Invitation from Anita McCormick Blaine to Emma Dryer, February 1915, Anita Blaine McCormick Correspondence and Papers.

Emma's Friendships and Acquaintances

request to end the presentation: "Why, I haven't done anything . . . it is these other people: please play the piano."[68]

Nettie's final days were spent at the *House-in-the-Woods*. On July 5, 1923, she entered into Christ's presence. With Anita, Cyrus Jr., and Harold beside her, her parting words, said three times, were "How lovely!"[69] Upon hearing the news of the loss of her friend, Emma penned the following letter on July 9 to Nettie's son, Cyrus, who resided at 101 East Erie Street in Chicago. She shared the blessed memories of Anita's mother:

> Dear Christian friend:
>
> Not a day passes without my prayerful repetition of the McCormick family whom I have been privileged to know so many years. I shall even keep sacred the day of your Mother's departure to Christ's presence & I shall miss her till I meet her. I have known friends . . . who saw the angels that bore Christians to Christ's presence. What a goodly company she met! What a great work the angels have to do! Read John 1 51. [1:51]. We are near the End of this dispensation. Christ's coming is very near. Then glorified, we the church shall return to Earth with Him, to work with Him forever . . . In this best of bonds, Cordially Yours, Emma Dryer[70]

Months later on April 3, 1924, Emma continued her correspondence with Anita:

> My dear Mrs. Blaine,
>
> Daily I repeat the names of your father and mother (& of their children so far as I know them) & I think of the Heavenly glories, opening to their view. 'Eye hath not seen, nor ear heard, neither have entered into the heart of man, the things which God hath prepared for them that love Him.' I Corinthians 2:9; Rev 22:20, 21[71]

A year after Nettie's death Emma once again expressed her endearment of Anita's parents. She wrote from her 4124 Jackson Boulevard residence: "My Dear Mrs. Blaine, We are entering on the memorable month of your Mother's translation. What glories have opened to her view & your dear Father's view since the angles [sic] came & took them away from us."[72] Emma's words of hope for Anita were fully realized when less than a year after writing these words of comfort, Emma herself would also enter into an angel-escorted eternity.

---

68. Roderick, *Nettie Fowler McCormick*, 299.
69. Ibid., 315.
70. Anita Blaine McCormick Correspondence and Papers, McCormick Collection.
71. Ibid.
72. Ibid.

WOMAN OF NOBILITY

Josiah and Lucy Rider Meyer: Co-Founders of the Chicago Training School

As Emma settled into Chicago life during the 1870s she must have been struck not only by the poverty, but the prolific population of European immigrants. She was not alone. God raised up other women to assist with the diversified needs of the city. One Methodist woman by the name of Lucy Rider Meyer (1849–1922), an associate of D. L. Moody, carried a burden for these disenfranchised groups.

Like Emma, Lucy affirmed Mayflower roots for her family. She was raised on a farm in New Haven, Vermont, and brought up by Christian parents.[73] As a young girl she began teaching Sunday school classes which groomed her for work from 1881 to 1885 at The Illinois State Sunday School Association. In 1872 Lucy graduated from Oberlin College, a school popularized by revivalist Charles Finney. Oberlin operated as the first college to award degrees to women, such as Lucy, at a time when the education of women was looked upon as an unnecessary exercise. Emma recollected and perhaps shared with Lucy the stories she also heard about Finney in 1855 at Mary Allen's seminary in Richmond.

Lucy served as a preceptress at Troy Conference Academy in Poultney, Vermont, before moving to Illinois in 1878 where she accepted a teaching position at the Cook County Normal School. As with Emma, the normal school background laid a foundation for Lucy in her plans to operate a training school. While serving as a professor of natural sciences from 1879 to 1881 at McKendree College in Lebanon, Illinois, Lucy obtained an honorary Master of Arts degree from Oberlin awarded in 1880.[74] She received a medical degree in 1887 from the Woman's Medical School at Northwestern University in Illinois after completing medical training at the Student Woman's Medical School of Pennsylvania from 1873 to 1875.

In 1885 Lucy and her husband, Josiah Meyer (1849–1926), established the Chicago Training School patterned after the methodology of the Methodist Episcopal Deaconesses. Lucy and Josiah believed along with Emma that Christian ministry for women should go beyond church and Sunday school to attending to the uneducated, destitute, sick, and orphaned.

TEMPERANCE AND HOLINESS ASSOCIATIONS

Emma and Lucy admired *spiritual reformers* such as Hannah Whitall Smith (1832–1911) and evangelist Dwight Moody as well as *social reformers* such as Frances Willard of the Woman's Christian Temperance Union.[75] In 1876 while attending Garrett Biblical Institute near Chicago, Frances Willard professed *sanctification* at a Phoebe

---

73. Meyer, *Deaconesses, Biblical, Early Church*, 2.
74. Horton, *High Adventure*, 62.
75. Ibid., 293.

Emma's Friendships and Acquaintances

Palmer (1807–74) holiness camp meeting.[76] Although Emma submitted to Moody's admonition to avoid association with the temperance movement, Lucy joined with Frances in some of her ideology. According to Methodist Bishop Nicholson, Lucy became one of many responsible for the passage of women suffrage in America.[77]

Although not an active temperance or suffrage advocate, Lucy remained a powerful influence for reform in the movement. She considered her friendship with Frances as a beloved gift. Likewise, Frances considered Lucy her *Dearest best Friend* in a letter written six months before Miss Willard's death.[78] In Frances's introduction to Lucy's 1892 book *Deaconesses: Biblical, Early Church, European, American* she wrote, "My friend, Lucy Rider Meyer, is as much raised up to pioneer the way for these, her younger sisters, as ever Phoebe was to help the Church at Cenchrea."[79] Miss Willard later served as a committed and influential member of the Meyer's Chicago Training School Board.

Both Emma and Lucy admired and respected the Holiness Movement advocate and Quaker, Hannah Whitall Smith. Emma would have anticipated hearing this key speaker at Moody's Northfield Conferences especially after reading Mrs. Smith's popular masterpiece, *The Christian's Secret of a Happy Life*, published in 1875. Mrs. Smith was also inspired by Frances Willard as evidenced in her introduction to Frances's 1889 autobiography, *Glimpses of Fifty Years*. Hannah acknowledged that it was a tremendous highlight of her life to have Frances as her friend. She stated that she had "been inspired by her genius . . . cheered by her sympathy . . . taught by her wisdom . . . led onward and upward by her enthusiastic faith."[80] Mrs. Smith viewed Frances as a role model and encourager to their women comrades as she taught them "the vast possibilities of a pure and holy womanhood, consecrated to God and to the service of humanity."[81]

---

76. Ruelas, *Women and the Landscape*, 7. Phoebe Worrell Palmer (1807-1874), known for her admonition to keep the cleansing fires on the altar continually burning, initiated and popularized the American Holiness Movement's *Tuesday Meetings for the Promotion of Holiness*. The movement freed women to assume positions of leadership with the empowerment of a second blessing that D. L. Moody experienced. Phoebe and her husband Dr. Walter Clark Palmer in Wesleyan tradition became intensely involved in evangelistic missions for prisoners and for urban poverty. She trained and encouraged other emerging women leaders such as Salvation Army cofounder Catherine Booth, temperance advocate Frances Willard, and Hannah Whitall Smith.

77. Horton, *High Adventure*, 205.

78. Ibid.

79. Meyer, *Deaconesses, Biblical, Early Church*, 6.

80. Willard, *Glimpses of Fifty Years*, v.

81. Ibid., vi.

D. L. Moody Influence

During his 1876 Chicago campaign—before Lucy came to Chicago and at the time when Emma was diligently laying the groundwork for Moody's Chicago Bible School—Moody became acquainted with Frances Willard.[82] Seeing her potential as an educated and well-known speaker, he invited her to participate in his ten week 1877 Boston campaign. She used her unique ability to minister in Moody's after meetings with genuine seekers in *inquiry-rooms*. She also viewed this as an opportunity to spread her cause for prohibition. However, this association did not last.

Despite good intentions Frances and Moody would find that their ability to partner in ministry would be hindered by numerous obstacles.[83] Moody requested that she cut her ties with a prohibitionist Unitarian speaker on her platform. She originally complied but later retracted her decision and indicated that the choice of speakers was hers to make and not Moody's. She wrote: "For myself I only knew that, liberal as he was toward me in all other things, tolerant of my ways and manners, generous in his views upon the woman question, devotedly conscientious and true, Brother Moody's Scripture interpretations concerning religious toleration were too literal for me; the jacket was too straight—I could not wear it."[84] Moody believed that her activist platform could inhibit the spreading of the gospel and give offense to participating clergymen and parishioners. Frances consequently sent a letter to the Moodys to which she never received a response.[85]

Meanwhile, Emma moved ahead with her *Bible Work* and became supportive of other women's ministries such as the Meyer's Chicago Training School and Frances Willard's WCTU. However, Moody resolved that the temperance movement no longer aligned with his revival agenda.[86] No record exists of Emma joining in the friendship between Lucy and Frances. Nevertheless, D. L. Moody made it very clear to Emma that he felt it was best for her to not associate with the movement.

In a letter written to Nettie McCormick on September 20, 1888, while visiting at Moody's Northfield schools, Emma wrote of a past situation in which she approached the platform in Farwell Hall to speak at a WCTU meeting. Moody told her: "If you speak on that platform I'll never take hold of that work." When she asked him how she could possibly avoid it since she was on the WCTU committee, he said, "I'll go & speak! That's enough! You keep away from them! . . . If you have anything to do with those temperance women I won't come to Chicago!" In response, Emma regretfully

82. Daniels, *His Words, Work and Workers*, 510.

83. Willard, *Glimpses of Fifty Years*, 356–61.

84. Ibid., 361.

85. Thirteen years later, in September 1889, Chicago would again witness a ten day Christian conference in which Moody gladly shared the platform with fifty year old Frances Willard at the Chicago Avenue Church. She proclaimed her delight in the dedication of the Chicago Bible Institute for both men and women. *Chicago Tribune*, "Moody is Here Again," 1.

86. Joiner, *Sin in the City*, 55.

submitted—at a personal cost of slowly fractured relationships: "So, I withdrew—no easy effort! I obeyed and bore the blame & hoped for *peace* . . . I had helped organize the W.C.T.U. & it was flourishing . . . I *believed* that God wanted him to come to Chicago and would make it right further on. I kept the peace & alienated—*not only*—from him."[87]

Lucy became acquainted with D. L. Moody through her and Emma's mutually shared vision of Bible training schools for women. Isabelle Horton, a close friend to Lucy, wrote regarding Lucy and Moody: "They had many a friendly discussion as to what form of work, educational or inspirational, would best meet the needs of the hour."[88] In 1884, years after he had secured Emma's commitment to begin the Bible Work, D. L. Moody commissioned Lucy to teach Bible at his school for girls in Northfield, Massachusetts, founded in 1879. Lucy traveled to Moody's Northfield schools for the winter months of 1884 to 1885. She became familiar with boarding school procedures and perhaps valued the time to pray through her disappointment, just as Emma had, in not yet seeing a fully operating Chicago training school.[89]

Upon Lucy's return to Chicago she met Josiah Shelley Meyer. It appeared that although she had been considering a position at Moody's school, her interests were now stirred elsewhere. She ultimately declined for reasons observed by her friend, Isabelle: "Notwithstanding her staunch and outspoken friendliness for Mr. Moody and his ideals, one knowing both parties well would see where their views must diverge."[90]

Chicago Training School

Josiah Shelley Meyer served as secretary for the YMCA from 1882 to 1884 and attended Cyrus McCormick's Theological Seminary in 1884. After their marriage in 1885, he envisioned with Lucy a Bible training school that utilized both residential teachers and outside support. Together they founded a deaconess school named the *Chicago Training School for City, Home and Foreign Missions* (CTS). Lucy became acquainted with Emma through the WCTU and knew of Emma's *Bible Work*. She was intensely satisfied to know of others in Chicago who were considering schools for home and foreign missions.[91]

Emma surely noted along with many others the degree to which Josiah unassertively accommodated Lucy in the founding of the CTS although not in the area of certain theological views such as millennialism. He walked beside his wife in such a way that even others observed "their shadows fell as one."[92] Lucy sought to assure

87. Emma Dryer to Nettie McCormick, 20 September 1888, Biographical File of Emma Dryer.
88. Horton, *High Adventure*, 77.
89. Ibid., 81.
90. Ibid., 77.
91. Meyer, *Deaconesses, Biblical, Early Church*, 92.
92. Horton, *High Adventure*, 118.

that women with advanced training, such as she and Emma, could indiscriminately go beyond the status quo of domestic duties.[93]

With Josiah's support, Lucy, like Emma, determined to use her skills to serve and help others. She accepted the call as a Methodist *deaconess*, a term Lucy simply defined as one who served and assisted those in need.[94] Moody encouraged Emma to visit a deaconess setting in England in order to observe activities in the field of urban evangelism. She carried out his suggestion in 1879–80, living for a number of weeks in the Deaconess House at Mildmay. She accompanied the women of that institution on their round of duties in London. With Moody's help Emma also contacted his friends associated with the Central YMCA in London. Thus, she studied firsthand the work of deaconesses such as Lucy Meyer and the work of other evangelical groups in England's metropolis.

Consequently, Emma could identify with Lucy's goal to pattern the CTS after the teachings of Reverend William Pennefather (1816–73). She also understood Moody's prior acquaintance and support. In 1864 Pennefather initiated the Mildmay conferences at Mildmay Park in England. D. L. Moody attended a memorable session with him during his visit in 1872 which contributed to the 1874 establishment of the Keswick Convention which Moody later popularized.[95] Moody recollected Pennefather's emphasis on the work of the Holy Spirit and the atmosphere of holiness surrounding him. He recalled how Mr. Pennefather's face would beam with *heaven's light* as he reflected the life of one living continually in God's presence.[96] Emma did not personally meet Pennefather since he died unexpectedly at the time Moody arrived in Liverpool on June 17, 1873. However, she most likely met his wife, Catherine, during her 1879 trip to England when she assimilated much valuable information regarding deaconess techniques to better train the ladies at the Bible Work.

With support and affirmation Emma accepted Lucy's invitation to participate in the October 20, 1885, dedication of the Meyer's new school.[97] She joined editor and Methodist bishop Dr. John Heyl Vincent (1832–1920), Dr. Alabaster, and Professor Bradley as they spoke on this grand occasion. The CTS's publication, *The Message*, recorded: "A memorable day, because this evening occurred our first Reception, very unlike the formal society gatherings that are called by that name. The girls had prepared a little lunch . . . and the company were discovering its merits . . . Dr. Alabaster also spoke during the evening, and so did dear Miss Dryer. And Prof. Bradley ended, with the crowning thought that all intellectual culture amounts to nothing without

---

93. Dougherty, "The Meyers," 96.

94. Meyer, *Deaconesses, Biblical, Early Church,* 154.

95. With worldwide impact, the Keswick Convention influenced the Holiness, Fundamentalist, and Pentecostal movements. For a brief history and literary references of the movement, refer to David Bundy's 1975 work, *Keswick: A Bibliographical Introduction to the Higher Life Movements* and his 1993 work *Keswick and the Experience of Evangelical Piety.*

96. Moody, *The Life of Dwight L. Moody,* 154.

97. Meyer, *Deaconesses, Biblical, Early Church,* 119.

the vivifying influence of the Holy Spirit. Surely the Blessed Spirit has been with us to-night."[98] In spite of Lucy's disappointment in the small turn out for the school's opening, Emma could knowingly have encouraged her to continue in faith to believe that God would multiply this small beginning of four young lady students. Perhaps she also willingly offered her services as an outside lecturer.

As educators, Emma and Lucy would have discussed social trends and how to keep current with curriculum in education and Bible studies. Like Emma, Lucy developed a curriculum that both supported the spiritual development of students and equipped them for service in the inner city. She initiated a comprehensive Bible study with courses in health, government, and the family in order to assist in establishing God's earthly kingdom.[99] First year training included a practicum at the city hospitals with readings from Hannah Whitall Smith's book *The Christian's Secret of a Happy Life* and Lucy's own materials on deaconess training. Second year coursework included foreign language and readings from the *Life of John Wesley* and Frances Willard's *Woman and Temperance* (1883). Studies were culminated with field experiences and written exams.[100]

Lucy required her students to be self-supporting by acquiring additional vocations especially in the area of nursing. She encouraged them to learn immigrants' languages, display principles of servanthood and sanctification, and establish a strong biblical foundation.[101] Lucy's methods for reporting visitations aligned with Emma's Bible Work techniques. From 1887 to 1888 Lucy recorded the following: "Number of calls made at homes, 5,287; Bible readings and prayer at homes, 575; Bible lessons given in Sunday-school, 19,113; Lessons given in Industrial Schools, 8,371; Tracts and cards distributed, 6,130."[102]

A Methodist bishop brought further affirmation of the effectiveness of Lucy's Bible training work: "Mrs. Meyer was a prophet of the modern era of religious education. She was doing that work before the leaders of the church thought very much about it. She was one of the leaders in the historical study and modern interpretation of the Bible. And no one who knew her power in prayer had any fears about the new method of Bible study affecting the vitality of her religion."[103]

In assuring further success of the school, Emma would have supportively collaborated with Lucy in her methods regarding the policies and financial backing of the young ladies at her school. In order to be easily identified with the CTS, the ladies wore simple black gowns with white cuffs and large white puffy collars notwithstanding accusations of Catholicism's nunnery replication. Lucy remained undaunted as

---

98. Ibid., 119–20.
99. Warner, "Toward the Light," 177–81.
100. Meyer, *Deaconesses, Biblical, Early Church*, 78.
101. Warner, "Toward the Light," 177–79.
102. Meyer, *Deaconesses, Biblical, Early Church*, 139.
103. Horton, *High Adventure*, 205.

she explained: "Here were the women ready and eager to do the work . . . so terribly needed—at the merely nominal cost of furnishing them a home and clothes. Our good friends Mr. Blackstone and Mr. Elderkin and the elect lady, Mrs. Hobbs, all stood by us."[104] This dress code policy did not impede the growth of the school. When Josiah and Lucy resigned from the CTS in 1917 approximately 5,000 women were certified deaconesses. They founded over forty primary Methodist establishments including nursing homes, hospitals, and orphanages.[105]

Emma most likely entertained discussions with Lucy regarding the subject of premillennialism which echoed her longing for the return of Christ. Undoubtedly, Lucy advocated that kingdom admonitions be the subject of continued prayer along with a demonstrative anticipation of the Lord's soon coming sovereign reign.[106] Lucy and those in the deaconess movement would have leaned more toward postmillennialism based on their Wesleyan and holiness roots. Despite this doctrinal difference, the Meyers secured the financial support and friendship of a Methodist Zionist supporter and premillennialist, William Eugene Blackstone.

Emma, also a friend of Mr. Blackstone, advocated the reading of his widely circulated book, *Jesus is Coming*. She more closely aligned herself with Blackstone's premillennial theology than Lucy. Blackstone disapproved of Lucy's Scripture interpretation regarding the return of Christ. Nevertheless, he elected to serve as the CTS secretary and chairman for special committees. He admitted that Lucy, like D. L. Moody, demonstrated the capacity to discover *spiritual truth* in the everyday occurrences of life.[107] Blackstone voluntarily lectured on foreign missions at the school based on his ubiquitous travels and firsthand knowledge of countries such as Israel, India, Africa, Korea, and Japan. He and his family's continued support, especially their gift of $2,000, greatly strengthened the faith of Emma and the Meyers as they continued their sacrificial ministries in Chicago.[108]

Changing Roles of Evangelical Women

Sarah Clarke, Nettie McCormick, and Lucy Meyer modeled with Emma the pivotal roles for women during a period in history when evangelical women were emerging as serious business competitors and educators. Emma's Bible Work provided for her an opportunity to use her skills to equip other ladies to morally, educationally, and socially impact their environment for Christ. Unlike Sarah, Nettie, and Lucy who embraced the fortifying roles of their husbands, Emma could not claim as a single woman the protection of a father or close male family member. Instead, she experienced at

---

104. Meyer, *Deaconesses, Biblical, Early Church*, 155.
105. Ruelas, *Women and the Landscape*, 17.
106. Warner, "Toward the Light," 179.
107. Horton, *High Adventure*, 207.
108. Ibid., 184.; Meyer, *Deaconesses, Biblical, Early Church*, 97.

Emma's Friendships and Acquaintances

times a certain amount of inequity and restraint from male evangelicals, businessmen, and religious leaders due to expectant female submission.

Historian Thekla Joiner posed a perspective in her gender analysis of Emma's ministry years in Chicago as that of "underlying contradictions within the normative evangelical gender ideals."[109] She suggested that Emma would have been constrained by the evangelical paradigm regarding the place of women missionaries. The prevalent evangelical identity for women during Emma's lifetime was that of domesticity with authority limited to the home environment. For those women, the qualities of submission and suffering were viewed as proof of their successful mission outreaches.[110]

Sarah, Nettie, Lucy, and Emma possessed an altruistic passion to serve their city by ultimately serving their Lord and Master. However, their leadership roles would at times lead to misunderstandings from their male counterparts despite their own extensive or superb qualifications in business, missions, and education. Yet they were determined to overcome workplace or ministry restraints as frustratingly expressed by Lucy Meyer:

> Think of the furnace of misunderstandings! Who has not felt its fiery breath? To say things meant to be kind and cheering—to know that you have spoken from a loving and a true heart—and yet to see your words go, all twisted, to their destination! Is not this a fire? To know that more words would be worse than useless, and to hold still, while blame and criticisms beat around your head . . . Yet if the Master can bring out in us 'his own fair form' by such pain, welcome all that shall make us more like him! But thank God that in Heaven we shall know as we are known![111]

Lucy's friend, Isabelle Horton, caught the extent of Lucy's pain when she wrote: "Often she was criticised, often misunderstood, often unjustly blamed, and, though she neither faltered nor failed in the carrying out of her purposes, because of this, the hurt was nonetheless keen."[112]

Mrs. Horton observed that Lucy was not capable of holding ill feelings toward others. She would forcefully advocate for the programs in which she so intensely believed. Lucy sorrowed over conflicts that would emerge while the severe disapproval of others only brought her pain. Yet in spite of *the opposers and criticisers* she extended an all-embracing kindness and compassion.[113] Lucy purposefully illustrated her feelings with the analogy of an anvil: "My life seems destined to be always a storm center . . . I am surprised my poor old heart doesn't get over aching from the hard knocks.

---

109. Joiner, *Sin in the City,* 44–45.
110. Ibid., 52.
111. Horton, *High Adventure,* 292.
112. Ibid.
113. Ibid., 293–94.

Blow after blow falls! . . . Is not this an anvil? . . . If only they will drive me nearer to God!"[114]

Similarly, Emma would struggle through the issues of submission in societal and evangelical conflicts as did the women in Frances Willard's WCTU. They lived in an age when the church often appreciated the usefulness of women for service rather than supporting them in leadership roles. Little had been written or propagated regarding the unique and valued differences between men and women for various roles according to God's design.[115]

D. L. Moody in his advocacy for women possessed a genuinely sincere heart desiring to understand, but he lacked critical insights to successfully support and implement their unique gender leadership roles. Therefore, the *hard knocks* and *blows* that lay ahead for Emma and Moody would seriously challenge the strength of their friendship and their love for God.

> "Many women have done noble work, but you have surpassed them all!"
> PROVERBS 31:20, 29 GWT

---

114. Ibid., 294.

115. Sandom, *Different By Design,* 2012. Carrie Sandom creatively and sensitively distinguishes the beauty of both genders in their God-given abilities to lead and to follow in mutual submission. Sandom provides supporting information regarding differences in brain structure, physical make-up, long and short-range vision, equal status without superiority, role diversity, and the complimentary completion of each gender.

6

Emma and Moody: Complementary Leadership Roles

"When one rules over men righteously, ruling in the fear of God, He dawns on them like the morning light when the sun rises on a cloudless morning."

~2 SAMUEL 23:3B–4A AMP~

NOT ONLY DID EMMA's circle of friends include individuals from Chicago, but her association with D. L. Moody broadened her contacts with his family and friends from Chicago to Massachusetts, to New York and beyond. After Moody left in 1873 for England where he secured new friendships, he and Emma continued to correspond regarding the school's development. Emma devoted herself to a new leadership role in the establishment of the Bible Work—with Moody's blessing. After his return from England in 1875 she began the first of many visits to Northfield, Massachusetts. Emma became more steadfastly included in the Moody family.

Moody Family Support and Ties

In August of 1875 Moody and his family permanently left Chicago for Northfield, Massachusetts, where he purchased a farm. Emma knew of their prayerful consideration for maintaining their residence in Chicago. Mrs. Moody shared with Emma her personal desire to reside in Chicago close to her own mother, brother, sisters and friends.[1] Granddaughter Emma Powell concurred in her book *Heavenly Destiny* that the year following the Chicago Fire her Grandmother Moody still felt more at home in Chicago than any other place.[2] However, Mrs. Moody gladly settled into the area of her husband's birthplace in Northfield near his own relatives.

---

1. Emma Dryer to Charles Blanchard, 1916, Biographical File of Emma Dryer.
2. Powell, *Heavenly Destiny*, 67.

With great interest, Emma closely followed Moody in his new leadership role in the 1879 establishment of a school for girls in Northfield and Mount Herman school for boys in 1881. The schools provided an education for poor and minority youth which bridged denominational, racial, and gender gaps. In 1880 Moody also made Northfield a major location for conferences with international leader participation. At Moody's request Emma traveled to New York City in the spring of 1876 during Moody and Sankey's campaign at the Hippodrome. While there, Moody met with Emma to discuss the Bible Work and to keep her encouraged during his times of absence. Their on-going plans included a permanent facility where her Bible workers could reside during their training.[3]

As she visited Northfield, Emma became better acquainted with the Moody family. She observed that even in the midst of Moody's busy schedule, he took time for his family with demonstrations of love and attention.[4] She wrote: "In these waiting years, it was my great privilege to attend annually the Conventions in Northfield, and to be at home in Mr. Moody's house. He enjoyed his vacations there, playing with the children, visiting his schools, and planning for his future work."[5] Emma recalled her admiration of Mrs. Moody who found that she was still able to spend valuable time in Chicago with her mother, her mother's family, and her sister Sarah Revell Holden. She also contributed to her husband's numerous enterprises. Emma wrote:

> Only a few knew of Mrs. Moody's invaluable influence with her husband and family. She was his educated adviser in the schools, his confidant and sympathizer in all his undertakings . . . and once he said he was so glad to go to his Home in Northfield; that when he came in sight of it, he *ran* to meet his family. He said, 'I thank God for my wife and family. What would I do if my wife was like Mrs.—?,—worldly! My, I could not do anything!' My own heart responded, 'You never spoke more truly.' God gave Mrs. Emma Revell Moody her position in her husband's affection, and her place in his work, for the advancement of Christ's Kingdom! And she was faithful to her high calling.[6]

Moody's son Will concurred that his father had found a soul mate that became his *balance wheel* to enhance his ministry with her "advice, sympathy, and faith . . . judgment, tact, and sacrifice."[7]

Emma also spoke of Mrs. Moody as "the beloved Balance-wheel of D. L. Moody's existence."[8] She heard others refer to Mrs. Moody as his *indomitable spouse*. At an early age Emma Revell and her family tenaciously emigrated in 1847 from England

---

3. Emma Dryer to Charles Blanchard, 1916, Biographical File of Emma Dryer.
4. Moody Bible Institute, "D. L. Moody's Story."
5. Emma Dryer to Charles Blanchard, 1916, Biographical File of Emma Dryer.
6. Ibid.
7. Powell, *Heavenly Destiny*, 54.
8. Emma Dryer's tribute to Mrs. D. L. Moody, Biographical File of Emma Dryer.

to America. Without hesitation she returned to visit her birthplace with her husband when they traveled to England in June of 1873 along with Ira Sankey and his wife. On this trip they inspired people to develop ministries for children and training schools for women just as Moody had encouraged Emma to do.[9]

Undoubtedly, Emma would have been thrilled to converse with yet another educator such as Mrs. Moody who taught in the Chicago public schools three years prior to her marriage. With her education background Mrs. Moody naturally supported her husband in his caring outreach for children by responding to Sunday school teaching opportunities. Emma would have noted that even after the birth of three children Mrs. Moody, a devoted mother and teacher, maintained an unfailing support of her husband while attending to their finances and written correspondence. Her granddaughter remembered her mother describing Emma Revell as an established linguist who mastered much of the Italian language in only six weeks.[10] Mrs. Moody's son-in-law, Arthur Percy Fitt, spoke in later years of Mrs. Moody as *a choice lady* with "a serious, beautiful face, indicative of a lovely character." He also described her as "reserved, well poised, thoughtful, much better educated, independent in judgment . . . [with] social grace and charm."[11] And Scottish evangelist Henry Drummond (1851–97) approvingly added: "I have never known her equal."[12]

When Emma visited the Moody family in Northfield she would have agreed with the caricature given Mrs. Moody as "a model of hospitality, friendliness . . . good breeding . . . retiring in disposition . . . a good neighbor . . . ready in time of sickness and need with sympathy and substantial help."[13] Emma knew that Moody valued his wife's input and gave her due respect. This was not always the case as Mrs. Moody recalled the early formative preaching years of her husband. She remembered how she would "cringe under his severity," but with the passing of years changes occurred in him where "a passionate note of tender appeal took its place."[14]

In 1881 Emma shared the following observations of Moody at Northfield as they made their Chicago Bible Work plans. She referenced the words of Samuel F. Smith's (1808–95) popular patriotic song written in 1831, *My Country Tis' of Thee*:

> Mr. Moody was building a great and good work in his own beloved home. He loved 'the rocks and rills, the woods and templed hills,' of that beautiful region, more than any other earthly place. He loved his family and friends there. Northfield meant rest and Home, as he followed his work in many places; but he still loved the work he had planned in Chicago, and he loved his Christian friends there. It was evident that our Bible-Workers, who had no home in

---

9. Moody Bible Institute, "D. L. Moody's Story."
10. Powell, *Heavenly Destiny*, 177.
11. Fitt, *Moody Still Lives*, 124.
12. Powell, *Heavenly Destiny*, 251.
13. Fitt, *Moody Still Lives*, 124.
14. Ibid., 125.

Chicago should be gathered into one family; and Mr. and Mrs. J. S. Helmer (later Directors of the China Inland Mission in Toronto) offered their home at 100 Warren Avenue, for that purpose. Moody was willing to accept the arrangement for one year; and offered to meet our immediate expenses, with the understanding that we move to the North Side, the following year.[15]

Emma recalled her visits with the Moody family when they prayed together and discussed plans for the Christian education of young people: "Mr. Moody's schools shed their increasing light, from the hill tops of Northfield and Mount Hermon—Schools which illustrate the Christian education the Church should secure to the worthy children of the masses; that they, by the grace of God, faithfully committing *the same*, be able to teach others also (II Tim. 2:1–3). And to that end, D. L. Moody 'endured hardness, as a good Soldier of Jesus Christ."[16] Emma prayed that the Northfield and Hermon students would imitate their founder's admirable example in serving and following the Lord.

Emma most certainly conversed with Mr. and Mrs. Moody regarding the 1871 Chicago Fire. Mrs. Moody shared the fears of that night when she fled with her two children. Her son Paul later remembered, "Her hair became streaked with white owing to the horrors of the Chicago Fire in 1871, when she got separated from her two children for twenty-four hours."[17] Emma heard of Moody's later regret when news of the raging fire arrived after his sermon at the Illinois Street Church in which he had missed an irreversible opportunity to present a definitive invitation for lost souls to receive the Lord Jesus.

Emma encountered first-hand the kind of tenderness Mrs. Moody herself experienced from her own faithful husband. Emma had not been home to see her parents in Victor, New York, for quite some time. In 1875 a YMCA friend named Sarah Cleveland expressed concern that Emma needed a time of rest. She handed her a railroad pass good for a year with unlimited stops, plus one hundred dollars.[18] A year later, Moody received a letter from a mutual friend of the YMCA, John Morrison, referring to Emma's recent *affliction*. She had suffered the loss of both her mother and father just days apart. Moody readily extended the invitation for her to come to New York. Emma never forgot this kindness as she repeated the story in 1916. She said, "A little later, I knew by his assurance, that I was going East to dear father and mother and home in Victor, New York; and also to New York City, to see Christian work there."[19]

Moody was positively impressed with Emma as a teacher who possessed a gift for working with the younger generation. He could see her deep devotion to instruct youth in God's word and recognized her competence as she ministered to young

---

15. Emma Dryer to Charles Blanchard, 1916, Biographical File of Emma Dryer.
16. Ibid.
17. Fitt, *Moody Still Lives*, 124.
18. Emma Dryer to Caroline Waite, 18 July 1924, Biographical File of Emma Dryer.
19. Emma Dryer to Charles Blanchard, 1916, Biographical File of Emma Dryer.

mothers and their children. She could evangelize in ways that Moody and other men could not.[20] He valued her deep devotion and ability to educate young people both spiritually and academically. Likewise, as Emma became acquainted with Moody, she saw the magnetism and love which drew him to the younger population.

Moody developed a charming rapport with kids in the slums. He related to them during week day and holiday outings as he cared for their emotional and physical needs. His granddaughter recalled how he would entertain the children with a bushel of apples. He would run through the meadows dropping the apples as he went. The children would gleefully gather the delicious fruit as they ran behind him.[21] Emma would have enjoyed reading the England newspaper report of how Moody successfully entertained 6,000 children with his own charismatic personality.[22] Moody himself possessed an "intense and almost womanly love for children."[23] Reverend Daniels in his own association with Moody witnessed this affection when he stated: "He never seemed happier than when in the midst of a crowd of boys and girls, with whom he romped in the wildest fashion, beating them at their own sports and games, until he won their fullest confidence, and came to be regarded by them as the biggest and jolliest boy of them all."[24] Clearly, Mrs. Moody's love for her husband deepened as she witnessed his love for children. She was assured their own children and grandchildren would be included in his vast circle of love.

Just as Illinois State Normal University called Emma to teach and minister to young men and women and children, so also did Moody follow a comparable summons. When he counseled and held inquiry meetings, he would reach out to the children and youth by holding special sessions for them.[25] Reverend Daniels recalled a meeting in which Mr. Sankey, knowing how much he and Moody loved the little ones, seated a swarm of children in the reserved seating area and filled the empty spaces surrounding Moody's pulpit.[26]

In her association with Moody, Emma now heard a first-hand account of his conversion and the formative background of this character—*Crazy Moody*—from Chicago. She heard the story of his spirited childhood devotion to his mother:

> There were few things he would not do for his mother: at her urgent entreaty he would even do a little studying. He would usually obey her; but she was the only person in all the world who ever was able to manage him. He was proud and willful to the last degree, but full of generous impulses. He was ungovernable, partly because he was a natural leader himself. Still there was nothing

20. History's Women, "Emeline Dryer: Christian Educator and Administrator," para. 10.
21. Powell, *Heavenly Destiny*, 41.
22. Ibid., 224.
23. Daniels, *D. L. Moody and His Work*, 37.
24. Ibid.
25. Ibid., 288.
26. Ibid., 299–300.

vicious in his disposition. If he could be made to see that he had wronged any one, he was ready to beg his pardon for it, and do better in the future.[27]

Emma learned that just as Moody began to take his studies seriously, it was time for him to get a job. Emma's friend, Reverend Daniels, shared: "With such little learning as had accumulated in him, he hardly knew how, he must go out and boldly face the world . . . with no other piety in him than the love of his mother, and a sturdy determination to be an honest and successful man."[28]

Despite a minimal education, Moody possessed an inner drive that motivated him to venture a hundred miles to Boston to work for his uncle. His Sunday school teacher, Edward Kimball of the Mt. Vernon Congregational Church, shared with him on April 21, 1855, the deep love of Jesus Christ—a love which Moody willingly embraced.[29] Thereafter, he left Boston for Chicago seeking to earn money by working in the shoe selling business. Yet he saw beyond his own success in business and provided Sunday school training for the poor and homeless children in the city. He started the school in a converted saloon. It grew beyond expectations. Moody was encouraged to establish a church for these children and other converts with whom he had shared the gospel. As a result, on February 28, 1864, Moody opened the doors to the Illinois Street Church with his new leadership role as the church pastor.[30]

Mutual Scripture Emphasis and Bible Teaching Leadership Roles

Moody gradually developed as a religious leader and expounder of God's word. At the same time Emma's deep love for the Bible flowed from her as she took every opportunity to instruct others. While teaching Bible classes at Moody's church and the Bible Work, Emma quickly gained the reputation as "a superb teacher with a deep and practical knowledge of Scripture."[31] On Bible Work stationary she included a schedule for different locations within the city featuring the Bible as the prominent emphasis: Bible Classes 8–11 a.m.; Office Hours 11–12 a.m.; Bible Readings, p.m. and evenings.[32] Also, on the stationary were texts such as "Search the Scriptures; for in them ye think ye have ETERNAL LIFE, and they are they which testify of ME."

Emma was drawn to Moody's passion for God's word. She eagerly assimilated his teachings regarding the importance of Scripture. She observed, as did Moody's close friend and associate, Reuben Archer Torrey (1856–1928), that Moody "was not

---

27. Ibid., 13–14.
28. Ibid., 14.
29. Ibid., 20–27.
30. Moody Bible Institute, *D. L. Moody's Story*.
31. Dorsett, *A Passion For Souls*, 166.
32. Emma Dryer to Caroline Waite, 18 July 1924, Biographical File of Emma Dryer.

a student of psychology; he was not a student of anthropology—I am very sure he would not have known what that word meant; he was not a student of biology; he was not a student of philosophy; he was not even a student of theology, in the technical sense of the term; but he was a student, a profound and practical student of the one Book that is more worthy of studying than all other books in the world put together; he was a student of the Bible."[33] Emma noticed the large crowds attracted to Moody's campaigns due in part to his thorough grasp of God's word. Torrey agreed: "Mr. Moody . . . did know the one Book that this old world is perishing to know and longing to know, and this old world will flock to hear men who know the Bible and preach the Bible as they will flock to hear nothing else on earth."[34]

Moody's proficient understanding of the Scriptures did not occur immediately upon his arrival to Chicago or during his early days of teaching young people in Sunday school and at the YMCA. Around 1873 Mr. Moorehouse from England, who claimed to be a man of *one Book*, heard Moody preach and afterward told him, "You are sailing on the wrong track. If you will change your course, and learn to preach God's words instead of your own, He will make you a great power for good."[35] Moody took up the challenge. Moorehouse introduced him to a higher level of Bible study involving the solitary use of the Bible by trained Bible readers. Mr. Moorehouse proceeded to train Moody, Emma, and others in a method of Bible study beginning with prayer for the Holy Spirit's enlightenment. Prayer was followed by singing, group Scripture passages centered around one theme of truth, an assignment of Scriptures for others to read, and the group leader giving illustrated explanations of the passages. The primary objective of Moorehouse's method was to allow the Lord to speak to his people for himself. In so doing Moorehouse believed that the Lord would honor his own word. From this point on, Moody's addresses were saturated with God's word and essentially void of self.[36]

Emma implemented Moody's directive for students to focus their studies explicitly on the Bible. He wholeheartedly approved of her laying this biblical foundation for her Bible reader trainees. She acknowledged with Moody that the *work* of reading the Bible truly WORKS in changing the lives of people; and thus the emphasis on the name *Bible Work* for the emerging Chicago ministry. For Moody and Emma the Bible

33. Torrey, *Why God used D. L. Moody*, 16–17. In his 1923 sermon, *Why God Used D. L. Moody* (also compiled and edited by James S. Bell in the 1997 edition of *The D. L. Moody Collection*), Torrey cited Moody's admonition for him to continue to preach the baptism of the Holy Spirit. From 1902 through 1905 Torrey, with one of the Bible Institute students, Charles M. Alexander, while attending the 1904 Keswick Convention, joined a worldwide revival extending to Wales where Evan Roberts led the fires of the Welsh Revival in 1904. Torrey's extensive absences from the Moody Bible Institute during these revival tours plus doctrinal tensions with James M. Gray, the acting director during his absences, led to Torrey's 1908 resignation and, according to L. W. Dorsett (1997), moved the school away from Torrey's emphasis on the work of the Holy Spirit and divine healing.

34. Ibid., 25.

35. Daniels, *D. L. Moody and His Work*, 177.

36. Ibid.

literally became the capstone for their schools with the placement of Scripture at the cornerstone of each future constructed edifice.[37]

Leadership Roles in Prayer

Both Moody and Emma acknowledged prayer as central to their leadership and ministry roles. Emma treasured the word of God which in turn prompted her to pray powerful prayers. On one occasion John Farwell returned with Attorney Horatio Spafford from Michigan evangelistic meetings of 2,500 in attendance and 300 conversions. He reported to Moody that he had just witnessed a tremendous harvest in which Miss Dryer's prayers must have reached the heavenly throne.[38]

Likewise, Moody clung to prayer as the *chief power* in ministry for impacting souls.[39] In the early 1890s Moody's new son-in-law, A. P. Fitt, emphatically declared his father-in-law as a true man of prayer. In 1923 Torrey maintained that the Lord used D. L. Moody because he was indeed a man of prayer. On one occasion after hearing him pray, Torrey realized that Moody was a greater man of prayer more so than an evangelist. He wrote: "Oh, I wish you could have heard that prayer! I shall never forget it, so simple, so trustful, so definite and so direct and so mighty."[40]

Emma internalized the powerful prayers of Moody and extended her own unwavering petitions to the Lord even when others gave up. In early 1883 Emma began a weekly prayer meeting at the Chicago Avenue Church with other Christians. These included Mr. Moody's close friend John Farwell, American evangelist William E. Blackstone, and Mrs. Moody's brother, Fleming H. Revell, who knew of Moody's vision for a Bible training school. They exercised consecrated prayer on behalf of the establishment of a Bible Institute—prayers for Moody's support. While Fleming and Emma taught adult Bible classes, they developed a strong teaching and prayer relationship. With the unity of these close prayer partners, they issued their appeals to heaven.[41]

Several years later, Emma wrote to Moody reminding him of her faithful prayers for him: "For more than 15 years *my* heart has been prayerfully set on city evangelization here . . . & I have *believed* through the years & before God that you must be led by the Spirit of God to purpose & *promise* & *re-promise* to push this work for the glory of His name . . . When others turned away, I prayed on . . . "[42] In response to the persistent prayers of Emma and her prayer friends, the Lord stirred Moody's heart.

---

37. Fitt, *Shorter Life of D. L. Moody*, 16.
38. Farwell, *Early Recollections of Dwight L. Moody*, 166.
39. Torrey, *Why God Used D. L. Moody*, 6.
40. Ibid., 14.
41. Dorsett, *A Passion For Souls*, 339.
42. Emma Dryer to D. L. Moody, 25 July 1887, Biographical File of Emma Dryer.

He began preparations for the ultimate manifestation of the envisioned Bible Institute birthed through the efforts of these two strong prayer leaders.

Leadership Likenesses and Differences By Design

During the twenty-nine years of their association, Emma and Moody ministered in leadership roles according to their unique giftings and design—for better and at times for worse. Reuben Torrey acknowledged that as a leader Moody was not a perfect man but possessed recognized shortcomings. "Nevertheless," he wrote, "I know that he was a man who belonged wholly to God."[43] Moody biographer Lyle Dorsett also noted that despite Moody's outstanding character, he displayed "enough flaws to remind us that our Lord uses people who are willing to confess their sins and truly repent."[44]

Likewise, those who knew Emma, as well as various historians, pointed out her strengths and weaknesses in leadership and ministry. Historian James Findlay indicated that Emma could be headstrong and impetuous while operating according to her highly sensitive nature. He wrote that she was very exact about details almost to her detriment.[45] Although she performed efficiently as an intelligent leader and thorough organizer, she was observed as being quite meticulous.[46]

These two separate compelling leaders worked side by side over a long period of time. Inevitably, the same complementary leadership qualities and vision that drew them together for the Lord's purposes would become dissimilarities reflecting their apparent weaknesses. A close examination of their designated leadership styles can be helpful in identifying and understanding the supportive and dissonant relationship they had with one another and others.

Visionary Leaders

Leadership may be characterized or defined as the method of persuasion by which an individual convinces others to accept ownership and commitment for setting and securing goals.[47] Both Emma and Moody exhibited high levels of leadership effectiveness when motivating people to assist them in achieving their visionary goals. Moody's leadership resulted in the effective accomplishments of his vision for evangelism and for numerous schools of education despite his own minimal education.[48] Moody's granddaughter, Emma Powell, attributed her grandfather's success in moti-

---

43. Torrey, *Why God Used D. L. Moody*, 9.
44. Dorsett, "Far From Perfect," 4.
45. Findlay, *Dwight L. Moody: American Evangelist*, 331.
46. Getz, *The Story of Moody Bible Institute*, 23.
47. Chemers, *An Integrative Theory of Leadership*, 1. Chemers is a social psychologist and researcher on leadership effectiveness.
48. Findlay, *Dwight L. Moody: American Evangelist*, 337–38.

vating Christian workers and missionaries worldwide to his establishment on a firm God-given visionary foundation.[49]

Upon meeting Emma Dryer in the summer of 1870 Moody perceptibly identified her as a uniquely religious woman with humanitarian aspirations.[50] He envisioned her as a dedicated woman equipped to not only organize special meetings and evangelistic training sessions for young mothers but to educate them in practical home-making skills.[51] With high ambition and vision herself, Emma could foresee linking up with this man. He held a God-inspired vision which he effectively used to encourage her to establish the *Bible Work* to train others to walk in evangelistic foresight.

Emma and Moody utilized various vision strategies on their trajectory toward effective leadership. First, they possessed and nurtured a *compelling* and *inspiring vision*. Then they created *organizational ownership* by attempting to *communicate* their vision to others. As principled leaders they held a mandate to personally demonstrate a *steadfast commitment and participation* in the vision. And with initial certainty regarding the success of the vision, they provided their own *resources* in time, energy, and financial sacrifices.[52]

Emma and many others aligned themselves with the Bible School vision that Moody possessed. He articulated to Emma this vision of training Bible readers to evangelize their city with best practices for teaching and preaching. When Moody first shared his vision with Emma, he realized that the seminaries could feel threatened by the establishment of the school. He therefore down played the idea of including men. With Emma's coeducational background, she envisioned a school including both men and women. In *The Story of Moody Bible Institute* Gene Getz concurred: "It was Miss Dryer who raised the idea of coeducational training at the Chicago school."[53] Nevertheless, Emma acquiesced in order to participate in Moody's initial vision.

When he departed for England in 1872, Moody recognized that Emma had embraced his compelling vision with a commitment to seeing it materialize. She was willing and ready to become a servant leader on behalf of this visionary leader. By sanctioning and communicating his vision, Emma received an ownership of that vision that caused her to persevere. Although the time for its fulfillment would lengthen into fifteen years, Emma continued to remain steadfast despite Moody's unclear, and oftentimes, reticent communication. His evangelistic work frequently overburdened him with staggering demands; yet he knew he could count on her faithfulness. Emma, in turn, relied on his steadfast commitment as she faithfully fought to keep their vision alive.

---

49. Powell, *Heavenly Destiny*, 70.
50. Findlay, *Dwight L. Moody: American Evangelist*, 321.
51. Moody, *The Life of Dwight L. Moody*, 194.
52. Bennis and Namus, *Leaders: The Strategies for Taking Charge*, 27.
53. Getz, *The Story of Moody Bible Institute*, 19.

Emma and Moody: Complementary Leadership Roles

During these nascent stages of visionary development, Emma secured an efficient *operational* staff. She held the administrative qualifications to tend to the day-to-day short term operations of the Bible Work with its daily challenges. However, she knew that the success of the organization would depend on the *conceptualization* of the vision maker, D. L. Moody. Emma was dreaming big dreams with him. Yet she needed not only his conceptual clarification, but his name and personal resources to implement long-term goals—assets without which an organization flounders. Mini-sporadic steps were approved by the traveling visionary leader for times of urgent funding.

Moody also displayed a commitment to the spiritual growth of his own workers and other believers. He contributed financial resources for Emma's 1879 overseas visit to the Mildmay Institute with her own personal resource of time. In 1883 he granted approval for Emma to conduct, with her renewed stamina, the annual May Institutes in Chicago for the spiritual training of many others. In great detail Emma reflected on the extent of Moody's support and commitment to the Bible Work:

> Mr. Moody . . . told me to select a site for the Bible-Work Home, and he would try to attend to its building, as he returned from the South, by way of Chicago. I selected the site next to the Church, North, with its still open lots . . . and presented the descriptions and prices to Mr. Moody. But he was overwhelmed by old friends, and many changes, and really had no time to do more than attend to the meetings and greetings of the Church, and the familiar affairs of former years. So he told me he was coming in October, for a long evangelistic campaign, and would then have time to attend to the prospective work, which we contemplated. He came in October. He asked me again for the site, and the related facts for the intended building. I gave him the same information. His frequent visits to the Church enabled him to see the unoccupied lots . . . He preferred property nearest to the Church, and on which the Institute now stands. He met with us in the Bible-Work room . . . and increased the number of the workers, asking individuals and churches to support them . . . Whenever this was done, church committees co-operated with us in their field work. It was still Mr. Moody's hope to fill Chicago with Christian workers, who should competently instruct, and who working from missions, and selected stations, by house to house visiting, distribution of the Bible, teaching in homes and missions, should do a continued work for Christ here, and also in foreign lands.[54]

During this phase of vision communication and participation Moody expanded his outreaches with his two Northfield schools, conferences, and campaigns. Perhaps these long-distant plans contributed to the conclusion that Moody appeared unable

---

54. Emma Dryer to Charles Blanchard, 1916, Biographical File of Emma Dryer.

to keep his word made to Emma in 1873 to develop and promote her Bible Work ministry.[55]

With Moody's fluctuating oversight and support, an ever-present leader was needed to directly and actively officiate with a board of directors to *conceptualize* or launch the vision.[56] As servant leaders Emma and Moody both needed a group of trustees to assist in casting the vision and creating policies. Such governance would help maintain a careful balance between visionary leadership and the day-to-day operations of the school.[57]

Moody made an attempt to receive board management training. In 1877 he visited Henry F. Durant, founder of Wellesley College in 1875. He gained board experience as a trustee on the Wellesley board in forecasting situation outcomes—a necessary quality for trustees.[58] Nevertheless, Moody's extensive absences and limited participation in the Chicago training school during the 1870s and early 1880s produced a void in the visionary concepts necessary to form the Chicago school. Without an established board supplemented by Moody's prominent and consistent involvement and backing, Emma realized that only with prayer and God's intervention could this vision unfold.

As the training program gradually developed, Emma frequently communicated with Moody's Chicago friends encouraging them to participate in the ownership of this inspiring vision. These friends included realtor Elbridge Gerry Keith (1840–1905), foundry and iron works businessman Nathaniel S. Bouton (1828–1908), YMCA friend John Farwell, philanthropist Nettie McCormick, and lumber businessman Turlington W. Harvey (1835–1909) who was also president of the Metropolitan National Bank. They prayed with her that Moody would return to Chicago for more than just short-term revival campaigns. Emma believed that the Lord would continue to place on Moody's heart the vision for a coeducational Bible school. Her prayer was answered in part when on his visits to Chicago he began inviting young people to the church to attend Emma's Bible classes as a continued effort to reach all the masses of people. In lingering yet faltering ways throughout the approaching years their intuitive vision—a characteristic of servant leaders—enabled them to learn from their past experiences, address present actualities, and determine future outcomes.[59]

Servant Leader Assessment

In *The Velvet Covered Brick*, the author examines the meaning of Christian leadership and affirms that leadership without definition cannot exist.[60] Emma and Moody

---

55. Findlay, *Dwight L. Moody: American Evangelist*, 332.
56. Spears, "Character and Servant Leadership, 28.
57. Ibid.
58. Findlay, *Dwight L. Moody: American Evangelist,* 309n7.
59. Spears, "Character and Servant Leadership," 28.
60. Butt, *The Velvet Covered Brick*, 6.

were called by God to serve as leaders. However, their leadership characterization at times lacked clarity and direction. With the present twenty-first-century leadership dynamics, the searching questions would be: What were Emma and Moody's leadership styles? How would their styles and personality profiles on instruments such as the *DISC* assessment (*Dominance, Influence, Steadiness, and Conscientiousness*) effect their communication, relationships, and productivity?[61] And what would have been their rating for emotional intelligence (EQ)—a defining issue for relational workability—on Daniel Goleman's (1946–) classic *Emotional and Social Competence Inventory* with its five components of self-awareness, self-regulation, internal motivation, empathy, and social competency?[62] Obviously, these evaluation instruments and other valuable leadership information from popular authors such as John W. Maxwell and Travis Bradberry[63] were not available during the nineteenth century to analyze or guide either of these leaders. However, some aspects of Emma and Moody's personalities and behaviors as nineteenth-century leaders can be assessed based on these and other twentieth and twenty-first-century leadership tools.

D. L. Moody and Emma Dryer lived during the era of the singular leadership theory of *The Great Man*. This theory stressed the prevalent view that males were inherently destined to lead rather than females. Thomas Carlyle (1841–1907) propagated this theory that *great men* were effective because of their spiritual giftings and true character.[64] By the turn of the twentieth century after Moody's death, numerous additional leadership theories began to emerge. Today's transformational theories, focusing on the relationship of leaders to their followers, include strong Christian leadership models such as the *Servant-Leadership Style*. This model, although introduced by Robert K. Greenleaf (1904–90) around 1964, originated in the heart of the Master Leader, Jesus Christ. He demonstrated this *old as the Bible* model with these instructions: "Whoever wants to become great among you will be your servant" (Matthew 20:26, *GWT*).

Larry C. Spears, head CEO of the Center for Servant-Leadership Incorporated, lists several qualities of a servant-leader: *conceptualization, foresight, awareness, listening, healing, empathy, commitment to the growth of people, building communities,*

---

61. Psychologist Dr. William Moulton Marston in 1828 presented his work on personality traits from which the DISC personality profile originated. Walter Clark developed the DISC assessment in 1940 based on Marston's 4 personality traits of Dominance, Influence, Steadiness, and Conscientiousness. This assessment is commonly used in work places to assist in developing more effective leaders.

62. For a detailed explanation of emotional intelligence and its five components refer to Daniel Goleman's 1995 work *Emotional Intelligence: Why It Can Matter More Than IQ. New York*: Bantam Books.

63. Dr. Maxwell (1947–), author of *The 21 Irrefutable Laws of Leadership (1998), Developing the Leader Within You (1993)*, and *The 21 Indispensable Laws of a Leader (1998)*, founded EQUIP, a Christian organization that has trained and equipped more than 5 million leaders in 191 countries. Dr. Bradberry, author of *Emotional Intelligence 2.0* (2003) and *Leadership 2.0* (2012), is founder of TalentSmart, a consultant/training program used by Fortune 500 companies.

64. Cherry, "The Great Man Theory of Leadership."

persuasion, and *stewardship.* Both Moody and Emma displayed certain aspects of servant leadership in the fore-mentioned section on *conceptualization* and *visionary foresight.* Their leadership methods can also be examined by applying Spears's additional servant-leadership qualities, particularly in the area of organization and communication.

Organizational Skills

A servant-leader must possess an *awareness* of the need for organization skills in order to lead effectively and to launch their vision with success.[65] This *awareness* contributes to the understanding of issues and situations from a balanced position. Yet for Emma and Moody such balance would come with a cost as they found that awareness serves both as an annoyance when discerning difficult situations and as an instructive enlightenment of one's inner motives and responses.[66]

Both Emma and Moody experienced the leadership organization *awareness* challenge associated with leading others in ministry. Emma inherently realized that she possessed a leadership mindset characterized by a propensity for organizational thoroughness. She was not always aware that her exercise of this leadership quality caused her to be perceived as unbending and meticulous to her detriment—a disturbing awakener when circumstances forged an awareness. At the same time, others praised her as an incomparable administrator.[67] She strongly possessed the *DISC-Conscientiousness* traits for being orderly, organized, detailed, and systematic. Her administrative organization, gleaned from her years as a preceptress and teacher at Ingham University, Knoxville Ewing Female University, and ISNU, equipped her with valuable skills. She successfully organized the activities, curriculum, funding, and marketing of the Bible Work and created the stage for fulfillment of Moody's vision for a Bible school.

According to some gender analysts women tend to focus on tasks and relationships; whereas, men focus on awareness of themselves and their power and ability to contribute most effectively by staying more objectively removed from a situation.[68] Emma concentrated on the administrative and relational aspects of her leadership. She supplemented these traits with her *DISC-Steadiness* personality involving loyalty, dependability, team player role, and patience. These propensities put her at odds with Moody's strong *DISC-Influence* and *persuasion* traits. He was contagiously spontaneous, *persuasive,* talkative, and enthusiastic. Combined with his *DISC-Dominance* traits Moody portrayed high productivity and aggressiveness accompanied at times by inflexibility and control. Yet Emma's leadership proclivity provided the impetus for

---

65. Spears, "Character and Servant Leadership," 28.
66. Ibid., 41.
67. Dorsett, *A Passion For Souls,* 166.
68. Statham, "The Gender Model Revisited," 409–29.

Moody to stay focused, at a distance, while he influentially controlled or dominated the decisions and plans for the proposed Bible School.

Emma, aware of their inherent differences, continued to point out both Moody's strengths and weaknesses:

> Organization was not pre-eminently, Mr. Moody's endowment. Founding, evangelizing, and quick execution, were emphatically his. Where he went, Christ was proclaimed; where he lived, Christian institutions would grow. As Elijah had no arguments against Baal, but 'thus saith the Lord,' and no methods to explain, beyond the sacrificial altar of the Lord, and the Divine Fire from Heaven, so worked Mr. Moody . . . He broke the enemy's centers, and in so doing, incidentally aroused new organizers, and was an inspiration to their constructive work. He once said, while we were speaking of a needy field, for Christian work, 'God forbid that I try to do all the work I see needs doing. But I do want to set others at it.' [69]

Moody thrived on recognizing and persuasively motivating others to put their hands to the plow in service to God. This was evidenced by the intensity of his dedication to organize campaigns to spread the gospel. Several individuals acquainted with Moody later in his life valued the specific *campaign* regulation skills they observed. When it came to his travel schedule, Moody possessed the foresight to organize and adhere to his well thought out plans. He systematically covered different sections of the country with his campaigns. He would type up lists documenting where and when he preached. He kept them in a notebook under *Sermons*. However, by the 1880s, even his own schedule overwhelmed him.[70]

From Emma's viewpoint, she received mixed messages from Moody which brought only confusion from the initiation of their vision. Perhaps Emma's organizational frustrations increased due to his inherent disinterest in organizational details, their personality differences that tempered joint efforts, or simply his long absences from Chicago. Or perhaps confusion occurred because Moody's vast scope of visionary projects created challenges beyond his own capability to implement.[71]

Moody's son-in-law, Arthur Percy Fitt (A. P.), emigrated from Ireland in 1892 as Moody's secretary. He observed that Moody's campaign organization abilities were stretched to capacity.[72] About the same time, evangelist John McNeill from Glasgow participated in Moody's evangelistic crusades. He wrote a tribute of Moody in 1899 declaring: "He was a tremendous organizer . . . I admired his genius and power in organizing."[73] Nevertheless, Moody's demanding campaign schedule often left him

---

69. Emma Dryer to Charles Blanchard, 1916, Biographical File of Emma Dryer.
70. Findlay, *Dwight L. Moody: American Evangelist*, 337.
71. Ibid.
72. Fitt, *Moody Still Lives*, 47.
73. Williams, *Life and Work of Dwight L. Moody*, 389.

without sufficient time to organize or obtain adequate information to make solid and informed institutional decisions.

When Moody was in his late fifties his organizational Bible skills were viewed by some as being quite systematic. A. P. Fitt wrote:

> All these years he was gathering a large stock of first hand anecdotes and illustrations . . . numerous references to his own early experiences . . . Sunday school experiences . . . Civil War . . . He was adept in the faculty of seeing illustrative material all along the way, and skillful in the use he made of it . . . he devised a system for preparing sermons . . . large blue linen envelope . . . measuring about 9 by 6 inches, and [would] write on it the title or the Scripture reference . . . In these envelopes he stored his own thoughts, outlines and anecdotes, cuttings from papers, extracts copied from other men's sermons and from commentaries and other writings . . . with his open bible in his hand . . . he had before him the outline of his sermon.[74]

A. P. did not view his father-in-law as an organizational procrastinator. He saw him continually working to prepare for each new calling—a different picture from his earlier years with the insurmountable demands on his time. One supporter during Moody's final years gave a similar report after his visit to Northfield. He reported that the opinion of others regarding Moody's lack of organization could not be correct. From his viewpoint he observed that Moody's organizational skills at Northfield included aptitude in planning for events, securing funds, and recruiting and inspiring others to fulfill his vision with similar passion.[75]

In any event, the more complex structural changes in American businesses potentially contributed to Moody's confusion and inability to focus organizationally. According to historian James F. Findlay, Moody had gotten out of touch with his rapidly changing world in his later years. He struggled to adapt to the institutional and religious changes that accompanied this cultural shift. These factors compounded the pressure for Moody to become organizationally aware of the Chicago Bible School vision. In the process, he would retreat from stressful Chicago situations to his Northfield schools and his beloved family.[76]

During this process Emma welcomed the opportunity Moody gave her to organize the Bible school. From her experience at ISNU with President Edwards and the co-ed faculty, she knew the need for leaders to organize their team players in a clearly understood environment while providing motivation, guidance, delegation of assignments, outlined expectations, and follow-up.[77] In essence, Emma perceived that in order for the goals of the Bible Institute to be attained, it would take unprecedented

---

74. Fitt, *Moody Still Lives*, 47.
75. Findlay, *Dwight L. Moody: American Evangelist*, 337.
76. Ibid., 413.
77. Chemers, *An Integrative Theory of Leadership*, 60.

organization on the part of all the leaders—Moody, an active governing board, and Emma herself.

Listening and Communication Skills

Just as important as organizational aptitude, effective leaders must develop and utilize good listening and communication skills. These prerequisites are characterized by a deep commitment to listen intently, empathetically, and receptively to others. This process helps leaders to identify the strengths and preferences of their followers and to assist in effectively utilizing and clarifying those recognizable distinctives. Emma and Moody desired to be vessels of *healing* through their listening hearts and communication, whether in the form of written literature, teaching, or service. Healing occurred as they reached out even in the midst of pain and conflict to make resolution.[78] Therefore, as servant leaders both Emma and Moody unfailingly, though not perfectly, desired to pursue the Prince of Peace when organization difficulties occurred.

Emma, in her letters to Nettie McCormick, communicated a listening heart with *EQ-Empathy* and a *DISC-Steadiness*: "We minister by *listening* to others griefs which only God can cure . . . I am Trusting Jesus whatever befall. Trusting Jesus That is all'. In Christian hope & love. Emma Dryer."[79] Emma and Moody loved the hymns. They equipped others through music training to bring comfort from hymns such as *Simply Trusting Every Day*. This song was composed by Moody's close traveling companion, Ira David Sankey, with lyrics by Methodist Edgar Page Stites (1836–1921). Moody was inspired to promote with *DISC-Aggressiveness* his crusades with the faith building and healing words of the hymn, *Simply Trusting Every Day*. He obtained the words from an 1876 newspaper clipping which he gave to Sankey to set to music.[80]

The healing of relationships through servant leadership is a powerful force for transformation and integration. Both Emma and Moody were passionate with their high *EQ-Empathy* components when it came to reaching out to those broken in spirit and suffering from spiritual and emotional hurts. As leaders they desired to see healing for those who received their instruction either through preaching, reading literacy, or the physical maintenance of proper hygiene. Healing came with Moody's ability "to communicate with souls at the deepest level" transcending "all natural boundaries including those of class and nationality."[81] His passion for souls was evident when he persuasively preached with his intense *DISC-Influence* traits. As so often characteristic of spiritual leaders, his heart was grieved when others would not listen and act upon the message he delivered to them from God's word.

---

78. Spears, "Character and Servant Leadership," 28.
79. Emma Dryer to Nettie McCormick, 20 September 1888, Biographical File of Emma Dryer.
80. Ibid.
81. Dorsett, *A Passion For Souls*, 19.

Moody was an ardent communicator of the gospel but unyieldingly resisted controversy.[82] Consequently, when conflict surfaced his responses were often impulsive or marked by avoidance rather than empathetically distinguished by open confrontation—a leadership weakness which Emma would inevitably witness firsthand. Even Moody's son, Paul, wrote about a conflicting dispute his father experienced regarding the Northfield land: "Disputes of this sort always distressed my father, and his solution was short and direct. He made an offer to the neighbor for his farm, impulsively and over generously."[83]

Moody was also described as being unclear and ineffective when it came to evaluating and addressing individual performances of his workers.[84] In 1890 Moody realized that the headmaster of his Mount Hermon school needed to be replaced. But his hesitancy and lack of initiative left uncertainty for at least three months before action was taken.[85] He often "stood back, begged for unity and hoped the problems would go away." This was viewed by some as relationally "weak or naive . . . hurtful and ultimately destructive."[86] However, when he aggressively and impulsively took action with his *DISC-Dominance* trait, he was labeled as an abrupt, insensitive, and rude person.

In various situations, Moody was known for stepping on toes and hurting people. Although in contrast to his Christ-loving nature, he nevertheless offended others with his thoughtlessness and unwarranted conduct causing some to distance themselves from his ministry.[87] At the same time, Emma with her *DISC-Steadiness* personality would intentionally address misunderstandings and pursue reconciliation and communication. Yet in the process she was criticized as being too outspoken, overly sensitive, and critical.[88] She and Moody's different communication styles appeared in opposition. Yet their distinct differences, when in harmony, produced a well-rounded and united front for effectively and incontrovertibly spreading the gospel.

In modern day organization terms, an institutional *chain of command* assures that conflicts are handled according to a structured and pre-identified process. Effective executives and board leaders anticipate and prepare for both conflict and conciliation.[89] As a servant-leader Emma built and surrounded herself with *community*—friends, interested church pastors, donors, and a board of trustees in the development of the Bible Work. She needed those who could look at various situations and assist her in addressing them. However, until the establishment of the Chicago Evan-

---

82. Marsden, *Fundamentalism and American Culture*, 33.
83. Powell, *Heavenly Destiny*, 100.
84. Findlay, *Dwight L. Moody: American Evangelist*, 368.
85. Ibid., n56.
86. Dorsett, *A Passion For Souls*, 370.
87. Findlay, *Dwight L. Moody: American Evangelist*, 368.
88. Ibid., 331.
89. Butt, *The Velvet Covered Brick*, 33.

gelization Society Moody would independently handle conflicting situations without a governing board or a broad spectrum of accountability leadership. Consequently, he lacked twenty-first-century requisite training regarding effective leaders who do not run from hassles but with the skill of effective communicators boldly confront conflict according to organizational structure and guidelines.[90]

Despite weaknesses in his conflict management skills, others continued to excuse these imperfections and viewed Moody—especially in his later years—in light of his strengths. One of Moody's assistants commented, "Moody is impetuous, and all the time committing blunders; but he never makes the same mistake twice."[91] Perhaps the key to Moody's times of conflict recovery was his attitude regarding human failings. His friend Reuben Torrey wrote that after praying about a difficult situation Moody said: "Torrey, we will let the other men do the talking and the criticising, and we will stick to the work that God has given us to do, and let Him take care of the difficulties and answer the criticisms."[92]

Conceivably, Moody's numerous scattered enterprises contributed to his impetuosity and short-circuited his ability at times to communicate effectually or to follow up on delegated matters. His vast array of projects inhibited effective contact with his constituency of believers and those in charge of his endeavors. Realizing her husband's communication weaknesses, Mrs. Moody loyally demonstrated *servant-leadership* to her husband. She filled in her husband's communication gaps by composing letters for his extensive mail and answering his phone calls when he was traveling abroad or conducting crusades.[93]

Their son Paul Moody recalled his father's communication struggles especially when others took advantage of him. When his father cut off communication with these individuals, they would then accuse him of being disloyal. Paul understood why his parents developed a lack of trust in some people and chose instead to no longer mention the incidents.[94] Mrs. Moody graciously and lovingly attempted to shield her husband from conflict and undue stress that could lead to potential burnout.

Leadership Burnout

Moses pushed beyond his limits as God's chosen leader of Israel until his father-in-law proposed the leadership tool of delegation. We also find that Emma and Moody, as servant leaders exhibiting *EQ-Internal Motivation* traits, held a deep commitment and drive to achieve. They went beyond all that could be humanly expected for those in ministry. Reverend Daniels conveyed his astonishment at Moody's jam-packed

90. Ibid., 61.
91. Daniels, *D. L. Moody and His Work*, 158.
92. Torrey, *Why God Used D. L. Moody*, 15.
93. Powell, *Heavenly Destiny*, 117–18.
94. Ibid., 268.

schedule: "It is amazing . . . how Mr. Moody can do so much and live. He attends and conducts a morning prayer-meeting at the Tabernacle; a second meeting at 4 p.m. for Christian instruction; preaches at 7:30 at the Rink; goes at a little before 8:30 to an inquiry meeting in the church opposite; rides thence down to the Tabernacle, and preaches to a congregation of clerks and salesmen and mechanics, a young men's meeting at 9 p.m. Then I suppose he goes to bed."[95]

During his last months on earth, Moody continued to pour himself out with great productivity (*DISC-Dominance*) without limits: "He forgot all about being weary and heavy laden with an amount of toil and care sufficient to prostrate three common men; but when the last service was ended, and the crowd pressed forward to grasp his hand and bid him good-bye, he actually broke down."[96] He explained to them that in his exhaustion he could no longer greet them and with a final distant handshake quickly departed. Moody's own granddaughter fittingly compared her grandfather to Rough Rider and President, Theodore Roosevelt: "He was burned out by his own flaming spirit."[97]

Similarly, Emma energetically exhausted herself after the first nine years of ministry in Chicago. By the fall of 1879 she could no longer physically cope with the rigor and unsupported demands of leadership.[98] Moody could readily empathize. When he heard of her distress, he immediately provided a six month sabbatical for her in Great Britain where she stayed at the Mildmay Deaconess Home. She extended her trip to include a visit to Scotland and returned to America physically invigorated and overflowing with new enthusiasm.[99]

Without a definitive organizational structure for delegating and sharing responsibilities, leader burnout increases, and the health of the organization is jeopardized. After an additional eight years, Emma again experienced stress from insufficient resources needed to assure growth and actualization of the Bible Institute. This severely impeded the execution of their vision. Leadership burnout resulted from the intensity of ministry that both Emma and Moody experienced. Jesus would frequently ask those He served, "What do you want me to *do*?" Both of these servant leaders were headed toward burnout due to their intense desire to *do* for others as Jesus did even when it was mentally and physically beyond their capacity to do so. Yet the passionate flaming spirit of God's love sustained them. They walked in obedience to the Lord in serving others and continued to faithfully spread the gospel in hope of the Lord's eminent return.

---

95. Daniels, 1876, *D. L. Moody and His Work*, 481.
96. Ibid., 482.
97. Powell, *Heavenly Destiny,* 230.
98. Dorsett, *A Passion For Souls*, 273.
99. Ibid.

Emma and Moody: Complementary Leadership Roles

Leaders in Evangelism and Education

Moody and Emma both possessed rich qualities as leaders in evangelism. However, Moody with his prominent *DISC-Dominance* and *Influence* personality excelled over Emma as an unrivaled evangelist and speaker. In contrast, Emma succeeded as an expressly designed master teacher and administrator with strong *DISC-Steadiness* and *Conscientiousness* traits. Their likenesses and differences uniquely worked together full circle to form a completed *DISC* pattern. They were equipped to cooperatively spread the gospel while securing the future Christian educational welfare of others.

As a revivalist Moody's leadership charisma and business aptitude perpetuated opportunities in the educational realm that must have appeased his and Emma's desire for evangelizing and training others in God's word. Emma reflected a magnificent prism of educational inspiration. Combined with Moody's passion for evangelization, their partnership was ripe for the creation of a religious training school that would fulfill their mutual vision.

When Emma moved to Chicago in 1870 she discovered Moody's profound consuming fervor for souls. He would not permit a day to pass unless he spoke to at least one person about the Lord.[100] In his earlier days in Chicago it was not uncommon for him to sit in *squatters' shanties* in the Sands district with a child on his lap reading Scriptures and praying for their conversion.[101] Even when Moody travelled abroad in 1873, Emma heard the testimony of revival among the YMCA young men in York, England. Moody intensely declared, "It is souls I want: it is souls I want."[102] One attendee of the York meeting reported the consuming impact of Moody's arrival: "I found the meeting on fire. The young men were speaking with tongues, and prophesying. What on earth did it all mean? Only that Moody had been addressing them that afternoon."[103]

Despite Moody's captivating revival influence one Catholic paper, *The Freeman's Journal*, negatively critiqued Mr. Moody as "being too intimate with the Heavenly Host . . . roaring too loudly and too furiously . . . appealing to the imagination, and speaking in a noisy, rhapsodical, haphazard style."[104] Still, Emma's Methodist friend Reverend Daniels reported that at the 1873 international meetings Moody insisted that all things be done with quiet and orderliness. He did not want any *wild excitements* that he knew could erupt during such times of revival.[105] Nevertheless, Moody was not as concerned about the personal and doctrinal opinions of men as he was about their souls.

---

100. Torrey, *Why God Used D. L. Moody*, 39.
101. Ibid., 50.
102. Daniels, *D. L. Moody and His Work*, 248.
103. Ibid.
104. Ibid., 318–19.
105. Ibid., 313.

Emma rejoiced to see God moving on the hearts of the saved and unsaved when she attended the North Side Tabernacle for protracted revival meetings during the winter months following the Chicago Fire. Desperate people traversed the snowy winter wreckage of the city in order "to see and to hear Moody and Sankey and Emma Dryer!"[106] In the midst of tragedy people were burning in their souls as "wave after wave of revival swept the people . . . crowds weeping over sin one day, shouting over pardon the next; dispirited men and women seemed to absorb Moody's overflowing gladness."[107] Even in the midst of relief efforts Moody continued to preach the gospel and refused praise for himself. He said, "Don't praise me,—bruise me rather; but if you love me, love Christ for my sake."[108] With great compassion he treated the poor from the perspective of rescuing their souls rather than simply consoling their flesh.[109] Moody judiciously encapsulated his soul-saving philosophy: "What is the use of keeping these poor people's bodies a little longer out of the grave and not trying to keep their souls out of hell?"[110]

Moody approached evangelism by going against the established status quo and ignoring rank and religion. In 1875 when he preached at the Royal Opera House in London an observer noted the compelling burden for all souls that Moody possessed. He stated that to Moody "a sinner riding in a carriage emblazoned with a coat of arms, was just as much in need of a Saviour as the poor dog-fighter himself."[111] Despite the fighting between the Catholics and Protestants in Ireland Moody ignored denominational backgrounds and continued to preach the word of God. As time went on both Catholics and Protestants admired a man used of God to bring revival.

When A. P. Fitt first met Moody in October of 1892, he warmly recalled: "Who could resist such generous pressure from so prominent a man, of whom I had heard all my life . . . my respect for his position and ministry as an evangelist."[112] As Moody's son-in-law traveled with him during the 1890s, he noted: "Living with him and sharing his confidence and comradeship, I observed his strong and masterful personality at all points and under most diverse conditions: aggressive, authoritative, but kindly, gentle, persuasive, magnetic; wholly concentrated upon bringing Christ to men and men to Christ . . . speaking with authority as the messenger of God, yet so humanly as to find entrance into people's hearts."[113] By the end of the 1800s as Moody's popularity

---

106. Day, *Bush Aglow*, 144.
107. Ibid.
108. Daniels, *D. L. Moody and His Work*, 153.
109. Ibid.
110. Ibid., 204.
111. Ibid., 369.
112. Fitt, *Moody Still Lives*, 10.
113. Ibid., 109.

began to diminish, he was still admired and considered a conciliatory individual who united the nineteenth-century middle class with Christian evangelicalism.[114]

Emma contagiously assimilated Moody's passion for spreading the gospel. Her heart for the souls of people motivated her to remain in Chicago after the fire. At once, with *DISC-Steadiness*, she conscientiously used her organizational skills to devise innovative plans for evangelizing Chicago's diverse population. She methodically laid out a Chicago map with grids to record progress and used regular schedules for tracking the responses and effectiveness of her Bible readers.[115] Like Moody, she used every opportunity to share the gospel. When writing letters she would include outlines of the gospel message in her lengthy correspondence. Consistently, she closed her letters with references to the gospel: "As always in the sweet hopes of the gospel"[116] or "Cordially in the Gospel."[117] In a letter to Moody she expressed her pleasure in hearing that he had received an urgent invitation to share the gospel in India: "For years I have hoped you would go. I wanted you used to bring in the great triumphs of the gospel, as a 'witness to the nations,' that the end might come—and I as much desired that you be used to kindle a flame of sacred zeal in our American cities that sho'd [sic] impel multitudes to 'go into the high-ways & hedges' to bring sinners to the great gospel feast."[118]

Emma knew of Moody's objections toward women preaching and his preference for men to evangelize. Yet she remained firm in extending her positive support. She regarded their vision of a Bible Institute as "a remarkable feature of evangelization in these 'last days,' which so closely precede *the Coming and Kingdom of Christ*."[119] She observed Moody's joy as he inspired others to serve the Lord: "And that he did, and is still doing, wonderfully doing, in the works that follow him."[120] Thus, both Moody and Emma evangelistically thrived in the mutually shared corner of the world where God placed them.

Education Background and Learning Styles

As an educator Emma possessed strong cognitive skills which coalesced with her ability to teach students at various grade levels in multiple subjects. In twenty-first-century terms she would have been a high functioning student and a highly capable teacher possessing upper levels of cognitive ability. In an 1877 edition of *Moody: His Words, Work, and Workers* the editor included Emma as one of Moody's biblically equipped associates acknowledged along with highly esteemed individuals such as William

---

114. Marsden, *Fundamentalism and American Culture*, 33.
115. Undated Paper written by Lowell K. Handy, Biographical File of Emma Dryer.
116. Emma Dryer to Nettie McCormick, 12 March 1888, Biographical File of Emma Dryer.
117. Undated Letter from Emma Dryer to Mr. Fitt, Biographical File of Emma Dryer.
118. Emma Dryer to D. L. Moody, 25 July 1887, Biographical File of Emma Dryer.
119. Emma Dryer to Charles Blanchard, 1916, Biographical File of Emma Dryer.
120. Ibid.

Erdman, Ira Sankey, and P. P. Bliss. She was noted for her excellent "knowledge of the Scriptures . . . and . . . devotion to the cause of Christ, together with her marked ability as a leader and instructor."[121] These qualities combined with Emma's high honors from Ingham University compelled Moody to recognize her as a vital evangelistic player. He willingly commissioned her to join his *team* despite, and perhaps even because of, his own educational limitations.

With Emma and Moody's education backgrounds they would have instructed according to their own individual learning styles—tactile-kinesthetic (movement), visual, and auditory. Emma employed diverse modalities for instruction drawn from her Model School days at ISNU. She would have appreciated how Moody excelled in captivating children through his auditory or verbally illustrated stories. He possessed a natural ability—not professional educational training like Emma. He explained that his story methods evolved due to his earlier lack of Bible comprehension.[122] As his knowledge of God's word deepened, his preaching became augmented with numerous descriptive illustrations from his home life and especially stories about children.

In the twenty-first century, educators and psychologists prominently assess the learning styles of students to determine methods of instruction especially for students delayed or struggling in their learning. In the nineteenth century, Moody's learning styles and struggles were not as easily identifiable. His family in today's realm of education would more than likely be classified as poverty-stricken and therefore *at risk*. At an early age he seemingly lacked educational motivation sometimes viewed as understandably characteristic of a student with learning difficulties. Negative school experiences only increased his unwillingness to study. Moody reflected: "When I was a boy, we had a teacher who believed in governing by law. He used to keep a rattan in his desk, and my back tingles now . . . [shrugging his shoulders] as I think of it."[123] Despite his unwillingness to study, his mother faithfully continued to encourage him to apply himself and to memorize Scripture even when his mind was elsewhere.

Moody, as a winsome leader among his friends, would often bring them into his own mischievous schemes that threatened to have him dismissed from school. Unfortunately, Moody's under-developed study habits displayed a lack of *EQ-Motivation* and his ungoverned disposition or lack of *EQ-Self-Regulation* abbreviated his educational advancement.[124] He continued with some of these struggles even until the 1890s when his son-in-law observed: "He was a practical, not a speculative student of the Bible. He had not an analytical mind or training . . . I never knew him to sit down with

---

121. Daniels, *His Words, Work, and Workers*, 504.
122. McClure, *D. L. Moody's Child Stories*, 23.
123. Chapman, *The Life and Work of Dwight Lyman Moody*, 53.
124. Daniels in 1877 noted that Moody finished the fifth grade; In 1876 Lobb cited Moody as attending school until 16: "When he left, his education was exceedingly imperfect" due to his inattentiveness and "the inherent love of fun and mischief." Lobb, *Arrows and Anecdotes*, 4.

pencil and paper to analyze a passage, or indeed any problem . . . his education was meagre at best, and its deficiency proved . . . a handicap all his life."[125]

Moody's educational strengths included effective speaking, auditory, and math skills—skills evidenced by his success as an evangelist and businessman. His early schooling included instruction and practice in declamation or a personification of a historical figure in order to persuade others to consider a different viewpoint.[126] Moody's participation in this rhetorical device later strengthened his evangelistic oratory and delivery skills. He electrifyingly captivated his audiences through appealing illustrations with his *DISC-Influence* traits. What he heard stuck with him. He could deliver touching stories with sincerity and genuineness. His son-in-law recalled that Moody also excelled in improvisation. Many of his most memorable and effective sermons contained inventive clever and concise statements. This ability resulted in part from his freedom to preach without the restraints of sermon memorization.[127]

Mr. Reynolds, a friend of Moody's from Peoria, Illinois, shared this unpretentious but self-disclosing conversation with Moody at a Canadian convention: "Reynolds, I have got only one talent: I have no education, but I love the Lord Jesus Christ, and I want to do something for Him; and I want you to pray for me."[128] Moody realized his need for prayer and that his greatest educational weaknesses revolved around grammar, spelling, and reading.

London editor John Lobb (1840–1921) wrote in his critique of Moody in 1876: "His education was exceedingly imperfect . . . indifferent reading and writing, worse spelling, with a very small modicum of arithmetic, were all the attainments he could boast of."[129] His reading was described by revivalist and co-worker John Wilbur Chapman (1859–1915), as "outlandish beyond description."[130] When attempting to read an unknown word Moody "mouthed his sense of it without full dependence upon his training, or made up a new word which sounded to his ear as suitable as the original."[131] He mispronounced words and misaligned subjects with their verbs. Moody incorrectly pronounced Jerusalem as J'ru-s'lem', Daniel as Dan'el, Israel as Is-rel, "they was" instead of "they were" and "done it" instead of "did it."[132] He used New England informalities and overpowering phrases from which scholars would have refrained.

Likewise, Moody's uncle, Samuel Holton, recognized his seventeen year old nephew's difficulty in reading while Moody briefly lived with him in Boston. He said:

---

125. Fitt, *Moody Still Lives*, 37, 141.
126. Chapman, *The Life and Work of Dwight Lyman Moody*, 52–53.
127. Fitt, *Moody Still Lives*, 140.
128. Daniels, *D. L. Moody and His Work*, 36.
129. Lobb, *Arrows and Anecdotes by Dwight L. Moody*, 3.
130. Chapman, *The Life and Work of Dwight Lyman Moody*, 53.
131. Ibid.
132. Daniels, *D. L. Moody and His Work*, 479.

"When Dwight read his Bible out loud he couldn't make anything more out of it than he could out of the chattering of a lot of blackbirds. Many of the words were so far beyond the boy that he left them out entirely when he read and the majority of the others he mangled fearfully."[133]

Nevertheless, Reverend Goodwin's First Congregational Church in Chicago heartily welcomed Moody despite the ridicule and closing of some pulpits due to Moody's traits of illiteracy. Goodwin's church members "never sneered at his broken, unpolished utterances, his faulty grammar" for they agreed that whether Moody was "taught in the schools, or taught only in the closet, ordained by the laying on of men's hands, or ordained only by the baptism of the Holy Ghost . . . he should have our heartiest fellowship, our sincerest prayers."[134] Despite Moody's humbling deficiencies, God awarded favor to this appointed evangelist.

By the 1880s A. P. Fitt had noticed improvement in Moody's skills attributed to time, training, and experience. He wrote in 1936 that he had heard early reports of Moody's fast-paced speaking; however, Fitt did not notice that mannerism or undue grammatical mistakes during Moody's later years. Daniels, in comparing the outcome of Moody's powerful and anointed messages on others, commented on the positive results of Moody's preaching: "What matters it that the Queen's English gets an occasional wound, while the sword of the Spirit is being thrust into the hearts of the King's enemies? It is all very well for Brother Moody to say modestly that 'there are plenty of ministers in Brooklyn who can preach far better than I.' But some of us know that there is not a minister among us who can pack so much soul-saving truth of God into a concise, probable form, and send it home with so much momentum as Dwight L. Moody."[135] Fitt knew that Moody's sincerity and *absorbing earnestness* overrode such errors and that during his later years even Moody's sermons needed little editing.[136]

Still, according to his friend, W. H. Daniels, Moody recognized his own handicap and personally was "mortified by his errors of speech and his lack of worldly wisdom" and "almost ready to sink."[137] Daniels continued his observations: "One great torment of his soul was the thought that he was an ignorant man, and yet was looked upon as a religious teacher." Nonetheless, as Moody yielded his *ignorance* and weaknesses to God, then he began ministering and displaying the power of the Lord. He traded his own self-consciousness and self-awareness for a ministry to all men regardless of their educational status—even that of Emma's. Moody realized that these circumstances were used in his life to deepen his understanding of the struggles of others. He learned to place his dependence on God alone: "In the saving power of rhetoric and grammar he had no faith at all; and the possession of these gifts by others never made him afraid

---

133. Chapman, *The Life and Work of Dwight Lyman Moody*, 56.
134. Quarter-Centennial of the First Congregational Church, 41.
135. Daniels, *D. L. Moody and His Work*, 480.
136. Fitt, *Moody Still Lives*, 50.
137. Daniels, *D. L. Moody and His Work*, 190.

of them, or hindered him from speaking his mind to them in his own plain and honest way."[138]

Educational Compensation and Impulsivity

With her nineteenth-century education background, Emma would have understood the need to teach low cognitive functioning students the necessary compensation skills. She noted how Moody wisely and humbly turned to the strengths of others to help him compensate for his own educational weaknesses. In 1857 he received assistance from J. B. Stillson[139] who quickly recognized that Moody did not possess the skills needed to even study the Bible.[140] Mrs. Moody greatly contributed to her husband's educational improvements with her own independent thinking and writing skills. Their granddaughter, Emma Powell, wrote of the tremendous help her Grandmother Moody gave to Grandfather Moody attributing his usefulness to her strong support and steadfast reassurances.[141]

Mrs. Peter MacKinnon, Mrs. Moody's close friend from Edinburgh, Scotland, wrote of Emma Moody's capability in assisting Mr. Moody: "She was not a mere unthinking echo of a master mind and will."[142] Even Mrs. Moody's sons recognized the impact of their mother on their father's education. Their older son William, in a letter to his mother on February 5, 1900, credited his father's learning and successful ministry to her counsel and teaching above all others—that which even his own father totally recognized.[143] Their son Paul added: "Till the day of his death he never ceased to wonder at two things—the use God had made of him despite what he considered his handicaps, and the miracle of having won the love of a woman he considered so completely his superior. He was impulsive, outspoken, dominant, informal, and with little education when they met. She was intensely conventional and conservative, far better educated, fond of reading, and self-effacing to the lst degree."[144] Mrs. Moody often edited his letters—letters that tended to be short, direct, and primarily penned in large script. Likewise, he gratefully received compensatory assistance from his son-in-law. Fitt answered most of his correspondence and even dictated answers for him while Mrs. Moody handled confidential correspondence.[145]

---

138. Ibid., 139.

139. Ibid., 55. Dwight Moody attended YMCA noon prayer sessions while receiving systematic Bible training through J. B. Stillson. Stillson introduced Moody to George Müller's Plymouth Brethren doctrine of expectant trust (*Life of Trust*) in God's provisions through prayer.

140. Ibid., 54.

141. Powell, *Heavenly Destiny*, 255.

142. Ibid., 269.

143. Ibid., 7.

144. Ibid., 258.

145. Fitt, *Moody Still Lives*, 139.

Moody had a reputation for being impulsive or spontaneous—a possible key component for those with *DISC-Influence* personality traits. Fitt viewed it more as Moody's premeditated and cautious consideration to all suggestions rather than impulse.[146] Impulsivity can be both a positive and negative quality by achieving immediate action or by acting on instinct with unpremeditated actions and little forethought. In the scope of today's educational trends, impulsive actions are oftentimes attributed to anxiety or attention difficulties. Moody's educational interference as a young student could perhaps have been due to the traumatic loss of his father at the age of four combined with his mother's grave responsibility to care for Moody's eight brothers and sisters. Also, his high energy levels could have appeared as impulsivity with a lack of concentration. Reverend John Chapman wrote of Moody's boundless energy as a young boy and his fondness for mischief. Contrasting Mr. and Mrs. Moody's dispositions, their granddaughter Emma Powell wrote of her grandmother's "calmness meeting so quietly his impulsiveness" and how her "dignity and serenity . . . counterbalanced her husband's impulsive, emotional nature and became the backbone of Moody's success."[147]

Early in Moody's Chicago work at the Market Hall Mission he was said to be "guilty of all sorts of vagaries, and would follow an impulse, without waiting for judgment."[148] This tendency was also noted by his son William. He wrote that his father impulsively moved to Chicago in 1856. Just as abruptly and impulsively in 1867 Moody made an announcement to those at the mission school that he was leaving for England that very week.[149] William knew that despite his father's impulsive nature, Moody still significantly maintained a quietness of strength, compassion, and thoughtfulness with an enthusiastic spirit as his dominant strength.[150] Moody himself looked positively at his own impulsivity: "I have always been a man of impulse . . . Almost everything I ever did in my life that was a success was done on the impulse, and I suppose when I get ready to die I will be up and off."[151]

Impulsivity was not a prominent trait for Emma. With her *DISC-Conscientiousness* she possessed strengths in analytical thinking. She administratively arranged and placed policies and strategies into a pre-planned organizational box. These strengths often conflicted with Moody's impulsive nature. Contrary to his insistence for immediate action, Emma believed that her lady workers needed time for intense training before they infiltrated the city with the gospel. Moody was an impulsive individual with general viewpoints and minimal follow-up.[152] He learned that Emma, as well as

146. Ibid., 11.
147. Powell, *Heavenly Destiny*, 255.
148. Daniels, *D. L. Moody and His Work*, 46.
149. Moody, *The Life of Dwight L. Moody*, 131.
150. Ibid., 502.
151. Ibid., 46.
152. Joiner, *Sin in the City*, 56.

other friends, did not always understand his charging ahead on an apparent sudden whim. Yet even Moody's son-in-law discovered the perception, awareness, and decisiveness that this strong leader displayed in his later years: "He seems to have had some reputation for acting on impulse, or by intuition, but in most cases . . . he had given careful thought and had previous knowledge on which to form a quick decision when the time came." Yet, Fitt knew that when his father-in-law had his mind set, he usually got his way.[153]

Emma's sound educational training and experience qualified her to work in Chicago using education as an evangelistic tool. By the time Emma met Moody, he had expanded his experience in teaching children with a gradual assimilation into a worldwide evangelical leadership role. His success was evident:

> The fact that he was not a scholar was forgotten. He evidently knew Christ and His Gospel and, because of this, the best people in London, including members of the royal household, pressed to hear his Bible readings and addresses; wept over his touching stories illustrating the love of Christ to lost sinners; sang with heartiness and rapture the sweet hymns and songs which the revival had already made familiar; and some of them, joining hands with him as one beloved of the Lord, gave him not only their personal friendship, but added the weight of their names and influence to help forward with the work.[154]

Just as others looked beyond his educational shortcomings, Emma also looked past Moody's deficiencies. She felt his evangelistic heart. Just as important, he looked beyond Emma's intense administrative focus and believed in her commitment and ability to fulfill their evangelistic and educational vision.

Outlook on Education

Without question Moody's educational perspective would have differed from Emma's. He never claimed to be an educator or an administrator. Frederick Meyer, one of Moody's closest friends, memorialized him not so much as a teacher or even as a preacher, but as a *prophet* and *herald* compelling souls to listen to God's word of truth.[155] At the same time, Moody's own incomplete experience in education prompted an intrinsic desire to see young people succeed. He did not want them to encounter the difficulties he had experienced. His Northfield schools gave him that opportunity as he left the teaching to teachers and the administration to the administrators. Through the lens of his own educational past he could knowingly advise and encourage others.

---

153. Fitt, *Moody Still Lives*, 11.
154. Daniels, *D. L. Moody and His Work*, 369–70.
155. Chapman, *The Life and Work of Dwight Lyman Moody*, xv–xvi.

He believed the best in them and they had faith in him as they eagerly sought his affirmation.[156]

As an educator Emma confidently defended and integrated *faith and learning*. Internally motivated, she heeded the call to Chicago's poor and unschooled. In so doing she satisfied her own desire to use the Bible as a tool. With her expertise she taught others to read as she utilized her *EQ-Self-awareness* and *EQ-Internal Motivation*. At the same time, Moody, as an evangelist, was also expected to be an intellectual purveyor of truth. However, he shied away from theological confrontational discussions requiring high levels of reasoning skills perhaps due in part to his own educational reserve. When it came to discussing the Bible he was immediately on board. However, he refused to go the route of debate and faithfully kept his call to preach the Bible and win souls. Another of Moody's close English friends, Henry Drummond, spoke of Moody's *non-theological* messages as pointed and direct. He said, "Every blow is straight from the shoulder and every stroke tells. Whatever canons they violate, whatever faults the critics may find with their art, their rhetoric, or even with their theology . . . they do their work with extraordinary power."[157]

Moody's evangelistic approach was at times viewed as either a sign of anti-intellectualism or an inability to respond to intellectual challenges. However, it could also explain why he avoided emerging himself in the popular teachings of the dispensational and holiness movements. In his attempt to deflect theological issues, Moody kept Scripture as the main topic of analysis while advocating openness with justice and Christian virtue. This could be seen in the contention he experienced at a Chicago YMCA meeting. L. Wilbur Messer, who led the YMCA into a new era of secularization during the 1880s, negated much of Moody's earlier evangelistic work due to theological differences. An observer at the meeting, who had no sympathetic ties to Moody, shared how impressed he was by Moody's notable character and non-reprising reaction. This observer noted that despite intense discourse and criticism, Moody was non-offendable.[158]

Emma did not disparage Moody due to his educational deficiencies. In spite of differences in their educational backgrounds, they became steady friends. "Moody saw more in Emma Dryer than robust faith; he saw a brilliant woman—one with extraordinary high intelligence. Whatever Dryer set her mind to, she did and did well."[159] She used education as an effective social tool to bring souls to Christ. Emma capably established an employment agency, banks for food and clothing and toys, an industrial education program, education and Bible reading in prisons, and Sunday school education for women. She used social issue approaches based on biblical integration principles.

156. Fitt, *Moody Still Lives*, 86.
157. Chapman, *The Life and Work of Dwight Lyman Moody*, xiii.
158. Findlay, *Dwight L. Moody: American Evangelist*, 410.
159. Dorsett, *A Passion For Souls*, 166.

Emma and Moody: Complementary Leadership Roles

B. F. Jacobs, one of the main speakers for Moody's Northfield conferences in September 1883, publicly acknowledged Emma's educational effectiveness. He encouraged churches to imitate her evangelistic method of taking the Bible and visiting the homes of others throughout their cities.[160] From Emma's education program Moody actually gained direction and organization for his own tract and Bible distribution program.[161] Consequently, Emma and Moody, by creative design, approached education and their passion for souls in complementary yet diverse leadership roles. For many years their contrasting styles were significantly neutralized against antagonizing competition and distrust.

Leaders Void of Prejudice and Bias

Emma cast aside a future of prominent feminist recognition as head of the ISNU Female Department. She willingly embraced a non-salaried position to minister to the needy in the streets of Chicago. In reverse, Moody, with lower class upbringing and mannerisms, scouted the streets of Chicago searching for the poor and destitute only to find himself promotionally destined to preach in colossal auditoriums throughout the world. Reverend Daniels observed: "His unpolished speech and manners were strong attractions for certain classes of people, who were glad enough of a chance to throw themselves into his sturdy arms, but would have been repelled by courtly manners and dignified address."[162]

Moody and Emma resolved to reach the unsaved masses with concentration on the lower-class immigrants, industrial workers, and the poor. Moody was known to ask what could be done to reach the great masses of people. With an inner urgency he pushed himself to hold *mass* revival meetings for all people. He did not cower to the wealthy or to royalty: "He never patronized the poor or sin-smitten, but had compassion on them. He was honest and to the point with all classes."[163] Without seeking social status, Emma and Moody chose to be servant leaders void of prejudice and bias by counting others better than themselves. And in the process they both obtained respectability among classes, races, denominations, and gender groups—one indication of their *EQ-Social Competency.*

Moody and Emma believed that the establishment of a Bible training school would provide the necessary workers to accomplish this mass evangelization task. Their work in training Swedes, Germans, and African Americans broadened their ministry among the racial and denominational communities. Moody was viewed as "a man of the people, and they opened their hearts to him . . . He was conscious of his power over those who were out of the reach of other men; but he never used blunt

---

160. Remlaf, *The Gospel Awakening*, 975.
161. Undated Paper written by Lowell K. Handy, Biographical File of Emma Dryer.
162. Daniels, *D. L. Moody and His Work*, 139.
163. Fitt, *Moody Still Lives*, 63.

words and phrases merely for sensational effect." He was naturally all things to all men and this attitude of heart caused him to be victoriously shielded from his own faults while at the same time protected from being "unduly mortified or cast down by reason of his many trifling blunders."[164]

Additionally, God created Emma and Moody in his own image and designed them with equal status while diverse in gender leadership roles. According to God's plan neither could count the other as superior; rather, they desired to assist and complement one another to fulfill their God-given roles.[165] They were equipped with different skill sets and abilities. Emma was designed as intuitive. She worked quite effectively with short-term plans for extended visions. Moody was a logical long-range visionary. Emma was task-oriented and administratively scheduled. Moody was non-compartmentalized and dealt more successfully with multiple and successive situations and visions.

God's plan brought them together during an intense struggle for equal gender rights. When disagreements such as the WCTU involvement occurred, Emma resorted to a submissive role as an evangelical woman. Moody recognized the need for Emma's assistance in fulfilling his vision for the masses. He viewed her position as a God-given role coupled with her discipleship of others. She beautifully personified the feminine side of God's creation. She was referred to as "a lady of extensive culture and thorough refinement."[166] Correspondingly, Emma recognized her need for Moody's influential male backing. Journalistic coverage on Moody reported: "No daintiness here . . . A spade is a spade."[167] Moody's public appearance demonstrated a physique of masculinity. He introduced "evangelical spirituality and middle-class respectability into his urban agenda with ideals of womanhood and domesticity."[168]

Despite their mutual gender respect, subordinate-dominant role struggles were apparent in Emma and Moody's organizational and leadership styles. Emma was described as being very detailed, precise, and careful especially when it came to the health and security of her lady workers.[169] Moody's minimal education and administrative background did not compare to that of Emma's. Still, the evangelical culture expected submission regardless of her organizational expertise and pragmatic education. With the establishment of the Chicago Evangelization Society and the Bible Institute, Emma would find herself severely tested in regard to her authoritative but secondary role.

The subject of gender difference was not a vogue consideration during Emma's time of leadership. Notably, studies of women in leadership were nonexistent until the

---

164. Daniels, *D. L. Moody and His Work*, 139.
165. Sandom, *Different By Design*, Kindle edition location 279.
166. Daniels, *His Words, Work, and Workers*, 503–4.
167. Joiner, *Sin in the City*, 43.
168. Ibid.
169. Emma Dryer to Nettie McCormick, 24 June 1886, Biographical File of Emma Dryer.

Emma and Moody: Complementary Leadership Roles

1970s.[170] Such studies still continue with a wide range of views. For example, research documents that women and men approach tasks differently which can undoubtedly result in disagreements and false impressions between genders particularly in places of employment.[171] Emma and Moody were not an exception. Deborah in Bible times needed the affirmation of male leadership to successfully complete her role as a judge over Israel. Likewise, Emma approached the establishment of the Bible Work with the need for direct affirmation from Moody and an understanding of his established parameters.[172] Moody expected the submission of women as exhibited in the evangelical culture of the times. Therefore, he considered Emma's cooperation as imperative to the success of his vision. She considered it imperative that he actively communicate to her his on-going support and direction for the Bible Institute.

Gender differences in leadership prevailed in Emma's era just as it does today. However, during the nineteenth and twentieth century, opportunities for women in leadership existed primarily in female organizations.[173] Evangelicalism tended to stereotype women as the helper expected to be compliant and reliant on male authority regardless of any exceptional leadership attributes. Leadership was perceived as an indispensable authoritative position of rule or control rather than the active input and involvement of followers.[174] Moody attempted to keep a balance by strongly supporting the work of women as limited by his evangelical covering. Emma recognized Moody's strong belief in women—such as Sarah Clarke, Frances Willard, and Lucy Meyer—to conduct urban evangelism within certain parameters. She also noted that Mrs. Moody was proudly supported by her husband. He approved her instruction of Sunday school classes which at one time included forty middle-age men older than her.[175]

With women in ministry and in his family Moody tried to balance what Howard Butt called the *velvet covered brick*. God makes the velvet area of submission and the brick of authority in order to create foundational unity. In their particular gender related case, Emma failed to recognize the potential damage that could come with non-acquiescence to male authority. Moody failed to recognize the conflict that his authority without humility and on-going communication and support would generate.[176] Until the time of their ministry separation in 1888, Moody and Emma would agree that equality consisted in their God-given value though not necessarily in their ministry roles.

---

170. Chemers, *An Integrative Theory of Leadership*, 135.
171. Moran, "Gender Differences in Leadership," 475–91.
172. Sandom, *Different By Design*, Kindle edition location 2436.
173. Moran, "Gender Differences in Leadership," 477–78.
174. Burns, *Leadership*, 50.
175. Powell, *Heavenly Destiny*, 45.
176. Butt, *The Velvet Covered Brick*, 163.

Persuasive Leaders

Leaders such as Emma and Moody held a persuasive and social influence that drew others to volunteer aid in order to accomplish good.[177] They relied on persuasion mingled with various degrees of social discernment. Moody possessed *DISC-Influence* and *EQ-Social Competency* traits. He also depended on his *DISC-Dominance* and positional authority status as a noted evangelist. Rather than using his servant leadership gift of *persuasion*, at times he used the traditional authoritarian model causing others to feel pressure from him to comply.

Emma persuasively attempted to build consensus among her lady workers with *DISC-Steadiness*. From her perspective she succeeded in managing and creating an atmosphere of camaraderie with her *EQ-Social Competency* skills during her many years at the Bible Work. Although receiving positive affirmation from organizations such as the Chicago Bible Society and from former students, she was still viewed by the daughter of Emma's friend, Mary Jane Moore Hitchcock, as a leader among women who used her persuasive authority in an exacting manner. Mrs. Ralph B. Grove in a 1958 interview stated: "Miss Dryer was a real stickler for rules. Had to report conversations . . . what they said to people, what people said to them in reply, etc. Rules as to what they wore, etc."[178]

Despite a perceived *EQ-Social Competency* weakness by some individuals, Emma was known for her "sensitivity and insight required for one-to-one ministry . . . dependable, energetic, and motivated to keep work going forward."[179] She sought to assist Moody in realizing his goals by persuading others to realize both hers and theirs. With Emma's persuasion she successfully built a *community* of servant leaders committed to her vision.

Moody used his gift of *persuasion* to win souls to Christ. When preaching he noticeably extended to the audience his opened Bible. He clearly spoke "to your heart in a voice flexible to every thought and emotion" while "an inner light illuminated his face as he touched the chords that sounded the music of human redemption" without any "suggestion of oratorical artifice, no striving for brilliance of phrase."[180] Even when working with his Sunday school classes, Moody exercised great alertness and ingenuity in handling the tough crowds of young people. He learned the value of persuasively dealing with them in novelty and with publicity devices that would challenge their attention.

Moody also used his influence and instincts to build a team of spiritually qualified individuals for leadership roles to bring about his evangelistic visions. On his vision team Moody included successful businessmen who were persuaded by his

---

177. Chemers, *An Integrative Theory of Leadership*, 77.
178. Interview with Mrs. Ralph B. Grove, 7 February 1958, Biographical File of Emma Dryer.
179. Dorsett, *A Passion For Souls*, 166.
180. Fitt, *Moody Still Lives*, 74.

Emma and Moody: Complementary Leadership Roles

sincerity and convinced of his ability as a leader.[181] As an effective leader, his greatness endowed them with greatness as well. Moody thrived on persuading individuals, including Emma, to give their lives to various ministries for the sake of the kingdom. Consequently, with his persuasive tendencies and ubiquitous vision even his son-in-law could foresee that Moody's dream of training young people to evangelize and share the gospel would inevitably come to pass.[182]

Emma and Moody were persuasive leaders of action—*DISC-Influence*. From time to time Moody acted on his commitment to Emma as she served as the spiritual leader among her Bible readers. He actively secured additional training for her at Mildmay, England. At the same time she proved her belief in Moody, as a spiritual guide with vision, by her continued support and faith in his dream of a Bible school. Emma did all in her power to nurture this vision and persuade others to participate as well. She took action with fundraising just as Moody did. He was not as interested in the Bible Work details and their implementation as he was in creatively casting the vision for advancing the kingdom of God. In a positive sense Moody and Emma's personalities of persuasion were primarily penetrating more than forcefully commanding.[183] They both took charge of meetings and encouraged young women and men to receive training for urban ministry. And they had followers who believed in them as they counseled and held inquiry meetings, training conferences, and children sessions.

At the same time, those qualities of active leadership expected from Emma and Moody involved openness and persuasion which could be interpreted negatively as *control*. The report from Mrs. Ralph Grove indicated an issue regarding Emma's leadership dominance or strictness over operations at the Bible Work. Moody's early YMCA ventures and his later establishment of the Chicago Evangelization Society also indicated a propensity—both positive and negative—toward control: "If any one offended his sense of honor, he would fly into fury at once; but the tempest of passion soon passed by. His habit of striking out right and left sometimes raised an uproar in the whole establishment; and there was no little difficulty in keeping the peace."[184] Nevertheless, the Lord used these experiences to equip Moody throughout the years in joyful service to fearlessly fight against the devil rather than the flesh of men.

Perceptions of control were also inevitable as long as Moody and Emma were viewed as the primary leaders of final committee voting on major decisions. Nonetheless, as servant leaders Emma and Moody learned through many difficult situations that submission, rather than control, gave them an enduring influence and authorization to serve as persuasive leaders.[185]

---

181. Ibid.
182. Fitt, *The Shorter Life of D. L. Moody*, 15.
183. Fitt, *Moody Still Lives*, 86.
184. Daniels, *D. L. Moody and His Work*, 20.
185. Butt, *The Velvet Covered Brick*, 163.

Woman of Nobility

Leaders of Morality, Character, and Integrity

With solid traits of *EQ-Self-Regulation*, Emma and Moody modeled the example of moral leadership producing moral ministries.[186] Moody expected Emma and his associates to maintain a godly character that aligned them with the purposes of his evangelistic endeavors.[187] Emma willingly trained her Bible readers in moral purity by warning them to avoid any appearance of evil. Likewise, Moody possessed an abundance of "contagious moral and spiritual enthusiasm."[188] He exhorted young men to moderation by encouraging them to look to Jesus and to access the inspiration and power that flows directly from God.[189] On November 12, 1875, Moody encouraged his many revival converts in a written letter:

> Your sphere of testimony may not be public; your place of usefulness may not be large; in your own homes 'adorn the doctrine of God your Saviour.' Keep one little thought in mind—'I have none but Jesus to please.' And so make your dress as simple as you know will please your Lord; make your deportment as modest as you know will commend itself to him . . . Your Brother In Christ, D.L. Moody.[190]

At times Moody provoked others with his *puritanical strictness*. He was viewed as a Puritan who "hated theaters, billiards, cards, and all such pastimes,—counting them so many enticements of the devil."[191] A fellow employee at one shoe store where Moody worked relayed the story of Moody's return after a church meeting. When he found other clerks playing checkers, he instantly grabbed the board and smashed it. Then, without a word, he fell to his knees in prayer. Also, while working at the Chicago YMCA Moody was incensed when the association rented the hall for dancing. When he resolved that he could not change the situation, he shut off their utilities and left them in the dark.[192]

Even so, when Moody's character and integrity were questioned several years later by churches overseas, thirty-six Chicago pastors dispatched the following declaration on May 21, 1874:

> WE, the undersigned, Pastors of the City of Chicago, learning that the Christian character of D. L. Moody has been attacked, for the purpose of destroying his influence as an Evangelist in Scotland, hereby certify that his labors in the Young Men's Christian Association, and as an Evangelist in this City and

---

186. Ibid., 27.
187. Fitt, *The Shorter Life*, 21.
188. Fitt, *Moody Still Lives*, 109.
189. Daniels, 1876, *D. L. Moody and His Work*, 495.
190. Ibid.
191. Daniels,1875, *D. L. Moody and His Work*, 30.
192. Ibid.

elsewhere, according to the best information we can get, have been Evangelical and Christian in the highest sense of these terms; and we do not hesitate to commend him as an earnest Christian worker, worthy of the confidence of our Scotch and English brethren.[193]

In response to such situations Moody admonished Dr. Charles F. Goss who was selected as pastor of the Chicago Avenue Church: "I have been misunderstood, misaligned, abused, but I made up my mind to keep sweet . . . You cannot do any good unless you keep sweet . . . My advice to you is to keep sweet."[194]

Leaders of integrity serve others—even in the midst of determining whether to maintain integrity through assertion or by yielding to others.[195] Emma and Moody sought to find the balance. Many acknowledged Moody to be "a rare Christian . . . deeply respected for his personal integrity and Christian commitment" and "quite unspoiled in character."[196] At the same time Emma was respectfully acknowledged for her beautiful smile and gracious spirit in her ministry to others.[197]

Character qualities of compassion, meekness, and love exemplified the hearts of these two leaders. Emma received news of the death of Wheaton College President Jonathan Blanchard's son. She wrote the following compassionate letter:

> Dear Christian friends: Appreciating somewhat your dreadful loss, in the departure of your son, Lewis. I wish to say that in your affliction, I am afflicted. I know that yet the sorrow grows no lighter as the days go. There is comfort in thinking that even his earthly work is not done, & that in the resurrection, in newness of life, he will work . . . for Christ. It is most sad to have him away. It is a great loss which only Christ knows how to make good to him and to you and to us all. How glad we are that our Lord calls our last *enemy* His *enemy*, & has promised to take away the victory from the grave. Which then we will go on through the gloom into the unclouded day *resting* in His unfailing promises. May our Lord send you great comfort. In Christian fellowship Your friend Miss E. Dryer.[198]

As Emma displayed compassion, Moody demonstrated meekness—a quality in which one uses self-restraint on behalf of another.[199] Others noted Moody's selflessness: "He is modest; ready to take a hint from any one; ready to let every man do his own work; and all the time full of anxiety to save somebody."[200] A. P. Fitt agreed that his

---

193. Ibid., 273.
194. Fitt, *Moody Still Lives*, 59–60.
195. Butt, *The Velvet Covered Brick*, 66.
196. Daniels, *D. L. Moody and His Work*, 369.
197. Undated Emma Dryer Obituary, Biographical File of Emma Dryer.
198. Jonathan Blanchard Papers, 17 March 1884, Wheaton College Archives and Special Collections.
199. Butt, *The Velvet Covered Brick*, 7.
200. Daniels, *D. L. Moody and His Work*, 263.

father-in-law in his later years displayed remarkable humility when it came to submitting to those younger and less experienced than himself.[201]

Furthermore, as an expression of maintaining a meek spirit, Moody instructed businessman H. N. F. Marshall against using his name to publicize the schools or placing it on seminary stationary. He didn't enjoy seeing his name in print.[202] Moody also refused to allow others to photograph him. Likewise, Emma shied away from the media of photography with only a few documented photos.

As Emma and Moody embraced a spirit of meekness, pride would closely follow. Moody's habit of outspokenness oftentimes negated his sincere quest for humility. Nevertheless, others noticed during his later years that a greater degree of meekness had begun to overshadow his battle with pride.[203] As for Emma, her tendency toward perfectionism caused prideful judgment of those who did not align with her organizational mindset and efficiency.

A spirit of conquering love permeated these servant leaders. After hearing Moorehouse preach on John 3:16 around 1873, Moody's sermons on love increased. Furthermore, he greatly influenced the distribution of Henry Drummond's 1 Corinthians 13 discourse entitled *The Greatest Thing In The World*. Moody responded: "I never knew up to that time that God loved us so much. This heart of mine began to thaw out; I could not keep back the tears. I just drank it in . . . I tell you there is one thing that draws above everything else in the world and that is love."[204] Fitt testified that in the final seven years of Moody's life he did not witness dishonorable actions, harsh words, or self-centered motivations. [205]

After the 1882 release of Scottish author and minister George MacDonald's (1824–1905) novel *Weighed and Wanting*, Emma placed a typed excerpt from the book inside her Bible at the beginning of the book of Matthew. It read: "The love of God is so deep, he can be satisfied with nothing less than getting as near as it is possible for the Father to draw nigh to his children—and that is into absolute contact of heart with heart, love with love, being with being." She wrote John 3:16 after the quote. Emma experienced the inward questioning of God's love during times of suffering. With her ministry to the poor and outcast she compassionately and lovingly related to Hester, one of the characters in MacDonald's book. Hester struggled with her own inadequacies while tending to an afflicted woman. Emma read the author's challenge to understand the suffering aspect of humanity which Emma herself had personally experienced: "As that must be wrought out from the deepest inside, divine law working itself up through our nature into our consciousness and will, and claiming us as divine, who can tell by what slow certainties of approach God is drawing nigh to the

---

201. Fitt, *The Shorter Life*, 21.
202. Findlay, *Dwight L. Moody: American Evangelist*, 369.
203. Ibid.
204. Day, *Bush Aglow*, 145.
205. Fitt, *Moody Still Lives*, 30.

most suffering of his creatures?"[206] Emma discovered that God's love flowing from her heart to the aching hearts of others would bring ultimate healing for those who served and for those in need.

Leaders in Doctrinal Issues

Emma treasured the word of God which she faithfully taught in her Bible classes and in her school. She took up Moody's challenge to learn more about the second coming of Christ beyond what the Lord had already taught her. Her position and hunger for truth regarding premillennialism inspired Moody. He sought to be surrounded with dispensationalists, fundamentalists, and even modernists such as Henry Drummond despite the urging of others to separate from them.[207] Moody also became associated with the 1875 Keswick Convention, a Reformed non-Wesleyan Higher Life Movement in England. Keswick advanced holiness and endorsed prominent Wesleyan-inspired figures such as Asa Mahan and Charles Finney.

When Moody began promoting Keswick holiness teachers at the Northfield conferences, also known as the *American Keswick*, he had those who opposed his conference speaker selections. He brought his life-long friend and Keswick teacher Fredrick Meyer to Northfield around 1891 despite a strenuous protest. With Holiness Movement advocates, Moody maintained a strong belief "in the baptism of the Holy Spirit as a gift of grace that was available to all people regenerated by the Holy Ghost."[208] He chose to take crisis situations and turn them into evangelistic crusades rather than employ an exclusivist Fundamentalist piety. Historian David Maas attributed Moody's nondenominational propensity along with his non-theological preparation as the reason for his laissez-faire church faith positions regarding popular nineteenth-century movements.[209]

Another doctrinal issue involved the place of the Holy Spirit in a Christian's life. In 1871 after the Chicago Fire, Moody experienced a *baptism of the Holy Spirit* on the streets of New York. He commissioned his pastor friend, Reuben Torrey, to preach on this subject with every possible opportunity. Beginning in 1886 Moody initiated college student conferences at his Northfield school with a primary emphasis on the power of the Holy Spirit. Many attendees, venturing to secluded areas to seek God's presence and pray for the Holy Spirit, departed from the conferences with an increased missionary zeal.[210] Moody knew that the anointing of the Spirit was a gift, richly given, to preach God's word throughout the world. He also realized what it meant to grieve the Holy Spirit. In his 1876 New York Hippodrome meeting he al-

---

206. MacDonald, "Weighed and Wanting," 81.
207. Findlay, *Dwight L. Moody: American Evangelist*, 411–12.
208. Dorsett, *A Passion For Souls*, 311.
209. Maas, "The Life & Times of D. L. Moody," 5–13.
210. Shanks, *College Students at Northfield*, 210.

lowed his flesh to interfere with the Spirit by impetuously and prematurely closing the campaign. Afterward, he confessed that he had grieved the Spirit and had gone against his better judgment.[211]

When Moody first met Emma he quickly sensed her profound and appealing understanding on the work of the Holy Spirit.[212] Like Moody, she had experienced the Spirit's presence in a profound way. With his encouragement Emma taught about the Spirit's work of comfort and counsel as the Helper who walked beside her. She also realized the Holy Spirit as her Healer when she was healed from typhoid at the time of her call to Chicago. On another occasion her friend Reverend Daniels unexpectedly appointed her to teach his weekly Bible class. He was suffering from double vision and asked her to take over his weekly Bible teaching program. Although Emma believed that the Lord would have her do this work, she struggled with her own eye disorder. She shared her dilemma:

> I could not, in my weariness, see clearly enough to read. I had severe, very severe, diplopia. I asked our Lord to heal me, if He would have me do such work. I had no idea by what ministry, the healing would come. And, to my surprise, He healed me, in a few minutes. He also *gave me the Scriptures* for the appointed meeting; and, by His Spirit, helped me as I talked. And he gave me a consciousness that this was an evidence of His will. He continued to give me evidences of His directing, and sustaining presence, and power.[213]

With believing faith Emma had knelt in her room and received healing instantly with 20/20 vision.[214]

Meanwhile, God used American Baptist Missionary Board member Adoniram Judson Gordon (1836–95) to bring a greater awareness to Moody regarding the subject of healing. This occurred through their partnership in student conferences, the mission field, and shared views on the disciplined life of the Spirit. Whereas Emma did not hesitate to make known her position regarding divine healing, Gordon cautiously approached Moody on the topic.[215]

Adding to his awareness of healing, Moody and his close friend John Farwell heard the testimony of a mutual friend, Mr. Field. Despite pain and lameness in his leg, Field assisted Moody at his North Market Sunday school in Chicago. His healing served as a strong confirmation of faith to Moody: "Like a vision of light and hope, to cheer the heart which was almost faltering, and to strengthen the hands which were

---

211. Dorsett, *A Passion For Souls*, 244.
212. Ibid., 166.
213. Emma Dryer to Charles Blanchard, 1916, Biographical File of Emma Dryer.
214. Dorsett, *A Passion For Souls*, 167.
215. Ibid., 251.

Emma and Moody: Complementary Leadership Roles

beginning to hang down . . . in the strength of this vision, Moody seemed to overleap all difficulties—he reached out his hand to grasp the hand of the Lord."[216]

Emma taught at the Bible Work that Christ brought divine healing through the power of his Spirit. Moody agreed that the Holy Spirit anoints, empowers, teaches, and guides, but he had to pray about the doctrine of healing. He was hesitant to make this teaching part of his platform. He continued to urge Torrey to do the preaching for him regarding the work of the Holy Spirit. Emma boldly shared with Moody and encouraged him to embrace a bigger picture of the Holy Spirit as the Healer.

In 1885 Moody and others joined Emma in narrating a book recording the wonders of prayer in which she reflected her position on divine healing. In a 1916 letter to her friend President Charles Blanchard of Wheaton College, written years after Moody died, she recalled: "I knew that our Lord had mercifully healed me for His service, answering prayer, and adding remarkable experiences of his guidance into Christian service, even when I had no understanding of the doctrine of Divine Healing. I could not neglect that experience! And similar healings were repeated."[217] Emma added that Moody's views regarding divine healing progressively altered by the time of his death in 1899.

Stewardship Leaders

Emma and Moody, as servant leaders, were known for their *stewardship* roles in which they held education and evangelism in trust for the good and service of others.[218] Such stewardship required a spirit of self-denial. Without expectation of any personal or financial reward, these leaders with *EQ-Internal Motivation* sacrificially removed the focus from their own needs. Moody appreciated Emma's audacious decision in 1870 to sacrifice financial gain for a higher calling. He marveled at her tenacious and faithful stewardship regarding the Bible Work.

Moody recalled how he wrestled with the decision in 1860 to leave business for the full time ministry of serving others.[219] He ventured from Boston in September of 1856 to a city on the verge of amazing industrial growth. Businessmen in Chicago were commandeering opportunities for financial investments. Three various shoe stores hired Moody as a salesman with traveling opportunities that expanded his territory to several states.[220] By 1860 he had become friends with businessmen such as John Farwell and entrepreneur Marshall Field (1834–1906). Initially, Moody thrived on the challenges of competition and developed the skill set for making quick sales. His name as a successful salesman was well-known. Henry Drummond wrote an article

---

216. Daniels, *D. L. Moody and His Work*, 86.
217. Ibid., 168.
218. Spears, "Character and Servant Leadership," 29.
219. Daniels, *D. L. Moody and His Work*, 81.
220. Fitt, *Moody Still Lives*, 43–44.

for *McClure Magazine* relaying a conversation he had with a well-known steamship merchant from Great Britain. This businessman told Drummond that Mr. Moody's *executive ability* and *business capacity* exceeded that of anyone he had ever known.[221]

Moody admitted that leaving business in 1860 for ministry was not easy: "I didn't know what this was going to cost me. I was disqualified for business: it had become distasteful to me. I had got a taste of another world, and cared no more for making money. For some days after the greatest struggle of my life took place. Should I give up business and give myself wholly to Christian work, or should I not? God helped me to decide aright, and I have never regretted my choice."[222] Without further hesitation, he left his salesman job telling his boss: "God is rich, and I am working for Him."[223]

From the early days of her acquaintance with Nettie McCormick, Emma possessed the gift of faith to trust God for favor and finances for the Bible school. That faith combined with her administrative background and skills, equipped her as an effective leader. She kept tight financial records on all funding with the help of businessman Nathaniel Bouton. Noting Emma's business abilities, Moody modeled for her his own ethical financial practices. Fitt observed that Moody did not keep money for himself. He faithfully gave his total earnings to his wife who served as his accountant.

Moody's financial philosophy involved his solemn responsibility to remain poor by giving away his wealth.[224] He kept none of the estimated million dollar royalties from the sale of his hymnals. Moody, along with his associate Ira Sankey, was poor like those around them. "They were so filled with hope and happiness that, though poor, they were able to make many rich, having nothing but possessing all things."[225] John Farwell declared that Moody left England no richer, and that his income remained lower than others in the pastorate.[226] According to Torrey, Moody exercised freedom from a love of material things and lived in contentment.[227] In a letter written in 1884 Moody pondered with gratitude his freedom from the snares of wealth that chained businessmen to the world. He experienced the pleasure that comes from giving to others in order to promote the gospel of Christ.[228]

Emma and Moody recognized that popular leaders without *EQ-Self-Regulation* could be exposed to the great temptation of leadership control resulting from undue wealth and personal preferences. Knowing his own business inclinations toward stubbornness and impetuosity, Moody confessed his self-focused responses in which he discharged verbal attacks on those close to him followed by a sincere repentant and

---

221. Powell, *Heavenly Destiny*, 40.
222. Fitt, *Moody Still Lives*, 23.
223. Daniels, *D. L. Moody and His Work*, 265.
224. Ibid.
225. Day, *Bush Aglow*, 144.
226. Daniels, *D. L. Moody and His Work*, 519.
227. Torrey, *Why God Used D. L. Moody*, 33.
228. Findlay, *Dwight L. Moody: American Evangelist*, 369.

humble heart.[229] Despite such temptations, as a stewardship leader he was vulnerable yet open. He learned from his mistakes and was impulsively quick to apologize publicly with what must have been humbling and costly acts of remorse.[230]

At his 1876 Hippodrome campaign he became offended with area pastors who were absent. Not perceiving their own weariness, he reprimanded them followed by his refusal to finish the campaign. This impulsive action resulted in financial inconveniences. He would always regret his actions and openly apologized and repented of his anger. Yet, a stringent temper continued to be a thorn in his flesh. At the same time Moody would occasionally reverse his dominant personality and would fear and avoid confrontation. This occurred when Moody did not reprimand Northfield theologian C. I. Scofield (1843–1921) for overriding the chief woman administrator and assuming control of the school's curriculum.[231]

As stewardship leaders, Emma and Moody served on various committees and boards. Emma was known to cautiously scrutinize indiscriminate financial matters to the extent that her emotions would at times interfere with her responses. On the other hand Moody would side-step board financial rulings and find himself trying to control and meddle in ministries which he originally initiated.[232] While at times lacking necessary delegation follow-up skills, his interference would jeopardize timely action. The Chicago Avenue Church held a high pastor turnover rate until Moody's death in 1899. One of those interim pastors, President Charles Blanchard, observed that the church was seriously fractured by Moody's inability to yield to those of the church the governance or ownership of duties and "no pastor found the freedom to develop his own vision without Moody interfering and upsetting the program."[233]

Despite obvious leadership limitations, Emma and Moody continued their mutual support. As an educator Emma possessed an inner instinct to walk nurturingly beside others, including D. L. Moody. As an evangelistic leader, he spiritually complemented Emma as she held in trust for him the Chicago Bible school that would one day carry on their biblical legacy.

"But for this very reason—adding, on your part, all earnestness—along with your faith, manifest also a noble character . . . "

~2 PETER 1:5 WEY~

---

229. Dorsett, "Far From Perfect," para. 7.
230. Findlay, *Dwight L. Moody: American Evangelist*, 368.
231. Dorsett, "Far From Perfect," para. 14–15.
232. Ibid., para. 12.
233. Ibid., para. 13.

7

Bible Work of Chicago, 1873–86

"Early in our work, he [Moody] gave me a Bible, in which he had marked II Timothy 4:1-5. As he handed it to me, he said, pointing to those words, 'This is your ordination.' It was surely his, and by it 'he, being dead, yet speaketh.'"

~Written by Emma Dryer 1916~

As an effective leader and follower, Emma embraced her ordination and calling to initiate the vision that had been presented to her. She received Moody's 2 Timothy 4:5 biblical charge to "keep your head in all situations, endure hardship, do the work of an evangelist, discharge all the duties of your ministry."

Initiation of a Vision

Emma and Moody believed in the power of God's word, the Bible, to *work* effectively in changing lives. Moody emphasized that the combination of God's word with God's work would result in strong and fit Christians.[1] As a visionary leader he initially articulated to Emma his ideals for a school in which the Bible *works*. He envisioned workers trained in God's word who would powerfully penetrate Chicago's urban city and assist in revivals, particularly in his one-on-one body ministry inquiry rooms. Moody suggested to Emma that they initiate a program similar to the Mildmay training of deaconesses which he had observed on his visit to England in 1872. He preferred that young men serve as evangelists and young women assist new believers—a strategy to potentially narrow the ministry distance between clergy and church members.

Moody conveyed this compelling vision to Emma one cold Chicago winter day in early 1873. She recalled meeting him on the Clark Street bridge on her way to church. He had just completed an evangelistic tour in the western states. Emma wrote:

---

1 Moody, *Pleasure and Profit in Bible Study*, 8.

> I said we had missed him, and hoped he could now remain with the Church. He told me about his meetings, and said he was going to another place. I said, there was a great work to be done in Chicago, and remarked, 'You say you have had more than a hundred converts; and all the churches in Chicago, have not, probably, had half as many, in your absence.' In his quick way, he said, 'One hundred converts! What's that? There ought to be thousands.' . . . Then he said, 'I want you to take hold of this work, and stay in it, all your life . . . unite with my Church, and help carry on this work.'[2]

As they approached the North Side Tabernacle Emma spoke with careful scrutiny regarding a full commitment to his church. She continued:

> He said he would tell me further about his plans, but only he and Mrs. Moody knew them yet. Later, he told me, that in the spring, he wanted to take P. P. Bliss with him, on an evangelistic tour, to England. Friends in England had asked him to come. He calculated that he should spend less than a year there,—perhaps eight months, but not more than ten, and he wanted the Christian work, like the Mildmay work, of which he had so much spoken, to begin before he went away.[3]

Moody expressed that upon his return he would assure that the school had a home. He reassured her that it would be a priority and *first work* for him. In response Emma asked him if this first work would even come before the YMCA. Moody emphatically affirmed that he would not let anything separate him from this important ministry. Emma took him at his word.

As they reached the church, Moody asked that she attend the communion service the following Sunday which would be his last service in the North Side Tabernacle before heading east. At that service, attended by Emma's friend David MacNaughtan and others, Moody reiterated to her that he wanted her to remain in his church and live and die in it as well.[4] At that point the church proceeded to hire Emma as superintendent. She led Bible classes and wholeheartedly embraced the large-scale inner vision that she and Moody had for a religious training school—that which would fully materialize in God's timing.

Until then, Emma continually sought to further clarify this vision. She believed that both young men and women should receive a Christian education in order to serve in the churches, Sunday schools, and missions, and to minister to families in all places.[5] On another occasion Moody indicated that the school would be only for women. In response, Emma asked him what could be done with the young men gathered at the YMCA and those at various missions who needed training if he envisioned

2. Emma Dryer to Charles Blanchard, 1916, Biographical File of Emma Dryer.
3. Ibid.
4. Ibid.
5. Ibid.

only educating young women. He said that he did not have any plan. She further pursued: "If you educate young women for Christian work, as done in Mildmay Institutions,—what will you do for the young men?" Moody responded, "Let the theological seminaries take 'em. We'd find ourselves in hot water quick, if we undertook to educate young men."[6]

Moody desired with Emma to create a training school for both young men and women. Yet over the next ten years he cautiously approached this idea of academically competing with seminaries. He did not want the proposed institute to be viewed as inferior training. When they met once again on another occasion to discuss this issue, Emma recalled: "I asked him about his plans for educating the men; and his laconic answer was characteristic,—'I intend to keep the school going, red-hot, all the time.' I asked no further! I only prayed. I believed the Lord was guiding him better than he knew."[7]

Despite Moody's hesitant and irresolute responses, Emma, with her coeducational credentials and normal school training, continued to encourage Moody to fulfill their dream of a training school in which men as well as women would be prepared for mission outreaches. Their friend Reverend Daniels noted that Emma, as a most judicious Christian, had already envisioned launching "a great school of Christ, equal in power and usefulness to Mr. Spurgeon's famous college in London" with students coming "from the level of the people, wholly wanting in professional training, but mighty in the Scriptures."[8]

Based on Moody's stated vision to her, Emma immediately initiated a training program. She laid the preliminary groundwork for a prominent training school that would ultimately have Moody's name on it—a joint vision, initiated by him, but first established by Emma as her work.[9]

Specific Objectives and Activities of the Bible Work

With her organizational gifting, Emma astutely laid out a program for the Bible training school. She publicized specific objectives for what she designated as the *Bible Work* in April of 1873. She included a succinct plan to provide a daily morning school for children unable to attend the public schools; a Saturday sewing school to teach both the Bible and sewing skills; and daily house to house missionary work with Bible readings and visitation of the sick.[10] The program merged personal evangelism and public ministry with immediate practicum or field training occurring primarily in the afternoons and early evenings.

6. Ibid.
7. Ibid.
8. Daniels, *D. L. Moody and His Work*, 188–89.
9. Ruelas, *Women and the Landscape*, 8–12.
10. Bible Work Flyer, April 1873. Biographical File of Emma Dryer.

As the work quickly developed, Emma published an 1875 mission statement for the Bible Work: "To make known salvation through Christ by reading the Bible to individuals in their homes and in small meetings collected for the study of the Scriptures."[11] Just as Moody claimed to be a *man of one book* so also God's word held a central place in Emma's life. The Bible took precedence in her ministry as workers canvassed the neighborhoods with tracts and Bibles donated by the Chicago Bible Society. The target population was limited primarily to women and children with whom the lady workers cordially and personally ministered. They entered homes where they would be naturally received—an evangelization strategy that even Moody knew would be beyond the reach of any man. Emma appointed specific districts for the workers to hold meetings and make visitations. She solicited cooperation from neighboring churches and other groups such as the WCTU, CBS (Chicago Bible Society), Chicago Training School, and the Pacific Garden Mission.

Emma assisted in organizing Bible reading and prayer circles. On the first morning of the 1876 New Year, Emma gathered with others in their Bible Work Room. They entered into a covenant alliance to read God's word together every Sunday for a year following a specific plan that began with the gospel of Matthew. The group published a paper that soon spread to the North Side Tabernacle Women's meetings. The publication included Emma's *Notes for Bible Study* with over three thousand copies distributed. Their group was officially called *The Bible Reading and Prayer Alliance* with Emma as secretary.

Numerous evangelists spread the work of the alliance to other areas. Individuals such as William Blackstone, Dr. William Erdman, Major Daniel Whittle, Mrs. Lucy Helmer, and Mrs. Emma Moody endorsed the Alliance. They procured Sunday school materials which included Emma's notes and calendar, question sections with Scripture references, daily chapters to read, and specific topics for the prayer meetings. Emma found that in time these materials became a self-supporting publication of the Bible Work. Her notes were additionally transferred to Canada for further publication by Mr. Roffe and renamed *The Lamp of Life and Notes for Bible Study*. Until 1914 Mary M. Jenkins from Kilbourn, Wisconsin, assisted by contributing to the Sunday school lessons primarily during a time when Emma was experiencing physical vision difficulties.[12]

As the school developed Emma added special Cottage and Mother Prayer Meetings to the Saturday Sewing Schools as effective extensions to the home front. Emma's friend from Victor, New York, Miss Mary Moore, who later married J. M. Hitchcock, kept a daily journal of 189 pages from January 1 to December 29, 1886. She recorded families that were visited, the number of cottage and Sunday school meetings, classes that were taught, and details of her experiences.[13] She documented the following re-

---

11. Getz, *The Story of Moody Bible Institute*, 43.
12. Emma Dryer to Charles Blanchard, 1916, Biographical File of Emma Dryer.
13. Bible Work Guidelines, Reports, and Bulletins. Biographical File of Emma Dryer.

warding accomplishments: thirty-six Bibles received; sixty-four given and sold; 3,273 papers and tracts received with 5,669 papers and tracts distributed; 337 garments received and 422 garments distributed; $66.25 money received and $65.25 money distributed; four conversions with three backsliders restored; 598 brought to the Bible study and 2,992 visits.[14]

Based on her own solid Sunday school background, Emma prepared Bible workers to teach numerous Sunday school classes at the North Side Tabernacle and Chicago Avenue Church. The annual Bible Work report from March 1, 1874, documented that a Chicago public school principal, Mrs. Gardner, assisted Emma. Other teachers included Emma's friend, Mary Moore Hitchcock, and a Bible worker named Miss Clara B. Wright.[15] The church's Sunday school classes had increased from the previous year's attendance of 1,500. This growth was due partly to the addition of a Chinese Bible class and the popularity of Emma's Bible class. Wheaton College President Blanchard's *Christian Cynosure* reported: "Miss E. Dryer, whose name has for many years been associated with the Bible work of Chicago, has 150 men and women every Sunday afternoon in her Bible class in Moody's church and there is room for more."[16]

At Emma's Bible class church members would pray and have open discussions regarding the Bible and the work of the church. Emma was especially interested in deepening the role of women in the Christian community as well as in their own families. It was with this goal in mind that she led the Ladies Bible Study. She urged women to take an active role in their children's education and upbringing. She exhorted them to participate in Christian service as an example to their children on how to serve Christ in their community.

On June 1, 1882, the Bible workers extended their Sunday school class experience to the county boys' jail. In conjunction with a jail day school, Sheriff Mann and his deputies gave their wholehearted attention and assistance.[17] The Bible Work entries from June 1882 to February 1883 presented a descriptive picture of this jail ministry:

> Miss Dryer had held a Sunday school there and took, by that means ascertained, the need among the boys of instruction in the elementary branches, and took measures in having them taught to read and write . . . The school commenced with 25 boys and about as many books of different kinds, that had been sent from various sources. Sheriff Mann was interested in the work and sent a Blackboard and a set of Outline Maps. Mr. Albert Day sent 55 school books and 2 large maps of Palestine and Bible Lands and has shown an active interest in the school. Mr. B. Norris sent a nickel clock and Mrs. Ferry of Lake Forrest sent 2 dozen slates. At Christmas and New Years, packages of handsome coats were sent to the boys by Mr. Schey who during the summer

14. Chicago Evangelization Society, 29 December 1886, Historical Collection.
15. Emma Dryer to Charles Blanchard, 1916, Biographical File of Emma Dryer.
16. *Christian Cynosure*, National Christian Association, 1884, 12.
17. Bible Work Report, 17 February 1882, Biographical File of Emma Dryer.

sent pretty cards with Scripture texts printed on them. Besides these gifts paper and books have been sent by different persons.[18]

Emma welcomed these gifts especially in the summer as the jail population increased with the courts on vacation. This break gave more opportunity for Emma and her workers to teach. She recognized the following individuals, including prisoners from the *Debtors Department*, for their assistance in the jail ministry:

> Mrs. [Lucy] Meyer of the city also helped 2 weeks, when the school was the largest. Since the 14th of Oct, Miss Ward of Lake Forrest has assisted in 2 or 3 days of every week. Among the boys in school at present are 2 Germans and a Chinaman who are learning to read and write our language. In the Woman's Dept. we frequently find a young woman who is unable to read or write. And during the winter some one of the ladies has given their instruction in those branches.[19]

The report detailed the daily jail program beginning with roll call, Scripture reading, recitation of the Ten Commandments, singing, and prayer. Academics included reading, arithmetic, geography, and writing. The 9:00 a.m. Sunday school class recited the catechism, the regular Sunday school lesson, and sang the doxology. The day school jail report recorded 221 lessons; complete attendance of 4,055; fifty-two Sunday school lessons; and an average attendance of twenty.[20]

For the most part Emma and her workers lived and operated in the near Chicago west side Haymarket and Union Park areas. Industrial factories were prevalent and close to their assigned districts.[21] Emma trained her workers to journal and record their activities and progress in these districts. For a time Nathaniel Bouton, Chicago's public works superintendent with whom Emma served in the relief efforts following the Chicago Fire, accepted oversight of the Bible workers' reports.[22] They would present reports at a meeting in the Bible Work Room where supporters and friends were invited.

In an attempt to develop constituency ownership and participation in the ministry's vision, Emma included the following invitation in her July 1874 report:

> The Bible Work, to which your interest is invited, began in the Spring of 1873, in the efforts of one person . . . We gratefully recognize the assistance which you have given this work. Will you not make yourself more intimately acquainted with the daily efforts. A morning meeting for prayer and study is held by the Bible workers at this place from 8–10 except Saturday. The meeting

---

18. Ibid., June 1882 to February 27, 1883.
19. Report of Jail Work, Biographical File of Emma Dryer.
20. Ibid.
21. See Ogorek, "Dryer, Emma," 251.
22. Emma Dryer to Charles Blanchard, 1916, Biographical File of Emma Dryer.

> Monday a.m. is a weekly report and prayer meeting. We shall be glad to see you at any of those meetings.[23]

At one meeting in 1873, Ella Stevens reported 123 children in the infant Sabbath school class and 100 girls in the sewing classes. In another meeting the workers delineated their progress in an outreach among *shopgirls*. These lower class, at-risk for prostitution salesgirls, worked at urban stores such as Marshall Field's. They would be approached by a Bible worker who presented the gospel. Emma believed that this was an innovative and interesting aspect of the Bible Work. She documented the progress in a February 1882 report. Her workers had visited twelve shops, held twenty meetings over a two month period, and had sold twelve Bibles while in the stores.[24]

The Bible Work highlighted another objective—retaining female respectability and morality. Emma experienced no trepidation for herself when walking the streets of a crime-infested city. However, she was extremely protective and conscientious of the safety and integrity of her workers. She sheltered them from areas potentially populated with inordinate individuals from saloons and prisons. She kept her ladies from hours after dark to avoid appearances of prostitution. Emma realized that in Moody's evangelistic zeal for souls he often overlooked such precautions. She reasoned: "I know that the Bible Work represents the legitimate work for women, but that such night work for young women is attended by dangers too many."[25] Emma tenaciously resolved that her Bible workers would honorably minister to others in order to transmit the societal spirit of godliness into the darkness of their surroundings.[26]

With Emma's education and Bible background she ingenuously aligned both a mission and a social service focus. She combined home evangelism with domestic training and integrated her sewing schools with a Working Woman's Home emphasizing both job and social skills.[27] Imitating her Massachusetts missionary predecessor John Sergeant, she utilized the tool of education to open doors into homes and hearts. Her training schedule for the workers included daily chores, two hours of study, and various training classes. By 1884 Emma added night school instruction for her workers who trained immigrants to read the Bible as they studied Sunday school materials. The sessions were held at the Chicago Avenue Church as well as the West Side Tabernacle at the corner of Indiana and Morgan Streets.[28] In November 1885 Emma explained to her friend, Nettie McCormick, the far-reaching extent of her work that included "preparatory studies for . . . women hoping to further their Christian training in order to enter the foreign mission field." In addition, two evening schools and

---

23. Bible Work Report, July 1874, Biographical File of Emma Dryer.
24. Ibid., 17 February 1882, Biographical File of Emma Dryer.
25. Joiner, *Sin in the City*, 51.
26. Ruelas, *Women and the Landscape*, 10.
27. Foster, et al., *Educating Clergy*, 201.
28. Getz, *The Story of Moody Bible Institute*, 73.

five other weekly meetings prepared young men for college. Emma proclaimed to Nettie the unceasing, yet satisfying, activity of this work.[29]

With Emma's background as a former college preceptress and instructor she quite capably directed the early curriculum development of the Bible Work. She patterned it after the ISNU Model School, Holyoke Schools,[30] Grattan Guinness's (1835–1910) East London Institute for missionary training of men, and the Mildmay Deaconess program in England. She had the privilege of entertaining Mr. Guinness at the Bible Work Home at 100 Warren Avenue. His daughter Geraldine married the son of China missionary Hudson Taylor. With these connections Emma received, with Moody in attendance, some excellent advice for structuring the Bible Institute.[31] Thereafter, Emma initiated training classes or clinics for her workers. She included Monday evening medical lectures at Central Music Hall with lessons on anatomy, physiology, and hygiene to prepare these workers for the mission field.[32]

Workers also received training in praying for the sick at weekly prayer meetings held in the YMCA Bible Work Room. Emma reported: "Many were healed. We taught and advised those that came,—seeking the truth for them, and for ourselves. We also secured instruction to our workers, by Lady Physicians, and put strong emphasis on healthful living, and proper care of our bodies (I Cor. 3:16, 17, and I Cor. 6:19)."[33] By 1878 seventeen of Emma's workers were either training others in God's word or serving as missionaries overseas.[34]

The June 8, 1882, issue of the *Christian Cynosure* reported an open invitation to these Bible Work training sessions at the YMCA. Reverend Hugh MacDonald Scott (1848–1909), professor of *Ecclesiastical History* at the Chicago Theological Seminary, would be holding allocation classes while lecturing on Wednesday afternoons with an *Introduction to the New Testament*.[35] While there, he attended other sessions and activities of the Bible Work home and the school's upcoming May Institutes. Professor Scott also lectured to an average attendance of seventy-five women from the Bible Work and west side churches on *Church History*.[36]

As Moody maintained his busy schedule conducting revival meetings at Oxford and Cambridge, Emma continued with the progress of the Bible Work. The October 14, 1875, edition of the *Christian Cynosure* reported that Miss Dryer, who conducted the Bible Work along with many others, held ninety-four cottage prayer-meetings

29. Joiner, *Sin in the City,* 48.

30. Mount Holyoke College in Massachusetts trained young ladies as educators. Northfield Conference and Bible Work speaker and Christian educator Andrew Murray founded his Huguenot Seminary in 1873 patterned after Mount Holyoke College.

31. Emma Dryer to Charles Blanchard, 1916, Biographical File of Emma Dryer.

32. Ibid.

33. Ibid.

34. Howat, *Ten Girls Who Made History,* 31.

35. *Christian Cynosure*, National Christian Association, June 8, 1882, 1.

36. Bible Work Report, 17 February 1882, Biographical File of Emma Dryer.

with many other varied activities.[37] Within just a few years of starting the work, Emma had overseen an incredible program with her Bible workers. They conducted not only their regularly scheduled hours for Bible study but also 673 cottage prayer meetings, 78 meetings for mothers, 165 school prayer meetings, 502 sewing school sessions, 2,820 Bible readings, 479 visits to the poor in health, and 10,628 tract and religious literature distributions.[38] The *Christian Cynosure* reported in 1882 a tremendous increase of the work:

> Miss E. Dryer, Superintendent of the Bible work of the YMCA in Chicago, reports that during 1881 they held 1014 cottage prayer-meetings, 206 mothers' meetings, 252 school prayer-meetings, 219 sewing-school sessions with an attendance of 18557; gathered into religions meetings 1999, into Bible classes, 752; Bible visits, 2895; scripture conversations and readings, 3882; Bible visits to the sick, 1460; persons induced to read the Bible regularly, 407; hopefully led to Christ, 182; errands to the poor, 658; Bibles donated and sold, 109; papers and tracts distributed, 8,117; garments received for distribution, 1958; money received last quarter, $970.[39]

Emma fondly remembered the participants of her early Bible Work classes with whom she maintained lasting relationships. She shared the orderly procedure of those classes held in the Bible Work Room at the YMCA: "We were accustomed to say the young men's names, at the head of the list, in the following order: Morrison, McLean, MacNaughtan, Kappeler, Lundgren . . . Johnson, Young, Caugherty . . . friends who attended Bible studies and prayer meetings together."[40] They would meet on the morning of New Year's day with the purpose of planning the Bible classes and selecting Bible passages for the year. They scheduled social gatherings for the afternoons.

On July 1, 1882, Emma detailed yet another open invitation on Bible Work stationary for the following meetings:

- Tuesday, Bible reading at 10 a.m. with the Bible Reading & Prayer Alliance
- Wednesday, Bible Workers' Reports, Normal Bible Class, International Sunday School Lesson, 10 a.m.
- Office Hours—10 to 12 a.m., Monday, Tuesday, Saturday. It is important to close the office at 12. Miss E. Dryer

Throughout these early days of the Bible Work others maintained that students envisioning work in missions had most certainly received appropriate Bible instruction and preparation.[41]

37. *Christian Cynosure,* National Christian Association, October 14, 1875, 9.
38. Daniels, *His Word, Works, and Workers,* 504.
39. *Christian Cynosure,* National Christian Association, February 23, 1882, 13.
40. Emma Dryer to Charles Blanchard, 1916, Biographical File of Emma Dryer.
41. History's Women, "Emeline Dryer: Christian Educator and Administrator," para. 9.

Bible Work of Chicago, 1873–86

Structure and Operation of the Bible Training School

While Moody traveled abroad from June 7, 1873, to August 14, 1875, Emma concentrated on the immediate implementation of her objectives with a formal structuring of the program. Nathaniel Bouton agreed to serve as the Bible Work's treasurer and auditor. He continued handling the Bible workers' weekly reports. Emma assumed the office of secretary and explained her early role: "I had called, as Secretary, every meeting of the Bible-Work, and had selected and nominated every officer of the Bible-Work Board, and Woman's Council, until the re-organization into the Chicago Evangelization Society. And so I knew our hopes and history. I praise God that... through those years, we had a united Board and Council of consecrated Christian friends."[42]

By 1877 Emma's appointed board adopted an official charter to govern the Bible Work. T. W. Harvey served as president, Emma Dryer as superintendent, Nettie McCormick and Emma Moody as co-vice presidents, E. G. Keith secretary, Joshua Helmer treasurer, and E. S. Albro as auditor.[43] Every Wednesday a leadership meeting with Bible instruction and prayer was held at the YMCA. Mrs. McCormick served with Emma on the board as the only other woman consecutively for many years. Other men were added including Nathaniel Bouton, Major Whittle, John Farwell, Henry Willing, Mr. Scott, Mr. Houghteling, and Cyrus McCormick.[44]

Encouraged by Moody's business expertise, Emma kept updated records to document contributors and maintain accurate accounts of the progress of the Bible Work. By 1877 Emma successfully implemented Moody's marketing and donor approaches with documentation that assured contributors of the security of their investments. Reverend Daniels registered his belief in Emma's ministry during the early years of the Bible Work. He promoted it as a flourishing enterprise and one that even Moody considered to be his most significant undertaking on behalf of God's kingdom.[45]

The structure and vitality of Moody's Chicago Avenue Church influenced the structure and progress of the Bible Work. From 1875 until Moody's death in 1899 seven individuals served as the pastor of the church with numerous interim pastors—J. H. Harwood (1866–69), Reverend William J. Erdman (1876–78), Charles M. Morton (1878–79), George C. Needham (1879–81), Charles Blanchard (Spring 1883–December 1884; 1891–93), Charles F. Goss (1885–90), and Dr. R. A. Torrey (1894–1906).[46]

---

42. Emma Dryer to Charles Blanchard, 1916, Biographical File of Emma Dryer.

43. Getz, *The Story of Moody Bible Institute*, 53.

44. Emma Dryer to Caroline Waite, 18 July 1924; Bible Work Report, 17 February 1882, Biographical File of Emma Dryer.

45. Daniels, *D. L. Moody and His Work*, 188.

46. Chapman, *The Life and Work of Dwight Lyman Moody*, 108; Charles Blanchard stated: "I came to supply the pulpit, in the Chicago Avenue Church in the spring of 1883 and continued with the church until December 1884." Charles Blanchard to William Norton, 4 June 1913, Biographical File of Emma Dryer.

Emma agonizingly watched this fluctuation of church leadership. In 1878 she expressed that Dr. Erdman's resignation had been difficult for her and her workers and that no one could possibly take his place.

Sometime after Needham's resignation Moody displayed once again his confidence in Emma by asking her to contact Reverend Moorehead. She wrote: "Mr. Moody asked me to secure Reverend Dr. W. G. Moorehead, as Pastor of the Church, and Teacher in the Bible-Work; as Dr. Erdman had once been. Dr. Moorehead was our Leader in our May Bible Institute . . . and he was greatly desired, as a teacher, by all who heard him. But he would not leave Xenia; and by diligent search Mr. Moody found Reverend Charles F. Goss, who was Pastor, until his health failing, he went to the Western Coast."[47]

Moody conducted a three month revival campaign in Chicago in 1876. Meetings were held at Dr. Goodwin's Congregational Church, the Centenary Methodist Episcopal Church, the Methodist Church on Western Avenue, and the Second Baptist Church.[48] When Moody returned to Northfield in 1875, his decision to no longer reside in Chicago created uncertainty for those at the Chicago Avenue Church. He continued brief ongoing connections with the Bible Work. However, his commitment and participation were viewed as sporadic and quite unpredictable[49]—thus diminishing the effectiveness of his visionary role for the CAC and the Bible Work.

Nonetheless, while at the Chicago Avenue Church dedication ceremony in July 1876, Moody made an appeal for support of the Bible Work. Thereafter, with Moody's assurance that she was a vital player in the permanent establishment of their envisioned Bible institute, Emma unflinchingly forged ahead with prolonged plans for publicizing the school. Blanchard's 1883 *Christian Cynosure* headlined a letter from Emma to members of the Prayer Alliances, established in the United States and Canada, with the heading *Christian Training school—Miss E. Dryer, Superintendent of the Bible Work in Chicago*:

> During the recent convention held in this city by Mr. Moody, he announced that measures are on foot for the establishment here of a Training-school for young men and young women in Christian work. Already young women are engaged in it, and we hope to see their numbers increase. The purpose is to fit Christian workers for the work of our Home Missions in our cities and on our frontiers, to visit from house to house, and, with open Bible, try to add souls to Christ, and to build up his cause. By this means many are excellently fitted for foreign fields, and our Lord will certainly lead his children to their best place of labor, if they will obediently follow his leadings.

---

47. Emma Dryer to Charles Blanchard, 1916, Biographical File of Emma Dryer.
48. Ibid.
49. Joiner, *Sin in the City*, 53.

With a renewed infusion of hope and vision, Emma continued with a charge for people of all ages and backgrounds to pray for these laborers to be sent forth: "Send them at home, send them here, send them all over the world, that this Gospel of the kingdom shall be preached in all the world for a witness unto all nations, AND THEN SHALL THE END COME." And with a special emphasis on young believers she urgently pleaded: "Who, among the multitude of young Christians in our land, is ready to seek first the kingdom of God, and his righteousness, trusting his promise to add all needed things?"[50]

Citywide Locations

After the Chicago Fire Emma found temporary residence with various individuals including educator and author Elizabeth Stansbury Kirkland (1828–96) and her sister, both originally from Geneva, New York.[51] Emma resided at their Kirkland School on the north side where new seminary buildings had just been constructed. Moody shared with Emma that some of his friends were living there and these new connections could prove beneficial for securing a location for the new training school.[52]

Meanwhile, under Moody's direction the Illinois Street Church set up a temporary building on the corner of Ontario and Wells Street known as the North Side Tabernacle with funds he had secured from his contacts in the East. The building, dedicated on December 24, 1871, was immediately used as a relief center for those in Chicago. With her educational background and Moody's urgent prompting, Emma quickly began setting up and leading evening Bible classes on the book of Genesis for young people at the Tabernacle. She used her prolific teaching skills to train women to read the Bible and scheduled regular home visitations for them to read God's word to others.

Moody's evangelistic crusades and newly elected position as president of the Illinois Sunday School Union consumed his time and energy. Nonetheless, Emma maintained contact with him and continued to focus on leadership of the Bible Work. Viewed as an *indomitable little lady*,[53] she unrelentingly urged Moody to secure a permanent residence for her workers. Emma pleadingly explained: "Our workers boarded where they conveniently could; and we felt the need of a Home where study and work could be more advantageously united, and the health of the workers, properly guarded; and we all prayed for the enlargement of the Bible-Work, as Mr. Moody ... had so hopefully planned."[54] As Emma began recruiting enthusiastic workers, she persistently felt a prodigious responsibility for them. After discussing this situation

---

50. *Christian Cynosure*, National Christian Association, November 1, 1883, 12.
51. Wanamaker, *Book News: A Monthly Survey of General Literature*, 28.
52. Emma Dryer to Charles Blanchard, 1916, Biographical File of Emma Dryer.
53. Day, *Bush Aglow*, 263.
54. Emma Dryer to Charles Blanchard, 1916, Biographical File of Emma Dryer.

with Moody she proceeded to rent space for her Bible workers next to the North Side Tabernacle.[55] The training school began to emerge as a reality although according to A. P. Fitt it was *a slow evolution.*[56]

Before Moody left for New York, Emma and her YWCA friend Sarah G. Cleveland met with him in the additional Bible Work space provided by the Relief and Aid Society in Room 1, Relief Block, 51–54 LaSalle Street.[57] They shared how rapidly the work was growing with their recent enlistment of Miss Ella Stevens as a new worker. Mrs. Cleveland and Emma were prayerfully listening to Moody's plans for his upcoming United Kingdom trip. He and Sankey believed they would be gone for only a few months. However, in spite of his envisioned plans for the training school, Emma recalled years later, "God's Plan contemplated larger usefulness for Messrs. Moody and Sankey than they knew."[58] Little did Emma realize that just as missionary David Brainerd experienced the burden and grief of time spent with seemingly no progress, she would be required to wait fifteen years for the manifestation of their mutual vision for a training school.

While at the North Side Tabernacle shortly before leaving Chicago, Moody told Emma about the purchase of land on the corner of Chicago Avenue and LaSalle Street. The construction of the new church building would progress slowly until Moody's return from the United Kingdom. He also explained the recent church name change to Chicago Avenue Church. Although Moody reasoned that the new name would more accurately locate the church, Emma expressed that she did not like the name. After Moody's death in 1899 she shared that the Chicago Avenue Church renamed Moody Church was now more properly identified.

With Moody's departure Emma received encouragement and financial backing from her friend Nettie McCormick. Nettie quickly secured additional rooms at the YMCA to serve as headquarters. YMCA superintendent William Van Arsdale provided main offices and rooms for the Bible Work. This arrangement yielded temporary financial and space relief for both the growing Tabernacle and the training school. It also helped to centralize the Bible Work and increased the visibility and recognition of Moody's interest and support for the school.[59]

By June of 1876 the Chicago Avenue Church was dedicated and the building paid in full by royalties from Moody and Sankey's hymnal sales. Meanwhile, the Bible Work spread to several diverse locations including vacant buildings, various church facilities, and hastily pitched tents. It was loyally characterized as "an amorphus thing

---

55. Day, *Bush Aglow,* 263.

56. Fitt, *Moody Still Lives,* 94.

57. Donation letter from Emma Dryer, 1 May 1874 from Room 1, Relief Bloc, 51 LaSalle Street, Chicago—a Bible Work flyer from April 1874 lists this address, Biographical File of Emma Dryer.

58. Emma Dryer to Charles Blanchard, 1916, Biographical File of Emma Dryer.

59. Ibid.

... [with] an annoying vitality."⁶⁰ Although still closely connected to the Chicago Avenue Church, the Bible Work incorporated in 1878 and moved operations to the YMCA in downtown Chicago. Bible classes were held in Farwell Hall at 100 Madison Street with another office located in 1884 on Randolph and Dearborn Streets.⁶¹ In the fall of 1881 Emma's friends, Mr. and Mrs. Joshua Helmer, donated their beautiful home in a prime residential area located at 100 Warren Avenue near Paulina Street. The location served not only as a home for Emma's volunteers, but also as a home for Chicago Avenue Church associates, itinerary missionaries, and visiting ministers.⁶²

Financial and Personal Support

During these years of waiting, Emma's faith journey demanded that she not rely on herself but on God's faithfulness and provision. From the beginning she refused to receive a salary. She wrote: "From year to year I had no salary, and by His gracious help, we never had debt, nor an empty treasury."⁶³ Realizing Emma's walk of faith and the financial needs of her Chicago friend, Mrs. Moody in 1880 wrote to their mutual friend Nettie McCormick. She explained that Emma's reason for being unsalaried was to highlight the spirit of servanthood among her co-workers and to prevent any perception of unfairness.⁶⁴ Mrs. William Shute, a coworker and friend of Emma who had initially introduced her to the McCormicks, suggested to Nettie and to Moody, that they not designate the money as a salary. In that way Emma would be more receptive and effectively able to maintain her integrity and autonomy.⁶⁵ They were correct.

Emma would not make financial appeals on her own behalf. She composed letters with requests for funds such as the following letter sent to her friend Nettie McCormick on November 11, 1881: "Please do not . . . think when I tell you about our money affairs that I am suggesting a place for me in your benevolence—not so . . . Do not give to the Bible Work what you should give elsewhere, and only you—not I, know where you should give to the Lord."⁶⁶ Emma could confidently state: "'Owe no man anything' has been strictly followed in the operations of the Bible Work & with the Lord's blessing."⁶⁷

---

60. Day, *Bush Aglow*, 263.

61. On Bible Work stationary, 16 September 1884, Biographical File of Emma Dryer. From this address Emma frequently gathered the latest news regarding the McCormick family's New York and world travels.

62. Blanchard, "Miss Dryer and the Moody Church," May 1925; *Christian Cynosure*, National Christian Association, June 8, 1882, 1.

63. Emma Dryer to Charles Blanchard, 1916, Biographical File of Emma Dryer.

64. Joiner, *Sin in the City*, 51.

65. Ibid., 52.

66. Ibid.

67. Emma Dryer to Nettie McCormick, 14 November 1887, Biographical File of Emma Dryer.

Emma's trust in the Lord as a faithful provider aligned her with the teachings she heard at the Northfield conferences from speakers such as George Müller. With experience for trusting God at his English orphanages, Müller testified: "Forsaking every other reliance but God . . . looking to him alone for the supply of every want, all that . . . [was] needed was furnished."[68] Similarly, Emma beheld God's faithfulness as funds and supplies emerged from numerous sources.

With her consistent and reliable communication skills, Emma would send out monthly reports to all who assisted in any way. In Emma's April 1873 Bible Work flyer she reported:

> In God's Providence this work originated with D. L. Moody, whose efforts to maintain and enlarge it were interrupted by his mission to England and Scotland. On his return he hopes to resume his connection with it. The subjoined report will give a clearer idea of the work. New features will be added as the Lord sends means to carry it on. This He has done from month to month, and greatly encouraged the hope of its permanent success.[69]

On the other side of this report Emma wrote by hand: "We are in need of clothing for children & adults; children whom we wish to send to S. School if decently clothed would attend church. We solicit your prayerful consideration of this work & of your relation to it, wishing you to contribute to its support only as our Lord shall direct you."

On July 1, 1874, Emma continued her reporting of the Lord's provision. Mrs. Horatio G. Spafford donated clothing, quilt squares, and ninety yards of calico material. Dr. George Shipman provided seventy tracts while the Bible Society supplied twelve Bibles.[70] On another occasion Emma listed furniture and numerous gifts from over thirty female donors including her friends Nettie McCormick, Mrs. John Farwell, Sarah Moore, Mrs. William Shute, and Sarah Clarke.[71] Ellen Blanchard, wife of Wheaton College President Charles Blanchard, also supported Emma and her Bible Work assistant Miss Parmelia Hand by volunteering to fix second-hand garments to distribute to the poor.[72]

When Moody's career as an international revivalist escalated, Emma's ministry was faithfully maintained. She received donations from her friends and acquaintances as well as from D. L. Moody. Characteristic of an effective visionary, Moody generously financed Emma's ministry by sending a thousand dollars annually.[73] Additionally, Moody graciously introduced Emma to his well-established business contacts

---

68. Müller, *The Life of Trust,* xxiii.
69. Bible Work Report, April 1873, Biographical File of Emma Dryer.
70. Ibid., 1 July 1874.
71. Ibid., 17 February 1882.
72. Charles Albert Blanchard Papers, Wheaton College Archives and Special Collections.
73. Dorsett, *A Passion For Souls*, 272–73.

and evangelical influences in the Chicago area. Even while Moody spent less time in Chicago, they willingly put their support behind Emma. At one point the Metropolitan Bank president, Mr. Keith, made a donation of five hundred dollars to provide housing for the workers. Emma gratefully acknowledged the support of this generous benefactor.[74]

On the Bible Work flyer of April 1873 Nathaniel Bouton acknowledged his support for the Bible Work: "I am acquainted with the work represented by Miss E. Dryer . . . and cordially endorse it to the public."[75] Emma shared her mutual endorsement of Mr. Bouton. He encouraged her to continue working with women and also with men who likewise needed instruction. She asked Mr. Bouton, "How could I go on with the work?" He told her not to stop her work but to leave it up to him to take the necessary steps. As one of the first contributors toward her Bible Work ministry, she described him as "an active, sympathizing friend, [who] raised money for us, gave kindly advice, and was one of the first friends to help in the enlargement of Mr. Moody's plans."[76] Mr. Bouton also introduced Emma to affluent businessman John Crerar from the Chicago firm of Crerar, Adams & Company. This Bible Work supporter was responsible for supplying railroad supplements such as lamps and lanterns to the burgeoning Midwest railroad companies.

Emma also received sacrificial backing from the families of friends and other ministries. When her YMCA friend, Sarah Cleveland, became ill and unable to assist at the Bible Work, Sarah requested that her annual salary of $1,000 be given to the other workers. Emma also gave thanks for the YMCA superintendents, Mr. Van Arsdale and his successor Mr. A. T. Hemingway. Likewise, she expressed her gratitude for Mr. T. B. Carter who was the CBS Secretary. Emma saw all these individuals as resourceful friends to whom she was indebted for their wise counsel and unfailing support.[77]

Emma frequently recognized the collaboration of Chicago's Christians throughout the burgeoning metropolis. She acknowledged the friendship of these early supporters: Mr. and Mrs. John Eberhart; Reverend and Mrs. William Daniels; Reverend and Mrs. Goodwin; Mrs. William Shute; Nettie McCormick; Sarah Cleveland; Nathaniel Bouton; Mr. T. B. Carter; John Crerar; Mr. and Mrs. Joshua Helmer; John Farwell; Mary Ann Hubbard; Mr. and Mrs. F. W. Savage; members of the YWCA and the YMCA, and members from numerous churches and missions.[78]

With years of denominational contacts Emma comfortably and inexorably reached out to other churches in the Chicago area. She reported on February 17, 1882, that the women at the First Congregational Church held a reception for other

---

74. Joiner, *Sin in the City*, 53.
75. Bible Work Report, April 1874, Biographical File of Emma Dryer.
76. Ibid.; Emma Dryer to Charles Blanchard, 1916, Biographical File of Emma Dryer.
77. Ibid.
78. Ibid.

west side churches. They took up a collection of food for the Bible Worker home. She gratefully noted:

> Occasional donations of canned fruit, vegetables & other edibles were generously presented to the Home. For these, & the liberal gifts previously bestowed, we are sincerely grateful & desire to say to the friends who have carried & who still carry this work on their hearts, that their generous Christian interest has contributed more largely than they know, both to encourage & to establish this work. The responsibility—of it would be overwhelming, but for your prayers & efforts.[79]

On the opposite side of her May 1, 1874, Bible Work donation letter Emma shared about their great need for funds with which to carry them through the summer months. There was a constant need for children and adult clothing and especially for money to buy milk for the children who attended the Sunday school and day school. Emma ended the letter by expressing that an ever abiding support for the needy comes from Christ. His provisions would draw them into a deeper relationship with him.[80]

Emma's earlier days as a preceptress at ISNU equipped her with a sensitivity toward the housing and work conditions of her Bible readers. Emma wrote to Nettie McCormick in 1881: "I find it difficult . . . to get places for some of them in their districts, on account of high prices for board on the one hand, and then the miserable accommodations which their means secure on the other." In 1877 a coworker and friend, Mrs. William Shute, wrote to Nettie that Emma was lacking adequate funds for her workers.[81] With a humanitarian heart Nettie unfailingly responded financially to this request.

Those in organizational leadership must purposefully and sensitively place an emphasis on supplying their workers with the assets and materials with which to become effective and dynamic in their professions and ministries.[82] Moody had spent many years in raising funds for a number of evangelical and educational purposes. In spite of his traveling schedule he continued to solicit funds on behalf of the Bible Work from philanthropists and those with an evangelistic passion for the poverty-stricken lower class.[83] In Moody's donation appeal letters, he stipulated that $600 would annually provide care for one Bible worker.[84] Similarly, in an appeal letter from Emma written on Bible Work stationary she trustingly quoted Scripture from Isaiah 4:10–11 and John 4:35–38:

79. Bible Work Report, 17 February 1882, Biographical File of Emma Dryer.

80. Bible Work Donation Letter Request from Emma Dryer, 1 May 1874, Biographical File of Emma Dryer.

81. Joiner, *Sin in the City*, 52.

82. Butt, *The Velvet Covered Brick*, 40.

83. Dorsett, *A Passion For Souls*, 169.

84. Bible Work Donation Letter Request from Emma Dryer, 1 May 1874, Biographical File of Emma Dryer.

> For as the rain cometh down, and the snow from heaven, and returneth not thither, but watereth the earth, and maketh it bring forth and bud, that it may give seed to the sower, and breads to the eater: So shall my word be that goeth forth out of my mouth; it shall not return unto me void, but it shall accomplish that which I please, and it shall prosper in the thing whereto I sent it.[85]

Emma believed in God's provision of joy toward those who sowed into God's harvest for souls and those who would reap through the ministry of the Bible Work. She was living what she had heard from China Inland missionary Hudson Taylor: "God's work done in God's way will never lack God's supplies."[86]

Spafford Support

Two other reapers for the kingdom were attorney and realtor Horatio Spafford (1828-88) and his wife Anna (1842-1923)—friends of D. L. Moody and supporters of the Bible Work. They also associated with premillennialist William Blackstone, WCTU activist Frances Willard, and Quaker-author Hannah Whitall Smith. Other mutual Chicago friends included Ira Sankey, P. P. Bliss, Major Whittle, Mr. E. W. Blatchford (1826–1915), Cyrus McCormick, and Charles M. Henderson. Henderson was the proprietor of C. M. Henderson and Company wholesale boot and shoe store where Moody previously worked.

In 1870 Moody, with the financial support of Horatio, initiated his well-known *Noon Prayer Meetings* attended by businessmen and other professionals. Horatio's daughter, Bertha Spafford Vester (1878–1968), recalled her father's early description of Moody as a poor self-supporting shoe salesman eager to share the gospel at every available opportunity.[87] Horatio, desiring to see Moody free to minister fulltime, approached him regarding his debt. He suggested that men such as Charles Henderson could supply advance quarterly contributions beginning the first month of that year.[88] Greatly encouraged, Moody recommended that perhaps Spafford could also oversee payment of the debt of their friend Major Whittle. This was expressed in Moody's letter to Whittle on January 30, 1874, with the intent of freeing Whittle for the ministry.[89] Horatio not only supported Moody financially but backed the work of the YMCA and the reconstruction process after the Chicago Fire.

Known as an autonomous and analytical free-thinker, Attorney Spafford found himself in a strained relationship with Moody's friend, Cyrus McCormick. He argued for a *conflict of interest clause* regarding donations for Mr. McCormick. He based this

---

85. Letter to Nettie McCormick from D. L. Moody, May 1873, Biographical File of Emma Dryer.
86. Taylor, *Hudson Taylor and the China Inland Mission*, 42.
87. Vester, *Our Jerusalem*, 20.
88. Ibid., 21.
89. Ibid. As a side note, this letter with an approximately two hundred word paragraph clearly displays Moody's carefree grammar style—no punctuation and very little capitalization.

on a questionable payback for support of the Theological Seminary that Cyrus had financially endowed. Nevertheless, Spafford's daughter recalled that despite their conflicting discrepancies and personal attacks, a respectful friendship continued.[90]

Horatio reached a season in his life when he chose to concentrate on Christian ministries and charities, especially those of his friend D. L. Moody.[91] This inspiration was due in part to the devastation of the Chicago Fire. At the time of the fire Mrs. Moody fled with her children and brother to Buena Park where they stayed with the Spafford family.[92] As a realtor Horatio realized the fire had brought a tremendous financial loss to Chicago although his family and their cottage in Lake View were spared.[93] He joined in the relief effort with Anna as a board member for the *Chicago Home of the Friendless*, an orphanage for abandoned infants.

Approximately two years later Horatio and Anna suffered yet another tragedy. *The Ville du Havre* on November 23, 1873, shipwrecked in the Atlantic Ocean with their four daughters lost at sea, and Anna alone surviving the debilitating experience. At this time Moody was in Paris en route to revival meetings in Scotland. He met Anna, unbearably devastated from the loss of her children, in a London hotel on December 24, 1873. Anna later reflected on Moody's response stating that she needed to console him in his grief over the death of her children even more so than her receiving his comfort. Anna's daughter Bertha, born five years after the shipwreck, accurately confirmed Moody as an emotionally demonstrative man while especially remembering his typically eighteenth-century lengthy black coat.[94]

During this difficult time Moody compassionately counseled Mrs. Spafford to lean not on her natural understanding. In his own persuasive way he encouraged her to join his Chicago work in order to forget her own despair in the activity of assisting others. Anna Spafford heeded Moody's advice and immersed herself in relief work—a charitable ministry for which she had not previously taken an active role.[95]

While visiting at Moody's Northfield home Emma wrote a compassionate letter to Anna Spafford assuring her of Moody's love and concern. She passed along Mr. Moody's suggestion that perhaps Mr. Spafford, in order to relieve some of his financial difficulties, could return to his former successful law practice until the difficult times were eased. Emma reassured Anna that comfort comes from God's promises which will not fail or disappoint.[96] Emma accurately reflected Horatio's heart when he later composed the words of the well-known song, *It Is Well With My Soul*. He knew that

---

90. Ibid., 20.
91. Ibid., 1.
92. Powell, *Heavenly Destiny*, 66.
93. Vester, *Our Jerusalem*, 9.
94. Ibid., 48.
95. Ibid., 49.
96. Ibid., 52.

when one is discomforted from the turbulent sea-billows of life, Christ's promises to never leave his children are unfailing.

Emma's letter served as a warm future welcome for Anna to join the Chicago Bible Work ministry. Moody foresaw an important role in the Bible Work for Anna and asked if she would be in charge of women's activities. However, Anna became frustrated with the excessive pressure she felt from him. She realized her own limitations and objected to his inability to accept her refusals to assume certain responsibilities. Rather than working administratively in Chicago with a distant authoritative figure such as Moody, she preferred a daily hands-on experience and ministry with the ladies in the Bible Work. She was relieved when Emma began mentoring her in the work. Anna gladly left the administrative tasks to this new advisor and friend.[97]

Anna later became quite offended over what she saw as Moody's ministry flaws when it came to rescue work among the poor. She recognized with Emma the need for a stable environment to disciple the poor and rescued wanderers. Emma realized her frustration but admiringly watched Anna's diligent devotion to the work of ministry. Anna added to the success of the Bible Work with her astute listening skills and sensible advice.[98]

At the same time, Horatio led the Moody noon prayer meetings in Farwell Hall. At one of his meetings his daughter recalled hearing her father's prayer for a release of fire and a baptism of the Holy Spirit in their midst.[99] And with that fire of God Horatio supported Anna in her mothers' weekly meetings. Women of diversified nationalities were experiencing serious financial concerns and home abuse. Horatio attempted to legally represent them. Unfortunately, the women would consistently back out due to their own fears.

The Spaffords continued their faithful support of the Bible Work and the Chicago Avenue Church. At the 1876 church dedication both Emma and Moody listened with deep gratitude to Horatio's devoted hymn written on behalf of the growing church: "Our Father, God, Eternal one! / And Thou, the living cornerstone! / And Holy Spirit—one and three— / We dedicate this house to Thee! / Take for Thine own, and write in power, / Thy name on wall and shaft and tower; / and make it, by Thy blessing given, / A house of God—a gate of heaven."[100]

Support from Charles Blanchard

As a young boy around twelve years of age, Charles Blanchard in 1860 moved with his family to Wheaton, Illinois, where his father, Jonathan, became Wheaton College's first president. Within a short time the Blanchard family began hearing stories of Chicago

97. Ibid., 49.
98. Ibid.
99. Ibid., 22.
100. Ibid., 51.

evangelist D. L. Moody. Charles's father also heard Horatio Spafford's memorial hymn as he participated in the 1876 Chicago Avenue Church dedication ceremony. He supported the advertisement of Moody's national tours and conferences in his school publication, the *Christian Cynosure*.

Charles remembered meeting Mr. Moody, shortly after their move, at a convention gathering in Wheaton where Moody gave a speech. Charles wrote:

> He was at that time in business and his Christian work was the natural outgoing of his irrepressible enthusiasm. In those days the criticisms which were made upon his diction, grammar and rhetoric had some foundation. He was too eager about his message to think particularly about the manner in which it was delivered. From that time until his death I was brought into more or less close contact with him and his work. While I was never intimately associated with him personally, I did have a relation to his labors . . . the Bible Institute.[101]

Charles's relationship to Emma and the Bible Work proved to be a critical component of the institute's future success.

When the Northfield Conferences in Massachusetts began, Charles received regular invitations from Moody to participate in the summer sessions. His father, Jonathan Blanchard, attended at least one conference with his son in 1881. Both Blanchards were adamantly opposed to Freemasonry. Moody's conferences served as a platform for them to spread the warning regarding secret societies.[102]

On November 11, 1887, the *Christian Cynosure* reported Dr. Evert's speech at the Sabbath Convention, held in nearby Elgin, Illinois, in which lodges and secret societies were opposed. The *Cynosure* recorded the tough opposition being received. Evert referred to Emma's supportive position on the subject: "The wretched men who have given up their lives were hardened against God; the appeals of Miss Dryer, of the Bible workers, and of Dr. Bolton were vain to penetrate their armor of unbelief and hardihood. They reached the 'seat of the scorner.'"[103]

When Charles became an interim pastor of the Chicago Avenue Church in 1883 he remembered Moody visiting the church like *a blessed hurricane* that whirled in and out of Chicago.[104] During these provisional times, numerous clergy would briefly fill the pastoral vacancy. Charles Blanchard shared about his own call to preach at the Chicago Avenue Church:

> I first preached . . . when Dr. Erdman was its teacher. He invited me to speak one Sunday evening which I did. The meetings of that time, as I remember, were held in what is now the basement, the building not having been completed . . . Shortly after this Dr. Erdman resigned and went back to Jamestown,

---

101. Blanchard, *President Blanchard's Autobiography*, 183.
102. Ibid., 184.
103. *Christian Cynosure,* National Christian Association, November 11, 1887, 20.
104. Blanchard, *President Blanchard's Autobiography*, 185.

New York, where he had been pastor of a Presbyterian church. After a few months (perhaps only weeks) I was asked to supply the pulpit regularly for a time, and did so.[105]

Charles's experience at Chicago Avenue Church gave him "blessings . . . far beyond my expectations."[106] He would faithfully commute from Wheaton to Chicago for the Friday evening weekly prayer meeting, stay for the weekend, and return to Wheaton College for his teaching duties on Monday morning.

During his pastoral itinerancy Charles became acquainted with Emma. With his own prolific educational background he immediately became impressed with her skills and abilities. He spoke highly of her as "a marvelous member of the Moody Church army."[107] He explained that the church had established a missionary group and Yoke Fellows Band of fifty to sixty young men who canvassed the Chicago streets for souls. He expanded on Emma's involvement: "These young people were in touch with Miss Dryer. Some of them were members of her class. All of them were inspired by her example and were the continual subjects of her prayers."[108]

Charles was greatly interested in Emma's weekly Adult Bible Class which became the largest Bible class in the church. He considered her to be an astute leader and "a very remarkable woman . . . with the instincts of a teacher born in her and cultivated with years of successful experience."[109] Not having any associate pastoral help, he considered Emma especially supportive: "Her relations to the church were also continually helpful. I do not think that there was any one person in the church who was more eminently useful than she. She was a great Bible teacher. She had fifteen or twenty ladies working under her direction . . . She was continually gathering up young men and women who had little or no education and starting them on the road to good English teaching work."

Charles and Emma would frequently enter into theological discussions regarding the issue of premillennialism. Under Emma's influence, Charles gave up his father's postmillennial views for a premillennial dispensationalist framework that influentially steered Wheaton College into the early twentieth-century era of fundamentalism. To show his gratitude, in his 1913 book on premillennialism entitled *Light On The Last Days*, Charles dedicated the book to Emma: "To Miss Emma Dryer, for years head of the Bible Work in Chicago, one of the founders of the Moody Bible Institute, the friend who first opened my mind to the dispensational teaching of the Word of God, this little book is gratefully dedicated."[110] As with Moody, Emma also influenced Charles's views regarding divine healing and holiness. Both doctrines had

---

105. Blanchard, "Miss Dryer and the Moody Church," May 1925.
106. Blanchard, *The Life of Charles Albert Blanchard*, 85.
107. Blanchard, "Miss Dryer and the Moody Church," May 1925.
108. Ibid.
109. Ibid.
110. Blanchard, *Light on the Last Days*, Dedication Page.

already been inculcated from him and his father's association with Charles Finney at Oberlin College.

Charles recalled his first introduction to the concept of a Bible Institute in Chicago when Moody was speaking at Farwell Hall during the 1876 revival. Moody spoke about needing the school to train evangelists along with their assistants but Charles did not recall any action being taken nor was the suggestion deeply planted in his thinking.[111] It was not until he met Emma that he heard an expanded vision of the school which he concluded was "born in the heart and mind of Mr. Moody [and] . . . part of the life of Miss Dryer who was called from her position to aid in establishing the work."[112] Charles stated that when they would occasionally meet, almost without fail Emma would mention the Bible Institute. Later Charles considered his involvement as part of his life story. He declared that it was "a great honor that I was permitted to aid in laying those foundation stones. Foundations are below ground and out of sight but they hold up buildings and I am glad that I had a share here."[113]

During Charles's pastorate at the Chicago Avenue Church Emma was led to discuss with him her vision for the Bible Institute. From her perspective she wrote: "As always, his ready sympathies were active in behalf of *Bible Study*. We talked of the characteristics of the proposed Institute. He asked me what would be the expense of such an Institute; and eager to increase the study of the Word of God, he immediately raised $500 for that work, and handed it to me."[114] Emma spoke of Charles as "God's consecrated instrument, to give the first great impulse to the Bible Institute, and to its subsequent prosperity."[115]

Charles justifiably questioned Moody's continued hesitation in establishing a Bible Institute which he alone had persuasively directed Emma to develop in 1873. Blanchard surmised: "Mr. Moody was an inspirer, not an organizer of work. He was so great a man that he could not debate with fellow workers. He directed them, and persons who did not care to do what he wanted them to were not associated for any length of time with him or his work. This is not a criticism, it is a statement of fact, the truth of which all who knew Mr. Moody personally will recognize."[116]

Despite Moody's delayed initiative regarding a Bible school, Charles filled the gap. He played a very important role in assisting Emma to fulfill her vision. He believed that Moody's interests in raising funds for the Bible school were no longer a priority due to a heavy and demanding schedule. Charles became financially and ardently supportive. He recounted at some length his own involvement and support:

---

111. Blanchard, *The Life of Charles Albert Blanchard*, 86.
112. Ibid., 87.
113. Ibid.
114. Emma Dryer to Charles Blanchard, 1916, Biographical File of Emma Dryer.
115. Ibid.
116. Getz, *The Story of Moody Bible Institute*, 23.

> I had only begun my acquaintance with Miss Dryer, when she began to speak of the Bible Institute and to express her regrets that something was not done to start it . . . She then told me of Mr. Moody's plans and of the fact that she had come to Chicago in the hope that such an enterprise would be inaugurated . . . As days passed, I was often reminded by Miss Dryer . . . that the Bible Institute was not started, that it ought to be started, and that she was in trouble about it . . . I said to her, 'How much would it take to make the test that you have in mind?' She said, 'If we had five hundred dollars, we could bring Dr. Moorhead [sic] here and the work could begin.' I said to her, 'If that is all you want, you may go ahead and make your plans. I will see that you have the money.' I spoke to Mr. Harvey, Mr. Farwell, and a few others, from whom I received the five hundred dollars, which I turned over to Miss Dryer according to my agreement.[117]

Charles wrote of their continued mutual interest: "Mr. Moody had urged her to turn from public school work, to organize such a training school, in 1873. She, Dr. William J. Erdman, and others had cooperated in Bible teaching and training; the Bible Work was an approved incorporation. And, with Mr. Moody's approval, it now had a family home. But something more should be done immediately."[118] Emma promptly began arrangements for the next stage of the Bible School. She inaugurated the *May Institute* with the five hundred dollar gift which paid for the first two winter sessions. Charles counted it a joy to participate in what he referred to as "pushing the boat into the stream."[119]

Charles and his wife made it a custom to frequently visit Emma and her workers on Warren Avenue when in the Chicago area. They looked forward to visiting *two gentle saints of God*—Miss Emma Dryer and Mrs. Tryphena Cecila Rounds, a member of the Hebrew Mission. Charles wrote how much he enjoyed counseling and praying with such saintly women.[120] On July 14, 1891, he wrote: "We went over to the Bible Institute and returning left at 10 as planned."[121] On yet another occasion Charles reported his visit to friends in Chicago, including Miss Emma Dryer.[122] Their friendship deepened over the years. Charles knew she had been orphaned as a child, and when Emma expressed her desire to be buried on his family grave site in Wheaton Cemetery, Charles kindly and compassionately consented.

---

117. Letter written by Charles Blanchard to A. P. Fitt, 16 November 1910, Charles Albert Blanchard Papers.

118. Blanchard, *President Blanchard's Autobiography*, 123.

119. Charles A. Blanchard to A. P. Fitt, 16 November 1910, Wheaton College Archives and Special Collections.

120. Blanchard, *The Life of Charles Albert Blanchard*, 183.

121. Charles Blanchard, 14 July 1891, Wheaton College Archives and Special Collections.

122. Charles A. Blanchard to his wife Frances Carothers Blanchard, 25 January 1909, Wheaton College Archives and Special Collections.

Connection With Evangelistic Meetings and Conferences

In 1875 Moody's activities in Northfield, Massachusetts, escalated as world renowned Christians visited his scenic mountain home. These individuals would discuss with him the momentum and state of God's kingdom and then urge him to schedule his campaigns in their specific countries or communities.[123] During the 1881 conference Emma and the Blanchards met the well-known evangelist Dr. Andrew Bonar (1810–92) of Glasgow along with other popular Bible teachers.

In many ways the Northfield conferences were Keswick in nature due to Moody's participation in the England conferences and his invitation for Keswick speakers to come to Northfield. Moody compared the two types of conferences by saying, "Northfield is general, Keswick is specific, but both are Biblical and practical."[124] Despite the fame and notoriety, Emma knew that Moody did not want the light and focus shining solely on *Northfield*. He emphasized, "Don't get up in prayer-meeting every week and tell about what you heard at Northfield! Everyone will get sick of the name of Northfield! Tell them about JESUS CHRIST. Tell them what He has taught you, what He had done for you. The world will never get tired of that Name!"[125]

Moody continued at an expeditious pace with the establishment of the Mt. Herman School for boys in 1881. His Northfield conferences were interrupted by his second major campaign in the United Kingdom which ran from 1882 to 1884 including two trips to Paris. From the summer of 1884 to the autumn of 1891 Moody ministered in America and Canada with a renewed focus on the Northfield conferences.[126] In the *Christian Cynosure* publication—initially designed to address the issues of secret societies—President Blanchard continued to contribute special reports regarding the Northfield conferences. He included the progress within area churches, missions, and the proposed Bible School.

Before Emma began attending these Northfield conferences, Moody sent her to Mildmay, England, in 1879. This was the location of the famous Mildmay conference that Moody had attended in 1873 which later inspired his Northfield Conferences. Moody told Emma about Mildmay and the England YMCA. She recalled:

> Mr. Moody had interested me much by telling me about Christian work in England. He said he could accomplish more there, and learn more of the Bible there, than in any other place. The Mildmay Institutions conducted by Reverend and Mrs. Pennefather, were to him, ideal. And he was also delighted with

---

123. Daniels, *D. L. Moody and His Work*, 274.
124. Fitt, *Shorter Life of D. L. Moody*, 55.
125. Ibid.
126. Powell, *Heavenly Destiny*, 171.

many of the YMCA evangelical, and *educational methods*. He desired to see such in America.[127]

Emma and Moody often talked about this special work in England and the vision of a similar training school in Chicago. In the fall of 1879 Mr. and Mrs. Helmer, Moody, and other friends made arrangements for Emma to travel to England. Emma mentioned that her health was *breaking*. Moody desired that she visit the Mildmay Deaconess Home as well as other places of interest for a much needed time of rest.

While in England, Emma met the new challenge of learning about the Mildmay Deaconess Home. Reverend William Pennefather, the rector in Bermet of St. Jude's Mildmay Park, pioneered the home in 1869. Emma attended sessions in a conference hall constructed next to the Mildmay Deaconess Home where she received additional training for home and foreign missions. This was not all new to Emma since her Methodist friends, Lucy and Josiah Meyer, had introduced her to the techniques implemented by the Deaconess Movement. Nevertheless, Emma witnessed firsthand the home mission assistance which the deaconesses provided through orphanages for children, aide to mothers, and Bible instruction. While at Mildmay Emma also gained experience in hospital and home care, lending libraries, food and garden kitchens, and houses of refuge for prostitutes.[128] She realized that her Chicago ministry could be expanded by providing foreign mission training for her workers. The Bible Work, patterned after the deaconess home, would provide a place where they could reside while voluntarily visiting and ministering to the poor.

Emma returned to Chicago a year later after a post-trip visit to the Moody family in Northfield. She was renewed and energized with a fresh momentum for implementing many of the deaconess techniques she had learned. Emma gave the following report:

> I lived many weeks in the Mildmay Deaconess' Home, and accompanied the Deaconesses to their fields and missions. I often attended meetings of the Central YMCA, and, by the help of its Superintendent, Mr. Hind Smith, and also by the advice of Mr. Robert Baton, Hon. Secretary and helper in Mr. Moody's Evangelistic Work, studied many lines of church work, of various grades, among men, and women, and children. It was a blessed education. In Scotland and England, my Christian life was greatly enriched by friendships which I long to renew in Christ's presence.[129]

For Emma, an added dimension of the Mildmay methods included training in *holiness*. Such instruction emphasized teachings from the newly developed 1873 Keswick movement as well as John Wesley's Methodism with its emphasis on small groups, piety, and perfectionism. Her Mildmay training was augmented by Moody's reception

---

127. Emma Dryer to Charles Blanchard, 1916, Biographical File of Emma Dryer.
128. Foster, et al., *Educating Clergy*, 202.
129. Emma Dryer to Charles Blanchard, 1916, Biographical File of Emma Dryer.

of other holiness teachers, such as Hannah Smith and Frederick Meyer, to his Northfield Conferences—often under protest.

Additional Mildmay training in biblical integration and character development gave Emma strong leadership tools for *faith and learning* instruction. Moody also desired that Emma make application of evangelism techniques learned from firsthand experiences in London and transfer them to her urban work in Chicago. Her Mildmay experience undoubtedly impacted her further development of the Bible Work.[130]

A few years later in September 1881 Emma served on the newly formed *Chicago Evangelistic Committee* which met at the YMCA's Farwell Hall. The desire of the committee was to see hearts lovingly bonded together on behalf of missions and to witness the fruit of the gospel in the lives of people.[131] She joined other Christians in the Chicago area to plan these revival meetings—Mr. and Mrs. Turlington Harvey, Eliphalet Wickes Blatchford, B. F. Jacobs, Reverend Edward Goodwin, Major George Clarke, John Morrison, John Farwell, Fleming Revell, Daniel Whittle, E. S. Albro, J. M. Hitchcock and Nettie McCormick. All of them either had, or would later play, a role in the establishment of the Bible Institute.

Major Whittle conducted the meetings in the thousand seat hall on behalf of the Chicago Evangelistic Committee. The meetings "secured for the Committee a good foundation for the building-up of their Gospel work in the city, and placed them under great obligation to himself and his co-laborers."[132] During the three weeks of revival meetings in Farwell Hall many rejoiced over the salvation of souls in response to the gospel of Christ. The revival led to daily noon prayer meetings and an association with the Pacific Garden Mission. Emma's friendship with Sarah and Colonel George Clarke was reinforced as she and other members of the Evangelistic Committee conducted meetings at the mission. This Committee also joined the Bible Work Committees to conduct follow-up training conferences three days a week during November. Emma led the Bible reading, soul winning, and Christian development classes. Following the November meetings she also conducted Tuesday Morning Bible Readings at 10:00 at the YMCA Bible Work Room. *The Evangelistic Record* welcomingly invited others to attend these meetings as a *source of unspeakable benefit*.[133]

The following December another Christian Convention was held at Paxton, Illinois, over one hundred miles south of Chicago. Chicago Evangelistic Committee member and speaker, E. W. Bliss, was used to kindle revival. "The interest has risen as a tide, and goes not out . . . [while] the spirit of praise employed the beautiful Gospel Songs. The hearts of the people were so full of heavenly love they poured it forth for Him who gave it." Emma joined in the testimony services and in the teaching sessions. The *Evangelist Record* cited that "the prevalent desire of hearts was met very effectually

---

130. Getz, *The Story of Moody Bible Institute*, 20.
131. *Evangelistic Record or Record of Christian Work*, December 1881, 9.
132. Ibid., 10.
133. Ibid.

by a Bible reading on being 'filled with the Holy Spirit,' given by Miss E. Dryer, Superintendent of Bible Work in Chicago."[134]

Toward the close of the convention Emma instructed a session specifically for women. She shared the importance of teaching God's word to their children in their homes and participating in mothers' prayer meetings. In reference to her previous Mildmay visit, she noted that the women in England appeared to be participating in more Christian work than American women. She encouraged them to become involved even in small ways such as visiting and praying for the sick while attending to the poor and needy. She concluded her message with a protective challenge for families: "Christian work would prove the great preventive of that restless desire for parties of social worldly pleasure."[135]

Adding to her already active participation in missions and conferences, on August 11, 1885, Emma joined other prominent individuals at the Northfield Convention to form a special missionary committee sanctioned to compose a written appeal for worldwide missions. The council included Reverend Dr. Pierson from Philadelphia, chairman; Reverend Dr. Gordon from Boston; L. W. Munhall from Indianapolis; Reverend C. F. Pentecost from Brooklyn; J. E. K. Studd (brother of Charles T. Studd) from London; and Reverend William Ashmore from Chicago.[136] With missionary enthusiasm Emma assisted in composing the August 14 letter sent to fellow believers throughout the world. The October 29 edition of the *Christian Cynosure* published the letter and listed Emma as representing the Chicago Avenue Church along with the same prominent individuals.[137]

May Institute 1883–89

In some ways, Emma and her Bible workers were a leaderless group without the consistent and committed involvement of the other Bible Institute visionary, D. L. Moody. However, they were not without guidance when it came to prayer. During the years 1883 to 1886 Emma led prayer meetings every Saturday morning in the Bible Work Room in Farwell Hall. Not only did she purposefully pray for the establishment of the school but also for a training program for home and foreign missionaries.[138] William Blackstone, Fleming Revell, and other faithful prayer warriors joined Emma. With this prayer support team Emma initiated a program vital to the establishment of her envisioned Bible training school—the annual May Institute. The Institute would hold annual coeducational systematic Bible studies with the following goal: "To reach

---

134. Ibid., January 1882, 11.
135. Ibid.
136. *Christian Cynosure*, National Christian Association, August 27, 1885, 12.
137. Ibid., 29 October 1885. Report of Northfield Convention August 14, 1885.
138. Beatty, "Emma Dryer and Her Unrelenting Prayer," para. 5.

the poor and neglected of this city, and to train Missionaries for Home and Foreign Fields."[139]

The May Institute met with Moody's full approval. In the early spring of 1883 he sent Emma a message asking her to prepare a speaking engagement for him in Farwell Hall during his stop in Chicago. Before a full audience he affirmed his support of the Bible Work: "I want it understood that I stand by the Bible-Work." After his message Emma remembered a man from Peoria giving ten dollars as a contribution for this work. Emma wrote: "Mr. Moody handed the bill to me, and in our cash box, we kept it, and thanked God, and took courage by this token of 'more to follow' in the Bible-Work."[140]

With this affirmation, Emma inaugurated the next phase of her training school—an institute with an open enrollment to be held in the month of May. During the first May Institute in 1883 around fifty male and female students registered from great distances and crowded into the YMCA lecture rooms. During these May Institutes Emma acquired the services of prominent Bible teachers who presented lectures for the morning and evening sessions. The students from this initial first year were said to be *eager and enthusiastic*. In 1884 attendance increased to over seventy. Once again the *Christian Cynosure* reported a similar deep and devoted interest from students, however, more intense.[141]

At last Emma's vision for training more than just women began to emerge. By now she had influenced Moody to think *coeducationally* in conjunction with her prior normal school training and background.[142] With this mindset, she secured the YMCA rooms and Farwell Hall for the institute that initially lasted for one week. She utilized her normal school training from ISNU to inaugurate a pedagogical religious training school for coeducationally low to middle class enrollees. Imitating her ISNU counterpart President Richard Edwards, Emma reached out to those who might otherwise not have had the opportunity to receive practical training in religious work. By the time Moody seriously began to take an active interest in the training school, Emma had conceptualized and set in motion her perception of Moody's vision for a religious training school—a vision which was quite unique for her generation.[143]

In preparation for the May Institute, Emma now possessed the expertise needed to network qualified individuals of both genders within diversified institutions—churches, Sunday schools, and seminaries—to serve the common people.[144] Her intent according to Charles Blanchard was to use the May Institutes as trial sessions

---

139. Getz, *The Story of Moody Bible Institute*, 44.
140. Emma Dryer to Charles Blanchard, 1916, Biographical File of Emma Dryer.
141. *Christian Cynosure,* National Christian Association, June 26, 1884, 13.
142. Foster, et al., *Educating Clergy*, 201.
143. Roderick, *Nettie Fowler McCormick*, 168.
144. Foster, et al., *Educating Clergy*, 200.

that would spur Moody to finalize their original vision of a Bible school.[145] Until then, Blanchard promoted her comprehensive advertisements in his *Christian Cynosure* publication in which she encouraged participation and preparation of students for the Bible school:

> We now hope to open this Training School in the autumn, and to receive into it ... such young persons as are prepared, by their Christian consecration and ability, diligently to study the Bible and successfully to give out its truths to perishing souls around them. Pray that our yet imperfect plans may be shaped according to the mind of the Lord, and that he will send out from this school not only scores, not only hundreds, but great multitudes of earnest Christians, mighty in the Scriptures, to proclaim the Gospel to the destitute. We are frequently asked, What scholastic education is desirable to fit young men and young women for ordinary Christian work? We believe that the Lord will use any consecrated Christian to give out his word, and that many an 'uneducated' man and woman is endued by the Holy Spirit with great power in the Lord's service, and we also understand, from the Scriptures, that there is no successful Christian service without the gracious power of the Holy Spirit. The POWER is of *grace*, and God's word is the gracious well-spring of salvation (Psa. 119), and whoever thirsts after righteousness may cry effectually, 'Ho, every one that thirsteth, come ye to the waters ... yes, come buy wine and milk without money, and without price.'[146]

Emma responded to letters she had been receiving from gentlemen inquiring about the school. She wrote from the Bible Work Room on Madison Street in June of 1884 that the first six week session in systematic Bible had been concluded by Reverend Professor W. G. Moorehead from Xenia, Ohio.

Emma first met William Gallogly Moorehead (1836–1914) in 1882 at a Believer's Meeting for Bible Study on Mackinac Island in Michigan. He was a tenured professor at Xenia Theological Seminary. She continued her acquaintance with him even after he became president in 1899. From the time she first met him, Emma could foresee his participation in her envisioned May Institute. She carefully studied him when he addressed the Michigan audience and was drawn to the subject matter of his presentation and his teaching style. She shared her thoughtful perception: "As I prayed the conviction was so strong, that I then spoke with our friend, Mrs. W. B. Shute about it. The Bible Institute, in which he might be of great service, was more and more impressed on my mind and heart."

After returning to Chicago she revealed her intuitive observations at the Bible Workers' prayer meeting. Her workers kept Dr. Moorehead in prayer.[147] Months later she invited Presbyterian minister Moorehead to participate in the May Institute to

---

145. Blanchard, *Life of Charles Albert Blanchard*, 85–86.
146. *Christian Cynosure*, National Christian Association, June 26, 1884, 13.
147. Emma Dryer to Charles Blanchard, 1916, Biographical File of Emma Dryer.

teach short-term courses for both men and women. These preliminary courses would eventually set the stage for the establishment of Emma's envisioned Bible school.

To further assist Emma, Blanchard advertised in the *Christian Cynosure* on April 16, 1885: "A Bible Institute will be held in Chicago in May and June for Christian workers. Rev. W. G. Moorehead, D.D., Xenia, O.; Rev. E. P. Goodwin, D.D., of Chicago, and Maj. D. W. Whittle are among the instructors. Inquiries should be addressed to Miss E. Dryer, Bible Institute, 150 Madison St., Chicago."[148] This report was followed on May 7, 1885, by a more detailed account of course instruction:

I. Christian Doctrine—some of the great fundamental truths revealed in Scriptures,—sin, justification, the mediatorial offices of Christ, the Holy Spirit's presence and work.

II. Biblical Exegesis—an analytical study of texts and passages in the English Bible.

III. Elementary Church History:—the planting of the church, fall of the Roman Empire; the Reformation.

IV. Practical work, meetings, inquiries, etc. The Institute will be held four and perhaps six weeks under the management of the Rev. Prof. W. G. Moorehead, D.D., who will be assisted by other ministers and Christian teachers.[149]

The report indicated endorsement by D. L. Moody, Reverend Goodwin, and Major Whittle. On May 28, 1885, an update for the institute was given. The Bible Institute organizers had met at the YMCA with Professor W. G. Moorehead who was in charge of the institute. Dr. Moorehead reported that fifty to sixty students attended the morning class during the week and 115 were present for the evening sessions. This show of attendance was viewed as a sign of tremendous success.[150]

On June 18 the *Christian Cynosure* summarized the successful and profitable institute meetings held in Farwell Hall for four weeks. Reverend Moorehead of Xenia had oversight with the assistance of "Miss Dryer, Rev. Mr. Goss and others."[151] A week later it was announced that the May Institute, under the guidance of the Bible Work had just closed as "evangelists, missionaries, Bible readers, colporteurs and other Christian workers met for the exposition of Scripture and the systematic study of doctrine and of church history, under the excellent leadership of Prof. W. G. Moorehead."[152]

The format of the 1885 May Institute included intense morning and evening sessions for four days weekly. The *Christian Cynosure* reported: "Most earnest attention was paid by the class, and their eager reception of the truth showed how deeply they felt the need of such an institute, and how much they appreciated its privileges. The

148. *Christian Cynosure*, National Christian Association, April 16, 1885, 12.
149. Ibid., 7 May 1885.
150. Ibid., 28 May 1885, 12.
151. Ibid., 18 June 1885, 12.
152. Ibid., 25 June 1885, 12.

enrolled members of the class attended regularly throughout, and the number of those who could attend for a few days only steadily increased."[153] The highest evening attendance was 119 with an overall average attendance of 176. The article ended by stating the desire to conduct yet another institute in the upcoming fall or in the early winter months. By 1888 the Institute would be expanded to three month sessions.

During the May Institute Emma and her workers had the privilege of hosting Dr. Moorehead at the Bible Worker Home. Emma recalled that Moody himself did not attend the first two institutes.[154] Nevertheless, she knew that he approvingly viewed the institute as being quite successful although he could not attend due to his prior campaign commitments.[155] By 1885 Moody was receiving pressure from the McCormicks and other Chicagoans to assist with this training institute. In April of 1886 Moody agreed to preside over the May Institute sessions. The location changed from the Bible Room at the YMCA to the Chicago Avenue Church. The month was changed to April in order to accommodate him. With Moody officiating, Dr. Moorehead continued as the primary speaker.[156] Impressed with an attendance of approximately two hundred workers, Moody's heart was inspired. He realized that the Bible Training School in Chicago must be launched and established as a year-round school. Land and buildings next to the Chicago Avenue Church would need to be purchased to launch the *Bible Institute for Home and Foreign Missions*.[157]

The May Institute called together many exceptional Christian instructors. Emma's vast network of qualified teachers included Reverend Samuel Ives Curtiss, Reverend Professor Hugh Scott, and Reverend H. M. Collison of Chicago. Emma also obtained the services of accomplished teachers such as President Blanchard and Dr. Moorehead whose efforts she acknowledged as "well united in the fundamental principles of that May Institute."[158] She saw her friend Charles as not only a contributing instructor but as the most helpful of all her friends in coordinating the institute. Emma wrote Moody's son-in-law, A. P. Fitt, that Charles also contributed numerous lectures and would have been even more involved if not for his own newly assigned duties as president of Wheaton College.[159]

Emma witnessed a growth in Institute and Bible Work attendance due to an enlarged prospective field of Christians from other countries. She wrote: "To these schools came Americans and foreigners, *always studying from the Bible*, comparing their Scripture with English, which language they were eager to learn. And from our

---

153. Ibid.
154. Emma Dryer to A. P. Fitt in N.Y. City, 24 November 1910, Biographical File of Emma Dryer.
155. Emma Dryer to Charles Blanchard, 1916, Biographical File of Emma Dryer.
156. Emma Dryer to A. P. Fitt, Biographical File of Emma Dryer.
157. Fitt, *Moody Still Lives*, 95.
158. Emma Dryer to Charles Blanchard, 1916, Biographical File of Emma Dryer.
159. Emma Dryer to A. P. Fitt, Biographical File of Emma Dryer.

school books learning the important facts of *practical* education."[160] The *Christian Cynosure* and other religious publications continued to advertise the school. Emma appointed Mr. Fred Jewett as school secretary and his uncle, Mr. Ensign, along with Mr. Hemingway, the YMCA superintendent, to work with advertising. She engaged the help of Chicago pastors such as Dr. Curtis and Dr. Scott from the Chicago Theological Seminary referring to them as *reliable helpers*. Her faithful friend from her early Chicago days—Reverend Goodwin from the First Congregational Church—joined the pastoral team. She fondly recalled how he continually assisted with the institute in cooperation with Dr. Goss, the pastor of the Chicago Avenue Church.[161]

The May Institute agenda consisted of daily Bible study and prayer marked by collaborative group discussions and religious instruction. Writing from her normal school and Bible Work experience Emma provided a lengthy discourse for the wide-circulating *Christian Cynosure* for prospective students interested in attending the Institute:

> We say to young people, try to finish a high school course of study with Greek. Such a course should give good menial training and prepare the way for future study and improvement: and in this country almost any young man and young woman with ability worth educating can educate himself or herself through a high school course of study, and if pecuniary means are limited, what of it? You are richer for that! You have, by this need, better opportunities for the exercise of ingenuity, wisdom, skill, economy, patience, vigorous efforts in many directions, and prayerful trust in our God, who has promised to equip for their work those whom he sends forth into his harvest. I Cor. 9:7 . . . Inability to do common things well is a most serious defect among any class of workers, and ought not long to exist among Christian workers. Young friend, desiring to do good Christian work, what is in your hand now? Do your best with that thing. It may, just now, appear to you like a small factor of life's great work, but on it hang great dangers, or great successes. If you will do that thing you may likewise will to do all to which it is related . . . 'heartily, as unto the Lord.' Young men and young women, on whom the work of life presses heavily, gratefully rejoice if you are obediently doing your work . . . for . . . 'he that is faithful in that which is least is faithful also in much' (Luke 16:10). 'Study to show thyself approved unto God, a workman that needeth not to be ashamed rightly dividing the word of truth' (2 Tim. 2:15). If you are willing to be led by him, ask him with reference to his service, 'Lord, what wilt thou have me to do?' and what he directs in his word and providence (Matt. 7:7). Young men, young women, boys and girls, who of you will pray and plan and work now that you may, in the remaining years, be most successfully used in Christ's service? In the fellowship of the Gospel, Miss E. Dryer.[162]

160. Emma Dryer to Charles Blanchard, 1916, Biographical File of Emma Dryer.
161. Emma Dryer to A. P. Fitt, Biographical File of Emma Dryer.
162. *Christian Cynosure*, National Christian Association, June 26, 1884, 13.

This article and Emma's choice of May Institute curriculum reflected her premillennial urgency for the spreading of the gospel. Courses consisted of Bible and music instruction with a premillennial mission-practicum emphasis for city outreaches including the Swedish school. Emma's diligent efforts in instructor and student recruitment, advertisement, and curriculum development proved instrumentally successful in initiating the May Institute which served as the foundation for the subsequent launching of the Moody Bible Institute.

Haymarket Riot: May 4, 1886

In the midst of Emma's successful annual May Institutes, the month of *May* also took on a negative connotation for Chicago as the country in 1886 headed into economically difficult times. Tensions began to mount between industrialists and working class employees. With the growth of the Knights of Labor and the influence of other unions, striking workers were encouraged to picket for critical labor issues such as eight hour days and higher wages. At the McCormick Reaper Works the management's conventional practice of replacing strikers agitated the union employees. Although the resulting violence could not compare with the fiery destruction of the city in October 1871, needless lives were nonetheless taken when displaced workers tauntingly protested on May 3, 1886.

A large group of Chicago policemen stationed themselves to protect the strike defectors. They inadvertently shot an unknown number of workers and civilians as they forced their way through to the strike breakers. Tensions mounted as another crowd of around 1,500 gathered the next day at the public Haymarket Square to protest police brutality. In the midst of the protest an unknown assailant threw a dynamite bomb, and police automatically shot throughout the crowd. This action resulted in the wounding of sixty officers with the death of seven policemen and an estimated four workers.[163]

This tragedy, known as *The Haymarket Riot*, occurred in the midst of Emma's Bible Work territory near Des Plaines and Randolph Street. Her close connection to a number of Chicago business friends, especially Nettie McCormick, brought her to the forefront of their financial concerns regarding this socio-economic dilemma. Emma also realized Josiah and Lucy Meyer's apprehensions regarding the delay in the construction of their Chicago Training School due to the riots. Lucy wrote: "This greatly delayed the work on the house and for a time it seemed that our summer suspension might become the sleep of death."[164]

The riot also resulted in numerous arrests and an internationally acclaimed trial. On October 8, 1886, Emma entered the courthouse as a spectator to listen to

---

163. Joiner, *Sin in the City,* 47–48; McNarmara, "The 1886 Haymarket Square Riot in Chicago: Anarchist Bombing at a Union Meeting Provoked a Deadly Riot," section 6.

164. Meyer, *Deaconesses, Biblical, Early Church,* 131.

the testimonies of these defendants—August Spies, Samuel Fielden, and Albert Parsons. Having worked in this district for many years, Emma realized the poverty and challenges for the poor working families. She also knew the hearts of industrialists such as Cyrus and Nettie McCormick who walked in integrity and concern for their employees. Emma later wrote to Nettie her response after hearing the defendants' unkind remarks regarding the McCormick family: "I hear the name McCormick frequently . . . There is no justice possible out of Christ. Law centers in Him and as I hear these arguments from a social standpoint my heart aches to have the church of Christ see where her work lies. Over and over, these men argue and plead for justice to the poor."[165] Nettie McCormick's friend, Stella Roderick, expressed her view that Emma "though unsympathetic with Fielden's views . . . was impressed with his long, passionate plea for justice to the poor (whom she served so well)."[166]

The Haymarket Riot proved to be a setback for the labor movement and unions.[167] A guilty verdict was reached for eight defendants with four men hung on November 11, 1887, while another committed suicide. Years later the trial was called a spectacle with fabrication of the evidence, judge and jury bias, and a miscarriage of justice. In reflecting on this dreadful event, Emma concluded that government, the judicial system, and the poor all needed Christian education as the ultimate answer to injustice.[168]

Bible Work Testimonies

In the aftermath of Chicago's Haymarket Riot, Emma continued with her Bible Work ministry which positively impacted the city and the whole country. In the 1880s Miss Parmelia Hand, daughter of Attorney O. Hand who had recently passed away, made the decision to retire as Emma's head assistant due to poor health. Upon her recovery she left for Utah where, having been sufficiently equipped by Emma, she taught in anti-Mormon schools. In 1886 just before the Haymarket Riot, Miss Hand returned to the Chicago area and spoke to students at President Charles Blanchard's Wheaton College chapel service on March 11. She shared her missionary experiences while under the New West Education Commission. She worked with sixty-two other teachers and 2,700 Hispanic and Mormon students with *wonderful successes*.[169] Parmelia's life, and that of many others, testified of Emma's training and nurturing of this effective missionary.

---

165. Joiner, *Sin in the City*, 49.

166. Roderick, *Nettie Fowler McCormick*, 151.

167. McNarmara, "The 1886 Haymarket Square Riot in Chicago: Anarchist bombing at a union meeting provoked a deadly riot," section 6.

168. Roderick, *Nettie Fowler McCormick*, 177.

169. *Christian Cynosure*, National Christian Association, March 18, 1886, 1.

Bible Work of Chicago, 1873–86

John L. Morrison

John L. Morrison became the first student from the Chicago Avenue Church to attend the Bible Study and Work program after returning from Scotland where he had assisted D. L. Moody. John came from a missionary family serving in India. He was skilled as a ship carpenter who on January 31, 1873, happened to see Moody's North Side Tabernacle. He explained that he had nothing else to do and no place else to go and had become assured of the truthful evidence of Christianity.[170] Upon his conversion he aligned himself with Emma's Bible Work missionary training program. After leaving the Bible Work he founded a Chicago mission in 1881. He served free Sunday breakfasts of beef and ham sandwiches with hot coffee followed by the message of the gospel through music. He also worked at the Chicago YMCA Railroad Mission. This program, which started in 1878, provided dormitories and saloon alternatives for railroad workers. Many of John's friends at the Chicago Avenue Church assisted him.

After the 1889 May Institute, John brought to Moody's attention a vacant lot and challenged him to prayerfully consider building a school there. The Institute trustees purchased that land plus three houses next to it. The timing was right as Moody had just witnessed the huge success of the 1889 May Institute. John went on to become a Pastoral Assistant. Emma, with great pleasure, wrote: "He . . . still goes on, going and growing."[171]

Reverend J. C. Crawford

Emma continually poured out her heart in prayer to the Lord regarding plans for the establishment of the Bible Institute. Meanwhile, J. Charles Crawford also cried out with a deep desire to train and equip other young men for God's service. He was a poor young working man from Boone, Iowa. Crawford's sister found Emma's advertisement for the May Institute in *Notes for Bible Study*. His heart was stirred as he headed to Chicago for the first term. He later told President Charles Blanchard that Miss Dryer assisted him in finding a home in the city where he could board and attend classes. At the Chicago Avenue Church Crawford eagerly listened to Charles Blanchard's preaching. He served as an assistant pastor to Reverend Goss and later affiliated with the Christian and Missionary Alliance. Emma wrote that his Christian service "forever endeared him and his family and his work, to our effectional Christian sympathies."[172]

---

170. Ibid., 6 April 1882.

171. Emma Dryer to Charles Blanchard, 1916, Biographical File of Emma Dryer; *Christian Cynosure*, National Christian Association, April 6, 1882, 12; Graves, "Evangelization Society to Storm Chicago," 5.

172. Emma Dryer to Charles Blanchard, 1916, Biographical File of Emma Dryer.

At the Institute Crawford was also nurtured under the teaching of Dr. Moorehead and acknowledged that he felt equipped for his life calling. Blanchard believed that Mr. Crawford was perhaps one of the first graduates of the school. When Blanchard visited Boone Biblical College in Boone, Iowa, several years later, he was amazed to learn the history of the school from Reverend Crawford, who had become president of the college.

Founded in 1891 with one hundred students, Boone Biblical College provided a home for the elderly, an orphanage, and a school for the orphans. President Blanchard had attended numerous college graduation ceremonies. He admitted that Boone Biblical College's commencement exercises surpassed any other that he had ever attended.[173] Blanchard most certainly expressed, to Emma's delight and gratitude, his amazement that a school 350 miles from Chicago had been founded by one of her Bible Work Institute graduates.

Crawford sent out scores of young people to the mission field. He provided a comfortable Christian home for the aged and orphans received shelter and training after being left homeless.[174] Emma proudly shared Crawford's testimony: "In his Bible Institute . . . he is now preparing missionaries for Home and Foreign Fields, also educating children of missionaries in the Public School . . . and in the Word of God. He also has a home for aged Christians. A great center of prayer and Christian Work is Boone Bible Institute."[175]

Mr. Fredrickson and Others

Mr. Fredrickson participated in the Bible Work program and attended the May Institutes. He was a student at the Chicago Theological Seminary and boarded with other workers at 100 Warren Avenue. Emma remembered him as one who "from those early days . . . moved by the Holy Spirit, more and more sought a Christian education for Home and Foreign Mission Fields, and studied in our Bible-Work and Night Schools in connection with the Bible Institute."[176] After leaving the institute Mr. Fredrickson instrumentally formed a mission in Alaska where according to Emma he labored in ministry with Swedish friends for a number of years.

Paul Gulander followed Fredrickson to the Bible Institute and was sent out as a Swedish missionary to South Africa. Additionally, Mr. John Bilhorn, a friend to Dr. Moorehead during Moorehead's eight year stay at the Bible Workers' Home during the May Institutes, preached and studied in a furnished barn. Emma truly valued his friendship and loyalty. John introduced her to his brother Peter who continued John's work in Chicago. Emma named other workers such as Mr. E. L. Vogel who worked

173. Blanchard, *President Blanchard's Autobiography*, 126.
174. Ibid.
175. Emma Dryer to Charles Blanchard, 1916, Biographical File of Emma Dryer.
176. Ibid.

in the area high schools. And foreigners such as Italian Evangelist Michele Nardi and Reverend Philippe Grilli utilized the practical education learned at the May Institute Night Schools for the Chicago Italian Missions.[177]

As Emma looked back on the years of preparation for the envisioned Bible Institute, she held sincere gratitude for the friendships that God, in her obedience to him, had given her. She wrote: "The Christian associations of these years were an unspeakable blessing. They awake my constant gratitude to God. My thanksgiving of them will be heard amid the melodies of Heaven. God wonderfully sustained us through trials;—trials which ultimately reveal his best blessings."[178]

Emma's desire to see the May Institute used as a tool to attract Moody's favor and involvement had been amazingly successful. As Emma had foreseen, when Moody recognized the success of the May Institute, his interest advanced with a characteristic passion. A. P. Fitt explained that although his father-in-law distanced himself from the oversight of the academics at his Northfield schools, when it came to the Chicago Bible Institute he determined a course of action and exactly how to achieve it.[179] Moody viewed the implementation of Emma's Bible Work and May Institute as the necessary groundwork for the training school and initially envisioned her work in the future Ladies Department of the school.[180] Others proclaimed her as the "brilliant Emeline Dryer, forerunner of the Bible Institute."[181] Her philosophy, educational training, and administrative oversight correctly calculated programs that would materialize into what continues to be known in the twenty-first century as the Moody Bible Institute.[182]

"A capable, intelligent, and virtuous woman—who is he who can find her? She is far more precious than jewels and her value is far above rubies or pearls. [He] trusts in her confidently and relies on and believes in her."

~ PROVERBS 31:10–11A AMP ~

---

177. Ibid.
178. Ibid.
179. Fitt, *Moody Still Lives*, 96.
180. Hassey, *No Time For Silence*, 35.
181. Day, *Bush Aglow*, 295.
182. Hassey, *No Time For Silence*, 35.

8

Emma's Spiritual Walk and Inspirations

"Imitate me, just as I also imitate Christ."
~1 Corinthians 11:1 NKJV~

Emma's parents followed their adopted daughter's missionary journey from Victor, New York, to Chicago from 1850 to 1876. Their hearts overflowed with the knowledge that they had given her not just an academic advantage, but also the mission background and spiritual surroundings she would need to courageously commit to God's calling on her life. Before Emma's move to Chicago, John and Lucinda Dryer supported her throughout her fearful recovery from typhoid fever. When seeking guidance from the Lord regarding her faith journey to Chicago, they provided their daughter with unremitting prayer. In answer to their prayers Emma was surrounded by new Chicago friends such as Methodists Josiah and Lucy Meyer, Methodist pastor W. H. Daniels, and other leaders who directed her on a new adventure of faith and holiness.

Emma lived during the time of the nineteenth-century American Holiness Movement. This movement adopted John Wesley's perfectionism doctrine through Methodism and later contributed to the holiness roots of non-Methodists such as the Salvation Army, Christian and Missionary Alliance, and the Church of God. Holiness experiences included personal conversions, various responses to worship, and acknowledgment of the sanctifying work of the Holy Spirit in individual lives via baptism, crisis, or a second experience blessing. God used D. L. Moody to lend the vision and challenge for Emma to become a forerunner of the Chicago Bible Institute. He also used this man to model even to a greater degree what it meant to walk in the power of the Holy Spirit. Moody expanded Emma's holiness contacts through the Mildmay deaconess program in England and through Keswick acquaintances appointed by God to deepen her spiritual walk. Moody introduced Emma to those with whom he had associated when attending the 1875 Keswick Convention—Andrew Bonar, George Müller, Andrew Murray, Hudson Taylor, and Henry Drummond.

Emma's Spiritual Walk and Inspirations
Power of the Holy Spirit

Moody passionately articulated and recognized the work of the Holy Spirit in his ministry. He served as an example and inspiration to Emma of a man seeking to be led daily by the Spirit of God. He urged: "Let us cry mightily to God that we may have a double portion of the Holy Spirit."[1] He shared with Emma and other Holiness Movement advocates his strong belief in the power of the Holy Spirit. In his book *Secret Power* he wrote: "I believe, and am growing more into this belief, that divine, miraculous creative power resides in the Holy Ghost. Above and beyond all natural law, yet in harmony with it, creation, providence, the Divine government, and the upbuilding of the Church of God are presided over by the Spirit of God. His ministration is the ministration of life more glorious than the ministration of law (2 Cor. iii.)."[2] Moody, reflecting the holiness and altar teachings of Phoebe Palmer, wrote: "If this love is in the heart, and the fire is burning on the altar, we will not be all the time finding fault with other people and criticizing what they have done."[3] Like Moody, Emma also desired to keep this fire of love burning in her own life and, with warmness of spirit, gave the hope of Christ to all around her.

Emma eagerly followed Moody's 1886 initiative for college student conferences at his Northfield school with a primary emphasis on the power of the Holy Spirit. Many attendees ventured to Northfield's secluded areas to seek God's presence and to pray for the Holy Spirit. They departed from the conferences with an increased missionary zeal.[4] It is also significant that the book *The Wonders of Prayer*, which originally appeared in 1881, had a lead essay by D. L. Moody, entitled *A Wonderful Answer to Prayer and Proof of the Existence of the Holy Spirit*. Likewise, his desire to minister to others regarding the power of the Holy Spirit is evident in his sermons and in his conversations with Emma and his Methodist friend, Dr. Reuben Torrey.[5] In his 1923 sermon *Why God Used D. L. Moody* (1923), Torrey cited Moody's admonition to continue preaching fully and regularly on the baptism of the Holy Spirit.

Emma recognized their mutual reliance on the Holy Spirit when she supportively wrote to Moody on July, 1887, "My loving, loyal zeal for you has without exception been immediate & constant & I have believed through the years & before God that you must be led by the Spirit of God . . . to push this work for the glory of His name."[6] As a leader and writer for the *Bible Reading and Prayer Alliance* Emma displayed her own dependence on God's Spirit. She placed at the heading of her publications the objectives of the Alliance: "Each member to read the same chapter daily praying *the*

---

1. Moody, *Secret Power,* 52.
2. Ibid., 12.
3. Ibid., 84.
4. Shanks, *College Students at Northfield*, 352–55.
5. Dorsett, *A Passion For Souls*, 311.
6. Emma Dryer to Mr. Moody, 25 July 1887, Biographical File of Emma Dryer.

Holy Spirit to guide us into all truth according to our Lord's promise. John 16:13." She added that the Lord's Day morning prayer time was "recommended for united weekly prayer, for Pastors, Ministers and Teachers of the Word, for all officers and members of the church that, *taught by the Holy Spirit*, they may understand and obey the Word of God."[7]

Emma's close relationship with friends such as President Charles Blanchard provided opportunities for her to hear their personal testimonies regarding the power of the Holy Spirit. She listened to Charles's declaration regarding his own inner struggle for a holy life. At one dark point in his life he cried out: "Soul-battle all day with the powers of darkness! God gave me His Holy Spirit anew for work."[8] Blanchard related yet another faith victory in sanctification:

> I remember my most easily besetting sin . . . How many times I prayed . . . and I never was freed. At last He spoke to me in this fashion, 'Why do you say "if" to Me? Do you not know that I wish you to live a holy life?' And I said, 'Yes, Lord.' 'Do you believe that any temptation ever overtakes you for which I have not provided a way of escape?' 'No, Lord.' He said, 'Why, then, do you say "if" to Me?' I said, 'I will not say "if." I promise not to commit that sin again.' That was nearly fifty years ago . . . I am sure that if I had kept on saying 'if' to God, I should never have been victor.[9]

Emma also listened intently to Charles as he explained his ecumenical philosophy and connections with revivalist Charles Finney. He would have shared with Emma in detail his memorable meeting with Finney at Oberlin College. His father lectured at Oberlin in 1839, and Charles also received an invitation to speak.[10] Finney's counsel to Charles involved advice on facing opposition that popularization with the world and a lack of holy works incur.

At this time Emma possibly shared with Charles the testimony of her former teacher and seminary preceptress, Miss Mary Allen, regarding the 1830 Rochester High School revival. She could also have relayed the story of Victor Presbyterian minister, Charles Furman, whose marriage was conducted by Finney. Ultimately, Charles's association with Moody and Emma culminated with her influence on both men's views regarding the Holiness doctrine of divine healing.

---

7. Insert in Emma Dryer's Bible: "Reading and Prayer Alliance Miss E. Dryer Sec. Bible Reading and Prayer Alliance Chicago Bible Society Room F 69 Dearborn St. Chicago" with 2 Tim. 3:15-17 and John 14:7 quotes in the top heading.

8. Blanchard, *The Life of Charles Albert Blanchard*, 190.

9. Ibid., 41.

10. Ibid., 58.

Emma's Spiritual Walk and Inspirations

Divine Healing

After Emma's personal healing experiences from typhoid fever and eye afflictions, divine healing continued to play an important part in her life. In conjunction with prominent authors George Müller, Charles Finney, C. H. Spurgeon, and D. L. Moody, Emma wrote a dramatic healing testimony for Major Whittle's 1885 book *The Wonders of Prayer: A Record of Well Authenticated and Wonderful Answers to Prayer.* Her testimony, entitled *The Prayer Of Faith,* reflected her position on healing.

Emma began her written testimony with an introduction to the James R. Jordan family whom she met in 1872. They resided in Lake View, Chicago, and attended the Lincoln Park Congregational Church. Following the death of Mr. Jordan in October, 1882, his family experienced numerous trials of their faith. Writing from the background of her healing experience, Emma maintained: "It is an instructive fact for Christian meditation, that when the exercise of intelligent faith was necessary to their cures, the faith was there ready for exercise."[11] Emma acknowledged the impacting influence of their faith on her own life. She knew that this family had learned, as she had, that "faith is trustful obedience to the Word of God; that it is not a determination to have one's own way, nor to expect the immediate gratification of a desire, simply because the desire has been made known to God."[12]

Emma quite frequently ended her correspondence with the phrase *living in the hopes of the Gospel.* She expanded on that phrase when writing about the Jordan family. She knew their hope was in heaven as their eternal home and final resting place. The youngest son in the family died suddenly in 1880 leaving the two daughters, Mrs. Furlong and Addie S. Jordan, to care for their mother who had fractured her hip in 1876. In 1884 another fall further debilitated her with a broken, dislocated wrist. Emma pointed out that despite assistance from the medical profession grave side-effects continued to incapacitate her. After being bedfast for eight weeks, Mrs. Jordan's vision and hearing had diminished. She experienced no hand mobility and had declined mentally.

Meanwhile, in January of 1883 Mrs. Furlong, the daughter, was stricken with paralysis and also found herself in a helpless and depressed condition. During this time she began to meditate on the healing miracles of Jesus. She considered that perhaps her reliance should be more on him than on the doctors. Emma detailed how the sister, with hope indescribable, considered the miraculous and unchanging power of Jesus. She stretched out her non-paralyzed hand and asked the Lord to heal her. Emma recorded her response: "Like an electric shock the life began to move in her arm, and the continued sensation was as though something that, previously, had not moved was set in motion. The feeling passed up to the head, and down the body to the foot. *She was healed! and she was grateful!*" The next morning she proceeded to walk

---

11. Whittle, *The Wonders of Prayer,* 21.
12. Ibid.

fifteen blocks to church as she expressed with fervency of spirit the touching nearness of the Holy Spirit.[13]

At this time Miss Addie Jordan, weighing a meager eighty pounds and with a five year history of lung disease, became chronically ill with tuberculosis. Although hearing of her sister's miraculous recovery Addie had no such assurance. On January 1, 1884, Mrs. Furlong declared that the Lord could and would heal Addie. Emma recorded: "Six hours of united waiting upon the Lord followed. They were hours of pain. From nine in the morning till three in the afternoon she suffered indescribable pain. A few minutes after three, the pain left her, and with a bright look she said, 'I believe I'm better.'"[14] Her health improved and her weight climbed to one hundred and twenty pounds. She was able to attend church services once again. In September of 1885 Addie became a missionary to freed slaves in the south. Emma witnessed how these two daughters in faith obeyed God and received from him "at such times and in such ways as God appoints; all of which truths they found . . . in the Holy Scriptures."[15]

Miss Jordan's mother at eighty-five years old also received hope from the Lord. On June 16, 1884, with humility she decreed that the Lord was her Helper as she recalled the testimonies of blind men seeing, lame men walking, and deaf men hearing. She knew that the Lord could heal her if he so willed it.[16] For eight years Mrs. Jordan had been greatly afflicted. Now she found that she could read without glasses, walk for blocks without assistance to nearby Lincoln Park, and kneel with thanksgiving before the Lord.

Emma exhorted, "Christian reader, stop here and think what a joyful family that was that June morning. That aged saint, of a little more than 85 years, was in good health again! And her two daughters had been snatched from the jaws of death!"[17] Emma left her readers with the hope and faith that nothing is too difficult for the Lord and that he withholds no good thing from those who walk uprightly. She ended her message by stating: "If we live by the Spirit, let us also walk by the Spirit. In the hopes of the Gospel, Miss E. Dryer."[18]

Although Moody read this testimony and others like it, he chose to maintain his focus on evangelization rather than divine healing. He knew of Emma's steadfast faith on this issue for which she had her own personal testimony. Emma believed in concentrating on the whole person which included both the spiritual and the physical aspects of man's design. With her regular prayer meetings held at the YMCA from the inception of the Bible Work she reported that many were healed. Therefore, from the lens of experience and with sincerity she explained this one doctrinal issue on which

13. Ibid., 23.
14. Ibid., 23–24.
15. Ibid., 21.
16. Ibid., 26.
17. Ibid., 27.
18. Ibid.

she and Moody differed: "Mr. Moody was opposed to the doctrine of Divine Healing, as he understood it. I favored it, as I understand it."[19]

Despite these early differences, Emma reported to Charles Blanchard that as the years passed, Moody embraced "a wider view of healing grace" as his "views of this subject changed somewhat, before he died."[20] D. L. Moody was influenced by Andrew Murray, author of *Divine Healing*. He also greatly encouraged his friend A. J. Gordon to publish the 1882 book *The Ministry of Healing*. Moody further displayed his progressive belief in healing when on Tuesday, January 13, 1891, he wrote a letter to a former Northfield student, Joshua Gravett, on behalf of his wife Charlotte Gravett. Moody performed their wedding ceremony at the Northfield Hotel just a few months earlier on November 5, 1890. Soon afterward, Moody received word that Charlotte had been smitten with terminal tuberculosis. He advised Joshua to take his wife to see Albert Benjamin Simpson (1843–1919), Canadian born founder of the Christian Missionary Alliance. Moody confidently encouraged them to ask Simpson to pray and anoint her as they held onto faith in God's healing power. The next Wednesday, on January 21, Dr. Simpson led an anointing service attended by the Gravetts. Charlotte lived for fifty-three more years.[21]

During the 1860s the groundwork for Moody's evolving faith in divine healing had already been laid. He witnessed the healing of a North Market mission school and business associate, Mr. Field, from Wisconsin. Field was unable to walk without support due to a crooked and lame leg. He had suffered with intense pain for an extended period of time. Known as a man filled with faith and the Holy Spirit, he meditated one evening after excruciating pain on the story of the man with palsy whom Jesus healed. He determined that he should also ask the Lord to heal him. That night, after dreaming that he had surgery on his leg, he actually awoke with no pain. He now walked on a straightened and healed leg. The following Sunday he shared his remarkable healing testimony with his friends, John Farwell and D. L. Moody.[22]

Moody did not join Emma with a wholehearted promotion and inclusion of healing in his ministry. She nevertheless had an advocate in her friend President Charles Blanchard. Blanchard attended meetings where he received instruction from Keswick pietists George Müller, Hudson Taylor, and Andrew Murray. With reality and humility he confessed that his own life of faith and holiness could not compare to the momentous callings and examples of Müller and Taylor; yet he realized that his educational and ministerial tasks were God's chosen callings and assignments for him.[23] Blanchard, like Emma, conveyed his own eyewitness accounts of healing for those in the throes of accompanying death—those healed through his own prayers of faith.

---

19. Emma Dryer to Charles Blanchard, 1916, Biographical File of Emma Dryer.
20. Ibid.; Dorsett, *A Passion For Souls*, 333.
21. Olsen, *Patriarch of the Rockies*, 41–44.
22. Williams, *Life and Work of Dwight L. Moody*, 77–78.
23. Blanchard, *The Life of Charles Albert Blanchard*, 114.

Inspiration of Andrew Bonar (1810–92): Free Church of Scotland

Emma valued the sincere welcome she always received at Moody's Northfield home. At the second Northfield conference in August 1881 she gladly renewed her acquaintance with premillennialist Dr. Andrew Bonar and his daughter from Glasgow, Scotland. Moody had previously made acquaintance with Bonar in 1874 and 1875. Emma met him during her own trip to England in 1879. She kept written correspondence with the Bonar family. After the Northfield conference, she received a letter from Isabella R. Bonar regarding Moody's continued work in England. To the delight of many, Emma allowed its publication in the June 22, 1882, *Christian Cynosure*.

At the age of seventy-one Dr. Bonar accepted Moody's 1881 invitation to conduct several meetings daily at the Northfield conferences with instruction from the Bible. Another of his daughters, Marjory, recalled that those who heard him, including Emma, "listened eagerly for the weighty words that fell from his lips."[24] Emma delighted in listening to this master storyteller. Even Moody, gifted in the art of telling stories himself, requested to hear *Bonar's fables* which were highlighted with colorful speculations regarding events in the Bible.

Having heard the stories of missionary David Brainerd since her childhood, Emma was pleased to hear of Dr. Bonar's request to visit the historic territory not far from West Stockbridge. Bonar sincerely desired to honor and respect the lives of Jonathan Edwards and David Brainerd with his visit. He and his daughter Isabella were accompanied to Northampton by Mrs. Moody and Moody's co-evangelist Major Whittle. Bonar wrote to his family on August 2, 1881, regarding this visit: "You know how much I desired to be there, and our visit was most interesting . . . We sat under . . . the two old elm-trees planted in front of his house by Jonathan Edwards, and I can *sell* you, when I return, a piece of the bark!"[25]

His tour was also highlighted with his visit to David Brainerd's tomb and historic scenes of past great revivals. Marjory recalled how much he enjoyed the fellowship of those whom he had enduringly admired and respected. He knew he could return to Scotland with an overflowing heart and thoroughly gratifying recollections.[26] And these memories of Bonar's visit to America were forever and inspirationally engraved on Emma's heart and mind.

Inspiration of George Müller (1805–98): Evangelist and Missionary to Orphans

As an orphan herself Emma compassionately, yet eagerly, listened to the stories told by Moody regarding a German-born man in Bristol, England, who walked by faith and

---

24. Bonar, *Reminiscences of Andrew A. Bonar*, xvi.
25. Ibid., 94.
26. Ibid., xvi.

trusted in God's faithfulness to supply the needs of thousands of orphans. Moody had been first introduced in 1857 to George Ferdinand Müller through Müller's book *Life of Trust* given to him by his pastor friend J. B. Stillson. George Müller in 1834 began a ministry with no material support. For forty-three years he witnessed God's supply of more than $500,000 for buildings and over a million dollars for the support of as many as 15,000 orphans.

Major Daniel Whittle accompanied Plymouth Brethren evangelist George Müller in June of 1880 on his journey across the Atlantic from Quebec to England. Whittle, also known as a hymn writer and Bible teacher, preached and taught at the Chicago Avenue Church where Emma made his acquaintance. He was born in Chicopee Falls not far from Emma's birthplace. He discussed with her the publication of her testimony on healing for his 1881 Müller inspired book, *The Wonders of Prayer*. Only the names of prominent men were placed on the cover. Whittle honored Emma by positioning her testimony of healing in the beginning pages of the book following evangelist George Müller's *chair* testimony on answered prayer.

Emma read the story of Müller's confident faith-filled prayer for his wife's chair, shipped from New York, to arrive before the ship set sail. Whittle confessed his concern that Müller was overreacting with these unwise faith confessions. Ten minutes after Müller boarded, Whittle observed a wagon pulling up with Mrs. Müller's chair loaded at the top. Whittle quickly delivered it to Mr. Müller. He watched in absolute admiration as Mr. Müller received the chair with the joy and heartfelt appreciation of a child. Müller quietly and respectfully placed his hat into his hands and lifted up a prayer of thanksgiving to God for hearing and answering his request for the chair.[27]

On Moody's earlier visit to England he determined to study from notable men such as George Müller. In the process he succeeded in orchestrating Müller's two visits to Chicago. On his fourth worldwide evangelistic tour Müller, at the age of seventy-three, travelled to Chicago in June of 1878. Emma eagerly anticipated the Sunday evening service at the Chicago Avenue Church (CAC) along with almost 3,000 others. They joined their voices to sing with the choir the hymn *Hold the Fort, For I Am Coming* written by Whittle's friend, P. P. Bliss. After prayer and Scripture reading, Mr. Müller preached for an hour. The next day he greeted some of his former orphans. Once again he spoke for over an hour at Farwell Hall to an audience of around 2,500. His last message to almost 2,000 in Farwell Hall was on the second coming of the Lord, much to Emma's intense satisfaction.

On Müller's sixth worldwide tour in February of 1880 he reached out to the Chicago German congregations. He addressed an audience of around 2,000 Germans at the CAC. Five days later he spoke to a thousand delegates at the Sunday school Teachers' Convention followed by messages from Major Whittle and Baptist minister B. F. Jacobs. A week after his arrival Müller preached at the morning CAC service

---

27. Whittle, *The Wonders of Prayer*, 8.

from 2 Timothy 4:7–8 "with great help and power."[28] He followed in the afternoon with another message on the return of the Lord and the parable of the ten virgins. He culminated his visit to Chicago by delivering a sermon at the First Congregational Church where Emma's dear friends, Dr. and Mrs. Goodwin, ministered.

Emma received inspiration from these close encounters with George Müller. She heard his faith building messages and with renewed encouragement continued in the way of faith that Müller had advocated: "How God supplies our needs, how he rewards faith, how he cares for those who trust in Him. How he can as well take care of his children to-day as he did in the days of the Prophets, and how surely he fulfills his promise, even when the trial brings us to the extremities of circumstances seemingly impossible."[29] Toward the end of Emma's association with the Bible Institute in 1889, she would once again receive inspiration from Müller's prophetic words regarding trials of faith. His words would have echoed in her mind and heart: "Our desire therefore, is, not that we may be without trials of faith, but that the Lord graciously would be pleased to support us in the trial, that we may not dishonor him by distrust."[30]

Inspiration of Andrew Murray (1828–1917): Educator and South African Minister

In his book, *Getting Things from God*, Emma's friend Charles Blanchard introduced each chapter with quotes from Reverend Andrew Murray regarding the sin of prayerlessness and the Holy Spirit's activity through prayer. Greatly influenced by the writings of this prolific author, Emma and Charles eagerly anticipated his arrival at Moody's Northfield Conferences. As a Dutch Reformed minister Murray actively participated in the Mildmay and South African Keswick Conventions. Emma heard how God had gloriously poured out his Spirit in Worcester, South Africa as Andrew Murray led this 1860 revival. It was reported that the renewal started when a young black girl of fifteen began reading Scripture and earnestly praying. This group of sixty young people suddenly heard a distant and unexplainable vibrating sound advancing toward them. The meeting gloriously extended into the early morning hours with singing in the streets and increased prayer. Andrew Murray's wife wrote about the unrelenting powerful outpouring of God's Spirit and presence.[31]

Emma unequivocally related to Andrew Murray. As a fellow Christian educator, he founded *The Huguenot Seminary* in 1873 to train young ladies as teachers for the African children. Murray patterned the seminary after Mount Holyoke College in Massachusetts where Charles Blanchard's own sister Maria attended.[32] After numer-

---

28. Müller, *The Preaching Tours and Missionary Labours of George Müller*, 148.
29. Whittle, *The Wonders of Prayer*, 203.
30. Müller, *The Life of Trust*, 194.
31. Douglas, *Andrew Murray and His Message*, 86–89.
32. Ibid., 119–26.

ous invitations from Moody, Andrew Murray finally agreed to visit Northfield in 1895 where he "exemplified in such remarkable degree the humility, purity and love which he urged upon his eager auditors, with the authority of a veritable prophet of God."[33] Much to Emma's elation, he extended his trip to visit Chicago where he spoke twice every day at a five day conference.[34]

Moody successfully promoted Murray's writings of over two hundred books in America through Revell Publishers and later Moody Press including Murray's books *The Prayer Life* and *The Deeper Christian Life*. As evidence of his inspiration on Emma's life, she wrote in her Bible, perhaps at his 1895 visit to Chicago, notes from his message regarding prayer: "How to pray: Intelligently according to the revealed will of God in His Word. Unremittingly without ceasing. Imperatively Gen. 32:28 I John 5:14–15 and contagiously & now Luke 22:40–46 Man ought always to pray and not to faint. Luke 18:1." Emma penned underneath those notes the words of Andrew Murray: "Prayer is the strategical point which Satan watches." She acknowledged that Andrew Murray spoke these words by writing his name, *Rev. Dr. Andrew Murray*, beside this quote.[35] Murray appealed to Christians to recognize prayerlessness as sin and to never neglect times of fellowship with the Lord. Through the years Emma received inspiration from Andrew Murray's admonition to remain watchful and steadfast in prayer with unbroken fellowship regardless of the heart wrenching circumstances of life.

Inspiration of Hudson Taylor (1832-1905): Founder of China Inland Mission

When Emma first moved to Chicago she stayed with her New York friends, Mrs. Lucy Flagler Helmer and her husband, who both carried a burden for mission work in China. This couple later became the directors for Hudson Taylor's China Inland Mission (CIM) in Toronto. With their influence Emma also actively supported the work of the China Inland Mission.

Emma heard glowing reports from Moody, Andrew Murray, and George Müller about this very special missionary to China—James Hudson Taylor. As the son of a Methodist preacher he settled in North London in order to touch base with Pennefather's Mildmay Conferences. In 1853 at the age of twenty-one he left for China convinced that God would meet his every need. Equipped with a medical background and ultimately assuming the Chinese dress, Taylor impacted China. He established the China Inland Mission, revised the Chinese New Testament, recruited over eight hundred missionaries, and established 125 schools.

In 1857 Hudson Taylor received a letter acknowledging monetary support from George Müller as they began a long-time missionary friendship. Like his

---

33. Williams, *Life and Work of Dwight L. Moody*, 257.
34. Du Plessis, *Life of Andrew Murray of South Africa*, 445.
35. Emma Dryer's Bible, Biographical File of Emma Dryer.

contemporaries—Müller, Murray, and Moody—he attended the Mildmay Conferences from its early days. He lived in London not far from Mr. Pennefather. Pennefather asked the young and fairly unknown Hudson Taylor to speak at the 1872 Mildmay Conference attended by 2,500 people. Taylor joined D. L. Moody on the platform to give the opening conference address.[36]

Even at that time Taylor had no idea that he would one day venture to America and Canada. He had not yet envisioned the CIM work greatly expanding through the cooperation of Mr. Moody. The efforts of Henry W. Frost, an American missionary to China, failed to convince him to plant an American branch of the CIM. Mr. Frost was later quite surprised when he heard that Hudson accepted an invitation to attend the premillennialist Niagara-on-the-Lake Conference. Frost immediately notified Moody regarding a possible request for Hudson to speak at Northfield.[37] Other invitations in America poured in. Hudson believed that providence had offered the means for his visit to America to meet Moody and over 2,000 mission-minded students eager to serve overseas.[38]

Hudson Taylor arrived at the Student Conference at Northfield in July of 1888. Mr. Moody met him and cordially escorted him in his buggy to meet Mrs. Moody and the family. Moody shared the news that two years previously over 2,000 undergraduates of the Student Volunteer Movement had signed a pledge to enter into missions.[39] One of those signers, Robert P. Wilder, attended the Hudson Taylor Northfield Conference of 400 students from over 90 colleges. Emma's heart would have been moved with others who heard Mr. Wilder's impressions of Hudson Taylor's visit:

> When he came to Northfield and appealed on behalf of China, the hearts of the delegates burned within them. And he not only made the needs of the mission-field very real; he showed us the possibilities of the Christian life. The students loved to hear him expound the Word of God. He was a master of his Bible, and his sympathy and naturalness attracted men to him. His addresses were so much appreciated that Mr. Moody had to announce extra meetings to be held by him in the afternoons—so many of the students were anxious to hear more from the veteran missionary . . . eternity alone can reveal the results of that life, and the effect of his words.[40]

It was reported that Hudson Taylor's vast knowledge, incredible trust, and steadfast faith in God's word deeply impacted the meetings proving him to be a missionary of unnatural strength and authority.

---

36. Taylor, *Hudson Taylor and the China Inland Mission*, 223.
37. Ibid., 439.
38. Shanks, *College Students at Northfield*, 12-13.
39. Taylor, *Hudson Taylor and the China Inland Mission*, 442.
40. Ibid., 443.

Hudson Taylor traveled across America holding over forty meetings. In his brief visit to Chicago in July 1888 he addressed the church for two successive meetings.[41] As Emma listened, she connected with the mission heart of this emissary to China. She would have agreed with her friend William Blackstone: "It was the almost visible presence of God in him that made his plain and simple words so powerful."[42]

Emma's Chicago friend, John Farwell, spoke of his trip with Hudson Taylor as he and Moody travelled to London. Farwell remembered that Hudson was preparing a group of young men for mission work in China. Hudson passionately shared with Farwell and Moody his vision to send missionaries to every China province. Hudson's trip to America deepened Moody's interest in the CIM. Moody made appeals for students to respond to the call to China. He gave his full support by providing his Northfield Hotel for training missionary candidates.[43]

Hudson delivered his final message from Toronto on September 23, 1888. His heart was encouraged by the aid and assistance given him. He witnessed a powerful manifestation of God resulting in an increased momentum for spreading the gospel to foreign lands.[44] After Emma's encounter with the unwavering faith of this missionary, she wrote in her Bible the words of Hudson's meaningful and inspirational poem that had become her prayer as well: "'Lord Jesus, be Thou unto me, A living bright reality: More precious to faith's vision keen. Than any Earthly object seen. More real, more intimately nigh Than e'en the sweetest Earthly tie.' Ask & ye shall receive. E.D."[45]

Inspiration of Henry Drummond (1851–97): Scottish Professor and Author

When Moody returned in 1885 from England he contacted Emma and requested that she include in the Bible training program Henry Drummond's reading of the Love chapter—1 Corinthians 13. While staying at Lord Aberdeen's home in England in 1884, Moody had been dynamically moved by this young man. He shared:

> I was staying with a party of friends in a country house... On Sunday evening as we sat around the fire, they asked me to read and expound some portion of Scripture. Being tired after the services of the day, I told them to ask Henry Drummond, who was one of the party. After some urging he drew a small Testament from his hip pocket, opened it at the 13th chapter of I Corinthians, and began to speak on the subject of Love. It seemed to me that I had never heard anything so beautiful... The one great need in our Christian life is love,

---

41. Ibid., 445, 471.
42. Ibid., 444.
43. Ibid.
44. Ibid., 442.
45. Emma Dryer's Bible, Biographical File of Emma Dryer.

more love to God and to each other. Would that we could all move into that Love chapter, and live there.[46]

Emma took Moody's request seriously as she also desired to move and remain in God's love. Her correspondence with others revealed the expanse of her Corinthian love: "I am with daily prayers & love"; "Thus, cheerfully, prayerfully, repentantly, forgivingly in Christian love hoping"; " In Christian love always"; "May His Word be our open Book—a living letter of His infinite love to you & yours always"; and "in the bonds of everlasting love."[47] Truly, the regular reading of Drummond's book at the Bible Work impacted Emma's life.

Drummond presented a reading of his book, *The Greatest Thing in the World*, in Stone Hall during the 1886 Northfield Conference. Moody responded with deep sentiment and prophetic awareness: "Young men, you have heard a great address. I prophesy that this will live and will be translated into twenty languages."[48] Moody began a friendship with Henry Drummond in November of 1873 on his tour to Scotland. When this twenty-two year old Edinburgh University student heard Moody's message he joined hundreds of other students involved in Moody's campaigns. Moody quickly discerned Drummond's talents. He had discovered another beloved assistant for his evangelistic work to serve in the inquiry rooms and to minister to other young men. Drummond spent two years following Moody and nurturing a friendship that would be life-long. During this crusade he joined the Moody family on Saturdays for their day of rest. He found a kindred friendship in Mrs. Moody with her granddaughter recording their mutually abundant respect and high regard.[49]

Emma closely followed this new friendship between Drummond and Moody. After ministering with Moody from 1873 to 1875, Drummond arrived at a difficult decision to leave the campaign trail to continue his education. He trained as a professor of science with a divinity background. He wrote the 1883 *Natural Law in the Spiritual World* asserting a logical extension of the material realm to the spiritual. This book quickly made his name popular throughout the United Kingdom and America. In 1894 he wrote *The Ascent of Man* in response to Darwin's 1871 evolution work *The Descent of Man*. Regardless of Drummond's fame he continued to be "the charming, unspoiled, youthful-spirited man the Moodys had first known."[50] Even with his heavy lecturing and professorship schedule, he remained supportive of Moody's future campaigns to the British Isles and received numerous invitations to visit American universities and Moody's schools.

---

46. Drummond, *The Greatest Thing in the World*, Introduction.
47. Anita Blaine McCormick Correspondence and Papers, McCormick Collection.
48. Powell, *Heavenly Destiny*, 170.
49. Ibid., 165.
50. Ibid.

Emma's Spiritual Walk and Inspirations

Emma could relate firsthand to the unexpected welcome she knew Moody's new visitors would receive on their first visit to Northfield. With Drummond's arrival in 1886 he had the prior advantage of having already met their sturdy farmerlike coachman driving a horse pulled buggy:

> As he drives you to the spacious hotel—a creation of Mr. Moody's—he will answer your questions . . . in a brusque, businesslike way . . . [W]hen you are deposited at the door . . . you ask the clerk whether the great man himself is at home . . . [H]e will point to your coachman, now disappearing like lightning down the drive, and—too much accustomed to Mr. Moody's humor to smile at his latest jest—whispers, 'That's him!'.[51]

In 1893, after several previous visits to America, Drummond attended the World's Columbian Exposition in Chicago. He was eager to view the Irish village exhibition funded primarily by his friends Lady and Lord Aberdeen. On his last visit to America, he toured various universities, including Harvard and Amherst College where he lectured against evolution and spoke on his book, *Ascent of Man*. In May and June he scheduled a time for sightseeing and lecturing in Chicago. Drummond also attended the October 8–14 Evangelical Alliance of the United States where he presented the lecture *Christianity and the Evolution of Society*. Emma and her May Institute friend, Professor Scott from the Chicago Theological Seminary, both judiciously observed Drummond's fondness for analytical reasoning and inquiry. Moody himself loyally believed in Drummond and although he did not agree with him in all of his suppositions, he esteemed him as a living Christian example of 1 Corinthians 13.[52]

Emma's spiritual life was influenced and inspired by these great minds and spirits of her day. The Lord used them to prepare her for an upcoming trial regarding her ability and willingness not necessarily to start an orphanage as George Müller; nor to stand on the missionary soil of China or South Africa; and not to return as a professor to a major university—but to test her willingness to let go of her envisioned dream and allow God to forge her destiny in total surrender to his perfect plan.

"She senses the worth of her work, is in no hurry to call it quits for the day."

~Proverbs 31:18 MSG~

---

51. Ibid., 107.
52. Ibid., 156.

9

Chicago Evangelization Society and Bible Institute, 1885–89

"May God, who gives you this endurance and encouragement, allow you to live in harmony with each other by following the example of Christ Jesus."
~Romans 15:5 GWT~

"Peacemakers are people who breathe grace."
~Ken Sande~

With the success of Emma's Bible Work and the May Institute, the groundwork had been laid for the manifestation of her dream—a full-fledged Bible Institute. After his fifth trip to England in 1883, Moody, characterized as *the powerhouse*[1] behind the vision, began more actively to promote the school's development and to push for its success.

During the years since first speaking with Moody about the Bible Institute, Emma had not failed to support this vision. In a July 25, 1887, letter to Moody she reiterated the long-lasting assistance of many others and her own steadfast relationship with him: "For more than 15 years I have planned & gathered the meetings for the work . . . so I *know* what was planned & done & what work was proposed to be done; & I know some warm, earnest hearts & willing efficient hands that have *for years* grown *weary* waiting to do this work with *you* . . . But in a loyalty to you & your expressed purposes all has been made to wait tho in pain for your continually promised coming."[2] Emma enduringly advocated for her Northfield friend: "Through loneliness and trouble, and constraint, wearing work, then I held on. When others shuddered, I believed. When others hurried away, I . . . worked on. When others said you were never meant to come

1. Joiner, *Sin in the City,* 53.
2. Emma Dryer to Mr. Moody, 25 July 1887, Biographical File of Emma Dryer.

here, I believed that God had made you speak The Truth, in preaching and planned purposes. And I prayed on."³

In 1872 the flaming evangelistic passion of D. L. Moody had totally captured Emma's spiritual devotion and commitment.⁴ In the process of their friendship, many believe that Emma's perception of the necessity of a Bible school emerged even before Moody's did and that she was *the driving force* behind its success.⁵ Historian Richard E. Day in 1936 urged others not to "lose sight of the heroic pioneering of Emeline E. [sic] Dryer, . . . [the] brilliant Emeline Dryer, forerunner of [the] Bible Institute."⁶

Even as recently as 2006, authors of a publication funded by the Carnegie Foundation regarding seminary education likewise concluded that Emma Dryer qualified as an innovator of a Bible school training program and was the hidden and unrecognized organizer of Moody Bible Institute.⁷ Current and former Moody Bible Institute students have likewise acknowledged Emma's place in the founding of the school: "While many people think that D. L. Moody founded my school, the driving force behind this wonderful institution was a largely unnoticed woman, Emma Dryer."⁸ In 1916 Emma more specifically and humbly acknowledged that neither she nor Moody founded the school, but rather "God founded and established that institute—a Child of the Moody Church!"⁹

Whether they be known as co-founders or shared vision-holders, neither Emma nor Moody desired to receive a founder's adulation or to make a name for themselves. Rather, for seventeen years Emma sought to safeguard, per Moody's direction, the mission of the school. She carefully abbreviated criticism against Moody in the public arena and purposefully kept ties with him and his family.¹⁰ Even after Moody's death in 1899 Emma still viewed their relationship, despite the challenges of the years, as one in which from its initiation they had *providentially co-operated*.¹¹

Emma's relationship with Moody went beyond that of a friend and Christian associate to that of his being her spiritual mentor and church pastor. However, her disappointment through the years eventually took the form of non-dispelled impatience and impending mistrust. She had inherently desired to fulfill the nineteenth-century cultural and evangelical expectations of submission to those in masculine and pastoral authority. Yet Emma's submission presented a dilemma. She could not move forward as long as Moody hesitatingly wavered and delayed the implementation of

3. Ibid.
4. Day, *Bush Aglow*, 263.
5. Beatty, "The City to Come," para. 3.
6. Day, *Bush Aglow*, 263, 295.
7. Foster, et al., *Educating Clergy*, 199.
8. Beatty, "The City to Come," para. 3.
9. Emma Dryer to Charles Blanchard, 1916, Biographical File of Emma Dryer.
10. Dorsett, *A Passion For Soul,* 273.
11. Emma Dryer to Charles Blanchard, 1916, Biographical File of Emma Dryer.

their vision.[12] With Emma's confident faith—though accompanied by uneasiness and setbacks—she submissively prayed for Moody's return to Chicago as he had promised.

The timely input of others helped Emma to understandably realize Moody's tremendous schedule and unending responsibilities. She remembered one conversation she had with Major Whittle:

> Major Whittle . . . came . . . confidentially to tell me, that the Chicago work was very hard for Mr. Moody; and he had so many 'irons in the fire' already, that he dreaded Chicago; and he loved Northfield more than any other place on Earth. When I answered, 'Why does he not say so?' he replied that Mr. Moody saw in the contemplated Institute, a great evangelistic work, and so wanted to undertake it; but with his many cares, this work perplexed him. Northfield meant rest and Home, and affectionate co-operation; and Chicago meant distance and an untried field. Mr. Moody was greatly beloved in Chicago; and he had so related himself to the contemplated Institution, always speaking of it, in Northfield Conventions, and other occasions, as our Bible-Work in Chicago.[13]

Supporters backed Emma in her determination to see Moody visit Chicago as an act of his unwavering support. By 1885 her encumbering frustration and disappointment began to temporarily ease when Moody presented what Emma resolved to be a surmountable, although burdensome, financial challenge. Once again Emma's faithful determination, maintained by her prayers and submission to the Holy Spirit, caused her to rise above these times of discouragement.

The $250,000 Challenge of 1885

Emma biblically portrayed Moody as an Elijah who was "a Divinely equipped 'flying artillery' on life's battle-field" and truly a man of accelerated action.[14] At the release time of the January 1, 1885, *Christian Cynosure*, the publication reported that Moody, true to form, hurriedly entered the city like a whirlwind with a one day lay-over on his trip from Cincinnati, Ohio, to St. Paul, Minnesota. Moody reportedly met at Farwell Hall in the Bible Work Room "to consider the question of founding here an institution for the training of lay missionaries . . . and making permanent the effort made last year by Miss Dryer, Pres. C. A. Blanchard, Prof. Moorehead and others."[15]

Emma's long-time friend, Charles Blanchard, who attended the Farwell Hall meeting, registered his earnest impression that this was unmistakably the providential

---

12. Joiner, *Sin in the City*, 56.
13. Emma Dryer to Charles Blanchard, 1916, Biographical File of Emma Dryer.
14. Ibid.
15. *Christian Cynosure*, National Christian Association, January 1, 1885, 12.

work of God.[16] He knew that many of Emma and Moody's other friends were involved. He recalled that Moody challenged those in attendance to raise $250,000 for the Bible Institute. Likewise, Emma also recollected this meeting with Turlington Harvey presiding. Mr. Kimball made a presentation followed by remarks from her dispensationalist friend, William Blackstone. Emma listened as Moody, true to his visionary tendencies, challenged the group to raise the $250,000 needed for the construction of a building to accommodate 150 to 200 people and to create an endowment fund. He also suggested that a temporary facility be obtained to get the school going as soon as possible. Moody would serve and oversee the business orientation of the workers with the help of a team of teachers and a committee to formulate and execute this new school project.[17] Yet with this challenge Moody insistently made it quite clear: "I am not going to shin around this city for money any more. I have done my share of that kind of work."[18]

After the meeting, as Moody prepared for a hasty departure, in confidence he told Emma: "I don't know but we had better take the school to New York. I don't feel sure, that Chicago is prepared for it." Although from New York herself, she responded with concern: "I hope, Mr. Moody, you will decide, for your indecision hinders other Christian work." Moody replied, "Wherever it goes, I want you to understand, that you and I keep this work in our own hands, while we live." Emma hid this promise in her heart while challenging his $250,000 request: "And may I say you will come, if that is raised?" He replied in the affirmative. As they approached the elevator he sensitively assured her that her difficulties would be over with the commencement of this new work.[19]

Emma sincerely believed that the home for the Bible Institute would be in Chicago and that the money would be raised. Years later she confided in Nettie McCormick the pain of Moody's financial request: "*It hurt* and my heart ached before the unexpected, added burden. But I soon remembered God's Almightiness & thought I would look at that until the money came."[20] As Moody had done previously in 1873 he confidently left the challenge to raise funds in Emma's capable hands. He compellingly mandated that she continue to hold the vision before the people because he would not come unless the $250,000 was raised.[21]

After Moody's departure Emma immediately contacted her friend Nettie McCormick and Nettie's son Cyrus Jr. She secured their pledge of $50,000. One of Emma's

16. Blanchard, *The Life of Charles Albert Blanchard*, 87.
17. *Christian Cynosure*, National Christian Association, January 1, 1885, 12.
18. Charles A. Blanchard to Mr. William Norton at the Bible Institute Colportage Association, 4 June 1913, Wheaton College Archives and Special Collections.
19. Emma Dryer to Charles Blanchard, 1916, Biographical File of Emma Dryer.
20. Emma Dryer written from Northfield to Nettie McCormick, 20 September 1888, care of Reverend Ed M. Williams, Biographical File of Emma Dryer.
21. Getz, *The Story of Moody Bible Institute*, 21.

faithful prayer partners, John Farwell, promised $100,000 in stock. By the spring of 1885 other Bible Work board members pledged $30,000, $20,000, and $10,000 along with further conditional pledges.[22] After a quite successful four week May Institute in Farwell Hall, Emma headed to the 1885 Northfield summer conference. While there, she suggested to Moody that he could perhaps obtain the fundraising services of Reverend Frederick G. Ensign (1837–1906) who specialized in making appeals to businessmen. She recognized that Ensign, as superintendent of the Chicago American Sunday School Union, successfully secured missionary resources for the union. He had also assisted Moody in raising funds to rebuild the YMCA after the Chicago Fire.[23] Mr. Ensign readily agreed to meet with Emma and Moody at the conference.

Emma knew Moody as a man of vision who continually sought out the potential in all with whom he associated. Therefore, she was not surprised when Moody encouraged them both to make interest in the school *red-hot* followed by the request that Mr. Ensign assist in superintending the upcoming school.[24] After the meeting, Ensign immediately began an extensive *red-hot* advertisement campaign by placing Bible Training School ads in Revell's publication, *Record of Christian Work*.[25]

Turbulent Years 1885 to 1889

With the establishment of the Bible Work in 1873 Emma invested her faith in the power and wealth of God rather than that of man. Full of hope, she successfully secured Moody's $250,000 requirement and credited it to the goodness of the Lord. In later years she privately wrote to her friend, Nettie McCormick, expressing her deep grief and lingering disappointment in Moody's reaction to this positive news:

> That strangely impossible condition . . . was a mistake, a wrong. But God sent the money & would have sent more! One would have thought that my Christian friend, dearly beloved in the Lord would have come to C. [Chicago] then with something like this:—'Well! Miss D—, you have waited here by this treasury more than 15 yrs & God has graciously sent the money for our work. Let us thank Him for all this goodness . . . ' and—'Now tell me about the subscriptions and how things stand & what you are doing & what you see to do'—and—'Now let's gather the friends & thank God for what He has done & try to understand what He will have us do.' Oh my rent soul! How sweetly we might have walked together with Christ to hasten His coming kingdom!'[26]

---

22. Ibid.
23. Rice, *The Sunday-School Movement*, 279–80.
24. Emma Dryer to Charles Blanchard, 1916, Biographical File of Emma Dryer.
25. *Record of Christian Work* (1883–1886). *The Evangelistic Record* (1881–82).
26. Emma Dryer written in Northfield to Nettie McCormick care of Reverend Ed M. Williams, 20 September 1888, Biographical File of Emma Dryer.

Chicago Evangelization Society and Bible Institute, 1885–89

During the remainder of 1885 following the Northfield summer conference, Moody showed little further affirmative regard concerning the training school. In spite of her unfulfilled expectations, Emma continued to work with perseverance and determination.

The following winter, from Sunday, January 17 to Monday, January 25, 1886, Emma gratefully anticipated Moody's return to Chicago en route from Cleveland, Ohio, to Knoxville, Tennessee. He had arranged revival meetings at the Chicago Avenue Church with a follow up meeting on the progress of the school.[27] The *Record of Christian Work,* a monthly chronicle first published in 1881 under the title of *Evangelistic Record* by Moody's brother-in-law Fleming H. Revell, reported that with the rise of crime in Chicago a greater need for Christian workers existed—thus, necessitating a training school. The question was posed: "Why shall not Mr. Moody be put at the head of such an institution at once in Chicago?" Those who were backing this project firmly believed with Emma and Moody that Chicago needed an educational institution which would train *gap-men* in urban ministry to work with the poor and labor classes. The *Record of Christian Work* optimistically proposed that men and women could achieve this with their $250,000 gift which would enable them to reach the *unevangelized* with the gospel in America and throughout the world.[28]

On January 22, 1886, at a Friday noon meeting Moody made an appeal to gain support from Chicago businessmen for city evangelism. Following his comments, a discussion began regarding the proposed Bible school. At this time Moody boldly sanctioned a training school for both men and women. With a deep show of respect for Emma's efforts at the Chicago Avenue Church and the Bible Work, he complimentarily stated that she was the most excellent Bible instructor in the country.[29] His wide-sweeping stamp of approval and words of affirmation most certainly touched Emma's heart, tempered prior discouragement, and reaffirmed his continued commitment to maintain their vision.

At this meeting Moody confidently suggested the following plan: "Take $50,000 and put up a building that will house seventy-five or one hundred people . . . Take the $200,000 and invest it at 5 percent, and that gives you $10,000 a year just to run this work. Then take men that have the gifts and train them for this work of reaching the people. But you will say: 'where are you going to find them?' I will tell you. God never had a work but what he had men to do it."[30] Moody affirmed the desire of those present by restating his vision for training individuals who would fill the gap that existed between the laity and clergy. This could be accomplished by their willingness to serve and give their lives to labor beside those in the ministry.[31]

27. *Record of Christian Work*, January 1886, 1.
28. Ibid.
29. Beatty, "The City to Come," section 7 para. 2.
30. Getz, *The Story of Moody Bible Institute*, 22.
31. Day, *Bush Aglow*, 264.

Moody went into action as board chairman. He selected prior Bible Work board members from the Chicago business community—Cyrus McCormick Jr. as secretary, Turlington Harvey as vice chairman, Elbridge Keith, John Farwell, and Nathaniel Bouton. Robert Scott, who went into the dry goods with a firm named Carson, Pierie and Scott, also joined this eager group of business-focused contributors with his own significant financial resources.

Board Tensions and Expectations 1886

At last Emma had the necessary team players committed to establish the Bible Institute. With her extensive administrative skills and the tremendous financial support of these Chicago businessmen, Moody confidently forged ahead with his dream of a training school for city evangelism. The board began to proactively scrutinize their investments while pinning down a viable location for the school.

Since Moody's departure, Emma, with the promised $250,000 in pledges, joined a specially appointed building committee consisting of Bouton, Farwell, and Nettie McCormick to begin the exploration of land possibilities for the proposed school. Reverend Charles Goss, pastor of the Chicago Avenue Church, also assisted in the search. The committee recommended real estate west of the church as well as property owned by Judge Anthony just north of the church. At the end of the 1886 May Institute Moody asked Emma to visit Judge Anthony, with whom she was acquainted, and schedule a meeting. In place of his father, Anthony's son met them at the Chicago Avenue Church. The newly formed board finance committee set a limit for Moody to offer no more than $25,000 for the property. Emma watched as Moody inquired as to the amount Judge Anthony would take for the land. He was told $40,000. Without hesitation Moody said, "I'll pay it."[32]

This marked the beginning of a two year turbulent season in which Emma found herself a troubled participant. These board members, who had been Moody's friends for years, were highly experienced businessmen who believed in conducting business according to protocol. Moody's lack of consultation and follow-through with them regarding the Anthony property caused them to either withdraw or limit their pledges. According to Emma the board entered into a *sharp discussion* with Moody which initially dispersed the board and detained the payment of pledges. This scenario created the early stage of a future dilemma for Emma and Moody. Moody, as an independent business-minded evangelist, now found that he was accountable to a full board of business-focused leaders. Emma, who had thrived primarily on total dependence for God's supply as the primary leader over her own Bible Work board of women managers, now found herself accountable to this same group of practically minded businessmen.[33]

32. Emma Dryer to Charles Blanchard, 1916, Biographical File of Emma Dryer.
33. Foster, et al., *Educating Clergy*, 204.

Chicago Evangelization Society and Bible Institute, 1885-89

This proactive board also wanted to know specific details of the work. They sought assurance regarding Moody's plans in order to secure reliable returns on their investments. They were looking to Moody for his valuable leadership, but according to Emma "they wanted to understand what they were about."[34] The board began asking detailed and significant questions such as "Who would direct them in their studies and work?—What was to be the theology of the Institute?—How should it be supported?"[35] As a businessman, Moody knew that these business magnates with their investments would not deposit their pledges until they received more concrete information. They required assurance that the vision aligned with their conservative investment strategies.

To increase their faith in this venture Moody, despite his prior assertion that he would not assist with fundraising, actively sought backing from other Chicago businessmen—merchants Levi Leiter, Marshall Field, and Potter Palmer along with meatpacker industrialists Philip and Herman Armour. During his four month Chicago campaign from January to April, he requested that they invest in the school by giving $50,000 each.[36]

The early months of 1886 brought unreserved fears regarding the financial and social conditions in Chicago. Conflicts between the working class and business management caused Moody's business associates to extend caution. While they understood his evangelistic thrust, they pragmatically viewed the mission of the Bible Institute from a social mission and business perspective. As businessmen they realized the significant spiritual changes in their own lives through his ministry. Consequently, they regarded the Bible institute as a tool to train workers who would embrace higher ethical standards and morality to a greater degree than before their conversion. This would result in increased worker productivity and a decrease in the risk of financial loss for their investments.

Support also came from board member and industrialist Turlington Harvey. In April 1886 he advertised Moody's reason for establishing the school as a defense against the rise of socialism stating that "the only way to convert this dangerous element into peaceful helpful citizens was through the transforming power of Christ."[37] These Christian philanthropists raised legitimate concerns regarding aspects of socialism and the increase of inner city crime. With the onset of the Haymarket Riot they more heartily recognized the urgent need to develop an Evangelization Society to spearhead the establishment of the Bible Institute. This society would prove to be the culminating work of Moody's vision as well as "Emma Dryer's energy and hard work, and the generous gifts of several Chicago philanthropists."[38]

---

34. Emma Dryer to Charles Blanchard, 1916, Biographical File of Emma Dryer.
35. Ibid.
36. Findlay, *Dwight L. Moody: American Evangelist*, 330–1n51.
37. Ibid., 27.
38. Dorsett, *A Passion For Souls*, 273.

Notwithstanding the conflicting difficulty regarding the purchase of the Anthony property, Emma and Mr. Ensign continued to investigate potential locations. They looked at the 75'x210' corner lot on Ohio and St. Clair which Nettie McCormick offered to donate. Emma expressed to Nettie her disappointment that the land was not closer to the church. She suggested that perhaps the lot on Ohio Street and LaSalle Avenue south of Superior might be a possibility.[39] After several months of further land search and a delay caused from board deliberations, Emma reported on July 21, 1886, with a sigh of relief, that Moody sent her a telegram with his final approval for purchasing the Judge Anthony property on Chicago and LaSalle.

Divergence in Vision and Objectives

Individuals who unite with a compatible vision and a clear mission provide protection for their organization from unnecessary obstacles while assuring a crossing of the finish line to success. Leaders can drift from their original purpose and mission due to cultural or ethical pressures and various other diversions. According to Greer and Horst (2014) in their work *Mission Drift*, leaders who do not clearly communicate and unite in those changes could face a crisis of devastating and often irreparable damage. Since the year of 1873, when Emma and Moody joined together with a common vision, a changed articulation of their previous united vision created obstacles for the establishment of the Bible Institute and for all involved.

The first change occurred in Moody's target audience. He initially foresaw a training school for women and, in order to avoid a conflict of interest, stayed clear of any indication of creating a seminary training school for prospective pastors. In 1886 Moody unmistakably expanded his vision to now include *gap-men* who would minister to the common people in ways for which he believed seminarians were ill-equipped. Realizing his determination to avoid conflict with the seminaries, Emma had previously discussed with him the possibility of a Bible Institute to serve as a feeder school for the seminaries while providing Bible courses and student interns for local clergy.

Ultimately, Moody chose to follow her advice and extend their vision for seminary training of common people despite potential conflict or rivalry with the established seminaries.[40] He shared with his friend Major Whittle that he knew this transition could be difficult but with the steadfast support of some of his friends it would work out.[41] In due course, by 1889 three classes of male workers would be targeted:

1. Those who already possessed Bible skills to become more efficient

---

39. Emma Dryer to Nettie McCormick, 21 July 1886, Biographical File of Emma Dryer.
40. Foster, et al., *Educating Clergy*, 203.
41. Letter written by D. L. Moody to Major Whittle from Northfield, 24 May 1889, Biographical File of Emma Dryer.

2. Those who found it too late in life to take seminary courses

3. Those at secular jobs—unacquainted with the Bible, Christian work, and soul-winning—who held no intention of entering fulltime ministry[42]

Moody also altered his message to Emma regarding a coeducational school. Although terming *gap-men* as gender inclusive, his vision now primarily focused on men. Perhaps his self-confidence for their inclusion had in part been securely affirmed due to his notoriety as an established and internationally acclaimed evangelist. For whatever reason, he expanded his vision to include the need for preparing men in specific areas where training had been minimized. The original vision of a women's training school with specific female instruction for service would serve as an addendum to the Bible Institute.

Just as Emma had predicted several years earlier to Charles Blanchard, the success of the May Institute had been quickly noted by Moody. However, she did not realize that it would present the impetus for Moody to expand his vision of pastoral short-term seminars to a full time school for men. In exchange, the original purpose and make-up of her training school would soon be altered and minimized.[43] By the spring of 1889, when over five hundred ministers attended the annual May Institute, Moody confidently envisioned over a thousand for the fall session as a springboard to the establishment of the year round Bible Institute.

With the creation of an umbrella organization known as the Chicago Evangelization Society in 1887, its board members also brought their own objectives for the Bible Institute. They realized that Moody's vision centered on an expansion of city evangelism. However, they continued to view the new Bible Institute as an opportunity to produce higher social and ethical standards. Potential labor unrest would be curbed, and productivity and assets would increase. Furthermore, although Mr. Harvey wholeheartedly agreed with the objective of city evangelism, he would not acknowledge the value of Emma's Bible Work. He did not believe that it met Moody's evangelistic objective. He opposed Emma's limited concentration of women workers to certain assigned localities, their exclusion from attending evangelistic services, and their limited assistance to the evangelist.[44] Harvey's perspective would later fuel an irreconcilable discord between Emma and the Society.

With Moody's rise as a revivalist and evangelist his vision also expanded. Perhaps without full realization, he distanced himself from the original distinctives of the Bible Work.[45] Emma's vision, backed by her normal school training, centered on education and mission work from a social perspective. Moody's evangelistic approach no longer corresponded with Emma's focus on social hands-on activities and involvement

---

42. Getz, *The Story of Moody Bible Institute*, 45–47.
43. Dorsett, *A Passion For Souls*, 306–7.
44. Joiner, *Sin in the City*, 54.
45. Ibid.

which Moody believed would only hinder his work of evangelism. Moody's vision now involved aggressive evangelism and a training of workers to support his gospel message.[46]

Emma's experience in education in an urban setting was a drawing card for women interested in social community involvement beyond evangelism. With Moody's prior direction, Emma continued to incorporate into the Bible Work her Mildmay training regarding foreign and home missions. Once again Moody, rather than now envisioning a school to train individuals for foreign missions, foresaw primarily the training of home missionaries to serve in metropolitan areas within the working classes although he did not completely eliminate overseas missions.[47]

The question now became—*Whose perspective would govern the Bible Institute?* Ultimately, the different viewpoints of businessmen, evangelist, and educator would create a dissonance and an unfolding mission drift for the Bible Work away from the objectives of the newly formed Chicago Evangelization Society in which Emma would find herself slowly and despairingly unanchored.

Chicago Evangelization Society and Bible Work Merger 1887

From the initiation of Moody's $250,000 appeal in January 1885, plans remained stagnant despite the pledges and increased fundraising. However, by 1887 an economic upswing eased concerns of Chicago business investors. On February 5, 1887, Moody met with Emma, Nettie, and the board in his Chicago Grand Pacific Hotel room. At this time they jointly and officially organized the Chicago Evangelization Society (CES). A charter was adopted for the founding of a Bible Institute. This meeting led to a motion made by Emma that the Bible Work be known as a training school called *The Bible Work Institute* with a new charter and a seven member board. The primary objective of the Society was "to educate, direct, and maintain Christian workers as Bible readers, *teachers and evangelists* (author emphasis); who shall teach the Gospel in Chicago and its suburbs, especially in neglected fields."[48] Charter members agreed to faithfully support the work and its objectives with annual contributions.

The organizational chain of command consisted of a board of trustees with the following charter members: Bouton, Farwell, Keith, Harvey, Cyrus McCormick, Moody, and Robert Scott. They appointed a general manager for marketing the school and a Board of Managers to manage the Society's affairs. Committees were board appointed for such tasks as hiring faculty to oversee the field work, the Bible Work Institute, special meetings, and office management. Now at last with the formation of the

---

46. Ibid.
47. Getz, *The Story of Moody Bible Institute*, 45.
48. Ibid., 44.

Chicago Evangelization Society Moody's vision of a Bible school was being actualized and formulated by Emma's resilience and persistence.

The process of incorporation began for Emma's Bible Work—a ministry originally established as an evangelistic and social program to reach Chicago's non-churched women and children. At this February trustee meeting Emma made a motion that the Bible Work with all its assets be merged into the newly formed Chicago Evangelization Society. The Society approved Emma's prior suggestion that the new training school be named the *Bible Work Institute*.[49] And with years of incorporation experience, Mr. Harvey began preparation to obtain the state required incorporation certificate for the CES. This corporate certification was received from the state of Illinois on February 13, 1887.[50]

On February 17 Bouton and McCormick formed a committee designated to merge the Bible Work into the CES with the stipulation that Emma receive a yearly salary of $1,000.[51] By February 23 they reported that the Bible Work was ready for its transitional merger with the CES as soon as its own organization was completed. An interim committee consisting of five women was also appointed to conduct a feasibility study for various forthcoming aspects of the merger and to watch over the current interests of the Bible Work home.[52]

The CES maintained management and sponsorship of not only the Bible Work Institute but also, with Moody's backing, the Temperance Gospel League and city tent meetings. Beginning on March 3, 1887, Major Whittle was employed to head up the Temperance Gospel League. Whittle secured the services of temperance evangelist Francis Murphy (1836–1907) for lectures at various locations and specifically at the YMCA. The business minded CES board who was behind the establishment of the Bible Work Institute struggled to understand how the temperance issue connected with the objectives of the institute. But realizing Moody's friendship with Whittle and his passionate evangelistic focus on the salvation of souls, they were not totally opposed to this addition.[53] At the March 23 trustee meeting Moody suggested that summer evangelistic work with daily tent meetings led by evangelist Merton Smith be conducted throughout various sections of the city. With his futuristic and firm evangelistic mindset Moody would later propose that communication begin with Reverend Benjamin Fay Mills (1857–1916) and other popular evangelists in order to secure their services for the winter months.[54]

---

49. Emma Dryer to Charles Blanchard, 1916, Biographical File of Emma Dryer; Board Minutes, 5 February 1887, Chicago Evangelization Society File.

50. Ibid.

51. Findlay, *Dwight L. Moody: American Evangelist*, 223n54.

52. Board Minutes, 23 February 1887, Chicago Evangelization Society File.

53. Ibid., April 20, 1887 and March 9, 1887.

54. Ibid., 15 March 1888.

On April 20, 1887, the board agreed to meet at noon every Wednesday in Mr. Moody's hotel rooms. They adopted the following: "The Executive Committees are instructed and authorized to take up the work of this Society, arrange and plan for building, arrange and plan for training school courses for the year 1887, take the general direction of the Society's work, except evangelistic meetings, until the new buildings are completed."[55] Mr. Alexander H. Lowden was contracted for the construction of the men's building. Moody asked Emma to follow up on the Anthony property and determine its suitability for occupancy by her lady workers. She and her friend Mary Moore Hitchcock checked out the houses. Emma remembered years later how she and Mary knelt on that property to ask the Lord for his continued blessings on the Christian work that would soon be established there.[56]

By May 11 Bouton and McCormick reported favorably regarding land on which to build the Bible Institute. At a cost of $50,000 it could be constructed by the first of August. Emma's hopes were further secured with the following announcement reported in the *Christian Cynosure* on May 12, 1887:

> Mr. Moody . . . told the Presbyterian ministers last week that on a lot at the corner of Ohio and St. Clair streets on the North Side he proposes to erect a training school for women city missionaries. The young men will be provided for elsewhere. Mr. Moody has $250,000 subscribed for the purpose, $50,000 of which will go into the building and $200,000 will be invested as endowment. The school will accommodate at least 100 girls, and Miss Dryer, so long and favorably known in the Bible Work of Chicago, will be at its head.[57]

At last it appeared that Emma's long and arduous work in establishing a Bible school was coming to fruition.

On June 16 the building committee reported a steady progress. By June 29 an additional committee consisting of Keith, Scott, Bouton, and Ensign was appointed. During this time Nettie McCormick reiterated that her $50,000 pledge was specifically for the Bible Work. Perhaps discerning a growing lack of support on the part of Mr. Harvey, she indicated her desire that "Miss Dryer be connected with that work permanently as had been proposed." She desired confirmation and assurance that Emma's long established and successful work, which Nettie had supported for many years, would continue in its effective outreach to the city's wage earners.[58]

During the remainder of 1887 the Board stood ready to go, according to Emma, with the funds and projected building plans. Nevertheless, Emma lamented: "But the hope of an *established system* of city evangelization did not increase, and the support

---

55. Ibid., 20 April 1887. The CES was chartered February 12, 1887, and the school officially opened on September 29, 1889.

56. Emma Dryer to Charles Blanchard, 1916, Biographical File of Emma Dryer.

57. *Christian Cynosure*, National Christian Association, May 12, 1887, 1.

58. Ibid., June 29, 1887.

of the Work did not increase; and some of the subscriptions, in whole or in part, were withdrawn. *I do not doubt* that Satan sought to prevent the Work!"[59] According to Nettie's friend Stella Roderick, the building project was brought to a standstill due to "labor troubles, money delays, and stress in the new society."[60]

During this time Emma sought consolation from her Christian friends, her faithful Bible workers, and members of the Bible Work Women's Council. She continued to declare God as her refuge and her strength especially when the summer of 1887 brought major board disagreements regarding building plans, board constitution, and board structure.[61]

Board Organization Conflict 1887

Conflict occurs when imperfect and inexperienced leaders attempt to exercise their authority over imperfect and unwilling followers.[62] When leaders and followers of an organization or ministry experience unresolved disagreements, their controversies hinder the establishment from growing into a vibrant organization. The advent of the summer of 1887 brought such challenges impeding organizational stability and dissipating relationships. When Nettie McCormick joined others on the CES board and on various committees, her business experience and expertise caused her to carefully scrutinize and review the CES's organizational constitution. Nettie noted some weaknesses regarding the governing power of a minority which could potentially present serious conflict of interest and operational issues.[63]

From her years of corporate experience with the McCormick Harvesting Machine Company Nettie McCormick realized the advantages of maintaining a large board in order to correct or avert potential difficulty. She also began detecting divergent changes from the original Bible Work vision and training school objectives. She held reservations regarding the vague and seemingly demeaning placement of the Ladies Department in the by-laws rather than in the constitution.[64] In a letter written to CES board member Nathaniel Bouton on July 12, Nettie contended: "The ladies' work . . . is a Constitutional and important part of this society—and none is more so."[65]

In late June, Nettie received a personal letter written on June 24 by an unidentified friend of Emma's from Kilbourn City—a resort town later known as the Wisconsin Dells. This letter could have further moved Nettie to push for a greater constitutional support for Emma's Ladies Department. Without Emma's knowledge, this friend felt

---

59. Emma Dryer to Charles Blanchard, 1916, Biographical File of Emma Dryer.
60. Roderick, *Nettie Fowler McCormick*, 169.
61. Emma Dryer to Charles Blanchard, 1916, Biographical File of Emma Dryer.
62. Butt, *The Velvet Covered Brick*, 45.
63. Roderick, *Nettie Fowler McCormick*, 63.
64. Findlay, *Dwight L. Moody: American Evangelist*, 333–34.
65. Joiner, *Sin in the City*, 58.

compelled to write Nettie on behalf of Emma who had spent time with this Wisconsin friend at the home of Mary Jenkins. Mrs. Jenkins, the writer of *Notes for Bible Study*, had assisted during Emma's eye-sight difficulties. Emma had discussed with this unnamed friend the uneasiness she was experiencing with the CES, particularly her feelings of exclusion in its plans. This friend bemoaned the fact that Emma, having given the best years of her life organizing and establishing this work and serving as a valuable Bible teacher, should now be superficially set aside. She imploringly wrote: "I am *full* with amazement, and indignation that she is so left to sink into oblivion by those who have profited by her instruction. Her personal friends must not let it be so."[66]

Consequently, Nettie and others proposed various areas of organizational and constitutional improvement. They suggested an increased board size to sixteen rather than seven to lessen the control and dominance of a few.[67] Nettie, with her extensive experience as a mediator in industrialist and workforce disputes, sensed the tensions developing between society board members faithful to Moody, those faithful to Emma, and those struggling to be faithful to both. Nettie's expertise and financial support was respected by all as she diplomatically attempted to curtail their on-going conflicts.[68] In July Nettie, serving as a spokesperson, wrote Moody a letter outlining their suggestions. She was definitely not prepared for his response.

Moody received her letter and responded on July 18. He stated his confidence in the ability of Nettie's son, Cyrus McCormick Jr., and Nathaniel Bouton both of whom were instrumental in writing the CES constitution. Furthermore, he stated his opposition to enlarging the board as Nettie had suggested—at least at that time. He wrote: "I think seven is far better than sixteen to get things in motion. I have had some experiences with large committees and I feel convinced that they are not so effective as small ones when there is any building going on." He offered two options—to either "go against my judgment and join with my board or stand aside and let the work go on without me." Moody's decision to resign over Nettie's suggestion to expand the size of the board was unexpected and implied either his own personal weariness or a huge power struggle taking place. He expressed his heavy heart due to the opposition he was receiving from some of his closest Chicago friends and said he was *tired and sick of it* and viewed this situation as a door that God was shutting in Chicago.[69]

According to some, Nettie was infuriated by what she perceived as power abuse or unreasonable control.[70] Moody became offended and resigned from the CES over what she believed to be a reasonable board appraisal.[71] Others believed that Nettie

---

66. Letter to Mrs. McCormick from unknown source, 24 June 1887, Biographical File of Emma Dryer.

67. Roderick, *Nettie Fowler McCormick*, 169.

68. Findlay, *Dwight L. Moody: American Evangelist*, 334.

69. D. L. Moody to Nettie McCormick, 18 July 1887, Biographical File of Emma Dryer.

70. Foster, et al., *Educating Clergy*, 204.

71. Joiner, *Sin in the City*, 58.

was insulted by his abrupt and unexpected resignation. She felt humiliated by his rejection of her judgment[72] and believed that his threat only came because things were not going his way.

Leaders who abnegate their authority and are not willing to lead openly with their God-given influence, set the stage for potential leadership collapse.[73] Moody impulsively washed his hands of the Bible Work Institute but not without the disastrous effect of a Pilate-style crucifixion. His action astonished the board and sent waves of presumed betrayal to both Nettie and Emma. When Nettie received Moody's written response on July 26 her close friend Stella Roderick recorded Nettie's reaction: "Mrs. McCormick, amazed and hurt, instantly resigned in turn from the work, protesting that his resignation would endanger the whole cause." Nettie conceded that Moody was "the cement that holds it together"[74] and that her position in the formation of the institute could not compare to his.

With an inexorable concern for God's honor, Emma's first reaction to this conflict was that of offering up a plea of intercession to God similar to that offered by Moses on behalf of Israel. In her letter to Moody she forthrightly pleaded with him to reconsider: "The decision *must* go to the public: & what will the enemies of Christ say when they hear that for a well considered *suggestion* which makes immediate work possible *your* decision is not only against it, *but* deliberately made fatal to a great Christian enterprise. And what will half-hearted Christians say? Who have so long predicted that you *never meant* to do this work?"[75] Without an inordinate concern for herself, she continued her intercessory role by appealing to Moody's relational and business sensibilities: "And what will Mrs. McC.s friends say to treatment so inconsiderate of her gentle, generous kindness? Not a lady friend will go on a board from which she has resigned for such a reason." And finally she reminded him of his own words: "You say that you never had so set your heart on any thing as on this Society. There, Mr. Moody, for no small provocation should you give it up."

In defense of her friend, Emma reminded Moody that Nettie was only attempting to do what was morally right and kind but that "the shock & the grief is too severe for any change of decision at present." She stated that Nettie had never been so mistreated and then proceeded to admonish him: "It was not *right*, Mr. Moody. It was a mistake!" Emma also defended the CES board who had placed their hopes in his cooperation but had become discouraged by such a gratuitous decision. More concerned about God's honor than her own welfare, she supported her defense with an impassioned spiritual and evangelistic appeal:

---

72. Findlay, *Dwight L. Moody: American Evangelist*, 334.
73. Butt, *The Velvet Covered Brick*, 67.
74. Roderick, *Nettie Fowler McCormick*, 169.
75. Emma Dryer to D. L. Moody, 25 July1987, Biographical File of Emma Dryer.

> How sad the shadow that this will cast upon your cherished memory!—And what a stumbling block it may be to men in this city & country whose salvation & Christian growth you desire. I am affectionately afraid to have you do this. If it were only I who had it to sorrow over I would take the burden & go away: but there are many to be astonished & grieved & I fear already lest the unsheathed sword of dissension be not soon returned to its rest. I dare not—tho the provocation be dangerously distressing leave my post, lest *the enemy* triumph. Do not you leave yours![76]

Emma culminated her letter of defense with the following appeal:

> I believe you have been unconsciously led to decisions which involve serious results to the cause you love for the Lord's sake. We live in 'perilous times.' Alas! That I have added to their trouble! To the end that you may be a blessing to others & your service for Christ multiplied manifold I ask in earnest Christian love that you prayerfully re-consider your decisions & stop the trouble which threatens to blight the faith & hope & love of so many through the years that remain. In the fellowship of the Gospel. Emma Dryer.[77]

Although Emma may not have fully understood Moody's reasons for resigning, she saw this crisis as yet another spiritual battle. She did not want to see the enemy thwart the work that she believed was God-ordained. She knew that God was using Nettie to protect and accomplish the vision which Moody had originated and Emma had nurtured. Therefore, she encouraged Moody to not give up. She pleaded, "There is no lack of money. Money has been ready for enlargement more than 3 full years. Mrs. McC. has been ready to give & to do a long time. This is too sad & cruel a blow to her good purposes! & Mr. Moody, many will have to know it. Do not let this be!"[78]

Moody's response to Nettie's letter written on July 18 demonstrated a willful determination and continued impulsivity even at the age of fifty.[79] Despite his traits of over-sensitivity to criticism and impatience with disagreement, he openly received correction from Emma and his own wife. Mrs. Moody quickly intervened on July 21 with written correspondence desiring to restore Nettie's confidence in Mr. Moody's heart-felt motives for the well-being of the Society.[80] She most likely prompted Moody's speedy telegram response to Mrs. McCormick and Miss Dryer on July 27 from Northfield: "Your two letters just received. Am very sorry for the letter. Will withdraw it. Tell the trustees to do as they please about the construction and push the building and I will come as soon as it is ready."[81] Moody presumably misinterpreted

---

76. Ibid.
77. Ibid.
78. Ibid.
79. Findlay, *Dwight L. Moody: American Evangelist*, 334.
80. Ibid.
81. D. L. Moody to Emma Dryer, 27 July 1987, Biographical File of Emma Dryer.

Nettie's purposes and suggestions. His quick impulsive decision could have been due to misconceptions and pressures that had been mounting within the Chicago Evangelization Society.[82]

Nevertheless, Emma's close friend had been deeply wounded by Moody. With his pattern of sincere and quick apologies, Moody provided follow-up correspondence to Nettie by openly admitting his mistake. She was intensely moved and willingly received his telegraphed and written regrets. She wrote that his response deeply touched her and revealed his kindheartedness.[83] Nettie, Emma, and the board members desired to see Christian harmony restored. They once again committed themselves to Moody in the development of the training school.

After this 1887 summer crisis the CES board continued to move—but on shaky ground. Few trustee meetings were held and even then heated discussions and highly contested differences of opinion resulted in an expansion of fractured relationships.[84] Although Nettie assured her support for the completion of a home for the Bible Institute, she withdrew her proposal of land and began to pull away from her significant involvement in the CES.[85] Moody also scheduled a short evangelistic crusade in Montreal leaving Emma and Major Whittle to "enter the fray to smooth feathers and salvage the program."[86] While in Montreal Moody wrote Nettie a letter on October 6 echoing Emma's intercessory words which he apparently took to heart: "I will . . . do all I can in the future to keep peace . . . I do not want anyone to rise up in judgment and say any act of mine has kept them from the Kingdom of God for that is my one aim day and night to get them into the fold."[87]

By late summer and early fall Moody realized the grave on-going tension of the CES and how the establishment of the Bible Work Institute could be jeopardized. He wrote to Mrs. McCormick from Montreal on October 15: "I find the committee feels discouraged and do not know what to do, and they think I am standing in the way, and if I am I want to get out of the road."[88] He offered a more detailed explanation for his prior resignation. He had been disappointed, and perhaps somewhat convicted, upon hearing from Major Whittle that Emma had made the statement, justifiably though perhaps inappropriately, that it was difficult for the Chicago work to continue when its president was located elsewhere. Although Moody should have recognized the necessity of having an ever-present leader to launch one's vision, he became offended by this remark. Moody's dismay deepened when he received Nettie's original letter contain-

---

82. Getz, *The Story of Moody Bible Institute*, 24.

83. Roderick, *Nettie Fowler McCormick*, 169.

84. Findlay, *Dwight L. Moody: American Evangelist*, 335.

85. Ibid., 334–35.

86. Dorsett, *A Passion For Souls*, 274.

87. D. L. Moody from Montreal to Mrs. McCormick, 6 October 1887 and 15 October 1887, Biographical File of Emma Dryer.

88. Ibid.

ing her own *reasoned criticisms* regarding constitutional changes and the need to give Emma's Bible Work a firm constitutional standing.[89] Talking over the situation with Major Whittle, Moody had then concluded that it would be best to resign in order to assist rather than hurt the CES. He also reiterated to Nettie his deep remorse over the situation: "If I have done wrong will you not forgive me? . . . I am willing to work at the front or behind, or outside, or inside, and will go where you say . . . only for the sake of the Master let us have the work finished."[90]

Upon receiving Moody's letter of October 15, Nettie took it upon herself to be a mediator—this time between both of her dear friends. Emma found that she had disappointed and grieved her Northfield mentor and that her troubles were only beginning to increase. In a November 14, 1887, letter to Nettie she explained about a difficult November 8 meeting with Moody and board member Elbridge Keith. By this time Emma was caught in a spider web of broken trust and suspicion between Moody and the CES Board. Therefore, she requested that her friend Mary Moore Hitchcock be present. Out of fear that Moody or others would mistake her remarks, she asked that notes be taken so she could later convey to Mrs. McCormick the actual contents of their conversation.

As the meeting began, her initial impression was that Moody was ill at ease. In a hurried attempt to make peace, he said, "I haven't much time & Mr. Keith hasn't either. Got to get off. Why can't you & I let the past go & stand anew?"[91] With her usual detailed precision Emma explained that it wasn't that difficult to let go of the past and to begin again if he meant that past events would not be repeated. She further explained that she too wanted to avoid further conflict and confessed that she could not bear to experience another season such as they had just encountered.

Quite familiar with Moody's tendency to avoid confrontation, Emma encouraged him to be open and frank with her. Emma and Moody agreed that they wanted the Bible Work Institute to go forward. She explained the seriousness of their conflict. Although she would continue to stand by the current practices of the Institute, she could not continue "if our purposes & methods are liable to be attacked & overturned & interfered with in a way that makes trouble." She expressed her belief that thus far the work of the committees and Bible workers had been open. She desired to see that that there be no secret and mysterious attacks from others—thus, implying board interference. Moody accommodatingly responded: "I see no criticisms [and] don't intend to make any. Go on with your work just as you & your committees like. I shant oppose anything that you say or do . . . & if there is anything I can do to help, I will

---

89. Joiner, *Sin in the City*, 58.

90. D. L. Moody from Montreal to Mrs. McCormick, 6 October 1887 and 15 October 1887, Biographical File of Emma Dryer.

91. Emma Dryer to Nettie McCormick, 14 November 1887, Biographical File of Emma Dryer. Hereafter, unless otherwise noted, the following information in this section is obtained from this source.

help." Emma agreed that his help was needed and that without the contributions of all involved the work could not peacefully resume.

At this point Moody, replying that he would never make reference to past situations, said, "I want you to forgive me. If I have done any thing wrong, I want to be forgiven." They mutually agreed to forgive. Emma had negatively referred to Moody earlier in the year in a personal letter to Nettie. In a spirit of unguarded criticism she wrote of her surprise regarding Moody's forgetfulness of things he had previously said and done.[92] Emma willingly acknowledged her own sin. She added that it should not be said *if* one has done wrong for she knew that she had sinned in this situation: "No Christian can be in such an affair & not sin. I have said some severe things about you which I thought you deserved. I hoped you would hear about them. I tried to say them to you. I did try to talk to you, very hard, but you would not hear." Moody fairly admitted that he had been so preoccupied with other business matters that he had not sufficiently heard what she had been saying. He said, "I've heard more today than I've heard all summer."

Moody proceeded to mention the situation in which he had acted on Major Whittle's advice that he resign. He supposed that the situation had been corrected. Emma stated that she realized Moody and Harvey attributed the delay in the society's progress to her, but that she did not consciously remember having caused it. She knew that Nettie had also been diligently working to accelerate the work at the time when Moody's resignation stopped it. Moody asked Emma to express to Mrs. McCormick that he hoped she would continue with her work.

Emma took this opportunity to mention to Moody a recurring and difficult situation with Mr. Harvey. She and Mr. Bouton had previously and personally spoken with Harvey. Obviously aware of the situation, Moody conveyed that Mr. Harvey was ready to withdraw right away if Emma requested that he do so. Emma sympathized and in reference to his prior resignation said that although it was difficult to change what had already occurred, it was best to go on and attempt to avoid them in the future. She suggested that this could be done by Moody asking openly and freely for honest advice from faithful friends who would help him to see what he should do. Moody touchingly responded: "I am like clay in the hands of the potter. I'm ready to be moulded what there is of me." They both agreed that nothing further could be done without unity.

At this point Emma intuitively warned that Mr. Harvey "in his exhausted, nervous & irascible condition was not as fit medium of communication between you & others." Emma shared with Moody her concerns about the management of the CES with Mr. Harvey working at such a distance from Nebraska with his business affairs. She referenced Moody's long distance commute from Northfield and his extended absences while on the road. He responded that they were willing to take any position that Emma would desire. She struggled to discern correctly the genuineness of this

---

92. Findlay, *Dwight L. Moody: American Evangelist*, 332n55.

act of compliance. However, she agreed that they should continue with their current official positions. Moody seemed pleased and hurriedly said, "Now it's all settled is it?" Emma agreed that it was but quite perceptively indicated that it would not be correct to think that it would not come up again. He asked what it meant then to have "all our sins put in the depths of the sea?" Emma suggested: "I believe all that implies, but *sins in the effects & the second of our sinning . . . are distinct things.*"

Emma later added to her own documentation of the meeting that it would be dangerous for Mr. Moody to set aside 2 Corinthians 5:10, Colossians 3:25, and Matthew 12:36–37. She realized the seriousness of these Scriptures which admonish all Christians to carefully weigh their words and actions as each person must give an account before the judgment seat of Christ of what is done in the flesh—both good and bad.

The conversation quickly ended and Moody *shot out the door* to travel to his meetings in Minneapolis. With a whirlwind of emotions Emma graphically expressed how she felt like a *beheaded maiden*. Mr. Keith tarried for a while and earnestly and gently responded affirmatively to Emma's hope that finally all secrecy would be halted. He accurately surmised that "less than harmonious words was distracting to our hopes & dishonoring to the Lord." Emma firmly agreed that united prayers would dispel their troubles and prayed that this *pasture* would be filled with love and Christian fellowship. However, she later sorrowfully confided to Nettie that she perceived with apprehension that greater troubles were ahead.

Women's Bible Institute and May Institute of 1888

After the November 8 meeting and before the end of 1887 Moody and the Chicago Evangelization Society board cooperatively managed another nine member council with two men as managers and seven women managers including Emma, Nettie, and Mrs. Turlington Harvey. Although the summer had created an unsettled beginning for the CES and the Bible Work Institute, they closed the year with anticipation of the first upcoming three month Bible Institute for Women.

Emma conducted the institute which began on January 8, 1888. According to the advertising brochure the Institute was "to give thorough instruction in the Word of God, and a practical training in various forms of Christian work."[93] The classes that were offered included *Bible Exposition by Books; Geography of Bible Lands and Mission Fields; Christian Evidences; Church History;* and *Methods of Evangelistic and Church Work*. Emma joined at least fourteen other instructors including Reverend Goodwin, Reverend Hugh Scott, E. W. Bliss, and Mrs. W. W. Wait. Mission training involved instruction in inquiry room methods, Sunday schools, industrial schools,

---

93. Ibid. The brochure included a circular of the Bible-Work Institute of the Chicago Evangelization Society with an application and contact address for Emma Dryer.

mothers' meetings, and kitchen-gardens. With pleasure Emma announced that no tuition would be charged with only the cost of $50 to cover room, board, and heating.

During the 1888 three month institute, the Bible Work gained legal incorporation with all property being transferred to the CES including the home used by the Bible workers. On March 12 Emma wrote to Nettie McCormick from the Bible Work address at 150 Madison Street: "My dear Mrs. McCormick: This am [a.m.] the long delayed transfer of the Bible-Work to the CES was effected. So you are now the Hon. Prest. [Honorary President] of the Ladies Council of the CES instead of the Bible-Work and on Thursday for me the new Board of managers . . . So hath the Lord ordained it!"[94] With relief Emma shared: "I certainly am ready to unite the work and the Board and all concerned."[95]

At the Monday March 15, 1888, board meeting in the Bible Work Room in Farwell Hall Emma was asked to open the meeting in prayer and to read her historical document of the Bible Work following the time of the Chicago Fire to its present day merger. After her presentation Nathaniel Bouton shared that "the Bible Work had by resolution adopted this day, transferred all its property to the Chicago Evangelization Society and had ceased to exist."[96] Bouton followed with the preamble and resolution: "Whereas, the Bible Work has voted to transfer its work & property to this Society, therefore, Resolved that this Society does hereby accept the transfer of said Bible Work, especially for this department of this Society's Work." A list of the personal property of the Bible Work included furniture, miscellaneous housing equipment, and total cash of $8,296.28. Transfer papers were signed by Mr. Harvey and by Emma who served as the CES secretary. These funds were earmarked for the exclusive use of the Bible Work or Ladies Branch of the Society.

The meeting also involved plans for the upcoming May Institute. Emma was asked to contact Reverend W. G. Moorehead who had conducted the institute the previous year. The April 26 edition of the *Christian Cynosure* announced that the 1888 May Institute would be held in Chicago by the Chicago Evangelization Society beginning the first day of May for Christian men and women who were students and workers.[97] The program included *Lectures on Practical Christian Subjects* and a three week plan for teaching and studies in *Christian Doctrine, Elementary Church History,* and *Sermons and Sermonizing*. Professor Moorehead, Evangelist E. W. Bliss, Reverend Goodwin, Reverend Goss, and others would serve as instructors. The article ended with notice that inquiries should be sent to Mr. F. G. Ensign or to Miss E. Dryer, Bible Work Institute, 150 Madison Street. This May Institute for men and women had grown steadily each year and would serve as a prototype for the 1889 full-time residential program of the Bible Institute.

94. Emma Dryer to Nettie McCormick, 12 March 1888, Biographical File of Emma Dryer.
95. Joiner, *Sin in the City*, 58–59.
96. Board Minutes, 12 March 1888, Chicago Evangelization Society File.
97. *Christian Cynosure,* National Christian Association, April 26, 1888, 12.

Woman of Nobility

Harvey Dispute 1887–88

Following a successful May Institute, tensions in the society escalated between Emma and Turlington Harvey. Harvey and she first became acquainted after the Chicago Fire of 1870. Emma worked with him when he served as the director and an executive committee member of the Relief and Aid Society. Harvey later served as president of the YMCA from 1871 to 1873 and again from 1876 to 1879. During this time he became friends with Emma and Moody. Emma furthered her acquaintance with him in 1876 in his position as the chairman of the executive committee for building the Moody Tabernacle. She knew him as an optimistic and efficient businessman. Harvey was "recognized as a man of forceful character, and of independent thought, having the courage of his opinions" and "respected for upright dealing."[98]

In 1877 Emma welcomed Mr. Harvey with his enthusiasm and talents to serve as president of the Bible Work. In 1881 she participated with him on the Chicago Evangelistic Committee. With her administrative skills and Harvey's business expertise and competence, they united their prayers on behalf of Moody's return to Chicago to establish the Bible school. However, Emma's conversation with Moody in November of 1887 regarding Harvey indicated that she now had some misgivings regarding him. A situation had occurred in which Emma, with Mr. Bouton's backing, addressed Harvey as a board member for unduly interfering with Bible Work operations. As she had expressed to Moody, she did not view Harvey as an able communicator between them. Without providing any defense for Harvey, who had been one of Moody's long-time advisors, Moody had shared with apparent uneasiness that Harvey was willing to resign with just one word from Emma.

The conflict deepened when in June 1888 Mr. Harvey personally sent Emma a judgmental and second-hand offense letter in which he stated that others were relaying to him her lack of submission to Mr. Moody and her refusal to allow her workers to do their job. He conjectured: "You are overworked and you are in a condition of mind unsuited to the discharge of the great work you are undertaking to do."[99] A letter written in response by Emma to Harvey on June 14, months after her November 1887 discussion with Moody, gives some further insight into this difficult situation.

Emma noted that Harvey's letter appeared to be personal correspondence rather than an official and representative business letter from the whole board. Therefore, she was uncertain regarding his purpose in writing to her. He proposed that she put in writing her readiness to comply and submit to the Chicago Evangelization Society's directives for a year. This act indicated his personal belief that Emma uncooperatively and independently acted contrary to board rulings. From a perspective of fairness and equality she asked whether she was being singled out or if the entire board had made this proposition. She wanted to know if there was an expectation that all board

---

98. Hotchkiss, *Industrial Chicago,* 390–91.
99. Harvey to Emma Dryer, 17 June 1888, Biographical File of Emma Dryer.

members should submit and abide by it as well. Additionally, she wanted to know if the pledge was being required of all the CES employees to be met before funds would be allocated to them. Critically, or perhaps astutely, she challenged him with a third leading question. She asked him if the note was "simply your way of saying that the CES organization will do nothing towards our long planned 'Training School' until Mr. Harvey is ready?"

Emma perceived an unbalanced issue of control. She reasoned that such a written guarantee of cooperation should not be required of Christians in order to assure full commitment and dedication to walking harmoniously with one another. She realized that her serving authority and reasoned challenges were being misinterpreted by Harvey as rebellion.[100] She responded: "To do that is every Christian's high calling— 'not Paul or Apollos or Cephas but we all are workers together with Christ, the Prince of Peace." Harvey had also asked her to push more aggressively the building project for the school. He believed that she was responsible for its delay and that more could be done.

Emma's response indicated her faith in God as the One to direct the building of the school for his glory. She acknowledged that the Lord would withhold no good thing to those who walk uprightly. Without faith she realized that she could not be an effective leader or a noble Proverbs 31 woman. She added, "He knows *when & where & how* to fulfill the dreams of His servants, giving them all they can use for His glory & in unity with Him a humble 'minority' or 'majority' will, be 'more than conquerors.'"

Although Emma did not communicate what Harvey's response was to her intense cross-examination, conflict in their relationship continued to escalate and spread beyond themselves. Harvey believed that harmony could only be achieved by Emma's complete acquiescence to himself and submission to Moody and the CES board.[101] Mrs. Harvey cooperatively joined her husband in adding to the consuming conflict: "We feel that quite outside of the differences in method between Mr. Moody and Miss Dryer, Miss Dryer lacks the breadth and sympathy to mother an extensive establishment, and that her experience in life has narrowed and set her convictions to such an extent that it is quite out of the question that she work with a Board, unless she is recognized as the absolute ruler."[102]

Mrs. Harvey's remarks only confirmed Emma's ongoing suspicions. She viewed Harvey as being mysteriously secretive and evasive while he sought to avoid the meticulousness of her constant inquiry. Emma realized that spiritual discernment was needed to detect the intent of the *prince of darkness* to obstruct God's plan. Yet with vulnerable humanness she succumbed to a spirit of intimidation and defensiveness. She subsequently wavered in courage and perseverance in the face of businessman or

---

100. Butt, *The Velvet Covered Brick*, 110.
101. Joiner, *Sin in the City*, 59.
102. Ibid.

industrialist control during an era in which women were discounted from important leadership roles.[103]

Bouton Resignation 1888

Nathaniel Sherman Bouton, the owner of the Union Foundry Works—a large foundry of architectural iron work—had ministered closely with Emma at the Bible Work since its inception. He observed firsthand how she managed her fiscal, administrative, and relational responsibilities. He stood by her during the years of waiting and celebrated with her when the Chicago Evangelization Society merged the Bible Work to form the Bible Work Institute. However, like Emma, as a CES board member he experienced some anxiety regarding the merger and the welfare of the Lady Council workers.

In a revealing letter written by Emma on March 25, 1888, she attempted to ease his anxiety: "Dear Nathaniel: Do not *you* be *anxious* about your hunches interfering with the new ladies of our board. Don't *you* be disturbed . . . Tell them, when you can, to set *their faces to the light* and march on & God's light will throw out our pains and dispel our fears." She went on to assure him of what he himself had witnessed. "For 16 years our ladies and I have been intimately there until it was *imported* and *forced on us.*"

Bouton, along with Emma, was concerned about board interference in the operations of the Bible Work Home since the merger. Seemingly, visitations were being made to find cause to question the work being done. Nonetheless, she resolved to guard against future attacks by lovingly speaking the truth. Emma closed her March letter to Bouton with a prayer that the Lord would keep him close and, as Caleb stood beside Joshua, he would fully follow the Lord until the day in which he would enter God's presence to behold and gaze upon God's face and image revealing his glory with unending hope.[104]

By August 16, 1888, Bouton could no longer serve on the CES board. He officially resigned and shared with Emma that his resignation was necessary due to Moody's indecisive actions. He observed that the work of the proposed school would be hindered as long as the CES continued to be inefficient and at variance in its objectives.[105] He likewise wrote to Mrs. McCormick: "The course pursued toward Miss Dryer is unchristian and has none of the Spirit of Christ. And agreeing in the main with Miss Dryer, I think best to withdraw."[106]

On August 29 Emma wrote Nettie regarding Mr. Bouton's resignation. She shared that he had advised Moody to change and restructure everything possible in order for the work to continue. After his resignation Emma spoke with gratitude that the Lord

103. Foster, et al., *Educating Clergy*, 204.
104. Emma Dryer to Nathaniel Bouton, 25 March 1888, Biographical File of Emma Dryer.
105. Joiner, *Sin in the City*, 59–60.
106. Ibid., 60.

had providentially protected him from the "straw blown by an ambitious wind that seeks by breeze or storms to show the presence and power to bring everything under its sway."[107] She expressed to Nettie that she believed that at least half of their difficulties materialized because of the power of this ambition.

Emma informed Nettie that not only had Bouton resigned, but others would also be doing the same. Two of her ladies on the council, Mrs. Ayres and Mrs. Shute, had given her their resignations to present at the next board meeting. For the first time Emma spoke of presenting her own resignation but was hesitant out of fear that her motives would be misunderstood. She deliberated: "They would then have *opportunity* to say that Miss D. did *this* & organized . . . to unite the 2 societies legally & *then* not a word having been said . . . went & resigned for nobody-knows-what reason . . . So I think I will remain quiet and keep our workings at their thorough, quiet work until God shows me what else to do."[108] Emma explained that in the past Nettie had the stabilizing position of the McCormick name, but that in their current Ladies Council Mr. Harvey primarily held control. She referred to it as a *religious boycotting* that symbolized a modern day collapse of circumstances in which even her faithful workers would not survive.

Emma also expressed her desire that all the board members be informed regarding the financial status and stipulations of the pledges or subscriptions given to the CES. She would later recall that during the October 1, 1888 meeting, subscriptions were being withdrawn, and the situation was disheartening.[109] She wrote to Nettie in her August 29 letter: "Mr. E[nsign] is easily swayed so by a strong power & Mr. H[arvey] guards like a sentinel." She expressed her desire to meet and speak with businessman Marshall Field, a donor to the CES and friend of the McCormicks, regarding the finances. Although she admitted that she did not know him well, she believed that he deserved to hear all the facts but knew her role was to pray that God would guide him.[110] Remorsefully, and with continued concerns regarding a balance in board governance, she added:

> It is an abnormal condition of a work whose foundations were for 15 years laid in prayer & humble, constant, loving effort & did I not know by the prophecies the characteristics of the last days, faith would well nigh fail. We could easily know God's will by unitedly waiting on Him & seeking to do His work in loving communion. Ambition & self-will must sooner or later destroy the ends they seek. Even a king enthroned in power & prosperity needs the advice & half of his humblest subjects & the foundations of his throne decay when he neglects the hard-handed lower stratus of his kingdom.[111]

---

107. Emma Dryer to Nettie McCormick, 29 August 1888, Biographical File of Emma Dryer.
108. Ibid.
109. Emma Dryer to Charles Blanchard, 1916, Biographical File of Emma Dryer.
110. Emma Dryer to Nettie McCormick, 29 August 1888, Biographical File of Emma Dryer.
111. Ibid.

Emma warned that CES independence would be quite dangerous if essential facts were to be set aside. She feared that success could still potentially end in failure.

Further Internal Board Conflict 1888

In a letter written to Nettie on September 8, 1888, Emma recognized the difficult position of her friend in trying to keep peace between all within the CES. She realized that the board respected Nettie and positively viewed her participation from a financial perspective. Emma also expressed to Nettie that she sensed once again Moody's reticence to start a school in Chicago: "Mr. M sends word that if he has to be 'opposed' in all his plans, he won't come; & he won't come anyway if they're going to keep up a quarrel!" She ended her letter with hopeful encouragement: "We shall all see alike further on in that Christian covenant for all."[112]

A few weeks later on September 20 Emma again corresponded with Nettie to share the approach of yet another crisis. She agonized over a silence from Moody that she could not explain. She wrote: "I tried to see him. He would not talk. He looked into vacancy. I tried again & again while others grew disturbed. I wrote. I suggested prayer. I urged. Silence there & nothing more while . . . attacks were set & operated."[113] She expressed how she had attempted to carry and abide by all the plans and suggestions of the CES board. She compared herself to a *galled steed* that winces and wrote that she was sorry for any wrongdoing. She mournfully reiterated that Mr. Harvey continued to accept little personal responsibility for his own mistakes.

Emma disclosed to Nettie another troubling situation in which Emma began receiving reports from others regarding Mr. Harvey. After Mr. Harvey joined the society, board member Robert Scott began noting some strange actions of Mr. Harvey. By way of illustration, Emma asked Nettie what she and Cyrus would have done if they had taken on a new worker at their Harvesting Machine Company only to find that he had begun to make unsolicited changes in the department. And then they found that he "misapprehends & misrepresents your cause & agitates discontent & has used emissaries to carry on a mysterious movement."

Still referring hypothetically to Nettie and Cyrus, Emma described the following scenario of Harvey's disinclined response toward Mr. Scott's attempts to open up channels of communication:

> Would you . . . take out your watch & say 'I haven't but a few minutes to see you—but I hope it will be all right' or 'Dear Mr. S[cott]. I have an unkind feeling in my heart towards you but I can't engage in controversy. I can only be responsible for myself!' And *suppose* Mr. S. should kindly send for Mr. H[arvey] & say 'I thought we may in conversation understand each other &

---

112. Ibid., 8 September 1888.

113. Ibid., 20 September 1888. Hereafter, unless otherwise noted, the following information in this section is obtained from this source.

make things better' & Mr. H should wildly say, 'That can't be done! & there's not a word of truth in what you say & you know it when you say it.

Emma was also told that one of Mr. Harvey's men overheard an associate who was firmly reproving Mr. Harvey and the Chicago Evangelization Society. Harvey's man promptly asked the associate what he would do when Moody and Miss Dryer finally decline to work with one another. This associate indirectly reprimanded Mr. Harvey by replying: "Do the decent & manly thing and address the meanness of your measures & your detestable [words] against a [fine] Christian work!" Yet another Christian man in a prominent position, according to Emma, viewed Mr. Harvey as *a [blight] to the church*. He grieved that there could be "no way of feeling kindly towards him or thinking what he would have been without the gospel."

Emma understood Moody's characteristic hesitancy regarding confrontation. He was more than likely receiving fractional or conflicting information from Harvey, and perhaps others, and had become reticent to intervene. Emma wrote to Nettie that Moody had been made aware of these events but had not at any time asked her about the situation, nor had he replied to her regarding the things that she had shared with him. From her viewpoint she felt that he was "responsible for letting them go on operating in this Soc[iety] when *he knows* that *he could stop it.*" Emma's prayer was that God would take away the obstacles and bring blessings to this work of God. The situation appeared to have no hope for peace with Mr. and Mrs. Harvey and two other contenders, Mr. and Mrs. E. W. Blatchford, who had previously served with Emma on the Chicago Evangelistic Committee.

Emma expressed her confidence that Nettie's upcoming visit to Northfield was proof that God was at work in Moody's life. Emma reiterated that she and Moody had no incessant difficulties with one another and that she chose to "let love flow & grow & bury the ambition & resentment—and say, 'Any where with Jesus . . . obey His loving will at any sacrifice." She was seeking to express love rather than indignation over injustice. Emma prayed: "May His will be done . . . May He give . . . peace & praise! . . . Daily asking God's blessing & guidance on all related *in any way* to the CES & our work."

After Emma wrote her September letters, Nettie and her daughter Anita visited Moody in Northfield to discuss the CES difficulties. Moody told them: "I will do anything on earth that you bid me do . . . I am tired. I am in a vise. The situation is locked."[114] At that time Nettie proposed a *separation* of Emma's Bible Work from the CES for a fixed amount. She encouraged Moody to meet with Emma to discuss the situation. Emma mentioned in her last letter to Nettie that she continued to look to Jesus who would ultimately bring reconciliation. "May His blessed will be done. Whatever he wills for good."[115]

---

114. Roderick, *Nettie Fowler McCormick*, 170.
115. Letter to Mrs. McCormick from Emma Dryer, 20 September 1888, Biographical File of

During this turbulent season Moody would have considerately realized Emma's spiritual battle with the flesh. So also did she note his fleshly struggles: "Stern & gentle, strong & broken, human & willful, wise & confused, practical & impracticable, loving & repelling, reliable & uncertain, effective & failing, progressive & propelling pious Christian life."[116] Despite his struggles, Emma and others would later recognize a deeper spiritual maturity in Moody as he entered the final years of his life. Moody biographer Richard Day referred to the indefinable change in him with his countenance appearing much more heavenly. Moody's intense longing to become like Christ materialized as "the human in him had lessened in power. Self was now far away and out of ken. Somehow one couldn't be with him half an hour without becoming conscious of—Another!"[117]

However, Moody had not yet reached this advanced spiritual state as Emma attempted to understand his actions during these struggling years of internal CES board conflict. She would strongly question his capricious decisions. From her perspective she could not understand why he continued to desire yet another Northfield school rather than investing his time in Chicago. She prophetically spoke of the destiny of Moody's Mt. Herman school to which Moody unendingly devoted his last years: "Strong institutions should stand where . . . sympathetic life will continuously flow. *Fancy* for Mt. Herman may fail to make it a *fruitful heritage*. The money that *mansions* those mountains . . . might marvelously multiply upward when the likes of growing life freely flow."[118] She intuitively judged God's calling on Moody's life to be, not so much that of a Samuel who writes "for the kings . . . the orders of the Kingdom in a book," but an Elijah "to lighten the curses by bringing the hearts of fathers & children to God!"

Furthermore, she compared Moody to the prophet Elijah and herself to Obadiah. Elijah sent Obadiah to deliver God's inspired message to King Ahab (2 Kings 18:12). Obadiah, who had protectively and sacrificially hidden away a hundred prophets, hesitated to do as Elijah said lest the Spirit of the Lord would snatch Elijah away and King Ahab would kill Obadiah. Emma used the Old Testament character Obadiah to illustrate her support for Moody and his message of a soon-coming school. Even in his absence she chose to reflect humility as she obediently "delivered his inspired messages to the King" and proclaimed in reference to herself: "So let Obadiah lower his head!"[119]

Emma remembered the earlier visionary years before Moody reached acclaim. "As the eyes of a maid to her mistress so even my practical eyes on his motions for

---

Emma Dryer.

116. Ibid.

117. Day, *Bush Aglow*, 287.

118. Letter to Mrs. McCormick from Emma Dryer, 20 September 1888, Biographical File of Emma Dryer.

119. Ibid.

15 varying hope filled years. My affections are appreciative of him again while *he was small* and the proposed work larger... [O]nly God could cause us to carry it!" In this letter to Nettie she expressed the grief she experienced during the long seasons of waiting by faith which at times produced a deep sense of loneliness. She shared how "the hopes of so many... were protected by [her] concealed loneliness" in which for her "it was sometimes dreadful to work and also be so alone!" Yet as a *prisoner of hope* she knew that God would be her shield as she waited and hoped and watched "so *alone* that He *must* carry the cause or it had dropped by the way." Even in the waiting of solitude when others no longer believed that Moody would keep his promise to bring a Bible school to Chicago, she knew that despite loneliness, God had kept her faith as she prayed and rested in his grace. Despite times of despondency, she continued to believe: "*God meant* that Mr. M should *finish* a good work in the city of his beginnings. So may it be. *So shall it be*, if God will that my living or dying, anywhere, any-way, secure it."[120]

Emma reflected on her willing submission to Moody's changes and his various contradictions. As she still pursued peace in the advancement of the school with Mrs. McCormick's support, Moody would protectively and dominantly tell her: "Keep every body's hands off till I am ready to take hold." When she asked if he wanted Nettie and herself to step down from the Board, he replied: "No! Let her stay with: but I want you to represent me on that Board." With this encouragement Emma pressed forward by informing the board of the Bible Work Institute's needs. And Moody continued to speak supportively to her: "Your strong hold is to keep it before them" and "you & I will keep the work in our own hands."[121]

Emma's confidence in Moody's past promises ultimately waned as they approached a board meeting that brought a crisis of great proportion. This life-changing October 1, 1888, meeting occurred as Emma returned from Northfield, Minnesota.[122] Moody and his wife were traveling through Chicago on their way to California. Emma held expectations that the CES board would operate as efficiently and openly as her own Bible Work with similar exactness and organization. However, on this day she reluctantly entered the meeting with only a two hour notice and heard that the board had met earlier in the morning.

Emma first greeted Mr. Ensign. Still having unresolved issues with Mr. Harvey, she acknowledged him with a pleasant bow but withheld her hand. She later stated that she could not disingenuously recognize his previously objectionable behavior. She believed that he needed to realize the full meaning of his conduct. Merton Smith, an evangelist associate of Mr. Moody, also entered the room followed by Mr. Moody. Emma most pleasantly greeted them. She finally was able to converse with Moody

---

120. Ibid.

121. Ibid.

122. Board Minutes, 1 October 1888, Chicago Evangelization Society File. These minutes were taken by secretary Emma Dryer.

although he only spoke uncomfortably and briefly about the hotel elevators and the elaborately designed windows. Emma asked Moody if his wife was traveling with him to California but sensed that he was not interested or comfortable in expanding the conversation.

During this time Emma had a strange feeling watching Mr. Harvey fly around, as she described it, *like a bee* whispering to Mrs. Mary Williams Blatchford in a secretive and clandestine manner. Her own insecurities emerged as she sensed that without the presence of Mrs. McCormick, Cyrus McCormick Jr., or Mr. Bouton she no longer had legitimate supporters on the board. Also in attendance were Mr. Keith, Mr. Blatchford, Mr. Albro, Mr. Ensign, Mr. Scott, Mrs. Harvey, and later on Emma's friend Mrs. Goodwin.

After the meeting began, Mr. Harvey reported that he had never seen a finer group of Bible workers at the Home and noticed a great need for their care. Then to Emma's amazement he proposed that Mrs. Sarah Capron, a middle-aged missionary possessing a fine Bible background and character, be hired to take over the Ladies Work. From the early days of the Bible Work most associates of the work, including Charles Blanchard, expected that Emma would head up the women's department.[123] Therefore, this sudden reversal amazed not only Emma but many others who later heard of the change in direction.

Reflecting the previously painful heart of her friend Lucy Meyer, she articulately expressed the *anvil-blows* she felt at this abrupt turn of events: "I simply hit another knock in the old place that makes the soul numb and quivery." A vote was taken with several voting yes and no one voting no. Moody immediately objected that he did not like this sudden change. "He didn't want someone 'on our hands.'" Furthermore, he would rather that Mrs. Capron just stay for a short teaching session.[124] To Emma's further dismay, Mary Blatchford objected to Moody's proposal leaving Emma with the perception that Mrs. Blatchford was acting in conjunction with Mr. Harvey. Moody stood firm—although unsuccessfully—with a ruling to turn the decision over to a committee of three ladies.

At this time Moody interjected his idea for establishing three homes on different sides of the city. In frustration he pleaded for them to simply agree in order to finally get things done. As Emma listened to Moody pressing the issue of unity and agreement, her heart began to ache even as she later expressed how she sought to display a pleasant countenance. Within her heart she was contemplating the sixteen years of lovingly attending to the Bible Work. She recalled that there was no "reproachful word or an unpleasant hour with never a animosity—never a debt nor empty treasury,

---

123. Charles A. Blanchard to William Norton of the Bible Institute Colportage Association, 4 June 1913, Charles Albert Blanchard Papers.

124. In October of 1890 Moody received a report from T. W. Harvey and assistant Gertrude Hurlburt regarding the "difficult personality" of the newly elected Ladies Department superintendent, Mrs. Capron. Dorsett, *A Passion For Souls*, 440n10.

never a serious illness or trouble in our Home" and now so quickly "without a kind word voted out!"[125] With inexplicable anguish she heard them toss aside the Bible Work along with its firm foundation and the financial seeds with which it had been sown. Yet with bittersweet faith she would later write: "God's encouragement to me abounds in the darkness of this night."[126]

Mr. Harvey proceeded to bring up the subject of his June correspondence with Emma in which he inferred that she could never find agreement with the actions and purposes of the Board. He also mentioned the negligence of Mr. Bouton in not fulfilling his pledge of property to the CES. He finally suggested that it would only be appropriate to return to Emma and the Bible Work the money which the CES had received at the time of the merger. He made a motion to that effect with a settlement of $6,000 plus interest. Emma sat silently stunned as she heard the motion carried with only a few voting yes. After this action Emma expressed that she could not take the interest money and that it would not be right for her to receive funds on behalf of a Bible Work charter that no longer existed.

Mr. Harvey returned to his previous conversation and referenced Emma's inability to get along with Mr. Moody and the CES. He indicated that Moody and Emma's disagreement gave reason to abandon the Ladies Home for the CES, and that the lady workers should secure their own places to live. In response Emma began by informing him of previous attempts to do just that. She was still disinclined to do so and realized the greater need for itinerate lady workers than for men to have a community home.

Next, Emma quickly pointed out that she and Moody over fifteen years had successfully come to mutual agreement when opportunities for valuable conversation occurred. Emma refused to take the responsibility for a situation that she believed Harvey had advanced. With a continued sense of committed ownership, she said, "I had as Mr. E.[nsign] knew sought to carry out every plan & purpose suggested to me by the Soc[iety] so far as I could & that I certainly desired the prosperity of that work: that I had not sought the enlargement 15 years without holding its interests sacred."[127]

By this time Emma noted that Mr. Harvey had become quite agitated and emotional. He reiterated to his own complete satisfaction that no agreement could possibly be reached based on his personal documentation. Emma attempted to explain her earlier conversations with Harvey, but both Moody and Harvey maintained that it was unnecessary. Emma replied, "You can't permit such an accusation to come before this Board without giving me an opportunity to reply to it." Emma was allowed to present her case. Mr. Harvey had spoken "fierce words . . . which could not well have been more severe except by the use of oaths and epithets" which had left her in shock. She contested that in her letters to him she had purposefully been careful to demonstrate

---

125. Emma Dryer to Mrs. McCormick, 12 October 1888, Biographical File of Emma Dryer.
126. Ibid.
127. Board Minutes, 1 October 1888, Chicago Evangelization Society File.

love and friendliness to both Mr. and Mrs. Harvey. In turn, she received treatment that was neither accommodating nor Christ-like.[128]

By now Emma fully understood that regardless of her defense, Mr. Harvey was determined that she no longer be on the Board. He brought up her *rudeness* to him when they first entered the room for the meeting. With non-obscured honesty she firmly responded: "I want you to distinctly understand that any man who conducts himself in such a fierce and ungentlemanly way cannot without an apology present a claim of familiar friendship." Emma gratefully noticed at this time that Moody appeared to have softened toward her. She now began to understand more clearly his silence from the past few months.

Longing to be a peacemaker, Emma continued: "I replied aloud that I desired the peace & prosperity of this Soc[iety] & wanted them to do whatever they thought best." However, she felt she could not so quickly agree when it came to financial decisions that had further ramifications. Moody encouraged her to make a decision, but Emma continued to be *firm and gentle* in her request for more time. She told him that if Mr. Bouton or Cyrus McCormick had been present, she did not believe several spontaneous and incorrect statements would have been permitted.[129]

Tension still mounted regarding Mrs. McCormick's pledge. Mr. Harvey insisted that her pledge had to stay with the CES. He proposed that a check for $1,000 be sent to Emma. Mr. Keith expressed that it would be in vain because he believed she would easily return it. Emma replied that she believed they could make a satisfactory arrangement. Mr. Harvey also reminded the board that Marshall Field's pledge would need to be returned if they did not use it for the building of a Ladies Home for the school. It was now quite apparent to Emma that the consensus of the board was to no longer recognize the Bible Work as part of the CES.

The meeting agenda changed to the topic of resignations. In Emma's opinion she felt that Mr. Harvey accepted Mr. Bouton's August resignation with *great satisfaction*. At this time Mr. Houghteling's resignation was officially received. Both men were immediately replaced by Reverend Goss and Dr. Goodwin. By now the intensity of the meeting caused Emma and others to forget about presenting Mrs. Shute, Mrs. Ayres, and Emma's own resignations. During this process Emma felt as if she was hearing her own death sentence and protectively expressed that she had not knowingly *perplexed any soul*.

At this point Mr. Harvey and his wife suggested that Emma needed to take a sabbatical. Mrs. Blatchford asked her whether she would "not do anything for the good of this work" and asked "what was she waiting for." Emma discerned that not only was Mrs. Blatchford irritated with her answers but that she was trying to manipulate her from an erroneous position. Emma later wrote Nettie McCormick on October 12 that as for her own reaction, her heart hurt as she tenderly yet decidedly responded.

---

128. Ibid.
129. Emma Dryer to Mrs. McCormick, 12 October 1888, Biographical File of Emma Dryer.

Moody conciliatorily added that after fifteen years without financial support he would like to see Emma take a vacation and offered her either a thousand dollars or some type of annuity. This spontaneous gesture of money and rest was disturbing for Emma since she had not consciously thought about it.

When Mrs. Goodwin arrived Moody suggested that Mr. Harvey be placed in the office of the presidency. Emma also urged such action with "kind courtesies [among] the friends."[130] She shared with Mrs. Goodwin the board's plan and her desire to wait before making a final financial decision. Mrs. Goodwin, favorable toward the Bible Work becoming independent in order to make peace, affirmed that she would continue to support the work. Not wanting to be involved any further in the discussion, Mrs. Goodwin left, and the meeting was adjourned.

Emma met the following morning with Mr. and Mrs. Moody, Mr. Keith, Mr. Goss, and Mr. Ensign in the Bible Work Room along with Mary Jane Hitchcock. Emma felt the liberty of sharing with Moody some *plain facts* of the situation. She also assured Mr. Ensign that she was his friend and encouraged him to take a stand. She recognized him as a friend of the Bible Work while knowing that they had both in the past impatiently spoken things they should not have.

At this meeting Moody shared a further revelation he received in the night hours that could perhaps help them out of their difficulties. He proposed once again a compromising plan involving the establishment of three homes scattered throughout the city. Mrs. Blatchford and Mr. Goss would be in charge of one home with Mrs. Harvey and Mrs. Capron caring for another. He asked if Emma thought the Ladies Council of the Bible Work would agree to take an arrangement for a west side location. She quickly conceded that if that would be best, then she would agree even if he proposed ten more houses. Mr. Keith, who according to Emma was such a faithful friend and supporter of the Bible Work, categorically refused along with the others to manage any of the suggested homes. Mr. Ensign and Mr. Goss were puzzled about such an arrangement. Moody's conciliatory plan, needless to say, did not receive board approval and proved adversely unproductive despite his noble intention.

Mr. and Mrs. Harvey told Moody prior to the meeting that they would not remain on the Board if Emma stayed. With this knowledge, both Mr. Goss and Moody concluded that the best solution would be for Emma to resign. Although Emma had experienced a dreadful and sleepless night, one of many for her in the past two years, by that morning she found a peace that passes understanding. She sympathetically realized that Moody also struggled with this crisis through the night. Remembering his prior admonitions to stay *sweet*, Emma chose to conscientiously remain calm and as "cheerful as a bright June morning."[131] Following the meeting Moody left immediately

---

130. Board Minutes, 1 October 1888, Chicago Evangelization Society File.
131. Emma Dryer to Mrs. McCormick, 1 October 1888, Biographical File of Emma Dryer.

for California. Emma wrote him a pleasant follow-up letter in which she benevolently referenced to him events from the past, present, and the future.[132]

The same day Emma also wrote a letter to Nettie and shared with extreme sensitivity and painful honesty: "I am numb & heavy with sorrow which I try to tell our Lord about & can only ask Him to lead us each & all." She expressed her concern that the pledges continue to be fulfilled to the CES. She even considered visiting Mr. Field to encourage him to not withhold his pledge until he meet with Mrs. McCormick. She continued: "I have carefully avoided introducing any perplexity to imperil this work." She expressed her desire to humbly follow the Lord wherever he would lead. She entreated Nettie to fulfill the pledge made to Moody of $300 a month for the Bible Institute as an ultimate loving expression of "a nail quietly secured."[133]

Within a few weeks after such a divisive meeting, Emma wrote Nettie another lengthy letter to express her after-thoughts regarding the actions of the board. Nettie had kindly suggested that Emma had most definitely not been accurately represented. Mrs. McCormick herself said for some time she had been sensing "a real divergence—just *where* it is, you cannot define—whether in method, or in want of harmony, but you cannot but feel it."[134] Emma agreed. She explained that Mr. Harvey brought allegations against her in which he had focused on her every movement to find cause for her dismissal. She quietly lamented, "What spirit so needlessly misrepresents trifles? And so unjustly?"

During the intense debate at that October first meeting, Emma had been accused of inappropriately and forcefully responding to Mr. Harvey. In her own defense regarding his allegations against her, she explained to Nettie that she naturally emphasized points she was making when she opened her hand and pointed to him saying that despite his denials, he had most definitely made certain statements.[135] From Emma's perspective she felt that any new posturing that she exhibited would only be perceived and presented as an uncalled for *cause*, not a *product* of others' actions.

Emma continued to explain that during the meeting she had silently listened to Moody's words and then to Mr. Harvey as he "made his careless, false statements about a 'correspondence' & a 'conversation' used to support his insistence that Emma would never submit to the CES board." Emma now viewed her own restrained quietness as no longer a positive trait: "I have not instituted an *attack* anywhere! I have poorly protected what I thot was God-directed work & did it *quietly* while others were anxious until I thought quietness no virtue." She questioned why Moody and the board had not approached her kindly and privately *before* the meeting regarding their intent to employ Mrs. Capron.

---

132. Emma Dryer to Charles Blanchard, 1916, Biographical File of Emma Dryer.

133. Emma Dryer to Mrs. McCormick, 2 October 1888, Biographical File of Emma Dryer.

134. Roderick, *Nettie Fowler McCormick*, 170.

135. Emma Dryer to Mrs. McCormick, 12 October 1888, Biographical File of Emma Dryer. Hereafter, unless otherwise noted, the following information in this section is obtained from this source.

Emma also suspected that Mr. Harvey or Mr. Blatchford held a *conflict of interest* regarding the hiring of Mrs. Capron to take over the Ladies Department. Emma realized that her strong belief that young ladies should not be sent out in the evenings to minister to or be with young men, especially in the jails, was now perceived as a hindrance by some on the board. Her strong views had aligned with that of her Pacific Garden Mission friends, George and Sarah Clarke, with whom she worked in the jail ministry without any reported conflict. She felt that this charge was yet another subtle reason used for replacing her.

Needless to say, short-circuited communication contributed to Emma's imagery of subterfuge, spying, and *modes operandi* as she believed that "affairs of their gains were incidentally spiked." With obvious offense, she openly shared with Nettie her deep feelings of rejection and misunderstanding while speaking of the "dusty talk about my improprieties ... the insanity!! ... I was quiet & still! Patient & still. It is their last weak resort." She sensed that Moody was simply following the expectant female gender consensus while she believed that her friend, Mrs. Moody, would not desire such actions but knew that she also must not interfere. Emma's ensuing response was compliantly poetic: "In quietness I will leave kind. Let us go on! Let us find the long peace of our ... hopeful days, flowing broad & ... lasting ... hidden & bridged under a new Capt.—[a] mountain whose snowy fields melted by the kisses of God's sun-light, swell its currents ... with added blessings to every land. Thus, cheerfully, prayerfully, repentantly, forgivingly in Christian love hoping."

After the October meetings Emma shared her struggle with her Bible Work helpers. She wrote, "*One* woman *can't* work on, so *alone* . . . to be *alone* is to be *weak* and liable to attack."[136] A month later after the separation of the Bible Work from the CES Emma reflected on the truth of the statement *the jaded horse winces*. She acknowledged how she wanted to shrink back in her weakness, weariness, and pain from a long journey. Pondering George MacDonald's book *Weighed and Wanting*, she wrote with a heart filled not only with regrets but with brokenness: "After 18 years of devotion to a work into which my life blood has gone—After 2 years of very trying circumstances as I concealed the peculiarities which I feared would alienate the friends of the work—The last 2 yrs of unwarranted attack & trouble have certainly proven that I am 'weighed in the balances & found wanting.'"[137] Emma admitted that she had experienced *a fierce battle* in which all she resented was the wickedness that came forth. She prayed to be better prepared to go through any other conflicts in the future.

Emma believed that at least two individuals knowingly brought opposition against her. Their impenetrable and mysterious cover-ups and *ipse-dixit* or opinionated and unsustainable methods were "executed by an ambitious instrument in wily

---

136. Joiner, *Sin in the City*, 60.

137. Emma Dryer to Mrs. McCormick, 15 November 1888, Biographical File of Emma Dryer. Hereafter, unless otherwise noted, the following information in this section is obtained from this source.

ways." She admitted that these events left her cast down, but that she was not depressed. She believed that it was not an unpardonable sin for her to oppose "mysterious, underhanded work." Emma lightheartedly mused that her unacknowledged attempts toward kindness had left her nothing else to do but "prepare myself for beheading."

Emma continued to believe that donor funding plainly formed the basis of unexplained maneuvering, and that Moody, as good a man as he was when he began, made a mistake in "imagining his facts & mysteriously concealing his purpose." Emma acknowledged that she did not object to working beside or with anyone else on the board but admitted that she was not very successful in *detective work*. She conceded that without her involvement the board now had a golden opportunity to position themselves as mighty pillars of integrity. She committed to holding them in prayer and forgiveness without cherishing any lasting resentment.

Board and Leadership Struggles and Conflict Resolution

Throughout these internal board conflicts Emma challenged astute businessmen who possessed their own objectives for the Bible Institute along with their strong inclination to govern with authority. In the final months when judgment and criticism escalated, neither Mr. Bouton nor Nettie or her son were present to advocate for Emma. No longer was she being upheld and honored for her moral goodness and expert skills as an educator nor for her deep Christian commitment to a vision long ago embraced. She could no longer sustain her position among the CES board who justified their final actions. She was no longer welcomed to align herself with the redirected vision of Moody or the imperial nature of his business associates. Disagreement and isolation of one who failed to meet their expectations became their response. The board knew that without Moody's endorsement and fortification the CES could not continue to exist. They also believed that without the services of Emma Dryer and the Bible Work, the CES would forge ahead.

The strength of any organizational board lies in its ability to address conflict. During Emma's lifetime, written resources in conflict management such as Ken Sande's (2004) *Peace Maker* Christian materials, had not been formulated. The CES board members—experienced in managing their own individual businesses—were industrialists in a day when attempted unionization and worker unrest brought conflict without the intervention techniques that management and governing boards possess in the twenty-first century. The CES board, including Emma and Moody, did not escape the slippery slope of conflict. They displayed the progressive steps that should not be followed in resolving conflict: unfulfilled desires leading to a justification of one's demands followed by judgment, criticism, and punishment of those who fail to align with one's perceived expectations.

Nettie came close in her attempts for resolution, yet even she felt helpless. Nettie wrote: "I had tried to help make peace—encouraging Mr. Moody—showing him that light was just ahead, for I could see at the Grand Pacific later meetings that he was distressed—and, also, I was certainly obliged to comfort Miss Dryer's deeply wounded heart." Nettie reassuringly affirmed, yet pointed out to her, the ways in which Emma unconsciously and perhaps emotionally misunderstood the intentions and meanings of others. Nettie spoke of her outreach to both Emma and Moody, not as an indication of choosing sides, but as her desire to "help reconcile the two—the *two leaders*."[138]

During conflict both Moody, with his primary leadership *dominance* traits in evangelization, and Emma with her primary leadership *conscientiousness* focus on education, operated out of the scope of their giftings in leadership. Since Moody's initial less-complex business days in Chicago during the 1860s, the Chicago businessmen bureaucracy had developed and morphed into a highly scientific corporate system beyond Moody's gradually outdated experience and expertise.[139] Emma's spiritual and educational influence spread to the area of business which blindsided her walk of faith and exposed her business and corporate leadership weaknesses. Yet her years of commitment to serving and educating the poor and outcast brought her an authority that led to the successful administrative planning and deep faith for the Bible Institute which some of the corporate leaders lacked.

Emma brought this authority with her as she stepped into negotiations for the merger of the Bible Work with the CES. Along with this authority she singly chose to scrutinize *male behavior* with a female empowerment that heavily depended on her compliance.[140] She temporarily and regretfully lost her expected quietness and unchallenging submission during this transition with the CES. When she forcefully moved beyond the board's perception of what was to be her limited gender authority, they systematically immobilized and cut short her authority.

Similarly, Moody struggled with his role as a benevolent evangelist who greatly valued the role of women. He mixed with his business associates who enthusiastically supported his ministry with their own financial resources, masculine ideals, and controlling interests.[141] When Emma questioned the business and procedural ethics of the board and challenged their integrity and spirituality, she met opposition. When she pointed out that "the underhanded element in which some *innocently* work & some, for *popularity,* is now at its height & doing its worst,"[142] these business leaders faltered. They were at a loss as to how to deal with her perceived *activism* and how to control her religious and individualistic tendencies and outspokenness.[143] Emma had most certainly benefited from their resources but would not submit to a controlling obligation to guarantee their support.

138. Roderick, *Nettie Fowler McCormick*, 170.
139. Findlay, *Dwight L. Moody: American Evangelist*, 336–37.
140. Joiner, *Sin in the City*, 61–62.
141. Ibid.
142. Emma Dryer to Mrs. McCormick, 15 November 1888, Biographical File of Emma Dryer.
143. Joiner, *Sin in the City*, 62.

Moody depended not only on Emma's resourcefulness and administrative talents to promote his evangelism, but also on the full backing of his business associates. He found himself caught between his commitment to Emma and their influence and perspectives. As their authority increased, Emma found the door closed on her journey as a coworker with the Northfield evangelist. Nevertheless, despite the apparent diversion of these two leaders whose paths had providentially crossed in 1870, God's eternal purpose for using earthly circumstances to mold them into his image and accomplish his will, would not be altered or diminished.

Time of Transition 1889

While operating with expected difficulties, the CES officially opened the Bible Institute for both men and women in October 1889. A year prior to Emma's parting with the CES, they hired Merton Smith, a Moody convert, as part of their continuing outreach. He conducted campaigns and held evangelistic meetings to support the citywide tent ministry. Emma knew of Mr. Smith's involvement in the tent ministry and remembered his presence at the devastating October 1888 board meeting. She would have had some continued association with him through the Chicago Avenue Church. Otherwise, minimal contact was made until around 1920 when he would cordially call on her for dinner with his wife and child.[144]

Until then, in February 1889 Mr. Harvey requested that Mr. Smith submit a report on his current work involving meetings at the Tyng Mission as well as children's prayer meetings, a mission band and choir practices, Thursday prayer meetings, cottage meetings, house to house visitations, and Sunday school and Bible classes.[145] His report included inquiries, conversions, and church membership applications along with his song leading outreaches. Merton also reported his heavy preaching and teaching schedule at the CAC and the Willard Avenue Baptist Church.

In his report Merton registered his concern regarding the CES which he understood to have been a *complete failure*. He felt a responsibility to show his faithful involvement in ministry as a successful tent evangelist. As with Emma, he meticulously outlined all the work that he had supervised including the successful revival meetings with Major Whittle. He recorded their disappointment in reaching out to a Jesuit gathering of close to 1,800 people with little results. However, this was followed by five months during 1888 when 486 people accepted Christ. At the conclusion of his affirmative and glowing report he humbly admitted a deep realization that even with success, he remained an unprofitable servant of the Lord.

---

144. Emma Dryer to Caroline Waite, 18 July 1924, Biographical File of Emma Dryer.

145. Merton Smith to the CES Board, 5 February 1889, Chicago Evangelization Society File. Hereafter, unless otherwise noted, the following information in this section regarding Mr. Merton is obtained from this source.

At the same time, Merton continued to confess his own personal loss of faith in the CES:

> I had hoped against hope that the day was coming in which the CES would recognize the marvelous work to which God had called it and launch out on His promises—and so I have held on when repeatedly my better judgment had told me to resign. Not that the work done has not been good work—nor that I have anything to complain of as to personal treatment—the CES has always treated me with the utmost consideration.

He then asked that he might humbly give the reason why he felt there had been a failure in the work of the CES. He wrote: "It is this; it has been done in the fear of man and consequently not with an eye single to the Glory of God." He pointed out that he had not been included in their meetings which forced him to speculate about what plans or course of action they were seeking to take. Due to this lack of communication and their fear of man, he concluded that their propensity was to take no action in order to avoid offending other churches. However, he knew that the denominations were already offended. He had observed along with information from other sources that they had been "laughing in their sleeves at our cowardice." He was asked if he believed that the churches were dying. When he responded in the positive, he was reproved for even suggesting that it could be a possibility.

After working in the CES's tent ministry for four years Merton concluded: "The poor and the church are in a state of Divorce by mutual understanding, and as regards any real consecrated effort to reach the masses the church is indeed *Dead*." He affirmed that studies verified that the church was overwhelmed with its own needs and had no time for follow-up and discipling converts. He only foresaw that the integrity and proof of the CES's ministries would continue to be discredited by the Chicago churches.

Emma, along with Merton Smith and Nathaniel Bouton, expressed similar concerns regarding the state of the church. Following Smith's report, Emma presented what she felt was the primary difficulty: "The *present* agitating questions resolve themselves into—Has the 'church' any power to adjust the moral & spiritual relations of its members? & 'Where is the power centered which decides the right & wrong of Christian conduct among church members?'"[146] With Emma's vast experience in established fundamentalist churches, she now believed that independent mission churches, such as the CAC, were more prone to experience difficulties regarding doctrinal and procedural control.

The church and society situation was amplified by the continued influence and interference of the Chicago Evangelization Society in the CAC. The church determined

---

146. Emma Dryer to Mrs. McCormick, 3 September 1889, Biographical File of Emma Dryer. Hereafter, unless noted otherwise, the following information regarding Emma's church reflections are obtained from this source.

that the CES was exercising "some peculiarly strange prerogatives involving members of that church" in which "a portion of the church are inclined to investigate & resist them." The society reportedly criticized the CAC for their involvement in situations that they considered to be inhospitable and adverse to some of the church members. The CES questioned the moral implications of those actions. Emma forewarned that if the church was to continue, changes needed to be made. She observed that an independent church lacked the power "to control the forces & no outside co-operating power is recognized & every commotion is likely to revolutionize them."

This church turmoil surely brought back memories to Emma of the division in the Proprietors' Church in her home town of Victor. Regretfully, she found herself pulling away from association with the CAC after sixteen years of membership: "I think a greater commotion is coming there than they have yet had." Emma communicated with Mr. Bouton and Mrs. McCormick that she no longer believed in independent mission churches. She concluded that such a church was "a short-lived institution which begins . . . to work out from the elementary processes the questions which sound doctrine has settled for ages. Such churches . . . under the fostering care of a mature eldership . . . can settle questions before the questions settle the church."

It is uncertain how Moody responded to the CAC difficulties or to Merton Smith's culminating letter. However, on March 15, 1889, with a continued focus on evangelization, Moody wrote Mr. Ensign at the CES regarding the tent meetings in which it was reported that thousands had been reached for Christ.[147] Moody continued to believe in this evangelistic work and wrote in his visionary style: "This work has been satisfactory as far as it has gone, but it should be increased twenty fold, and instead of having 10 trained workers, we must have one or two hundred, if we would reach and rescue these people . . . who are drifting so rapidly yet so surely to destruction."

In 1889 Moody began to actively promote the May Institute planned for April at the Chicago Avenue Church. The goal was to employ fifty trained women and men to work with people in the Chicago slums in the transformation of lives. While in San Francisco Moody asked the leaders in Chicago planning the Institute to actively promote and endorse the upcoming May Institute.[148] The headlines of one newspaper announced: *Inauguration of the Training of the Chicago Evangelization Society*.

Moody elaborated in a follow-up newspaper interview: "On the fourth day of April, 1889, I will begin holding in Chicago a Convention of Christian workers similar to those held in the summers at Northfield. These meetings will continue from 30 to 60 days, and instruction will be given by well-known leaders of Christian thought and action . . . this is the beginning of a movement . . . [for] a permanent school." He explained that this program would involve a practical approach of morning Bible study and lectures opened to the public with modern day application. For the rest

---

147. Letter to the CES from Moody to Mr. Ensign, 15 March 1889, Biographical File of Emma Dryer.

148. Getz, *The Story of Moody Bible Institute*, 25.

of the day participants would personally take the gospel to the unchurched and to those who had formerly rejected the good news of Christ. He invited pastors, Sunday school teachers, urban missionaries, students, and others engaged in or preparing for Christian ministries.

Moody also participated in a press conference in San Francisco regarding the training school. Deviating from his remarks to Emma in 1873, he now confidently stated that the school would not alienate the seminaries but rather serve as a feeder school—a move that Emma had previously suggested. The goal was to increase enrollment in seminaries by actively encouraging students to seek further training. He also assured churches regarding the nondenominational nature of the work while targeting the evangelical churches. He desired that all classes of dedicated men and women as well as lady seminary graduates and students of theology could take time to attend his school in preparation for the pastorate. He advertised the April and May Institute as a free trial session for individuals seeking to find their calling and direction. He believed that such nondenominational training had been neglected by the church with at least seventy-five percent of the working force in the urban population being unreached.[149]

Moody expanded the institute agenda by including Bible drills and home visitations with reports in the afternoon. Small evening cottage, hall, and church meetings were also held. These events followed the methods practiced in Paris at the McAll Mission. In 1882 Moody campaigned in Paris at Oratoire during which time he visited the mission. In 1885, in preparation for the Bible Institute, he had recommended the McAll Mission to a group of Chicago businessmen. Andrew Bonar's brother, Horatius (1808–89), quoted Moody as saying:

> I consider the McAll Mission as a model Mission for the world . . . Mr. and Mrs. McAll, giving themselves so completely, and without salary. It is the best-run Mission I know. That is just what we need here in Chicago . . . a mission not of churches, nor of chapels, but of shops or stores right on the busy thoroughfares where the people are . . . with a band of devoted workers, men and women, who go from station to station, thus giving a needed variety, and who have but the single aim to win lost souls to Christ.[150]

Moody gave assurance that he would personally lead the institute with classroom instruction conducted by pastors and teachers from the United States and other countries.

In April of 1889 the Institute registered a record attendance. From 1887 to 1889 many notable speakers and teachers highlighted the institute—Frederick Meyer, Major Whittle, Chicago Avenue Church pastor George Needham, Irish evangelist Grattan Guinness, E. W. Bliss, and Dr. Moorehead.[151] Moody capitalized on these institutes to

---

149. Ibid., 27.
150. Newell, *A Cry From the Land of Calvin and Voltaire: Records of the McAll Mission*, 71.
151. Bible Work Reports from Emma Dryer, 1887–89, Biographical File of Emma Dryer.

announce the 1889 fall opening of the new full time Bible Institute with three women's dormitories and another currently under construction for men.

At this time, on May 15, 1889, the CES trustees—Scott, Harvey, Keith, Cyrus McCormick, and Ensign—met with Moody at the cafe of the Grand Pacific Hotel at noon in a private dining area. Moody discussed the previous disharmonious stalemate regarding Emma and the Bible Work as well as Nettie's original $50,000 offer. He mentioned that Mrs. McCormick had rejected his suggestion to give Emma the total pledge. She requested that her original $50,000 pledge be divided equally between the CES and Emma's work. A board motion was made and approved to return $25,000 to the McCormicks to fund the Bible Work: "Resolved that the action of the Board of Trustees taken March 12th 1888 incorporating the Bible Work with the CES be rescinded and that the Treasurer is hereby instructed to return to Miss Dryer such money as now remains in his hands of that which was received from said Bible work."[152] The Society also agreed to pay Emma $1,200 a year for two years.

After this trustee meeting Emma joined Moody as they met with Scottish friends at the 143 Locust Street home of Mrs. Mary Ann Hubbard, wife of a prominent Chicago businessman and early settler Gurdon Saltonstall Hubbard (1802–86). They met to discuss plans for the Institute building.[153] Moody appeared content that Emma had temporarily remained connected with the CES in order to assist Mrs. Capron in the transition. The following day, on May 16, 1889, Emma officially resigned and later merged her Bible Work with the Chicago Bible Society. In this new association she would accept the challenge as a single woman to work successfully with an even larger CBS board.

In a letter to Nettie written the following fall, Emma expressed how relieved she was to be *out of the turmoil* associated with the Chicago Avenue Church in reference most likely to the church concerns voiced by Merton Smith and herself.[154] Likewise, on May 24 Moody wrote to Major Whittle that he had experienced "about the darkest 40 days and nights I have ever passed thru at Chicago, and I had no heart for anything but I am in hopes now I have got our society so it will go on."[155] Satisfied also with Bouton's departure, he was now hopeful for smooth and easy progress.

Months later, on November 9, Moody wrote to his son Will—who so lovingly through the years referred to Emma as his *Auntie Dryer*,[156]—that he hoped never to experience again three such years of turmoil. At the same time Moody stated that he had no problem with Emma and that he believed the storm was past and everything

---

152. Board Minutes, 15 May 1889, Chicago Evangelization Society File.

153. Emma Dryer to Charles Blanchard, 1916, Biographical File of Emma Dryer.

154. Letter to Nettie McCormick from Emma Dryer, 3 September 1889, Biographical File of Emma Dryer.

155. D. L. Moody to Major Whittle from Northfield, 24 May 1889, Biographical File of Emma Dryer.

156. Interview with Miss Emma MacNaughtan, 14 June 1958, Biographical File of Emma Dryer.

was now straightened out.[157] With a sense of closure, Emma was pleased that she and Moody had truly put the past behind them with anticipation of God's future. Most certainly, she would have wholeheartedly awaited the opening and dedication of the Bible Institute's first residential buildings for both men and women on October 1, 1889.

As Emma gradually withdrew from the work at the Bible Institute, her departure did not weaken her distinction or future standing with the institute or her impact in forming its initial ministry.[158] Even to this day, Emma is remembered for her humble and heartfelt recollections of the school in which her contributions to founding the Institute are still warmly referred to as *secure*.[159]

During their final years together in ministry, Emma and Moody experienced what Thomas Merton (1915–68) portrayed as "the resetting of a Body of broken bones" in which even the righteous ones experience grief and distress in their opposing interactions with other Christians.[160] Their differences with the pain of separation presented two choices—to love or to hate. By God's grace Emma and her God-ordained friend, D. L. Moody, ultimately and faithfully chose to cover their multitude of sins with God's divine love.

Sarah B. Capron and Reuben Archer Torrey

The April 1889 Institute became the springboard for the September 26, 1889, opening of the school designated as the *Bible Institute for Home and Foreign Missions of the Chicago Evangelization Society*. Dr. Reuben Archer Torrey headed the school as superintendent with Mrs. Sarah Brown Capron (1828–1919) presiding over the Ladies Department. At the opening of the school Emma would have supportively listened as Moody, with his continued flair for words, articulated: "We want men who can do something uncommon. Any man can eat soup with a spoon, but the man who can eat it with a one-tined fork is a marvel."[161]

As Mrs. Sarah Capron took on her new position, Emma, free from the shackles of controversy, sincerely prayed that the Lord would fill Sarah with his blessings and peace. Emma wrote: "The long contemplated Bible Institute and Work, according to God's purpose, moved on to its establishment. Praise God from whom that blessing came!"[162] This transition of leadership roles officially began in October 1888 when Mrs. Capron was elected by the CES board as the new superintendent of the women's department with her new assistant Gertrude Hurlburt.

157. Pollock, *Moody: A Biographical Portrait*, 270.
158. Hassey, *A Time For Silence*, 36.
159. Belmonte, *D. L. Moody—A Life: Innovator*, 163.
160. Merton, *New Seeds of Contemplation*, 72.
161. *Chicago Tribune*, "Moody is Here Again," 1.
162. Emma Dryer to Charles Blanchard, 1916, Biographical File of Emma Dryer.

As a missionary Sarah headed up a female boarding school in India with her husband Reverend William Banfield Capron (1824–76). They served as missionaries with the American Board of Commissioners for Foreign Mission for sixteen years. After a visit to America from 1872 to 1875 they returned to India. Despite Mr. Capron's death a year later, Sarah remained in India until 1886 before returning to America.[163]

On November 13, 1888, Mrs. Capron received an invitation to visit Chicago to view the site for the new Bible Institute and to participate in a December conference. During the period of the CES conflict Emma had met Mrs. Capron and favorably commented in a letter to Nettie: "I wished when I saw her here, that we were in peace so that I could employ her in our work!!" Nettie had counseled Emma to treat Mrs. Capron as a friend. Emma did just that as she assisted Sarah in the transition. With Emma's input, Mrs. Capron wisely implemented initiatives from the solid program that Emma had expertly established. Years later Emma amiably commented: "She and I were intimate friends while she lived."[164]

After Sarah Capron joined the CES, Moody approached Dr. Torrey, an intelligent Yale graduate and theologian, about heading up the Institute. Moody's attempts to hire Dr. Moorehead to direct the Institute had failed. He knew that the selection of Dr. Torrey (1856–1928) would lend credibility among the seminaries. He chose Torrey as a man who would theologically emphasize the work and power of the Holy Spirit.[165]

Torrey provided a sound foundation for the curriculum and other school programs while reducing the prior extensive emphasis on field work. The students were drawn to this motivational and inspiring teacher with his deep ability to pray. He was known to be an outstanding teacher with a solid biblical doctrine.[166] Torrey also played a vital part in the 1893 Chicago World's Fair Evangelistic outreach.

Just as Emma passed the mantle to Mrs. Capron, ten years later Torrey quite capably received Moody's mantle when Moody in 1899 was unable to finish his Kansas City crusade. Despite this leadership change for the Bible Institute, the new school could be described as a transitional mosaic of *a host of Great Hearts* including "Emeline E. [sic] Dryer, Reuben Archer Torrey, James Martin Gray, and a host of equally dedicated men and women."[167]

During this transition Emma worked very closely with Reuben Torrey just as she had with Moody, Dr. Moorehead, and Sarah Capron. With the opening of the Bible Institute she genuinely wrote: "May the present excellent gospel ministry in

---

163. Congregational Library, "Capron, William Banfield (1824–76) and Sarah Brown Capron (1828–1919)."

164. Emma Dryer to Caroline Waite, 18 July 1924, Biographical File of Emma Dryer.

165. Dorsett, *A Passion For Souls*, 311.

166. European-American Evangelistic Crusades, "Reuben Archer Torrey," para. 13–14.

167. Day, *Bush Aglow*, 262.

these united institutions, continue *until Christ comes!*"[168] She believed that God had faithfully directed Torrey and Mrs. Capron and other institute staff *for Christ's sake!*[169]

While a full picture of spiritual and situational causes and factors behind the poignant CES controversy cannot be clearly determined, there appears to have been a weakness in conflict management and a tremendous breakdown in communication between the key players. Furthermore, leadership burnout was inevitable especially for Moody with his demanding schedule and for Emma with her unfulfilled expectations. Within a few years even Mr. Harvey's business ventures took a toll on him when, unfortunately, the panic of 1893 created a financial collapse for his businesses which necessitated the selling of his property in order to pay off his debts.[170]

Notwithstanding, Emma peacefully acknowledged that those with the CES and the Bible Work ultimately desired God's guidance. She knew that "through an untried way, of remarkable difficulties, He guided that Institute" just as he directed and led Israel in crossing the Red Sea for his divine purposes. Emma was convinced that God guarded Moody and the CES Board *better than they knew*.[171]

In later years Emma gratifyingly reported that the Bible Institute continued to flourish and grow in its instruction of Christ's unsearchable riches. She sincerely prayed that God's "presence and blessing abide there, even until Christ's Kingdom comes, and God's will is done on Earth."[172] She believed that it was easier to trace the development of the Bible Institute not so much to the work of the CES as to the clearly identifiable hand of God who founded and sustained such a grand Christian institution.[173]

God touched D. L. Moody's heart with inspiration and vision while sanctioning Emma and the Bible Work to prepare the way for the founding of the Bible Institute in Chicago. Emma's educational and administrative skills, coupled with her deep love for the Lord and genuine care for people in need, secured a firm and noble foundation for the establishment of the Moody Bible Institute.

"I know your [record of] works and what you are doing. See! I have set before you a door wide open which no one is able to shut; I know that you have but little power, and yet you have kept My Word and guarded My message and have not renounced or denied My name."

~Revelation 3:8 AMP~

168. Emma Dryer to Charles Blanchard, 1916, Biographical File of Emma Dryer.
169. Ibid.
170. Nebraska State Historical Society. "Harvey, Turlington," para. 3.
171. Emma Dryer to Charles Blanchard, 1916, Biographical File of Emma Dryer.
172. Ibid.
173. Emma Dryer to A.P. Fitt, 24 November 1910, Biographical File of Emma Dryer.

10

Chicago Bible Society and Retirement, 1889–1925

"For I know the thoughts and plans that I have for you, says the Lord, thoughts and plans for welfare and peace and not for evil, to give you hope in your final outcome."

~Jeremiah 29:11 AMP~

By the end of 1888 Emma nobly sought out and found purpose beyond the Bible Institute. With this unanticipated, yet heavenly guided detour, friends from the Chicago Avenue Church encouraged her, though unsuccessfully, to consider using her expert skills to start a school at the church for missions.[1] Miss Livonia E. Ketcham, Emma's friend from her earlier days at ISNU, along with many others, offered their support. They made provision for her as she branched out into newly directed ministries such as the Italian and Hebrew Missions and the Chicago Bible Society.[2] As Emma placed herself under God's anointing and authority, she experienced his unending promotion and favor.

Expanded Mission Opportunities

With consistent loving support, Nettie McCormick sent contributions to Emma's special mission interest groups and area schools—the Pacific Garden Mission ($300 from 1899 to 1911), the Salvation Army ($300 from 1894 to 1911), and Wheaton College ($2,100 from 1911 to 1918).[3] Nettie also contributed $13,300 to the Chicago Bible Society from 1890 to 1896 after they welcomed Emma's Bible Work as one of their departments. Nettie donated $500 for the Bible Work Department from July 1889 to December 1889. McCormick finance records indicated a specified salary for Emma of $3,500 from 1896 to 1900. Additionally, according to the McCormick accountant

---

1. Emma Dryer to Nettie McCormick, 3 October 1888, Biographical File of Emma Dryer.
2. Ibid., 15 November 1888.
3. Financial File, Nettie Fowler McCormick, McCormick Collection.

ledger from agent John A. Chapman of the Chicago Stock Exchange, Emma was assured of a financial provision of $83.33 the first of every month from January 1912 to April 26, 1918.[4]

Nettie also purchased a California and Auburn railroad ticket for Emma on May 18, 1899, for $29.70 as they traveled together to California to visit Nettie's daughter, Virginia, who had suffered from mental illness since the age of nineteen.[5] With solid support from her friends, Emma held on with full assurance and trust in God's provision. She confidently wrote in reference to Psalm 76:10: "We shall doubtless be provided for. God is *in the future* as in the past . . . *The Lord will provide*. My soul rejoices in the Lord who maketh the wrath of man to praise Him & restrains the remainder thereof. I am not worrying."[6]

Emma became involved in the *Italian work* in Chicago through her long-time friends, Joshua and Lucy Helmer.[7] The work consisted of an evening school for Italian men and boys with Bible study and instruction in the English language. With great satisfaction Emma conveyed compelling stories of this work. One testimony involved a broken and needy man with hunger for the word of God who was asking many questions. His teacher invited him to the Italian prayer meeting where he received his first Bible. He had never read a Bible before coming to the school. Emma found that for him God's word became the light of life and the fountain which filled his thirst for knowledge.[8]

Emma and her friend, Charles Blanchard, were connected with the *Hebrew Mission* and its various Hebrew conferences for several years. They held a common association with its treasurer, Mrs. Tryphena Rounds, who was affectionately known as a *Mother of Israel*.[9] In January 1891 Emma corresponded with Nettie's daughter Anita sharing a report from the annual Jewish Christian Convention held in Chicago—the first of its kind. The Hebrew Mission was founded on November 4, 1887, by William Blackstone, Reverend Goodwin, Turlington Harvey, and Professor Hugh Scott. As an outreach to the Russian Jewish immigrants the Mission sponsored the convention with the purpose of exposing anti-Semitism and familiarizing Christians with their own Jewish background. Charles Blanchard, with his influential position as president of the Chicago Hebrew Mission from 1913 to 1925, encouraged Emma's participation at its Solon Street location.

In a 1915 letter Emma informed Anita once again about the upcoming Hebrew Christian Conference to be held on Tuesday, November 16 to Friday, November 19. She announced prominent speakers such as William Blackstone, (vice-president of

---

4. Ibid.
5. Roderick, *Nettie Fowler McCormick*, 178.
6. Emma Dryer to Nettie McCormick, 15 November 1888, Biographical File of Emma Dryer.
7. Ibid., 12 October 1888.
8. *Sixty-Second Annual Report of the Chicago Bible Society*. Chicago: Chicago Bible Society, 1902. Biographical File of Emma Dryer.
9. Blanchard, *The Life of Charles Albert Blanchard*, 183.

the Chicago Hebrew Mission), Reverend Cyrus Ingerson Scofield (dispensationalist author of the Scofield Reference Bible), Albert Simpson, Reverend Paul Rader (narrator for the conference and pastor of the Moody Church), and Dr. James M. Gray (Dean and President of the Moody Bible Institute). Emma held a steadfast allegiance to the Jews and to the Hebrew Mission. She encouragingly wrote: "This is an important time in Israel's history; and the Jewish Nation is watching events, with their eyes hopefully fixed on the prophetic promises of God's Word, to the children of Abraham. May the day of Israel's glory, and the triumph of Christ's blood-bought Church, hasten to this sin-sick world."[10]

Chicago Bible Society Affiliation

Not only was Emma involved in the Hebrew and Italian Missions, but in 1889 she led the Bible Work into a partnership with the Chicago Bible Society.[11] Nathaniel Bouton, her friend since the early days of the Bible Work, encouraged her to affiliate with the CBS. He unwaveringly promoted her during this transition. As former president of the Chicago Bible Society he was one of the first to support what CBS characterized as a thoroughly evangelical and humanitarian work. Under this covering Emma continued with the ministry incorporation name of *The Bible Work of Chicago*. The CBS provided assistance with mutual Bible distribution and extensive house-to-house visitations. Emma retained her practice of assigning Bible workers to various districts. With the approval of the CBS she implemented the *Ten Dollar Missionary Share Program* to provide salaries of $400 annually for her workers. These workers trained CBS missionaries and held prayer, Bible readings, and Bible studies in cottage meetings covering the YMCA, Haymarket district, and Union Park.[12] The goal continued to be that of evangelization by introducing families to God's word, bringing them to Sunday school, and involving both women and children in Industrial Meetings.

The Chicago Bible Society, an extension of the American Bible Society (ABS) in New York City, maintained oversight of the Bible Work. Without doubt Emma was impressed with the rich heritage of the ABS presidential selections. Founded in 1816, the ABS appointed Elias Boudinot (1740–1821), who was President of the Continental Congress, to be ABS's first president. John Jay (1745–1829), the U.S. Supreme Court's first Chief Justice in 1821, followed as the next president. National Anthem composer Francis Scott Key (1779–1843) also served as vice president from 1817 to 1843.

Since the early days of the Bible Work Training School, Emma valued the CBS's faithful support and generous provision of needed equipment, property, workers, and

---

10. Anita Blaine McCormick Correspondence and Papers, 15 November 1915, McCormick Collection.

11. *Sixty-Second Annual Report of the Chicago Bible Society*, 1902, Biographical File of Emma Dryer.

12. See Ogorek, "Dryer, Emma," 230.

officers.[13] The CBS, organized ten years after the 1830 founding of the city of Chicago, provided Bibles for Emma's Bible Work. The Society also supplied Bibles for schools, hotels, the military, passenger ships, train depots, jails, and rescue missions with their goal of placing a Bible in the hands of every person.

In their Bible worker reports the CBS reiterated the Bible Work's missionary emphasis, church and pastoral benefits, and utilitarian values as an important branch of the society. The CBS picturesquely portrayed the Bible Work's mission as a "personal ministry of angels to the poor, the sick, the brokenhearted; so free from race or denominational bias, so flexible and winning in its spirit and endeavor."[14] To Emma's complete satisfaction the ministry was referred to as a gift from the God of the word with its connection to over twenty-one nationalities including the South Side Blacks, Syrians, Polish, and Bohemians.

Emma continued to submit regular reports, as she had done for the Bible Work since 1873, and served as an adviser on the CBS council. The council noted, "We have observed the model methods of teaching the Bible, its doctrines, its historical and geographical facts, and the persistent efforts by which its vital truths have been made practical in families won by a kind Christian ministry to the study of the Word of God." They also expressed their admiration for Emma's exceptional fiscal management in superintending and directing the Home and Field Departments of the Bible Work. They communicated their gratitude and resolute assurance of Emma's Christ-centered commitment to her Bible workers and the unfailing actions performed heartily as to the Lord.

13. American Bible Society. *History of American Bible Society*.

14. *Sixty-Second Annual Report of the Chicago Bible Society*, 1902, Biographical File of Emma Dryer. Hereafter, unless noted otherwise, the following information regarding the CBS is obtained from this source.

Emma reported the activities of her thirteen workers in the 1902 CBS report: 1901 visitations 13,324, Family Bible readings and prayer 1,996, Bibles sold or given 790, and meetings 8,576; 1902 visitations 24,502, Family Bible readings and prayer 5,347, meetings 23,265, and 20,084 tracks distributed. In the report the CBS acknowledged that these recorded figures did not come close to revealing a complete picture of the lives touched by Emma's Bible Work ministry. They movingly stated, "We are unable to photograph the heart's joy; the praise of a forgiven soul; the happiness of a redeemed home; the love of a regenerated life; the sweetness of a new found hope."

Testimonies of the Bible workers presented an unfeigned snapshot of this work unendingly close to Emma's heart. Her workers kept their own *Field Books* which were made available to church pastors and other Christian workers. Testimonies included ministry to religious groups such as the Quakers and Catholics.

One worker wrote about a lady who refused the offer of a Bible saying that her husband would only burn it. In another report a mother in an unkempt house with a young boy agreed to attend the Mothers Meeting which was similar in outreach to the twentieth and twenty-first-century MOPS or Mothers of Preschoolers. The mother received ministry while the son received supervision and Sunday school training. The testimony continued: "The house began to look more tidy and care was shown in personal appearance. One day the mother said she had given her heart to Jesus Christ as her Saviour, and though her husband does not yet believe, he no longer forbids his wife going to church but rather encourages it." This mother's heart was overflowing with thanksgiving to the Lord for these workers and their commitment to fulfill the Great Commission of Jesus Christ.

Emma read a report from yet another Bible worker's Field Book. The worker hesitantly approached a run-down building with an enduring trust in the promise of God's word that he would always be with her. She discovered a sick woman and her intoxicated husband whose five unattended children played in the dirt. The mother watched as the worker cleaned the room and the children. She quietly asked why she was doing that. The worker replied that her motivation was the love of God's only Son crucified for all mankind. She then asked the mother if she knew the Lord. The woman replied that she had at one time, but now she had not even tried to think of him since she had been married to the tavern owner. The worker continued her visits and later reported the triumphant Sunday in which the five children, accompanied by their mother, excitedly ventured to Sunday school. The worker later discovered that the family had departed from the tavern. Her husband left his saloon business and returned to his skilled trade as a carpenter assuming a comfortable and godly life style for his family.

The CBS portrayed Emma's Bible Work Home as a ministry with a Christian family environment. Workers were trained by a faculty of qualified teachers with instruction on using the Bible to minister to backsliding Christians. Emma continued to implement a daily schedule, as she had formerly done, which included the following courses combined with various ministries, music, and lectures:

- Wed. 9–10 a.m. *Reports and Conference Meetings/Personal Work* taught by Reverend R. D. Scott teacher
- Wed. 10–11a.m. *Sunday School Work and Lessons* taught by Mrs. L. Hyatt
- Every other Thursday 9–10 a.m. *Old Testament Books* and 10–12am *Church History* taught by General S. L. Brown
- Every other Thursday 9–10 a.m. *New Testament Books* and 10am–12 *Life of Christ* taught by Reverend C. V. LaFontaine

Lady workers attending these classes wore serge navy blue dresses and matching bonnets. On October 17, 1903, at a special reception the CBS stated that the initiation of this new sturdy attire was received with admiration and approval from those in the position to evaluate fairly based on their experience. With Emma's background in fabric design, she suggested that the Bible workers wear this specially designed costume to identify themselves with the Bible Work. She witnessed the positive differences made in ministries when *costumes,* such as those used by her friends Lucy and Josiah Meyer in their ministry with the Chicago Training School, were worn.

The CBS gladly extended the Bible Work outreach to the Relief and Aid Society, area hospitals, and other institutions. Emma solicited students from the McCormick Theological Seminary as well as women from the Ladies Department of the Bible Institute. In 1903 she gratifyingly worked with the Bible Institute's new supervisor, Miss Strong, in placing five institute students in the district between North Avenue and Division Street. These assigned districts overflowed with dance halls, saloons, and breweries which created fertile conditions in which the Bible workers could operate. With her collective years of experience Emma skillfully trained these workers in the word of God—a powerful tool which effectively enlightened veiled minds and softened stony hearts.

With Emma's educational qualifications and her prior committed love and assistance to Nettie McCormick's handicapped daughter Virginia, she did not hesitate to reach out and educationally assist individuals with special needs. She also continued her close connections with churches in Chicago. She encouraged them to provide furnishings for worker rooms at the Bible Work relocated from Warren Avenue to 49 South Ada Street. The home was officially opened on December 10, 1891.[15] Some of these contributing churches included the Jefferson Park and Third Presbyterian Churches, the Warren Avenue and Union Park Congregational Churches, First Congregation Centinary Church, Methodist Episcopal Church, and the Second Baptist Church. Emma solicited financial support for her work from various ladies' societies, schools, numerous donors, and approximately 120 churches with sixty percent identified as Methodist Episcopal.

Emma maintained her contact with Joshua and Lucy Helmer who were serving at the China Inland Mission in Toronto. Influenced by Hudson Taylor's 1888 visit to the Chicago Avenue Church and her own continued contact with the Helmers, Emma began training some of her workers as candidates for the China Inland Mission. On November 20, 1891, the CBS Council satisfyingly approved its first CIM candidate for training at Emma's school.[16]

During her twelve years at the Chicago Bible Society Emma maintained correspondence with many ministries and groups beyond Chicago. She also continued her relationship with Moody and his family[17] and kept regular correspondence with Nettie McCormick's daughter, Anita McCormick Blaine. On January 7, 1891, she wrote Anita from her 69 Dearborn Street office with a continued motherly affection: "Not

---

15. *Fifty-Second Annual Report of the Chicago Bible Society*, 13 January 1892, 8.
16. Undated Emma Dryer Obituary, Biographical File of Emma Dryer.
17. See Ogorek, "Dryer, Emma," 230.

wanting Baby Blaine to go hungry for want of a spoon to eat with, I send him one, with unnumbered spoonfuls of best wishes for this & all the New Year." On June 19, 1892, after the sudden death of Anita's husband, Emma compassionately, and perhaps with her own past reflections, wrote from the 49–55 South Ada Street Bible Work residence: "In your unutterable sorrow, you have my constant loving sympathy. May God help you at the point where human help is weak and fails while love sorrows within you. Somewhere, End [sic] will turn sorrow into joy! He says so. In the gloom of terrible grief the hope seems too good . . . But He says so! Hoping, most of all, in *His promises*."[18]

Retirement

By 1901 Emma realized that she could not keep pace with all the ministries she held so dear. A special July 15, 1901, tribute edition published by the CBS reported that due to enfeebled health Miss Dryer would be resigning her position as superintendent of the Bible Work which she had for so many years faithfully developed, managed, and sustained by God's grace. She would now be leaving the work for others to continue while she attended to various Christian ministries with her dedicated and heartfelt prayers.

18. Anita Blaine McCormick Correspondence and Papers, McCormick Collection.

The CBS acknowledged her dependable and thorough organization of the Bible Work and her arduous ministry responsibilities since 1872. Some members of the Council, who had known her since that time, registered their "deep appreciation of her Christian work and their personal, affectionate regard for her . . . [as] a very useful laborer in the Lord's Vineyard." The council and Board of Directors gratefully observed how Emma had conducted the citywide Bible Work with *consecrated thoroughness*. With their own compelling Bible mission call they added their joy and gratitude for the Bible Work's extended emphasis on the foreign mission field.

In 1901 the council and board recommended that Emma be given *Superintendent Emeritus* status. They gratefully acknowledged that her continued prayers and sympathies would be cherished: "We pray that God will tenderly guard and guide her until he calls her to higher service in His presence." The council consisted of Mrs. C. H. Case, President; Mrs. J. M. Sherman; Mrs. James Frazer; Mrs. W. W. Storey; Mrs. William Ripley; Mrs. I. R. Krum; secretary Mrs. L. A. Shute; and Emma's good friend since her 1870 Chicago arrival, Mrs. Goodwin. The Board of Directors included President Charles H. Mulliken; Vice-President Frank E. Spooner; Reverend Thomas B. Arnold; Secretary Reverend J. A. Mack; Auditors Josiah Simms and Frank E. Page; Henry W. Dudley; Reverend R. D. Scott; and as Treasurer her life-long friend, Elbridge Keith. After her official retirement from active service the CBS gave her unlimited residency at the Bible Work Home on Warren Avenue.

In 1908 Emma received a special reunion invitation along with other former members and acquaintances of the Chicago Avenue Church, renamed Moody Church after D. L. Moody's death in 1899.[19] This first Moody Church reunion was held for a week from Sunday October 25 to November 1. The Moody Church web site article records, "What a home-coming it was for those old pioneers of an early day." Former pastors and teachers in attendance included the church's first pastor Reverend J. H. Harwood; Moody's brother-in-law and Emma's former prayer partner Fleming H. Revell; Thomas McMillen; T. S. Fauntleroy; Swedish church associate Reverend John S. Okerstein; former Moody Church pastor Charles Morton; and Emma's steadfast friend and supporter from Wheaton College, President Charles Blanchard.

On Thursday following an afternoon social gathering, a six o'clock *Reminiscence Day* banquet was held at the Bible Institute. This banquet primarily included former Moody associates. Emma attended the event. She received recognition for being one of the most highly regarded Moody Church workers and Bible teachers. Approximately four hundred individuals attended this Thursday session including J. M. Hitchcock, David MacNaughtan, D. B. Towner, John Morrison, A. P. Fitt, William J. Erdman, J. H. Harwood, William Moody, George C. Needham, A. F. Gaylord, C. M. Morton, and E. L. Vogel—a momentous gathering of Emma's beloved friends.

---

19. *Moody Church Reunion: Church History*, 1 November 1908. Hereafter, unless otherwise noted, the information about the reunion is derived from this article.

A few years after this memorable reunion of Moody Church forerunners, attendee A. P. Fitt wrote Emma asking her to document some of her reminiscences of his father-in-law, D. L. Moody. On November 24, 1910, Emma responded.[20] She shared a comment that Moody so concisely, yet humbly, spoke to her that notably impacted her life. She realized that Moody was referring to his passion to do God's business when he simply told her: "*This one thing I do.*" Emma acknowledged that his definitive act as God's servant to initiate the Bible Institute continued to bring blessings to all even after his death in 1899. She also recalled that Moody did not desire to publish results of his campaigns. He acknowledged that his devotion to God's will explained "his otherwise unexplained purposes." Emma concluded by affirming that the source of the school's success lay in his statement—"This *one* thing I do"—the fulfillment of God's will for his life. Emma unfailingly continued to pray for blessings on this *one* important work accomplished through the lives of Moody and herself: "Thru the darkness of these last days may the Moody Church & Institute remain true to Christ, 'until He comes.'"

Anita McCormick Blaine Correspondence

After retirement Emma's days were filled with written correspondence to individuals throughout the country—especially letters to Anita McCormick Blaine. After joyously accepting Anita's invitation to celebrate her mother Nettie's eightieth birthday on February 8, 1915, she continued her correspondence with an April letter. Emma, with an unrelenting passion for the state of Israel, sent Anita a copy of Reverend Sabeti B. Rohold's (1876-1931) book, *The War and the Jew*.[21] Emma and Anita were later privileged to hear Reverend Rohold speak on the topics of *The World Situation and the Jew* and *The Threefold Betrothal of Zion* at the November 16-19, 1915, Hebrew Christian Conference. During the same year Emma informed Anita that her friend Mary M. Jenkins had joined Anita's father and mother in the presence of the Lord. Mrs. Jenkins had devotedly served with her on the Prayer Alliance Team, edited Emma's *Bible Notes*, and studied with her the topic of the second coming of the Lord.

In 1917 Emma extended her congratulations to Anita, who lived at 101 East Erie Street in Chicago, upon the marriage announcement of Anita's son, Emmons, to Miss Eleanor Gooding. On March 21 Emma sent a letter of thanks to Anita for mentioning to her sons the papers written by William Blackstone. She expressed her gratitude that so many of Anita's family and friends held an interest in Blackstone's Christian work. Emma offered to send samples from a packet of flyers that he had sent her. She mentioned that his widely circulated book, *Jesus is Coming*, had been published in various languages. In view of end time prophecy and news of the ongoing World War, Emma

---

20. Emma Dryer to A. P. Fitt, 24 November 1910, Biographical File of Emma Dryer.

21. Rohold, *The War and the Jew*. Reverend Rohold was pastor of the Christian Synagogue in Toronto and president of the Hebrew Christian Alliance of America at the time of publication.

reported that the British were near Bagdad. She thought that perhaps Anita and her son would be interested in reading Blackstone's account of his visit to that region. She reminded Anita that the *fig tree* was "putting forth its leaves—above the clouds of God's purpose for Israel shed[ding] their radiance on our dampened world."[22]

On January 31, 1921, several years after the end of World War I, Emma sent condolences to Anita and her family over the passing of Anita's sister-in-law, Mrs. Harriet Hammond McCormick. She knowingly wrote:

> You, with others of your family have met another great affliction. How many earlier ones *you* have had to bear! We all have seen many of our Earthly lights go out in darkness, when those we loved, pass from our sight. Only faith in Christ sustains us. In His promises we rest our hopes of endless life in His presence, & in theirs . . . But this affliction is a heavy one to your Brother & to all the members of your great family . . . Those who are left have suffered but not those who depart to be with Christ.

Emma expressed her hope that Anita and her daughter-in-law and granddaughter were in good health along with her mother Nettie who was still residing at both the Rush Street and Lake Forest homes.

Emma received a letter written by Nettie from the McCormick Rush Street residence, which was to be her last, written on November 8, 1922. Nettie shared with Emma her continued fond memories of her husband Cyrus. She reminiscently wrote of the memories she cherished in every part of her house and the closeness she felt with her husband. Nettie shared her own difficulty with physical immobility. Nevertheless, she expressed her joy that Emma could rest at Nettie's Lake Forest home and be refreshed by the air upon her return visit from Cedar Rapids, Iowa, where Emma's cousins resided. Nettie ended her letter to Emma by writing that she herself was afflicted with Emma's weaknesses and expressed once again to her friend: "I love you & think of you many times. Every day—Every day."

After returning from a hospital visit to a friend at Alice House in Lake Forest, Emma wrote Anita about stopping at the McCormick House-in-the-Woods. The McCormick's housekeeper, Louise, had kindly escorted her around the beautiful outdoors. Louise expressed what a lovely and remarkable Christian Anita was. Shortly thereafter on July 5, 1923, Emma received word that her dear friend, Nettie, had gone to be with the Lord. On August 3 Emma wrote Anita that she had not experienced such bereavement and heaviness since her own dear parents had passed away. "Your sore trials have been many and severe and you have carried their heavy sorrows for others. How you needed them!" She assured Anita of her continued prayers. Closing with 1 Thessalonians 4:13–18 Emma reminded her of their reunion someday with their loved ones when their work on earth was complete.

---

22. Anita Blaine McCormick Correspondence and Papers, McCormick Collection. Hereafter, unless otherwise noted, the following information in this section is obtained from this source.

Two months later Emma followed with another letter of encouragement for Anita. She wrote that she had risen before dawn wearing her Japanese kimono which had more than likely been a gift from Anita. She remembered her last visit the previous year to the House-in-the-Woods. Louise gathered fall flowers and leaves for Emma to take to Nettie who was staying at a 4124 Jackson Street *flat* or apartment where Emma also resided. Louise mentioned that one of the tracts which Emma had given Nettie, entitled *Christ's Last Week,* brought conversion to William who was one of the house servants. Emma spoke daily to others regarding Anita and considered the McCormicks as her own family. She recalled how Nettie loved their times of prayer in that home with both Anita and herself.

Emma supported Anita in her unrelenting mission work in the country of Japan where on September 1, 1923, a 7.9 magnitude earthquake in Great Kanto brought great destruction with the loss of approximately 143,000 lives. Emma reiterated to Anita in her letter that devastating earthquakes would proceed the return of the Lord in the last days according to the prophesies of Matthew 24:7–14, Mark 13:8, and Luke 21:11. Emma closed her letter by apologizing for her scribbled writing due to her failing eye sight but expressed the release she felt in being able to write Anita about her parents.

With the coming of a January 8, 1924, Chicago snowfall Emma described the *fresh prostrating cold* as she painstakingly wrote another letter cherished by Anita. Despite her right arm being consumed with neuritis, Emma expressed how much she likewise valued Anita's letters. She kept them continually inside her Rotterham New Testament. Emma wrote of her prayer list which still included Anita's mother's name as the head of the McCormick family. She assured Anita that she would continue to keep it there until she joined Nettie in the presence of the Lord. With ongoing thoughtfulness Emma included in this letter copies of the tracts and booklets which she had last sent to Anita's mother.

In her February 7, 1924, correspondence to Anita, Emma addressed the letter with clear recollection: "My constantly and forever dear Anita McCormick Blaine:— whom I have never forgotten a day, since you & Virginia, led by your now glorified Mother, (two 'twin sisters') appeared at Danville, New York, where I first saw your noble father." She hoped that she would get to see Anita again on this earth but warmly acknowledged that she would be with Christ along with Anita's "father & mother, & mine, & other saints of all ages!" She reminded Anita of the Lord's last prayer from John 17:2–4: "Father, I will, that they also, whom thou hast given me, be with me where I am." She closed the letter with the blessed assurance that the angels escorted Anita's precious mother into his presence.

On April 3, 1924, Emma wrote to Anita expressing her gratitude for friends from the Baptist Church, Moody Church, and the Presbyterian Church who had assisted her during a long sickness. She described how she awoke after a time of unconsciousness to see three of her friends and her doctor at her bed side. She was hoping that with the assistance of her long-time YMCA friend and caregiver, Miss Alison Anderson, she could walk to the Baptist Church despite her weakened condition.

Emma praised God for her recovery and for news from her friend William Blackstone who was residing in California. She mentioned Anita's father-in-law, James G. Blaine who served as the twenty-eighth and thirty-first Secretary of State under Presidents James Garfield and Benjamin Harrison. Mr. Blaine had assisted Blackstone in traveling worldwide. Emma conveyed the Christian love she and Blackstone held for one another and their deep belief in the Bible, particularly the doctrine of Christ's return. She concluded her letter by mentioning to Anita that she had seen Mrs. James Blaine with Anita's mother before Nettie's death less than a year ago.

In spite of a year of la grippe or influenza and nine months of neuritis, Emma's handwriting in her letter to Anita on July 1, 1924, had noticeably improved since her April letter. She was glad that she would soon be able to write William Blackstone a letter as well. Emma constantly marveled at the great and powerful assurance of the resurrection: "What a multitude have died, in Christ, since He arose from the dead! (Acts 7:56). What glorious victories will follow, with His glorified Church, when, together, they reign forever, in our purified Earth!" On July 18, 1924, in a letter written to Caroline Waite, Emma once again with unending praise reiterated her hope of Christ's return: "Jesus Christ is coming soon to take His ransomed people Home. There we shall see His glorious face and praise God for redeeming grace, where heaven to Earth forever sings Christ is Lord of lords and King of kings."[23]

With a continued unfaltering commitment to the vision that the Lord had given in 1873 to Moody and herself, Emma maintained her heartfelt interest in the Bible Institute declaring that the Bible Work "finally gave way to the larger and better Work of the Institute."[24] Characterized as greatly admiring D. L. Moody,[25] Emma frequently mentioned his numerous virtues and her own amiable association with him through many years. It would appear that Emma, in faithful submission to her Lord, graciously put the past conflicts behind her. She focused on the glories that she would experience in the presence of her *soon coming Lord*.

"Speak out, judge fairly, and defend the rights of oppressed and needy people . . . she speaks with wisdom and on her tongue there is tender instruction."

~Proverbs 31:9, 26 GWT~

---

23. Emma Dryer to Caroline Waite, 18 July 1924, Biographical File of Emma Dryer.
24. Ibid.
25. Getz, *The Story of Moody Bible Institute*, 24.

11

With Christ Our Soon Coming Lord, 1925 Throughout Eternity

"Where I am there shall you be also. When Christ shall appear then you also shall appear with Him in Glory."

~JOHN 14:3; COLOSSIANS 3:4~

EMMA'S FINAL YEARS WERE spent quietly at her 4124 West Jackson Street home. Although it could have appeared that she experienced loneliness in her last years, a greater loneliness would have been for her to discover in her heart that the Lord to whom she had dedicated her life was not there for her. But for Emma that was not so. She knew the One in whom she believed. She anticipated and experienced God's presence in her communion with and dependence on Him through her faithful study of God's word.

A photograph of Emma, taken in 1922 at the age of eighty-seven, shows her tranquil contentment while reading her Bible in the garden where she enjoyed continued times of prayer and fellowship with the Lord. She securely held the Bible that had become so precious to her. On November 20, 1925 copies of the photo were sent to her friends including the McCormick family.[1] Anita McCormick Blaine cherished this picture which years later would be found in Anita's personal correspondence among her treasured letters from Emma now archived at the Wisconsin Historical Society in Madison, Wisconsin.

Numerous friends who frequently visited Emma commented on her eloquently sharp and descriptive stories of Mr. and Mrs. Moody, John Farwell, Major Whittle, the Helmers, and others. They were amazed at her "remarkable power of mind, and her beautiful and gracious spirit up to the time of her last and very brief illness."[2] Charles Blanchard and his family visited her at various times. During the last few months of Emma's life he watched his friend decline in health. She again expressed to him her desire to be buried at the Wheaton Cemetery close to his grave site. Why would she make such a request? With a tranquil finality she explained: "I want to rise with President Blanchard when the trumpet sounds." Charles's wife, Francis Carothers Blanchard, realized Emma's impact on Charles's life, especially his views regarding the return of Christ. She wrote in 1932—after the December 20, 1925, death of her own husband—that Emma's wish had been granted as "it is here the frail body rests till the resurrection morn."[3]

Emma's Homecoming

So it was that on Friday, April 16, 1925, at 11:00 in the evening Emma at the age of ninety went home to be with the Lord after experiencing a stroke.[4] Emma's hometown paper, the *Victor Herald*, respectfully reported:

> One of the best known, best loved and most distinguished nineteenth-century daughters of Victor, Miss Emma Dryer, died in Chicago, April 16, 1925,

---

1. Alison A. Anderson wrote: "My Dear Mrs. Blaine, It was almost the *last* request made by Miss Dryer that her friends should be given copies of the enclosed photographs. One was taken about thirty years ago and the other recently, about 3 years since. As Miss Dryer would wish to have done I am sending these pictures to each one of the McCormick family. Miss Dryer kept ever fresh the sacred memories of her long association with your family and their kindness and interest, continued to the close of her life. With warm appreciation of what all these things meant to the one who has gone." Alison A. Anderson to Anita McCormick Blaine, 20 November 1925, Anita Blaine McCormick Correspondence and Papers.
2. Undated Emma Dryer Obituary, Biographical File of Emma Dryer.
3. Blanchard, *The Life of Charles Albert Blanchard,* 205.
4. Mr. V. H. Gaylord to Caroline Waite, 22 April 1925, Biographical File of Emma Dryer.

having just passed her ninetieth birthday. Sophronia Emeline Cobb, daughter of Hiram and Emeline (Wilson) Cobb, was born at West Stockbridge, Mass., January 28, 1835 . . . She was devoted to her family and friends . . . Her strength of character was equaled only by its sweetness and she kept both undimmed to the day of her death. She looked daily for the second coming of the Lord and prayed that she might be spared to welcome Him. Surely, for such as she are meant His words, 'Inasmuch as ye have done it unto one of the least of these my brethren, ye have done it unto me.'[5]

President Charles Blanchard with Dr. James Gray, president of Moody Bible Institute, officiated at the funeral service conducted at Emma's home the following Monday. Moody Church Pastor Peter Wiley Philpott (1866–1957) extended the prayer along with Reverend E. Augusta Shulls, the pastor of the neighboring Garfield Park Baptist Church where Emma regularly attended.[6]

Many of Emma's close friends from her early Chicago days, including her housekeeper Miss Alison Anderson and members of the McCormick family, filled her house on this meaningful occasion. Miss Anderson had stayed beside Emma in faithfully caring for her until her death. President Blanchard expressed the beauty of seeing many of the McCormick family at the funeral who had been faithful participants in her life and work from her early days in Chicago.[7] With a deep expression of heartfelt love for Emma, Cyrus and Nettie McCormick's son Harold with others from the McCormick family, attended and duly cared for the expenses of Emma's funeral. Memories were still fresh from the death of their own mother less than two years earlier. Harold and his family provided an automobile loaded with exquisite flowers and floral arrangements along with Anita's special red rose bouquet given in honor of their mother's dear friend.[8]

---

5. Town of Victor, New York, Archives, 8 May 1925, *Victor Herald* Newspaper Obituary.
6. Ibid.; Mr. Gaylord to Caroline Waite, 22 April 1925, Biographical File of Emma Dryer.
7. Blanchard, "Miss Dryer and the Moody Church," May 1925.
8. Mr. Gaylord to Caroline Waite, 22 April 1925, Biographical File of Emma Dryer.

Sometime after the grave site service following the funeral, Emma was moved at the request of the Blanchard family from her burial plot to a grave located on the Charles Blanchard site at the Wheaton Cemetery in Wheaton, Illinois.[9] At the same time, her friends in Victor, New York, at Emma's prior request, erected a monument at Boughton Hill Cemetery on the plot owned by Emma. Scriptures were engraved, which she would have so carefully selected, from John 14:3 and Colossians 3:4: "Where I am there shall you be also. When Christ shall appear then you also shall appear with Him in Glory."

Not far from this memorial stood Emma's beloved parents' grave sites with markers also inscribed with God's word: For her father, John M. Dryer, the words from Psalm 17:15, "As for me I will behold thy face in righteousness. I shall be satisfied when I awake with thy likeness," and for her mother Lucinda C. Dryer 2 Timothy 4:8, "Henceforth there is laid up for me a crown of righteousness which the Lord the righteous judge shall give me at that day and unto all them also that love His appearing."[10] To the very end of her life Emma possessed a rich Bible heritage obtained from own parents' faithful respect and honor of God's word.

---

9. This information was obtained through the assistance of the personnel at the Wheaton Cemetery in Wheaton, Illinois. They show from their records that she had been moved from her original burial plot #626 to site 6 in the Charles Blanchard family grave site with no reasons being cited.

10. Town of Victor, New York, Archives, Historian's Office, Grave site photos are compliments of the Historian's Office.

With Christ Our Soon Coming Lord, 1925 Throughout Eternity

Memorial Service

Weeks later, on Sunday, May 31, 1925, at 4:00 p.m. many of Emma's friends held a separate memorial service in Keith Hall at the Moody Bible Institute to "call fresh attention to the beautiful and fruitful life of the saint whom God has taken home."[11]

Hymns and Prayers: Reverend E. Augusta Shulls and Miss Maby

With Emma's heart for worship, she would have deeply appreciated the program that Dr. Gray officiated in her honor. He began the service by reciting the first verse of Augustus Montague Toplady's (1740–78) 1776 hymn, *Rock of Ages*, "for the glory of God and for the honor of our sister, Miss Emma Dryer." The participants joined in that song followed by their recitation of Psalm 1 and the 1844 doxology *Gloria-Patri* with music by Charles Meineke (1782–1850): "Glory be to the Father, and to the Son, and to the Holy Ghost; as it was in the beginning, is now, and ever shall be, world without end. Amen." Reverend Shulls, on the faculty at Northern Baptist Seminary, offered this prayer:

> Oh my God, this afternoon we thank thee for the blessing that is ours, to look up into thy face in gratitude and thanksgiving for this hour . . . Grant that in all things thou mayest be honored and, dear Lord, we do want to thank thee for the memory of her in whose honor we have gathered. This afternoon, we thank thee, first of all, for that beautiful life, for the far reaching influence of that life, and what thou hast done through that life. We thank thee for the faith exemplified in that life and we thank thee for the establishment of this institute, as a direct result of her faith and the faith of others with her . . . And, dear Lord, we thank thee especially this afternoon for that wonderful hope that was hers, the hope of living to see Jesus in the flesh, and . . . we do know that she now is with her Lord . . . God, bless this institute in its mission, its far and wide-reaching influence over the world . . . May we with joy remember thy goodness and thy great mercies and the life that lived among us. We ask these intercessions in the Name that is above every name, our coming Lord. Amen.

---

11. Undated Emma Dryer Obituary, Biographical File of Emma Dryer. A handwritten note initialed only with F.A.S. wrote the words *Apr. 17, 1925* on this newspaper article (clearly published after the May memorial service) in an apparent attempt to give the exact date of her death since the article only says she died in April at her home. The following details recorded in this section regarding Emma's memorial service were found at the Billy Graham Center Archives Collection 330, Box 58, Folder 3 in Wheaton, Illinois, in a stenographer's notebook. The twenty pages of Gregg shorthand notes were methodically transcribed by Diana Zielinski with reference to the *Gregg Shorthand Dictionary* from the University of Chicago. The full transcription may be accessed from the BGC archives.

Woman of Nobility

Miss Maby, a faculty member of the Moody Bible Institute, followed Reverend Shulls's prayer by singing the hymn *Watchman Tell Me* with uplifting words regarding the signs of Christ's coming that will expel all unbelief.

Extracts from Emma's Paper or Journal by Dr. Gray

President Charles Blanchard of Wheaton College had been scheduled to recite from a paper or journal written by Emma. However, due to his delay for unknown reasons, Dr. Gray presented her paper. She wrote it at Dr. Blanchard's request in 1916. Emma initially recounted her Mayflower ancestry and birth in the Berkshire Hills of Massachusetts where she first heard of the unfaltering American Indian missionary endeavors of David Brainerd and Jonathan Edwards. Dr. Gray read about her teaching skills and the moral impact she made on her students. Emma's typed memoranda also included her account of Moody's early work in Chicago and her first encounter with him. Dr. Gray read her accounts of Mildmay, the May Institutes, Blanchard's $500 gift to start the Bible Institute, Moody's $250,000 challenge, and the establishment of the Chicago Evangelization Society.

Written Tributes From Friends

Reverend Sterling, assistant secretary of the China Inland Mission, read three letters of tribute on Emma's behalf. The first came from Ellis L. Vogel who served as the president of the Gideons in Illinois. In 1882 Emma taught him God's word and influenced his life as both a teacher and friend. He attended her night school where he "learned to reference the Book of all books, the Holy Bible." He considered her to be his spiritual mother and faithfully kept in contact with her throughout the years. He attributed his success in distributing Bibles to Emma's encouragement and training.

A second letter was received from Reverend A. Strange, representing the China Inland Mission, written around May 27. He became acquainted with Emma through J. S. Helmer and gratifyingly acknowledged her training of their first missionary candidates for service to China by 1891. The third letter came from William Blackstone dated May 14. He wrote, "My acquaintance and intimate relationship with Miss Dryer has been one of the most [rewarding] of my life. I could write of the blessed work which she successfully accomplished for my Lord and Master." He mentioned the powerful results of the Bible Work prayer circle which consisted of Fleming H. Revell, Miss Dryer, and himself for the creation of a Bible school in Chicago. He praised God for hearing and answering their prayers and rejoiced that one day he would again meet her "over there, in the presence of our Lord and Master."

Some of Emma's former students testified of her influence as an instrument of their conversion during her ministry at the Moody Church. Those who were present at the service included Ellis Vogel and David MacNaughtan (1850–1941). MacNaughtan attended Moody's church service on the evening of the Chicago Fire. Although he did not present an oral tribute for Emma at the memorial, his daughter Emma MacNaughtan in 1945 presented a written testimony in which she referred to Emma as a "lovely, gracious woman with a keen intellect and unusual gifts and ability, all consecrated to the service of Him, her Lord and Savior."[12]

Charles Blanchard's Message and Prayer

Before the scheduling of this spring day memorial service, Charles Blanchard had written in the May 1925 *Moody Church News* this tribute for Emma and her friend D. L. Moody: "She never worked for personal recognition, but always for the salvation of men and there are thousands more who have been glad today that she . . . lived and labored in connection with that great Christian who gave his name to the Chicago Bible Institute and to the Church which he organized."[13] Charles's friendship with Emma displayed itself further when Dr. Blanchard willingly accepted the invitation to officiate at this memorial service for Emma.

Upon the late arrival of Dr. Blanchard, Dr. Gray introduced Emma's unfaltering friend and acknowledged the change in the program. Dr. Blanchard would now take Dr. Gray's place by sharing the message of the second coming of Christ. Dr. Gray spoke: "We all know that Dr. Blanchard is abundantly capable of speaking on the Second Coming of Christ and we shall all be glad to listen. Come and pray for him and for ourselves, as he speaks."

Dr. Blanchard began by recalling the tremendous wisdom of Mr. Moody and especially his knowledge of Christ's return. He also recalled the moment when Emma asked Dr. Blanchard: "Would you be willing to spend a little time in looking over Scriptures about the coming Lord?" After these conversations he likewise concluded: "Miss Dryer was a wise person . . . a teacher born, a teacher always . . ." He explained how they would search out Scriptures on specified subjects. He expressed that he had been "intimately associated with Miss Dryer and those years having now grown, I have been more in touch with her personally." He shared her unfailing desire to meet the Lord and gaze upon his face. He spoke of her life as a *noble gospel teacher* who was quoted repeatedly as saying, "There is no repentance that will avail for the lack of an English education."

Dr. Blanchard reiterated Emma's determination to seek out and bring in young people to teach. As he sat in her classes he frequently saw her cover a whole blackboard with Scripture and noted that Emma consistently placed God's word as the highest priority. Then he shared the impact of Methodists Josiah and Lucy Rider Meyer of the Chicago Training School for City, Home and Foreign Missions and other

---

12. Miss Emma MacNaughtan to Dr. Wilbur M. Smith, 8 October 1945, Biographical File of Emma Dryer.

13. Blanchard, "Miss Dryer and the Moody Church," May 1925.

influential schools preceding MBI. He carefully noted: "The Moody Bible Institute was first, originally the work of Miss Dryer" who "came up from Normal where she had a life position with a good salary in the State University for teaching." He restated the fact that it was Moody's request that Emma organize this school specifically for young people to study the Bible.

Dr. Blanchard closed his message with a prayer that continues to its fulfillment even today on behalf of Emma and Moody's God-given vision:

> Dear Lord and Father, we give you thanks for the Moody Bible Institute and we give you thanks, Father, for the Moody Church and for all the people that have been brought in Your Providence into the institute and church through all the years past and we praise You that so many hundreds and thousands of people have been saved by the work of this great person of ours, who has been these years with Thee . . . to whom we shall one day talk face to face . . . Give us a lot of men and women who shall be like Mr. Moody and Miss Dryer.

As the memorial service came to a close, one of Emma's favorite hymns, *How Firm a Foundation,* reminded God's saints to lay up their faith, as Emma had, in the excellent word of the Lord.

After this hymn Reverend Sterling closed the service with this benediction: "May the God of peace, who brought again from the dead, our Lord Jesus . . . Shepherd of the sheep . . . the prince of the heavenlies . . . comfort now us, perfect in us good work to do His will, working in us that which is well pleasing in Your sight through Jesus Christ, to whom be glory forever and ever. Amen." On the firm foundation of Christ the memory of Sophronia Emeline Cobb Dryer would never be forgotten as one who securely grounded her life in the ever-enduring word of God.

Emma's Legacy as a Great and Noble Bible Teacher

The story of Emma's life would not be complete without some representation of her legacy as a Bible teacher. President Blanchard and numerous friends and associates considered Emma a valuable and distinguished teacher of God's word. They were blessed with the privilege of hearing the notable presentation of her Bible lessons in person. Although we do not have that same blessed privilege today, some idea of her teaching can still be understood by looking into her well marked Bible.

Emma's marking method was highly encouraged by D. L. Moody.[14] She sketched numerous red, black, and green ink marginal notes in her Bible with well secured inserts used when teaching her classes.[15] The Bible which she primarily used for teach-

---

14. Remlaf quoted Moody as saying: "There is another thing which has wonderfully helped me. That is, to mark my Bible whenever I hear anything that strikes me." Remlaf, *The Gospel Awakening*, 596–97. Moody wrote a chapter in an 1899 book *Golden Counsels* called "Bible Marking" with suggestions on how to deepen your Bible study.

15. Emma Dryer Bibles, Biographical File of Emma Dryer. Hereafter, unless otherwise noted,

ing contains a card insert displaying a graphic of D. L. Moody which reads: "Bible owned by Miss Emma Dryer: An early co-worker of D. L. Moody in the Chicago Avenue Church, who also had an important part in the founding of MBI. D. L. Moody Memorial Exhibit. 'He that doeth the will of God abideth forever.' (I John 2:17)."

Through the research efforts of Moody Bible Institute archivist Bernard R. DeRemer, the donation of Emma's Bible was received on Saturday, June 14, 1958, from Mrs. MacNaughtan. Emma had personally given it to Mrs. MacNaughtan some time before her death. This well marked King James Oxford University Press Bible contains the following preface: "Translated out of the original tongues; and with the former translations diligently compared and revised by His Majesty's special command" and "appointed to be read in churches." A copy of Emma's New Testament, also located at the Moody Bible Archives, includes a gold engraving of her name on the inside cover.

the following information in this section is obtained from this source.

Woman of Nobility

The Bible, published by S. Bagster and Sons in London and James Pott & Company in New York, is titled *The New Testament of our Lord and Saviour Jesus Christ with a copious and original selection of References to parallel and illustrative passages.* From Emma's Bibles we can still vicariously receive the living words that penetrated and inspired Emma's heart and life.

Emma's Bible Studies

Throughout her life Emma respectfully held God's word as the supreme authority for all truth. Inside the first pages of her Oxford Bible under the words *Old and New Testaments* she wrote that the Bible was *the court of final appeal.* She also penned these words: "More than all other books, the Bible is its own interpreter. Never read it between the lines. Compare Scripture with Scripture, by memorized or by marginal references." She created her own system for "'codifying' biblical teachings according to her views of Christ's second coming and her own doctrine of spiritual healing."[16]

Recognizing the importance of unreservedly living out God's word, Emma wrote the following statement which she attributed to President Charles Blanchard: "A partial morality is essencial [sic] minority." Following the teaching of her Wheaton College friend she also affirmed in her Bible classes the necessary work of the Holy Spirit in the revelation of truth. She cited 1 Corinthians 2:13 and John 16:13: "Which things also we speak, not in the words which man's wisdom teacheth, but which the Holy Ghost teacheth; comparing spiritual things with spiritual" and "Howbeit when he, the Spirit of truth, is come, he will guide you into all truth: for he shall not speak of himself; but whatsoever he shall hear, that shall he speak: and he will shew you things to come."

Study of Christ's Second Coming

Along with her own marginal notes, Emma primarily utilized a topical approach to the study of the Bible. She included studies on Christ's Second Coming, the Family and Women in the Church, Jewish Roots, Prayer and Faith, God's Glory and Image, and Prominent Bible Dates. From the first day that Moody asked her view of the return of Christ, Emma became zealous regarding the topic. She wrote a note in her Bible that there were 318 New Testament references to Christ's return. She would frequently underline end time passages such as "for he cometh to judge the earth" from Psalm 98:9 to which she added in the margin "*When He comes* Revelation 10:4–11."

Emma diligently searched the Scriptures regarding the topic of judgment. She instructed on the *Four Great Judgments* beginning with the first *Judgment of Sin* through Christ's death on the cross followed by the *Judgment of the Saints* at Christ's appearance using passages such as Romans 8:4, 1 Peter 2:24, and 1 Thessalonians 4:10–18. She

---

16. Dorsett, *A Passion For Souls*, 168.

taught: "The Lord himself shall descend from heaven with a shout, with the voice of the archangel, and with the trump of God: and the dead in Christ shall rise first: Then we which are alive and remain shall be caught up together with them in the clouds, to meet the Lord in the air: and so shall we ever be with the Lord. Wherefore comfort one another with these words."

In the third *Judgment of Living Nations* at Christ's appearing, Emma explained passages such as Matthew 13:40, Matthew 24:31–32 and Joel 3:1–13. She imploringly shared her concerns for the destiny of nations at the end of the ages—those gathered and separated by the Lord, the wheat from the tares, and the righteous from the unrighteous. With heartfelt thanksgiving and praise she also expressed the hope given from Revelation 17:14: "These shall make war with the Lamb, and the Lamb shall overcome them: for he is Lord of lords, and King of kings: and they that are with him are called, and chosen, and faithful."

Emma included in her study a fourth *Judgment of God's Enemies* which would occur at the end of the Millennium. She read from Revelation 20:12: "And I saw the dead, small and great, stand before God; and the books were opened: and another book was opened, which is the book of life: and the dead were judged out of those things which were written in the books, according to their works." Emma personalized her teaching on God's judgment by addressing the hindrances of *self* in a believer's life: "For if we would judge ourselves, we should not be judged." (1 Corinthians 11:31). She pointed to 1 Peter 4:17: "For the time is come that judgment must begin at the house of God: and if it first begin at us, what shall the end be of them that obey not the gospel of God?"

With her proficient expository skills Emma expounded on the translation of Enoch and asked a question regarding the death of the apostle John: "Did John die? Was he translated like Enoch?" These questions would have created a provocative discussion among her students as Emma referenced Luke 9:27: "But I tell you of a truth, there be some standing here, which shall not taste of death, till they see the kingdom of God." She shared Peter's question to Jesus (John 21:21-23) regarding how John would die: "'Lord, and what shall this man do?' Jesus saith unto him, 'If I will that he tarry till I come, what is that to thee? follow thou me.' Then went this saying abroad among the brethren, that that disciple should not die: yet Jesus said not unto him, He shall not die; but, If I will that he tarry till I come, what is that to thee?" Emma emphasized the words *Tarry till I come* followed by reiterating the missionary call of "professing again before many nations" (Revelation 11:7).

Emma addressed the timing of the Lord's return by focusing on the use of the word *one*. Her background in drawing inspired her use of a star design which also appeared in her earlier Bible Work publications. She marked 2 Peter 3:8 with this star for emphasis and, perhaps reflecting on D. L. Moody's deep influence on her own life, she wrote the word *one* before "this one thing" with the passage "One day is with the Lord as a thousand years & a thousand years as one day is." Emma added a footnote in which she taught that Genesis 2:17 was "the first unchangeable announcement!"—a passage regarding the event of death in the day that God's word is disobeyed. She asked "How many [days] do we count?" until his return and concluded that "Christ will keep with His bride & the Jews . . . His Bride & He will forever work together."

Emma explained that the *Elect* of God were those "chosen from among dear ones." She cited Romans 8:33: "Who shall lay anything to the charge of God's elect? It is God that justifieth." She read of the elect's responsibility to "prophesy again before many nations" (Revelation 10:9-11). At the same time she spoke of the end time spirit of the beast while citing Ecclesiastes 3:21: "Who knoweth the spirit of man that goeth upward, and the spirit of the beast that goeth downward to the earth?" She asked, "What is it that goeth?" Perhaps with reference to her earlier New York training regarding the errors of such teachings as necromancy, she challenged believers to exercise discernment of truth by concluding: "If promises are unbearable, the conclusion is untrue" and "by this test false religions & the numerous 'isms' of these last days" could be discerned.

Study of the Family and Women in the Church

With Emma's own ministry as a background, she knowingly taught about the position of women in public ministry within the church. She cited 1 Corinthians 11:23-26 for participation of women in communion and 1 Corinthians 14:34-35: "Let your women keep silence in the churches: for it is not permitted unto them to speak; but they are commanded to be under obedience as also saith the law. And if they will learn any thing, let them ask their husbands at home: for it is a shame for women to speak in the church." Emma, understanding the challenge of this directive, cited 1 Timothy 2:3: "For this is good and acceptable in the sight of God our Saviour" and also 1 John 3:2: "Beloved, now are we the sons of God, and it doth not yet appear what we shall be: but we know that, when he shall appear, we shall be like him; for we shall see him as he is."

From the early days of the Chicago Fire, Emma never lost concern for the welfare of young mothers and young people—for all families. In her Bible on the *Register of Births* page, although Emma never married,[17] she quoted words from Reverend Dr. Amos R. Wells (1862-1933), a prolific author on topics of the family and other Christian endeavors. Wells, a professor of Greek at Antioch College in Ohio, was also the 1892 editor of *The Christian Endeavor World,* a publication representing the United

---

17. An interviewer recorded the following: "On a visit here 5/12/59, Mrs. Grove said that her mother was Miss Mary Jane Moore (Later Mrs. J. M. Hitchcock). Married about 1888. She was a student in Emma Dryer's school before that . . . She said Emma Dryer was involved in romance! Someone who didn't respond. No other details. This would help to account, perhaps, for the suggestions in the letters around 1887 in the McCormick papers that Miss Dryer wasn't well, needed a vacation. May have been the result of an unhappy love affair . . . 803 Cherry St. Wheaton, ILL. MO.5-1589." Interview of Mrs. Ralph B. Grove, 12 May 1959, Biographical File of Emma Dryer. No other sources outside of this oral history substantiate this information.

Society of Christian Endeavor promoting Christian work in the church. He influenced Emma's written comment: "Family life is at the heart of National life and the life of this world." With her deep love and appreciation for the nation of Israel, Emma added: "The national unit of Israel was the family" referencing 1 Chronicles 21 and Joshua 7 and 19:5.

Study of Jewish Roots

With the irrefutable influence of Israel proponents such as William Blackstone, Charles Blanchard, and the Chicago Hebrew Mission, Emma compellingly instructed her students regarding the Jewish roots of Christianity. She covered the topics of the Passover, Jewish names for God, and God's Covenant. She referenced Psalm 96 as the Messianic and Millennial Anglo-Israel followed by citations from Genesis 22:16–18; 48:18–20; 49:22–26; Deuteronomy 33:13–17; and Micah 5:7–8. She included in her Bible a copy of her teaching entitled *Christ Our Passover* based on 1 Corinthians 5:7: "Christ Our Passover is sacrificed for us."

Emma credited the information for her teaching on *The Order of the Passover* to a Messianic Jew, with a background in Jewish feasts, who copied the material from a book written by Jews specifically for the Jewish feasts. Emma knew that he had approved the use of the references and types that she used for the study—the *Order or Succession of the Five Cups*. She instructed that the first cup began with the announcement of the Passover by the head of the family. This was followed by the standing positions around the table, reclining at the table, and the service of praise or *Hallel* from Psalm 115–118 and ending with the final cup of *The Utmost Limit*. Emma encouraged the reading of additional passages such as John 5:39, 46, 47; 2 Peter 1:19–21; 1 Corinthians 2:15; and John 16:13.

Emma could have explained the Jewish concept of *covenant* based on her own life's commitment to seeing Moody's vision for a Bible Institute fulfilled. Surely with this in mind she defined *covenant* in the margin of her Bible in this way: "A Covenant is a Divinely-appointed meeting place for the assured fulfillment of the gracious promise & purposes of God." Her instruction on *covenant* included the scriptural background of four types: Adamic Covenant, Noahetic Covenant, Abrahamic Covenant, and Christian Covenant.

With a deep reverence for the multi-faceted name of God, Emma taught that covenant meant "God in Personal relation" and included at least four revelatory Hebrew names:

- Jehovah–Elohim Genesis 2:3. Creator
- Jehovah–Jireh Genesis 22:14. The Lord will provide
- Jehovah–Nissi Exodus 17:15. The Lord our Banner

- Jehovah–Shalom Judges 6:24. The Lord our Peace

Emma also acknowledged God as Jehovah–Rapha, the Healer, in her marginal notes for the passage from Luke 5. Before these verses on the healing of the paralytic whom Jesus forgave and healed, she marked with blue ink the words "Forgiven +... Healed to glorify God." Emma could certainly have been referring to her healing from typhoid fever in 1870 and to her own times of requested forgiveness. Regardless, she recognized her indispensable need for God. She wrote at the top of the page these words from a popular hymn: "We need Thee every hour, Most Gracious Lord."

Study of Prayer and Faith

As a woman of *prayer and faith* Emma quite naturally taught on these topics. She emphasized that the Bible has 32,000 unfailing promises of God that should be prayerfully read and believed. Emma added: "No word God hath spoken can ever be broken." She cited the first spoken promise of God as Genesis 3:15: "And I will put enmity between thee and the woman, and between thy seed and her seed; it shall bruise thy head, and thou shalt bruise his heel." The last promise came from Revelation 22:20: "He which testifieth these things saith, Surely I come quickly. Amen. Even so, come, Lord Jesus." She underlined the words *faith* and *nature* in the Hebrews 11 Bible heading of that chapter which was subtitled "The nature and fruits of faith." Emma would have recalled, and perhaps shared, the many challenges to her faith when she wrote in the Bible margin: "Active obedience to God (not to man) is *faith*" and "Faith is obedient reliance on the word of God. Not the word of man."

This effective Bible teacher asked many questions including, "What were Christ's prayers?" She considered his prayers as contagious and ever present especially during times of temptation as exemplified in Jesus' experience in the garden:

> And when he was at the place, he said unto them, Pray that ye enter not into temptation. And he was withdrawn from them about a stone's cast, and kneeled down, and prayed, Saying, Father, if thou be willing, remove this cup from me: nevertheless not my will, but thine, be done. And there appeared an angel unto him from heaven, strengthening him. And being in an agony he prayed more earnestly: and his sweat was as it were great drops of blood falling down to the ground. And when he rose up from prayer, and was come to his disciples, he found them sleeping for sorrow, And said unto them, 'Why sleep ye? rise and pray, lest ye enter into temptation.' (Luke 22:40–46).

She cited Matthew 7:7–12 regarding the need to seek, ask, and knock along with the admonition from Mark 11:22–25 to exercise forgiveness and persistence in prayer. Based on the example of Jacob's persistence in receiving a blessing from God, Emma referred to prayer as "*Unremittingly* without ceasing." She encouraged prayer as *imperative* based on 1 John 5:14–15: "And this is the confidence that we have in him, that, if we ask any thing according to his will, he heareth us: And if we know that he hear us, whatsoever we ask, we know that we have the petitions that we desired of him." As she instructed from these verses, her heart surely spoke from the deep well of personal experience.

Study of the Glory of God and His Image

The topic of God's glory had been prevalent in Emma's training since her early days. She would have shared with her Bible Study students the experience of David Brainerd as he beheld the glory of a *Divine Being* as well as Miss Allen's youthful drawing of two saints encircled with beams of glory. She took black and green ink to sketch on the blank note page of her Bible a penetrating definition of *glory* to share with her class: an "effulgent substance visible, tangible, mighty, powerful, diffusive omnipotent . . . a Divine, personal *quality* and property."

In her study on the glory of God Emma described his manifested presence as revealed in Ezekiel 1:28 and 10:4: "As the appearance of the bow that is in the cloud in the day of rain, so was the appearance of the brightness round about. This was the appearance of the likeness of the glory of the Lord. And when I saw it, I fell upon my face, and I heard a voice of one that spake" and "Then the glory of the Lord went up from the cherub, and stood over the threshold of the house; and the house was filled with the cloud, and the court was full of the brightness of the Lord's glory."

Emma referenced numerous other passages including Proverbs 3:5; John 17:1–5; Mark 9:2–10; 2 Peter 1:17–18; John 17:20–24; Acts 9:1–22; Colossians 3:4; Hebrews 2:10, 9:3; and Jude 24. She recognized the words *The God of Glory* as eternally distinguishing the triune God as pictured in Psalm 24:7–10: "Lift up your heads, O ye gates; and be ye lift up, ye everlasting doors; and the King of glory shall come in. Who is this King of glory? The Lord strong and mighty, the Lord mighty in battle. Lift up your heads, O ye gates; even lift them up, ye everlasting doors; and the King of glory shall come in. Who is this King of glory? The Lord of hosts, he is the King of glory. Selah."

Emma referred to the God of glory as coming from one who thundered—a God who would guide men with his counsel and afterward be received into glory (Psalm 29:3; Psalm 73:24). She encouraged Christian fellowship as a means of experiencing this heavenly glory when she wrote: "God's commands imply meeting places." With her own conviction regarding the glorious splendor and the eternal weight of God's noble character, she gave this challenge to her students: "No Christian should use the word glory as a common term. The significance should be exclusively *Divine*."

Emma viewed one's image of God and man as a critical component for understanding a glorious God and oneself. While visiting her friend, Mrs. Gallup, from Victor, New York, on September 29, 1911, she copied a reference to the word *image*. She obtained it from a Bible Dictionary (1880) written by New York's Union Theological Seminary Professor Phillip Schaff (1819–93). She taught that according to Genesis

1:26–27 God created man in his own image with Christ as the image of the invisible God (Colossians 1:15), Jesus as the express image of God (Hebrews1:3), and the Father as known through those who have seen Christ (John 14:8–9). Emma quoted specifically from Schaff: "The term used of our Lord imports a complete likeness, like that which exists between a seal and its impression when the original is perfectly in the representation. Used of man, the tense refers especially to man's knowledge and capacity to comprehend God."

Referencing Colossians 3:10 and Ephesians 4:24 Emma taught that the new man was designed after the express image of the Creator in his righteousness. She summarized in her own words that living in his image meant "being like God in the tone of His moral nature & in the dominion over the creatures of the earth." With this likeness of God in every believer, Emma realized what she and Moody and so many others had experienced—that only the reflection of his love could ever bring completeness to mankind.

Bible Inserts

Emma carefully attached inside her Bible a copy of the 1891 *Bible Reading and Prayer Alliance* pamphlet, for which Emma was one of its writers. The insert described this publication as a Scripture calendar containing daily readings, topics for weekly meetings, and Sunday school lessons. It was published by the Toronto Willard Tract Depository, Toronto, Canada, at a cost of fifty cents per hundred and five cents per ten. When churches ordered more than 500, their name and the program of their weekly meetings would be added for the cost of ten cents per every extra one hundred copies. Another request was made that a two cent stamp should be sent for the receipt of additional information or samples and addressed to Miss E. Dryer, Secretary of the Bible Reading and Prayer Alliance, Chicago Bible Society Room 7, 69 Dearborn St., Chicago, IL.

Other Bible inserts included Emma's listing of *Prominent Scripture Dates and Events* taught in her Bible classes at the Bible Work. She inserted it next to the Jewish weights and coins information. She also compiled the following list of names and events for the number *twelve* as representing *government*—the twelve Patriarchs, twelve New Testament Dates, twelve Apostles, and twelve Caesars, and *seven* as representing *completion*—First seven Church Deacons, the seven Churches of Asia, the seven Dispensations, and the seven Herods.

Emma's Bible contained a copy of her published work entitled *Brief Harmony of the Life of Jesus Christ Reckoned from Passover to Passover*. Henderson and Company in Chicago and Toronto, Canada published this teaching and distributed it for five cents per ten copies or forty cents per 100. She arranged her abbreviated harmony by *Passovers* and *Mid-year Events* with the purpose of assisting her students in readily memorizing the material and assuring "a fuller interpretation of the facts of Christ's public ministry." With this publication she taught that the Christian dispensation began after Jesus turned four years of age and that the abbreviation BC meant *Before the Christian Era*. She added the following subtopics with numerous relevant Scriptures:

- Annunciation
- The Passover when he was twelve years old
- Baptism of Jesus
- First Passover of Christ's public ministry
- Second Passover of Christ's public ministry
- The great event of the first midsummer—Jesus' return to Galilee with his visit with the woman of Samaria at the well
- Third Passover with the great event of the midsummer: the Galilean circuit
- Fourth and last Passover

Emma's last teaching to be printed before her death was a comparison of Christ and his Church with Christ's Death as the Death of Death:

Christ and His Church	Christ's Death is the Death of Death
Genesis 2:23–25	Isaiah 25:8
John 1:51	Hosea 13:14
Matthew 25:10	Romans 8:11
John 3:29	1 Corinthians 15:52, 53
Ephesians 5:23, 27, 32	Philippians 3:20, 21
Revelation 4:1	2 Timothy 1:10
Revelation 19:6, 7, 8, 9; 21:9	Revelation 21:4

A Noble Poetic Tale That Is Told

Along with her great love for God's word, Emma often displayed her great passion for the arts, including music and poetry. In her Bible she secured either typed or handwritten copies of poems and songs. With a continued acknowledgment of her Mayflower roots, she copied Felicia Dorothea Hemans's (1793–1835) poem *Our Pilgrim Fathers, 1620* in which Emma identified with her forefathers who "sought a faith's pure shrine" and called it "holy ground, the soil first they trod; they have left unstained what there they found—Freedom to worship God." She also reflectively wrote out by hand the words to Dorothy Greenwell's 1873 song, *I Am Not Skilled to Understand*, with music in 1885 by William J. Kirkpatrick: "I am not skilled to understand / What God hath willed, what God hath planned; / I only know that at His right hand / Is One Who is my Saviour!"

A typed and anonymous poem insert, entitled *I Am Chief*, paralleled events from Christ's death to man's own sin and blame. Upon reading these poetic words to her students, Emma would have been moved by the knowledge that each of us have spilled the Savior's blood, have slept during the night hours, have denied his name as Peter did—much more than three times—and have driven in the nails with our sins. "These are sins, not spikes; and those / Those are crimes, not thorns; his woes Mine iniquities. That spear / In *my* heart was forged! And here Pilate, Herod, both were born— / Cross, and spike, and spear, and thorn."

The song *How Happy Are They* displayed Emma's familiarity and appreciation for Methodist Charles Wesley's hymns. This song assured Emma of the worthiness of her Savior.[18] Likewise, she appreciated the words of Charles Bacchius's untitled poem expressing humble gratitude for the privilege of being "among the blood-bought throng that fall before thy glorious face."

In her Bible Emma included a typed copy of another anonymous poem entitled *The Better Land* which surely brought comfort to her as she approached the ending years of her life on this earth: "They grow not old in that better land, / No staff for the aged is needed there. / Nor the wrinkled brow, nor the misled hand / Is found in that country, so bright and fair. / Be full of gladness, thou lingering one, / For soon we shall rest in the Heavenly Fold, / And burdens that bow us shall be undone / Then our years are spent as a *tale that is told*."

All those who have shared in Emma's life through this biography—*her noble tale that is told*—have surely heard her longing heart for others to know the One in whom she placed her unmitigated faith. Her life story is truly connected to ours for we hold in our hands the undying evidence of her prayers that reached the throne of God generations ago. All who have been connected to the Moody Bible Institute, the Chicago Bible Society, and other significant ministries and missions in service to the King of Glory have surely heard her imparted prayers resounding in their own hearts to take up her torch and teach God's word to all people. Let us continue to cry out with Emma, as united champions of *nobility*, the endless story of salvation as we await the eminent return of Christ, our soon coming Lord.

---

18. *How Happy Are They* with words by Charles Wesley 1749 and music by William H. Monk 1889.
"It is Heaven below my Redeemer to know / And the angels can do nothing more. / But to fall at His feet and the story repeat / And the Saviour of sinners adore."

WITH CHRIST OUR SOON COMING LORD, 1925 THROUGHOUT ETERNITY

"Now these ... were ... more noble ... entirely ready ... and welcomed the message concerning the attainment through Christ of eternal salvation in the kingdom of God with inclination of mind and eagerness, searching and examining the Scriptures daily to see if these things were so."

~ACTS 17:11 AMP~

Bibliography

Album of Genealogy and Biography: Cook County, Illinois With Portraits. 8th ed. Chicago: Calumet Book and Engraving, 1897. https://archive.org/details/albumofgenealogy 1897calu.

American Bible Society. "History of American Bible Society." Accessed August 13, 2014, http://www.americanbible.org/about/history.

Atkinson, P. "Notes of Travel." *Weekly Pantagraph*, 11(29 August 1857). Accessed March 18, 2013, http://www.illinoisancestors.org/knox/Township_Histories/Galesburg_Twp_ history.html.

Backus, Clarence W. *Historical Sketch of the First Presbyterian Church of Victor, N.Y.* Rochester: J. A. Gillies Print (2 July 1888). https://archive.org/stream/historicalsketooback#page/n5/mode/2up.

Ball, C. H. "Sale of Ingham University. A Protest Against the Unfeeling Language of Yale's Treasurer." *New York Times* (18 December 1906). Accessed March 5, 2013, http://query.nytimes.com/mem/archive-free/pdf?res=9A02E5D7123DE433A25753C1A9649C9464 9ED7CF.

Beatty, Caleb. "The City to Come: Emma Dryer." (blog), (24 June 2010). Accessed October 9, 2011, http://calebbeatty.blogspot.com/2010/06/emma-dryer.html.

———. "Emma Dryer and Her Unrelenting Prayer." (blog), (11 August 2011). Accessed January 2, 2012, http://insideMoody125.blogspot.com/2011/08/emma-dryer-and-her-unrelenting-prayer.html.

Belmonte, Kevin. *D. L. Moody—A Life: Innovator, Evangelist, World-Changer.* Chicago: Moody Publishers, 2014.

Bennis, Warren G., and Burt Namus. *Leaders: The Strategies For Taking Charge.* 2nd ed. New York: HarperBusiness, 1997.

Biographical File of Emma Dryer. Historical Collection. Henry C. Crowell Library Archives, Moody Bible Institute.

Blaine, Anita McCormick. Anita Blaine McCormick Correspondence and Papers, 1828–1958. McCormick Collection. Wisconsin Historical Society Archives. Accessed April 10, 2012.

Blanchard, Charles Albert. *Light On the Last Days.* Chicago: The Bible Institute Colportage Association, 1913.

———. "Miss Dryer and the Moody Church." *The Moody Church News*, 10(3) May 1925. Wisconsin Historical Society Archives. McCormick Collection.

———. *President Blanchard's Autobiography: The Dealings of God With Charles Albert Blanchard, For Many Years a Teacher in Wheaton College, Wheaton, Illinois.* Boone, IA: The Western Alliance, 1915.

Blanchard, Francis Carothers. *The Life of Charles Albert Blanchard.* New York: Fleming H. Revell, 1932.

Bonar, Marjorie. *Reminiscences of Andrew A. Bonar.* London: Hodder and Stoughton, 1895. https://archive.org/stream/reminiscencesofaoobonauoft#page/n5/mode/2up.

Brainerd, David, and Jonathan Edwards. *The Life and Diary of David Brainerd With Notes and Reflections,* 1749. Published by ReadaClassic.com, 2010.

Bundy, David D. *Keswick: A Bibliographical Introduction to the Higher Life Movements.* B. L. Fisher Library: Asbury Theological Seminary, 1975.

———. "Keswick and the Experience of Evangelical Piety." In *Modern Christian Revivals* edited by Edith L. Blumhofer and R. Balmer, 138–44. University of Illinois Press, 1993.

Burnham, John H. *History of Bloomington and Normal in McLean County,* Illinois. Bloomington: J.H. Burnham, 1879. https://archive.org/details/texts?and[]=Burnham,%20J.%20History%20of%20Bloomington%20and%20Normal%20in%20McLean%20County%20Burnham.

Burns, James MacGregor. *Leadership.* New York: Harper and Row, 1978.

Butt, Howard. *The Velvet Covered Brick.* New York: Harper and Row, 1973.

Campbell, O. L. "Knox Township." 1919. Accessed March 11, 2013, http://www.usgennet.org/usa/il/county/knox/annuals_knox_6.htm.

———. "Knox Township History, Educational Institutions." 1899. Accessed March 11, 2013, http://genealogytrails.com/ill/knox/1899_twp_historiespg10.html.

Casson, Herbert Newton. *Cyrus Hall McCormick: His Life and Work.* Chicago: A. C. McClurg, 1909. https://archive.org/details/cyrushallmccorm00cassgoog.

Catalogue of the State Normal University For the Academic Year Ending June 28, 1866. Peoria, IL: N.C. Nason. https://archive.org/stream/catalogue186465186970illi#page/n7/mode/2up.

Central Library of Rochester and Monroe County. **1855** Rochester City Directory, 33, 146. http://www.libraryweb.org/rochcitydir/images/1855/1855complete.pdf.

Chapman, Charles. C. *History of Knox County, Illinois.* Chicago: Blakely, Brown and Marsh Printers, 1878. https://archive.org/details/historyofknoxcou00chas.

Chapman, John Wilbur. *The Life and Work of Dwight Lyman Moody.* London: James Nisbet and Company Limited, 1900. https://archive.org/details/lifeofdwightmoodoochapuoft.

Charles Albert Blanchard Papers and *Jonathan Blanchard Papers.* Wheaton College Archives and Special Collections. Accessed July 2012.

Chemers, Martin M. *An Integrative Theory of Leadership.* Mahwah, New Jersey, London: Lawrence Erlbaum Associates, 1997.

Cherry, Kendra. "The Great Man Theory of Leadership." Accessed on January 17, 2014, http://psychology.about.com/od/leadership/a/great-man-theory-of-leadership.htm.

Chicago Evangelization Society File. Historical Collection. Accessed June 18, 2012, Henry C. Crowell Library Archives, Moody Bible Institute.

The Chicago Manual of Style, 16th ed. Chicago: University of Chicago Press, 2010.

Chicago Tribune. "Moody is Here Again." September 27, 1889. Accessed November 18, 2015, http://archives.chicagotribune.com/1889/09/27/page/1/article/moody-is-here-again.

Bibliography

Child, Hamilton. *The Gazetteer and Business Directory of Genesee County, N.Y. for 1869–70*, compiler, 92–101. Syracuse: Hamilton, 1869. https://archive.org/details/gazetteerbusineso7chil.

Christian Cynosure. National Christian Association. Chicago: Ezra A. Cook, 1875–87. https://archive.org/search.php?query=Christian%20Cynosure.

Clark, Francis Edward. *Christian Endeavor in All Lands: A Record of Twenty-five Years of Progress*. W. E. Scull for the United Society of Christian Endeavor, 1906. https://archive.org/details/christianendeavoooclar.

Congregational Library. "Capron, William Banfield (1824–1876) and Sarah Brown Capron (1828–1919)." Papers, 1830–76. http://www.congregationallibrary.org/finding-aids/CapronWilliamSarah0044. Processed August 2002 by Jessica Steytler.

Conover, George S., ed. *History of Ontario County, New York*. Syracuse: D. Mason, 1893. https://archive.org/details/historyofontarioooaldr.

Cook, John Williston, and James V. McHugh. *A History of the Illinois State Normal University: Normal, Illinois*. Bloomington, IL: Pantagraph Printing and Binding Establishment, 1882. https://archive.org/details/historyofillinoioocookiala.

CWP and Regents of the University of California. "Contributions of 20th Century Women to Physics: Whiting, Sarah Frances 1847–1927." 1999. http://cwp.library.ucla.edu/Phase2/Whiting,_Sarah_Frances@944123456.html.

Daniels, William H. *D. L. Moody and His Work*. Hartford: American Publishing, 1875/1876.

———. ed. *Moody: His Words, Work, and Workers*. New York: Nelson and Phillips, 1877. https://archive.org/stream/moodyhiswords wooounkngoog#page/n8/mode/2up.

Davenport, Reuben Briggs. *The Death-Blow to Spiritualism Being the True Story of the Fox Sisters*. New York: G.W. Dillingham, 1888. https://archive.org/details/deathblowtospirioodaverich.

Day, Richard Elsworth. *Bush Aglow: Life Story of Dwight Lyman Moody, Commoner of Northfield*. Philadelphia: The Judson Press, 1936.

Dewey's Rochester City Directory for 1855–56, 146. Rochester: Lee, Mann and Company, Daily American Office. http://www.libraryweb.org/rochcitydir/images/1855/1855complete.pdf.

Dorsett, Lyle W. "Far From Perfect." November 13, 2005. http://www.sermonindex.net/modules/newbb/viewtopic.php?topic_id=8037&forum=34&2.

———. *A Passion For Souls: The Life of D. L. Moody*. Chicago: Moody Press, 1997.

Dougherty, Mary Agnes. "The Meyers: Josiah Shelley and Lucy Jane Rider." *Methodist History* 37(1) (October, 1998) 48–58. http://archives.gcah.org/xmlui/bitstream/handle/10516/6248/MH-1998-October-Dougherty.pdf?sequence=1.

Douglas, W. M. *Andrew Murray and His Message: One of God's Choice Saints*. Grand Rapids: Baker, 1981.

Drede, J. L. "Who Are the Mohican Indians?" 2013. http://www.wisegeek.com/who-are-the-mohican-indians.htm.

Drummond, Henry. *The Greatest Thing in the World and Other Addresses*. Chicago: Fleming H. Revell, 1898. https://ia801403.us.archive.org/32/items/thegreatestthing16739gut/16739-8.txt.

Du Plessis, J. *The Life of Andrew Murray of South Africa*. London: Marshall Brothers Limited, 1919. https://archive.org/stream/TheLifeOfAndrewMurrayOfSouthAfrica-ByJ.DuPlessis-Dated1919/TheLifeOfAndrewMurrayOfSouth AfricaByJ.DuPlessis-1919.

Edwards, Richard. "Decennial Address: Delivered at the State Normal University. Board of Education. Published by Order of the Board," (27 June 1872).

———. "Normal Schools in the United States." Edited by Merle L. Borrowman, *Teacher Education in America: A Documentary History*, 74–85. New York: Teachers College Press, 1965.

Emma Dryer Bibles. Historical Collection. Henry C. Crowell Library, Moody Bible Institute, Chicago. Accessed June 18, 2012.

Emma Dryer Obituary. Biographical File of Emma Dryer. Historical Collection. Henry C. Crowell Library, Moody Bible Institute, Chicago. Accessed June 18, 2012.

European-American Evangelistic Crusades. Faith Hall of Fame. "Reuben Archer Torrey 1856–1928: American Evangelist, Pastor, Educator, and Writer." Accessed November 24, 2015, http://eaec.org/faithhallfame/ratorrey.htm.

Evangelistic Record or *Record of Christian Work*. Chicago: Fleming H. Revell, 1881–86. http://biblebelievers.com/ROCW/index.html.

Farwell, James Villier. *Early Recollections of Dwight L. Moody*. Chicago: The Winona Press, 1907.

Felmley, David. *Semi-Centennial History of the Illinois State Normal University: 1857–1907*. Illinois State University History Books, Book 7, 1907. http://ir.library.illinoisstate.edu/isuhistorybook/7.

Fifty-Second Annual Report of the Chicago Bible Society. Chicago: Chicago Bible Society, 13 January 1892, 8–9. http://faith.galecia.com/resource/report-field-chicago-bible-society.

Findlay, James. F. *Dwight L. Moody: American Evangelist, 1837–1899*. Chicago: University of Chicago Press, 1969.

First Presbyterian Church: LeRoy, New York. Accessed January 12, 2012, http://www.leroyfootball.com/presbylr/leroyny.htm.

Fitt, Arthur Percy. *Moody Still Lives: Word Pictures of D. L. Moody*. New York: Fleming H. Revell, 1936.

———. *Shorter Life of D. L. Moody*. Chicago: Bible Institute Colportage Association, 1900.

Foster, Charles. R., Lawrence A. Golemon, Lisa E. Dahill, and Barbara Wang Tolentino. *Educating Clergy: Teaching Practices and Pastoral Imagination*. San Francisco: Jossey-Bass, 2006.

Freed, John B. "The Founding of Illinois State Normal University: Normal School or State University?" *JISHS* 101 no.2 (Summer 1998) 106–26.

French, Justus H. "Profile of Palmyra. Wayne County, New York From the 1860 Gazetteer of the State of New York," 1860. http://wayne.nygenweb.net/townships/palmyra.html.

Getz, Gene A. *The Story of Moody Bible Institute*. Chicago: Moody Press, 1969/1986.

Goleman, Daniel Jay. *Emotional Intelligence: Why It Can Matter More Than IQ*. New York: Bantam, 1995.

Graves, Dan. "Evangelization Society to Storm Chicago." May, 2007. http://www.christianity.com/church/church-history/timeline/1801-900/evangelization-society-to-storm-chicago-11630617.html.

Greer, Peter, and Chris Horst. *Mission Drift: The Unspoken Crisis Facing Leaders, Charities, and Churches*. Minneapolis: Bethany House, 2014.

Gustafson, David M. *D. L. Moody and Swedes: Shaping Evangelical Identity Among Swedish Mission Friends 1867–1899*, 2008. http://www.openthesis.org/documents/D-L-Moody-Swedes-Shaping-430486.html.

Bibliography

Handy, Lowell K. Biographical File of Emma Dryer. Historical Collection. Henry C. Crowell Library, Moody Bible Institute, Chicago. Accessed June 18, 2012.

Harper, Charles A. *Development of the Teacher College in the United States With Special Reference to the Illinois State Normal University.* Bloomington, IL.: McKnight, 1935. Illinois State University History Books. Book 8. http://ir.library.illinoisstate.edu/isuhistorybook/8.

Hartzler, Henry Burns. *Moody in Chicago or the World's Fair Gospel Campaign.* New York: Fleming H. Revell, 1894. https://archive.org/details/moodyinchicagoor00hart.

Hassey, Janette. *No Time For Silence: Evangelical Women in Public Ministry Around the Turn of the Century.* Grand Rapids: Zondervan, 1986.

Henry, Carl Ferdinand Howard. *The Pacific Garden Mission: A Doorway to Heaven.* Grand Rapids: Zondervan, 1942.

History's Women. "Emeline Dryer: Christian Educator and Administrator." Accessed February 8, 2013, http://www.historyswomen.com/womenoffaith/EmelineDryer.html.

Horton, Isabelle. *High Adventure: Life of Lucy Rider Meyer.* The Methodist Book Concern: New York, 1928.

Hotchkiss, George W. *Industrial Chicago: The Manufacturing Interests Vol. III.* Chicago: Goodspeed, 1891. https://archive.org/details/industrialchicago1good.

Howat, Irene. *Ten Girls Who Made History.* Scotland: Christian Focus, 2003.

Huber, Babette. "Victor: A Brief History." Accessed January 11, 2012, www.victorny.org/index.aspx?nid=127.

Hutchinson, William T. *Cyrus Hall McCormick: Harvest 1856–1884.* New York: D. Appleton Century, 1935. https://archive.org/details/cyrushallmccormi000264mbp.

Illinois State Board of Education. *Proceedings of the Board of Education of the State of Illinois.* Peoria, Illinois: N. C. Nason, 1865–66; 1868–69; 1871. http://ir.library.illinoisstate.edu/univpubs/?utm_source=ir.library.illinoisstate.edu%2Funivpubs%2F7&utm_medium=PDF&utm_campaign=PDFCoverPages.

Internet Archive. https://archive.org/.

Joiner, Thekla Ellen. *Sin in the City: Chicago and Revivalism 1880–1920.* Columbia, Missouri: University of Missouri Press, 2007.

Ketcham Family Papers. Grand Rapids History and Special Collection Archives and Public Library Collection 293. October 2009. http://grplpedia.grpl.org/wiki/images/293.pdf.

King, Mary B. *Looking Backward or Memories of the Past.* New York: Anson D. F. Randolph, 1870.

Lawson, J. Gilchrist. *Deeper Experiences of Famous Christians.* Kensington, PA: Whitaker House, 1998.

Leffingwell, Charles. "St. Mary's School." USGenNet, 1912. Accessed January 11, 2012, http://www.usgennet.org/usa/il/county/knox/schools_st_mary.htm.

Lennox, Cuthbert (1901). *Henry Drummond: A Biographical Sketch.* Toronto: William Briggs, 1901. https://archive.org/stream/cihm_81003#page/n9/mode/2up.

Linehan, Mary. "Erring Women's Refuge." Encyclopedia of Chicago. http://www.encyclopedia.chicagohistory.org/pages/434.html.

Lobb, John. *Arrows and Anecdotes By Dwight L. Moody.* London: Folkard & Sons, 1876. https://archive.org/stream/arrowsandanecdo00moodgoog#page/n13/mode/2up.

Maas, David E. "The Life & Times of D. L. Moody." *Christian History*, 9(1) (1990) 5–13.

MacDonald, George. *Weighed and Wanting.* London: Edwin Dalton, 1908.

Bibliography

Marsden, George M. *Fundamentalism and American Culture,* 2nd ed. New York: Oxford University Press, 2006.

Marshall, Helen E. *Grandest of Enterprises: Illinois State Normal University 1857–1957.* Chicago: R. R. Donnelley and Sons, 1956. https://archive.org/details/grandestofenterpoomars.

McClure, J. B., ed. *D. L. Moody's Child Stories.* Chicago: Rhodes and McClure, 1877. https://archive.org/details/dlmoodyschildstoomoodgoog.

McCormick, Nettie Fowler. Financial File, 1843–1923. Wisconsin Historical Society Archives. Accessed April 10, 2012.

McNarmara, Robert. "The 1886 Haymarket Square Riot in Chicago: Anarchist Bombing at a Union Meeting Provoked a Deadly Riot." 19th Century History. Accessed January 13, 2012, http://history1800s.about.com/od/organizedlabor/a/haymarket01.htm.

Memorial Service for Miss Emma Dryer. Moody Church Collection 330, Box 58, Folder 3. Billy Graham Center Archives.

Merrill, Arch. "Rochester Sketchbook: The Roar of the Crowds." GenWeb of Monroe County, New York, 1946. http://mcnygenealogy.com/book/sketchbook-2.htm#crowd.

Merton, Thomas. *New Seeds of Contemplation.* New York: New Directions Publishing Corporation, 1961.

Meyer, Lucy. *Deaconesses, Biblical, Early Church, European, America: With the Story of the Chicago Training School, for City, Home and Foreign Missions, and the Chicago Deaconess Home.* Cincinnati: Cranston and Stowe, 1892.

Miles, Lion J. "The Mohicans of Stockbridge." Accessed October 29, 2012, http://www.berkshares.org/heroes/mohican.

Moody, Dwight Lyman. *Pleasure & Profit in Bible Study.* Chicago: Fleming H. Revell, 1895. https://archive.org/stream/worksofdwightlm004mood#page/8/mode/2up/search/healthy.

———. *Secret Power or the Secret of Success in Christian Life and Work.* Chicago: Fleming H. Revell, 1881.

Moody, William R. *The Life of Dwight L. Moody.* Chicago: Fleming H. Revell, 1900.

Moody Bible Institute. "D. L. Moody's Story." Accessed July 1, 2009, http://www.Moody.edu/edu_mainWF.as px?pageid=101256.

———. "Emma Dryer." Crowell Library Archives. Chicago. Accessed July 1, 2009, http://mmm.moody.edu/GenMoody/default.asp?SectionID=BEF05288304D486581D608CC3DC4EC31.

"Moody Church Reunion: Church History," 1908. http://www.moodychurch.org/150/teachings/moody-church-reunion/.

Moran, Barbara B. "Gender Differences in Leadership." *Library Trends* 40, no. 3 (1992) 4, 75–91. http://citeseerx.ist.psu.edu/viewdoc/download?rep=rep1&type=pdf&doi=10.1.1.204.5982.

Mount Holyoke. *Schools in the United States Associated with Mount Holyoke College*: Ingham University. Accessed January 12, 2012, https://www.mtholyoke.edu/archives/history/associated_us_schools.

Müller, George. *The Life of Trust: Being a Narrative of the Lord's Dealings with George Müller.* Boston: Gould and Lincoln, 1861. https://archive.org/details/thelifeoftrustbe27288gut.

Müller, Suzannah. *The Preaching Tours and Missionary Labours of George Müller of Bristol.* London: J. Nisbet, 1889. https://archive.org/stream/ThePreachingToursAndMissionaryLabours1889OfGeorgeMuller/The_preaching_tours_and_missionary_laboursByMrs.GeorgeMuller#page/n5/mode/2up.

BIBLIOGRAPHY

Nebraska State Historical Society. "*Harvey, Turlington,*" 1999. http://www.nebraskahistory.org/publish/publicat/timeline/harvey_turlington.htm.

New York GenWeb Project. *Census Records. LeRoy Town, Genesee County.* http://www.rootsweb.ancestry.com/~nycleroy/Census/1860/pgj0001.txt.

Newell, William W. *A Cry From the Land of Calvin and Voltaire: Records of the McAll Mission.* London: Hodder and Stoughton, 1887. https://archive.org/details/cryfromlandofcaloolond.

Ogorek, Cynthia L. "Dryer, Emma." In *Women Building Chicago 1790-1990: A Biographical Dictionary,* 230-32. Edited by Rima Lunin Schultz and Adele Hast. Bloomington, IN: Indiana University Press, 2001.

Olsen, Margaret Hook. *Patriarch of the Rockies; The Life Story of Joshua Gravett.* Denver: Golden Bell Press, 1960.

Ontario County New York Genweb. "Industry and Commerce in Victor, 1913." Accessed February 18, 2013, http://ontario.nygenweb.net/VictorNYBusinessmen1913.htm.

Perry, Albert James. *History of Knox County, Illinois.* Chicago: J. Clarke, 1912. https://archive.org/stream/3911940.1-2#page/n3/mode/2up.

Pollock, John C. *Moody: A Biographical Portrait of the Pacesetter in Modern Mass Evangelism.* New York: MacMillan, 1963.

Powell, Emma Moody. *Heavenly Destiny: The Life Story of Mrs. D. L. Moody.* Chicago: Moody Press, 1943.

Quarter-Centennial of the First Congregational Church of Chicago. Chicago: Culver, Page, Boyne and Company, 1876. https://archive.org/stream/quartercentennia00good#page/n0/mode/2up.

Remlaf, L. T. *The Gospel Awakening Comprising Sermons and Addresses, Prayer-meeting Talks and Bible Readings of the Great Revival Meetings Conducted by Moody and Sankey.* Chicago: Fairbanks & Palmer, 1883. https://archive.org/stream/thegospelawakeni00mood#page/n9/mode/2up.

Rice, Edwin Wilbur. *The Sunday-School Movement (1780-1917) and the American Sunday-School Union (1817-1917).* Philadelphia: American Sunday-School Union, 1917. http://babel.hathitrust.org/cgi/pt?id=nyp.33433068276231;view=1up;seq=5.

Roderick, Stella Virginia. *Nettie Fowler McCormick.* New Hampshire: Richard R. Smith, 1956.

Rohold, Sabeti B. *The War and the Jew.* Toronto: MacMillan of Canada, 1916. https://archive.org/details/warandjewabirds00rohogoog.

Ruelas, Abraham. *Women and the Landscape of American Higher Education: Wesleyan Holiness and Pentecostal Founders.* Eugene, OR: Pickwick Publications, 2010.

Sande, Ken. *The Peace Maker: A Biblical Guide to Resolving Personal Conflict.* Grand Rapids: Baker, 2004.

Sandom, Carrie. *Different by Design: God's Blueprint for Men and Women.* Scotland and Great Britain: Christian Focus Publications Ltd, 2012.

Sawislak, Karen. "Chicago Relief and Aid Society." Encyclopedia of Chicago. Accessed October 26, 2013, http://encyclopedia.chicagohistory.org/pages/1054.html.

Sawyer, William. "The Six Nations Confederacy During the American Revolution." National Park Service U. S. Department of the Interior. http://www.nps.gov/fost/historyculture/the-six-nations-confederacy-during-the-american-revolution.htm.

Shanks, T. J., ed. *College Students at Northfield* or *a College of Colleges.* Chicago: Fleming H. Revell, 1887.

Sheldon, Edward Austin. *Autobiography: Edward Austin Sheldon*. New York: Ives–Butler, 1911. https://archive.org/details/autobiographyofeoosheliala.

Sisk, Don. *Joyful Giving*. Murfreesboro, TN: Sword of the Lord, 2003.

Sixty-Second Annual Report of the Chicago Bible Society. Chicago: Chicago Bible Society, 1902. Biographical File of Emma Dryer. Historical Collection. Henry C. Crowell Library, Moody Bible Institute, Chicago. Accessed June 18, 2012.

Southold Historical Society. "Wiles Family Papers, 1850-1991." Southold, New York. http://media.wix.com/ugd/f19472_5b5cbaff329a4071a30bd1db75223282.pdf.

Spears, Larry C. "Character and Servant Leadership: Ten Characteristics of Effective, Caring Leaders." *JVL* 1 no. 1 (2014) 25–30. http://www.regent.edu/acad/global/publications/jvl/vol1_iss1/Spears_Final.pdfon.

Statham, Anne. "The Gender Model Revisited; Differences in the Management Styles of Men and Women." *Sex Role* 16 no. 7/8 (1987) 409–29.

Swift, John. *Landmarks of Wayne County, New York*, 1791. http://ontario.nygenweb.net/VictorNYBusinessmen1913.htm.

Taylor, Hudson. *Hudson Taylor and the China Inland Mission: The Growth of a Work of God*. London: Religious Tract Society, 1918. https://archive.org/details/hudsontaylorchinootayl.

Torrey, Reuben Archer. *Why God Used D. L. Moody*. Chicago: Bible Institute Colportage Association, 1923.

Town of Victor, New York, Archives. Historian's Office. Emma Dryer files, *Victor Herald* Newspaper Obituary, and Grave Site Pictures.

Truesdale, Dorothy S. "The Younger Generation: Their Opinions, Pastimes and Enterprises 1830–1850." *Rochester History* 1 no. 2/2 (1939) 1–24. http://www.libraryweb.org/~rochhist/v1_1939/v1i2.pdf.

United States Census, 1870. "Emaline Dryer in Household of Thomas Loer, Illinois, United States." *Family Search,* 12, family 73, NARA microfilm publication M593, FHL microfilm 000545758. https://familysearch.org/pal:/MM9.1.1/M6HF-TCM.

Vester, Bertha S. *Our Jerusalem: An American Family in the Holy City, 1881–1949*. Garden City, NY: Doubleday, 1950.

Vital Records of West Stockbridge, Massachusetts to the Year 1850. Boston: New England Historic Genealogical Society, 1907. https://archive.org/details/vitalrecordsofwesoowest.

Wanamaker, John, ed. *Book News: A Monthly Survey of General Literature*, 1897. https://archive.org/stream/booknews03britgoog.

Warner, Laceye. *Toward the Light: Lucy Rider Meyer and the Chicago Training School*. Garrett-Evangelical Theological Seminary, April 2005. http://archives.gcah.org/xmlui/pdfpreview/bitstream/handle/10516/6632/MH-2005-April-Warner.pdf?sequence=1.

Whittle, Daniel Webster, ed. *The Wonders of Prayer*. Chicago: Fleming H. Revell, 1885. https://archive.org/stream/wondersprayeraroomlgoog#page/n3/mode/2up.

"Who Led Billy Graham to Christ?" Billy Graham Center Archives. http://www2.wheaton.edu/bgc/archives/faq/13.htm.

Willard, Francis. *Glimpses of Fifty Years: An Autobiography of an American Woman*. Chicago: Chicago Woman's Temperance Publication Association/H. J. Smith, 1889. https://archive.org/details/glimpsesfiftyyeoowillgoog.

Williams, Augustus Warner. *Life and Work of Dwight L. Moody: The Great Evangelist of the XIXth Century*. Philadelphia: P. W. Ziegler, 1900.

BIBLIOGRAPHY

Women's Society of the Western Presbyterian Church. *Palmyra, Wayne County, New York*. Rochester: The Herald Press, 1907. https://archive.org/details/palmyrawayneco unoopalmrich.

Woodward Memorial Library. "Ingham University 1837–1892." Accessed January 12, 2012, http://www.woodwardmem oriallibrary.org/university.php.

Index

Albro, E. S., 143, 160, 216
Allen, Mary
    Allen Female Seminary preceptress and founder, 17
    divine healing experiences of, 24, 52
    education experiences of, 18–20
    family background of, 17, 20, 25
    Fox sisters and spiritualism, 23–24
    Looking Backward or Memories of the Past, 17
    missions, support of, 20–21
    revival conversion, 18
    Rochester revival, 21
    social issues addressed by, 23
    Sunday school experience, 20
American Bible Society, 12, 234
American Board of Commissioners for Foreign Mission, 230
Anderson, Alison, 244, 246n1, 247
Antioch College, 256
Auburn Theological Seminary, 11, 12

Bacchius, Charles, 262
Backus, Clarence, *Historical Sketch of the First Presbyterian Church*, 9
Beecher, Henry Ward, 59
Bible Institute Colportage Association, 9, 64
Bible Reading and Prayer Alliance, 137, 142, 144, 173, 241, 260
Bible Work
    Chicago Bible Society, affiliation with, 228, 232, 234–40
    Chicago Evangelization Society, 143, 196, 197, 204, 206–7, 210
    Chicago locations of, 73, 92, 145–47, 150, 167, 207
    developed by Emma Dryer, 60, 68, 101, 104, 143
    foundation for the Chicago Bible Institute or Moody Bible Institute, 171, 186, 244
    funding of, 79, 143, 144, 150, 198
    incorporation of, 157, 197, 207
    mission outreaches, 140, 142, 161, 168
    objectives of, 59, 97, 136–42, 195
    prayer at, 75, 161, 176, 250
    publications for, 137, 141, 142, 148, 207, 255
    reports of, 138, 139, 142, 148
    structure of, 108–9, 143, 192, 216
    students of, 169–71
    support from
        Blackstone, William, 98, 161, 189
        Blanchard, Charles, 188–89, 216
        Cleveland, Sarah, 94, 149
        Daniels, W. H., 143, 149
        Erdman, William, 61, 157
        Farwell, John, 102, 143, 149, 157
        Farwell, Mrs. John, 148
        Goodwin, Edward, 149, 166
        Goodwin, Nellie, 149, 219
        Keith, Elbridge, 102, 143, 192
        McCormick, Cyrus, 74, 143
        McCormick, Nettie, 69, 102, 146, 148, 189, 215
        Meyer, Josiah and Lucy, 85
        miscellaneous sources, 199
        Moody, Dwight, 78, 93, 101, 144, 162, 191
        Moody, Emma Revell, 143, 147
        Revell, Fleming, 98, 161, 240, 250
        Spafford, Horatio and Anna, 151, 153
        Swedes, 64
    workers, training of, 86, 141, 142, 160, 184, 196
Blackstone, William
    endorser of the *Bible Reading and Prayer Alliance*, 137
    friendship with Emma Dryer, 88, 244, 250
    Hebrew Christian Conference speaker, 233–34

Index

Blackstone, William *(continued)*
    Hebrew Mission founder, 233
    Horatio Spafford association, 151
    Jesus is Coming, 75, 88
    McCormick family association, 241, 244
    opinion of Hudson Taylor, 183
    Chicago Training School involvement, 88
    premillenialism, promotion of, 54
Blaine, Anita McCormick (daughter of Cyrus and Nettie McCormick), 56, 80–81, 213, 238, 241–44
Blaine, Emmons (husband of Anita McCormick), 71
Blaine, James (father of Emmons Blaine), 71, 244
Blanchard, Charles, 153–57, 254
    Chicago Avenue Church pastor, 133, 143, 169
    Christian Cynosure editor, 144
    Getting Things from God, 180
    Hebrew Mission connections, 233, 257
    May Institute, support of, 162–63, 164, 165, 195
    memorial service speaker for Emma Dryer, 251–52
    Moody Church 1908 reunion, 240
    Mount Holyoke College, 180
    Northfield Conference attendee, 158
    officiating at Emma Dryer's funeral, 247
    opinion of Dwight Moody, 156
    opposition to freemasonry, 154
    report from Bible Work students, 169–71
    views on divine healing, 177
    Wheaton College president, 138, 168, 240
Blanchard, Ellen (first wife of Charles Blanchard), 148
Blanchard, Francis (third wife of Charles Blanchard), 246
Blanchard, Jonathan (father of Charles Blanchard), xviii, 30, 127, 154
Blatchford, E. W., 151, 160, 213, 216, 221
Blatchford, Mary, 213, 216, 218, 219
Bliss, E. W., 160, 206, 207, 227
Bliss, P. P., 69, 114, 135, 151, 179
Boldt, Niclaus, 79–80
Bonar, Andrew, 158, 172, 178
Bonar, Horatius, 227
Boudinot, Elias, 234
Boughton, Claudius Victor, 5
Boughton, Jared, 5, 10
Bouton, Nathaniel
    Bible Work supporter, 143, 149, 210, 216
    Chicago Bible Society, president of, 234
    Chicago Evangelization Society participation, 192, 196–200, 207, 210, 211, 212
    Chicago Fire relief efforts, 139
    church concerns of, 225
    foundry and iron works businessman, 102, 132
    Harvey dispute, 205, 208, 217, 218, 222
Bradberry, Travis, 103n63
Brainerd, David
    influence on Emma Dryer, 10, 50, 55, 146, 178, 250, 259
    Life and Diary of David Brainerd, 2
    missionary to the Indians, 1–3
Butt, Howard, *The Velvet Covered Brick*, 123

Calkins, Norman Allison, *Primary Object Lessons*, 40
Capron, Sarah, 216, 219, 220, 221, 228–31
Capron, William, 230
Carse, Matilda, 76
Central Music Hall in Chicago, 79, 141
Chapman, John, 67, 115, 118
Chicago Avenue Church
    1876 dedication ceremony, 144–54
    formerly the Illinois Street Church, 55
    ministry of Emma Dryer at, 55, 135, 138, 140, 155, 161, 191
    pastors of, 127, 133, 143n46, 143–44, 154, 240
    prayer meetings at, 98
    Swedish Free Mission, sponsored by, 64, 65
Chicago Bible Institute
    Blanchard, Charles, involvement in, 154, 156, 157, 252
    board members, 106–7, 192, 217, 222
    Dwight Moody involvement, 106, 123, 161, 165, 196, 241
    financial support of, 188–90, 192, 220
    foundation of, 104, 110, 172, 192, 227, 231
    Grattan Guinness counsel regarding, 141
    Moody Church Reminiscence Day location, 240
    Moorehead, William, 144, 163
    opening of, 224, 229, 230–31
    support for, 160, 203, 231, 244
    vision of, 99, 113, 156, 187, 194–96, 257
Chicago Bible Society, 12, 60, 124, 137, 232–39
Chicago businessmen. *See also* Harvey, Turlington; Keith, Elbridge
    Armour, Philip, 78, 193
    Crerar, John, 63, 149
    Deering, Charles, 75
    Field, Marshall, 131, 140, 193, 211, 218, 220
    Leiter, Levi, 193
    Marshall, H. N., 128
    Palmer, Potter, 193
    Scott, Robert, 192, 196, 212, 216, 237, 240

Index

Chicago Evangelistic Committee, 160, 208, 213
Chicago Evangelization Society
    1888 May Institute, sponsor of, 207
    board of, 206, 210, 215, 222, 228
    board resignations of, 211
    conflict within, 201–6, 208–24
    constitution of, 199–200
    Dwight Moody involvement, 125, 196, 201, 214, 231
    divergence from Bible Work objectives, 196, 197
    formation of the Chicago Bible Institute, 193, 196–98
    funding of, 211, 220
    organization of, 195, 196, 207
    report on tent meetings, 226
    separation from the Bible Work, 213, 216–19, 223, 228, 231
    transition from the Bible Work, 228–30
Chicago Fire of 1871. *See under* Bouton; Dryer, Emma; McCormick, Nettie; Moody, Dwight; Sankey; YMCA
Chicago Interior, 80
Chicago Relief and Aid Society, 61–63, 72
Chicago Theological Seminary, 72, 144, 166, 170, 185
Chicago Times, 46, 57
Chicago Training School, 82–88, 137, 167, 237, 251–52
Chicago World's Fair, 79–80, 230
Chicago-Bladet, 64
Children's Lend a Hand Missionary Band, 13
China Inland Mission. *See under* Helmer; Taylor
Christian Cynosure
    Bible Work advertisements in, 138, 141–42, 144, 166
    Chicago Bible Institute advertisement, 198
    freemasonry reports, 154, 158
    May Institute advertisements in, 162–165, 207
    mission reports from, 161
    reports of Dwight Moody, 154
    Wheaton College publication, 138
Christian Endeavor World, 256–57
Christian Union Magazine, 59–60
churches
    Baptist, 26, 34, 144, 224, 238, 243–44
    Catholic, 14, 111–12, 236
    Congregational, 16, 34, 51, 64, 96, 238
    Episcopal, 16, 26, 30, 31, 144
    Lutheran, 30, 65
    Methodist, 30, 34, 46, 144, 238
    Presbyterian, 5, 9–13, 30, 67, 243
    Protestants, 112

Quakers, 236
Universalist Society, 14
Civil War, 30, 48, 54, 63, 66, 106
Clarke, George and Sarah, 66–68, 76, 88–89, 123, 148, 160, 221. *See also* Pacific Garden Mission
Cobb, Emeline C. Wilson (mother of Emma Dryer), 3n7, 4, 247
Cobb, George Hiram (brother of Emma Dryer), 4
Cobb, Hiram (father of Emma Dryer), 3n7, 4, 247
Cobb, Rufus and Lydia, 7–8
Conover, George, *History of Ontario County*, 9
Cox, Samuel Hanson, 26
Crosby Opera House, 77
curriculum
    Bible Work, 59, 87, 104, 141
    Chicago Bible Institute, 230
    Chicago Training School, 87
    Illinois State Normal University, 37–41
    Ingham University, 26–28
    Moody's Northfield schools, 133
    Palmyra Union School, 16

Daniels, W. H.
    Dwight Moody associate, 47
    Emma Dryer association, 50, 54, 58, 66, 136, 172
    First Methodist Episcopal Church, pastor of, 14
    opinion regarding Dwight Moody, 58, 95–96, 109–10, 111, 116, 121
    premillennialism, 54
    YMCA connections, 63
Dartmouth College, 18, 20
Day, Richard, *Bush Aglow*, 187, 214
DeRemer, Bernard, 253
DISC assessment, 103n61
Dorsett, Lyle, xviii, 61, 97n33, 99
Drummond, Henry
    Greatest Thing In The World, 128, 184
    inspiration to Emma Dryer, 183–85
    Keswick Convention, 172
    relationship with Dwight Moody, 120, 129, 131–32
    Scottish evangelist, 93
Dryer, Emma. *See also* Chicago Bible Society; Haymarket Riot; Spafford. *See also under* Bible Work; Holy Spirit; Moorehead
    Allen Female Seminary attendance, 12, 17, 21–23, 82
    Bible studies of, 102, 138, 145, 254–61
    birth of, 1, 3n7, 4, 28n1
    burden for souls, 21, 53, 55, 62, 64, 71

277

Index

Dryer, Emma *(continued)*
    Chicago Evangelistic Committee member, 160
    Chicago Evangelization Society, 122, 143, 196, 208, 209
    Chicago Fire, xvii, 4, 23, 56, 58, 94
    church background of, 9–14, 149
        church concerns of, 225, 228
        churches attended, 16, 26, 34, 54, 70–71, 247
    Civil War contribution, 31
    communication skills of, 102, 107, 108, 148, 221
    conferences, 37, 79, 160
    conflict management, 75, 90
    conversion of, 9
    DISC assessment, 104, 111, 113, 118, 124–25, 223
    divine healing, 24, 52, 130, 144, 155
    doctrinal issues, 23, 51, 88, 155
    Dwight Moody introduction, 47, 48, 50–52, 100
    early years of, 4–17, 27
    education background. *See also* curriculum; Illinois State Normal; Ingham University; Knoxville Ewing
        classroom management and discipline, 44–46
        courses taught, 27–28, 37, 161, 206, 236–37, 280
        early school years, 5, 14–15
        evangelization and education, 196
        faith and learning, 12, 120, 140, 160
        high school years, 16–17
        learning compensation, 117
        teaching methodology, 22, 55, 59, 61
        teaching skills, 40, 96, 113, 252
    educational leadership of, 111, 133, 167, 231
    Emotional Intelligence, traits of, 107, 109, 124, 131, 132–33
    evangelical identity of, 89
    evangelical submission of, 122, 187–88, 209, 215, 221
    evangelism, 111, 113, 160
    faith of, 132, 148, 151, 175, 188, 190
    final days of, 157, 246–47, 249n11
    finances of, 68–69, 77, 78, 101, 235, 238
    friendships of. *See also under* Blackstone; Daniels; Goodwin, Nettie; Helmer
        Blanchard family, 30, 127, 155–57, 233, 240, 246, 251
        Bouton, Nathaniel, 149, 234
        Clarke family, 67
        Erdman, William, 54, 61, 144, 157
        McCormick family, 57, 68–77, 80–81, 147n61, 201, 239
        Meyer family, 85, 167
        Moody family, 91–96, 159, 187, 228
    gender differences, 68, 82, 88–90, 122–32
    Harvey dispute, 195, 205, 208–10
    inspiration from others. *See* Bonar, Andrew; Drummond; Müller; Murray; Smith, Hannah; Taylor
    leadership style of, 99, 102, 124, 125, 128, 131–33
    learning style of, 114
    May Institute, 101. *See also* May Institute
    Mayflower roots of, 3n8, 4, 20, 82, 250, 261
    Methodist and Holiness influence, 14, 159, 172
    Mildmay Deaconess Home, 86, 110, 125, 158–60
    mission background, 1–5, 9–10, 13, 49, 50, 55
    mission interests, 21, 57, 61–65, 141, 243. *See also* China Inland Mission; Hebrew Mission
        Erring Women's Refuge, 59
        Industrial Schools, 62, 87, 206
        Italian Missions, 171, 232, 233–34
        jail ministry, 67, 69, 76, 138–39
        sewing schools, 59, 136, 137, 140
        shopgirl ministry, 140
        support of Israel, 233–34, 241, 257
        Swedish school, 64–65
        Women's Aid Society, 55, 57, 61–62, 62n42
    missions and education, 2, 120
    Moody Church Reminiscence Day participant, 240
    morality, character, and integrity of, 160, 184
    music and the arts, 16–17, 107, 167, 236–37, 249, 261–62
    Northfield, Massachusetts, 54, 91
    organization skills of, 104–6, 240
    parents of, 4, 13, 19, 42, 172, 248
    photo sent to Anita Blaine, 246n1
    preceptress position of, xviii, 16, 23, 35, 45, 104
    publications of. *See Bible Reading and Prayer Alliance*; *Christian Union Magazine*; *Notes for Bible Study*; *Victor Herald*. *See under* Bible Work; *Christian Cynosure*; ISNU: housing proposal; Whittle, Daniels: *Wonders of Prayer*
    relationship with Dwight Moody, 4, 51–52, 213–215, 224, 228–29
    resignations of, 47, 31, 211, 218, 228

Index

retirement of, 239–44
Reuben Torrey association, 230–31
role of prayer, 98
    prayer for the Bible Institute, 102, 161, 169, 198, 213, 241
    prayer for the McCormick family, 73, 243
    prayer with the Moody family, 94
sacrifices of, 2, 50, 53, 56, 121
salary of, 147, 197, 228, 232–33
scripture emphasis
    Bible studies, 96–98
    Emma Dryer's Bible, 74, 246, 252–54
    valued by, 98, 134, 137, 248, 251, 254
second coming of Christ, views on, 243, 244, 246, 254–56
social issues, 8, 12, 17, 44, 67, 154
spirituality of, 58, 76, 133, 173, 185, 229
strengths of, 99, 122
student association with, 44, 45, 169–71, 250–51
students of, 30, 145–46, 168, 251
Sunday school involvement, 20, 69, 76, 120, 138, 155
typhoid fever illness, 47–48, 50, 56, 130, 172, 175
U. S. Census 1870, 35n26
Victor Park School District, 14, 16
vision of, xvii, 134–36, 186–87, 189, 202, 252
WCTU (Woman's Christian Temperance Union), 84, 122, 137
weaknesses of, 99, 122, 125, 223
Women's Bible Institute, 206–7
World War I, awareness of, 241–42
Dryer, John (adoptive father of Emma Dryer), xviii, 4, 17, 172, 248
Dryer, Lucinda Cobb, (adoptive mother of Emma Dryer), xviii, 4, 9, 17, 172, 245
Dryer, Rufus, 7, 8, 10
Durant, Henry, 102

East London Institute, 141
Eberhart, John, 50, 56, 149
Eberhart, Matilda, 50, 56, 149
Edwards, Jonathan, 2, 3, 50, 178, 250
Edwards, Richard
    assistance and support of Emma Dryer, 35–36, 42–43, 45, 47
    classroom management, views on, 44–46
    Illinois State Normal University president, 35
    religion and politics, views on, 46–47
    staff support, 36–37
Emotional Intelligence EQ traits, 103n62, 114, 120, 121, 124

Ensign, Frederick, 166, 190, 194, 215, 217, 219
Erdman, William
    Charles Blanchard association, 154
    Chicago Avenue Church pastor, 61, 143
    Dwight Moody associate, 113–14
    endorser of the *Bible Reading and Prayer Alliance*, 137
    Moody Church Reminiscence Day participant, 240
    premillennialist, 52, 54
    Presbyterian pastor, 54
Evangelical women, changing roles of, 88–90
Evangelistic Record or *Record of Christian Work*, 160, 191

Farwell, John
    Chicago Bible Institute, supporter of, 210
    Chicago Evangelistic Committee member, 160
    Chicago Evangelization Society participation, 192, 196
    dry goods merchant, 63
    Dwight Moody associate, 78, 130, 131
    Emma Dryer association, 98, 246
    trip with Hudson Taylor, 183
    YMCA contributions, 63
Fell, Jessie, 33–34
Findlay, James, *Dwight L. Moody, American Evangelist*, 99, 106
Finney, Charles
    Blanchard association, 156, 174
    divine healing, views on, 175
    Charles Furman marriage conducted by, 11, 174
    conference in Bolton, England, 25
    Keswick Convention, 129
    Oberlin College, 21, 82
    revival, 21
Fitt, Arthur
    Bible Work, view of, 146
    Chicago Bible Institute, Dwight Moody's commitment to, 171
    Irish immigrant, 93
    Moody Church Reminiscence Day participant, 240
    description of Dwight Moody, 98, 106, 116, 127–28, 132
    introduction to Dwight Moody, 112
    son-in-law and secretary for Dwight Moody, 105, 117
Freeman's Journal, 111
French, Justus, 15, 16
Frost, Henry W., 182

Index

Gallup, Marilla, 27
Garfield, President James, 244
Genesee Wesleyan Seminary, 71
Getz, Gene, *The Story of Moody Bible Institute*, 100
Gideons, 250
Goleman, Daniel, *Emotional and Social Competence*, 103n62
Goodell, William, 20
Goodwin, Edward
    Chicago Bible Institute, endorsement of, 164
    Chicago Evangelistic Committee member, 160
    Chicago Evangelistic Society participation, 218
    Chicago First Congregational Church, pastor of, 51
    friend of Dwight Moody, 60, 116, 144
    Hebrew Mission founder, 233
    May Institute instructor, 164, 206, 207
    visit by George Müller, 180
Goodwin, Nellie
    Chicago Bible Society council, 240
    Dwight Moody's introduction to Emma Dryer, 51
    friendship with Emma Dryer, 216
    introduction of Emma Dryer to Erdman, 54
    premillennialism, 51
    visit by George Müller, 180
    wife of Reverend Dr. Edward Goodwin, 51
Gordon, Adoniram, 54, 130, 161, 177
Gorham, Nathaniel, 5
Goss, Charles, 127, 143–44, 164, 192, 207, 218
Graham, Billy, 67
Grand Pacific Hotel in Chicago, 196, 223, 228
Gravett, Joshua and Charlotte, 177
Gray, James
    funeral and memorial service of Emma Dryer, 247, 249, 250, 251
    Moody Bible Institute, dean and president, 97n33, 230, 234
    premillennialist, 54
Great Man theory by Thomas Carlyle, 103
Greenleaf, Robert, 103
Greenwell, Dorothy, *I Am Not Skilled to Understand*, 262
Greer, Peter, *Mission Drift*, 214
Grove, Mrs. Ralph, 124, 125, 256n17
Guinness, Geraldine, 141
Guinness, Grattan, 141, 227

Ham, Mordecai, 67
Hand, Parmelia, 148, 168
Harrison, Carter, 80

Harrison, President Benjamin, 244
Harvesting Machine Company, 68, 70, 72, 79, 199, 212
Harvey, Mrs. Turlington, 160, 206, 209, 219
Harvey, Turlington. *See also under* Bouton; Dryer, Emma
    Bible Work support, 143, 157, 189
    Chicago banker and lumber businessman, 102
    Chicago Evangelistic Committee member, 160
    Chicago Evangelization Society participation, 192, 193, 196–97, 206–7, 224, 228
    Hebrew Mission founder, 233
    loss of Bible Work support, 195, 198, 205, 211
    personal business collapse, 231
Haswell, Dr. and Mrs. James, 16
Haymarket Riot, 74, 167–168, 193
Hebrew Christian Conference, 233–34, 241
Hebrew Mission, 75, 157, 232, 233, 234, 257
Helmer, Joshua and Lucy
    Bible Reading and Prayer Alliance, 137
    Bible Work support, 143, 147, 149
    China Inland Mission, 93–94, 238, 250
    friendship with Emma Dryer, 48, 50, 147, 159, 181, 246–48
    Italian Missions, 233
    marriage, 48
Heman, Felicia Dorothea, *Our Pilgrim Fathers*, 261
Hewett, Edwin, 37, 41, 42
Hippodrome campaign, 92, 129, 133
Hitchcock, J. M., 137, 160, 240
Hitchcock, Mary Moore, 124, 138, 198, 204, 219, 256n17
Holden, Sarah Revell, 92
Holton, Samuel, 16, 115
Holy Spirit, view and work of. *See also under* Torrey
    Allen, Mary, 20
    American Holiness Movement, 172
    Bible Work, 170
    Blanchard, Charles, 174
    Chicago Evangelistic Committee convention, 160–61
    Dryer, Emma, 54, 98, 130, 173–76, 188, 214, 254
    May Institute, 163
    McCormick, Nettie, 69
    Meyer, Lucy Rider, 86–87
    Moody, Dwight, 30, 58, 116, 129–30, 173, 177
Moorehouse, Harry, 50

Index

Murray, Andrew, 180–81
Pennefather, William, 86
Spafford, Horatio, 153
Horst, Chris, *Mission Drift*, 194
Horton, Isabelle, *High Adventure*, 85, 89
Houghteling, James, 143, 218
Hovey, Charles E., 34
Hubbard, Gurdon, 228
Hubbard, Mary Ann, 149, 228
Hurlburt, Gertrude, 216n124, 229

Illinois State Normal University, 32–47
    courses taught by Emma Dryer, 39
    housing proposal by Emma Dryer, 42–43
    impact of Emma Dryer on students, 46
    Model School, 37–41
    Pestalozzi training method, 40n53, 40–41, 42
    salary of Emma Dryer, 36
Illinois Street Church, 53–55, 59, 60, 94, 96
Ingham University, 13, 25–28, 31, 50, 104, 114

Jacobs, B. F., 121, 160, 179
Jacobs, William Palmer, 76
jail and prison outreaches, 62, 67, 76, 120, 138, 140
Jay, John, 234
Jenkins, Mary, 137, 200, 241
Jewell, Reverend Joseph, 14
Joiner, Thekla, *Sin in the City*, 89

Keith, Elbridge
    Chicago Bible Society, treasurer, 240
    Chicago Evangelization Society participation, 192, 204, 206, 219
    Chicago realtor, 102
Keswick Convention, 86n95, 97n33, 129, 158, 159, 180
Ketcham, Emily, 17
Ketcham, Livonia, 40, 232
Key, Francis, 234
Kirkland, Elizabeth, 145
Kirkland, Samuel, 5, 10
Kirkpatrick, William, *I Am Not Skilled to Understand*, 262
Knoxville Ewing Female University, 27, 29–31, 65, 104

Ladies Missionary Society of Victor, New York, 13
Lane Theological Seminary, 12n13
leadership roles and assessment, 96–133
    burnout in leaders, 37, 109–10, 231
    control in, 125
    doctrinal issues among leaders, 129–31
    giftings of leaders, 223
    learning styles, 114
    morality, character, and integrity, 20, 126–29, 140
    persuasiveness of leaders, 124–25
    prejudice and bias, 121, 162
    social competency, 124
    stewardship, 131–33, 150
    training of, 103n63
Leffingwell, Charles Wesley, 31
Lewis, Leo, 39
Lincoln, President Abraham, 29, 30, 31, 32
Lobb, John, *Arrows and Anecdotes by Dwight L. Moody*, 114n124, 115
Lowden, Alexander H., 198

Maas, David, *The Life & Times of D. L. Moody*, 129
Maby, Miss, 249
MacDonald, George, *Weighed and Wanting*, 128, 221
MacNaughtan, David, 135, 240, 250–51
MacNaughtan, Emma, 251, 253
Mahan, Asa, 129
Mann, Horace, 33
Mason, Roswell, 61, 62n42
Maxwell, John, 103n63
May Institute, 161–67
    agenda, 166–67
    attendees, 170
    forerunner to the Chicago Bible Institute, 161, 164, 167, 171, 186, 207
    inauguration of, 157
    instructors of, 141, 164, 165
    locations of, 162, 165, 190
    promotion of, 169, 207, 227
    supported by Dwight Moody, 101, 195, 226
    the 1888 institute, 207
McAll Mission, 227
McCormick, Cyrus
    friend of Horatio Spafford, 151, 152
    friendship with Dwight Moody, 69, 77–78
    introduction to Emma Dryer, 69–70
    inventor of the reaper, 57
    philanthropist, 56
    political candidate, 78
McCormick, Cyrus Jr, 71, 189, 192, 196, 200, 216, 228, 247
McCormick, Harold (son of Cyrus and Nettie McCormick), 71, 80, 81, 247
McCormick, Harriet (wife of Cyrus McCormick Jr), 76, 242
McCormick, Nettie. *See also under* Haymarket Riot; Dryer, Emma: friendships of

McCormick, Nettie *(continued)*
   business aptitude of, 71, 74–75, 89, 167
   Chicago Evangelistic Committee member, 160
   Chicago Evangelization Society participation, 192, 194, 196, 198, 212–13, 228
   Chicago Fire, 56–57, 71–72
   conflict with Dwight Moody, 199–205, 211
   death of her husband Cyrus, 74
   Dwight Moody support, 60, 79–80
   final days of, 242–43
   mediator of board conflicts, 200, 204, 220, 222–23
   missionary ventures of, 75–77, 232, 233
   philanthropist, 56
   wife of Cyrus McCormick, 56–57
   Woman's Christian Temperance Union, 76
   worldwide travels of, 73
McCormick, Virginia (daughter of Cyrus and Nettie McCormick), 70, 73, 233, 238, 243
McCormick Theological Seminary, 76, 77, 237
McKendree College, 82
McNeill, John, 105
Merton, Thomas, *New Seeds of Contemplation*, 229
Messer, L. Wilbur, 120
Meyer, F. B., 67, 119, 129, 160, 227
Meyer, Josiah, 82, 159, 237
Meyer, Lucy Rider, 14, 82–90, 159, 237, 251
Mildmay
   conferences, 86, 101
   holiness contacts, 172
   pattern for the Bible Work, 134, 135, 136, 141, 196
   speakers for, 172, 180–82
Miller, James Russell, 66
Mills, Benjamin Fay, 197
Moody Bible Institute. *See also* Chicago Bible Institute
   Bible training school in Chicago, 14
   founding of, 61, 155, 171, 187, 231, 252
   Keith Hall, Dryer memorial service, 249
   Moody Bible Archives, 253
   staff, 229–30, 247, 249–50, 353
Moody Church, 155, 187, 234, 240
Moody Church News, 251
Moody Monthly, 74
Moody, Dwight
   Bible background of, 97
   Bible marking method of, 252n14
   birthplace of, 4
   Chicago Fire, 56–58
   children, concern for, 95
   Clarke family association, 67
   conversion of, 25
   DISC assessment for, 103–4, 107–8, 110–11, 118, 124–25, 223
   divine healing, views on, 130–31, 176–77
   Emotional Intelligence assessment of, 103
   England crusades for, 55, 60, 92–93, 135, 186
   Farwell Hall, involvement at, 56, 63, 156, 162, 188
   Frances Willard association, 84n85
   impulsivity, traits of, 108, 117–19
   influence of J. B. Stillson, 31, 117n139, 179
   inspiration to Emma Dryer, 53, 54, 55
   interest in education, 59, 92, 214
   Josiah and Lucy Meyer association, 84–85
   Keswick Convention, 86n95
   leadership roles of, 96–99
   learning difficulties of, 114–19, 114n124, 151n89
   learning styles of, 114
   nineteenth century evangelist, xvii, 54, 105, 111–13, 120
   premillennialism, 54, 55
   role of prayer, 98–99
   Swedish ministry, 64
   women, advocate for, 90
Moody, Emma Revell
   description of, 93, 109
   endorser of the *Bible Reading and Prayer Alliance*, 137
   English immigrant, 92–93
   wife of Dwight Moody, 27, 30, 92
Moody, Paul (son of Dwight and Emma Moody), 109
Moody, William (son of Dwight and Emma Moody), 117, 118, 240
Moorehead, William
   Chicago Avenue Church, pastor invitation, 144
   Emma Dryer association, 163–64, 230
   May Institute involvement, 163–65, 170, 188, 207, 227
   Moody request to direct the Bible Institute, 230
Moorehouse, Harry, 52, 97, 128
Morgan, J. Pierpont, 74–75
Morrison, John, 94, 142, 160, 169, 240
Mount Holyoke College, 141n30, 180
Müller, George. *See also under* Taylor
   author, 175
   Dwight Moody association, 55
   evangelist and missionary, 178–80
   inspiration to Emma Dryer, 178
   Keswick Convention, 172, 177
Mulliken, Charles, 240

Index

Munhall, L. W., 161
Murray, Andrew, 141n30, 172, 177, 180–81

Native American Indians, 1–5, 21, 26
North Side Tabernacle
    Bible Work support, 94, 138, 146
    Illinois Street Church, previous name of, 55, 145
    women's meetings at, 137
Northfield Conferences
    advertising of, 158
    attendees of, 154, 158, 161, 190
    Chicago Bible Institute, promotion of, 188
    college student participation in, 129
    Dwight Moody's organization of, 106
    Holiness Movement and, 83, 129
    inspired by Mildmay Conferences, 158
    international participants in, 92
    speakers of, 54, 121, 148, 159–60, 178, 182
Northwestern University, 82
Notes for Bible Study, 137, 169, 200, 241

Okerstein, John, 64–65, 240
Osband, Margaret E., 35

Pacific Garden Mission, 66–68, 76, 137, 160, 221, 232
Palmer, Phoebe, 82–83, 83n76
Palmyra Union School, 15–16
Peck, Henry Everard, 21
Pennefather, Catherine, 86
Pentecost, G. F., 54, 161
Phelps, Davenport, 16, 26
Phelps, Oliver, 5
Philpott, Peter, 247
Powell, Emma, 91, 99, 117, 118
premillennialism, xviii, 51, 53–55, 88, 129, 155
Proseus, Antionette, 31

Rader, Paul, 234
Rawson, Marietta, 10
Revell, Fleming
    Bible Work prayer participant, 98, 161, 240, 250
    Chicago Evangelistic Committee member, 160
    Moody, Dwight (father-in-law), 191
    Moody, Emma Revell (sister), 27, 98
    Moody Church Reminiscence Day participant, 240
    prison tract publications of, 67
    publisher of Andrew Murray books, 181
    Record of Christian Work publication of, 190
    Swedish publications of, 64

revivals
    Andrew Murray in 1860, 180
    Businessman's Revival of 1857, 63
    Chicago Evangelistic Committee in 1881, 160–61
    Chicago Fire, 58, 112
    Dwight Moody, 84, 102, 111, 112, 121
    Great Awakening of 1858, 62–63
    Great Revival of 1799, 10
    Swedish meetings at Chicago Avenue Church, 64
    Victor, New York in 1876, 13
Revolutionary War, 3, 5, 29
Rochester Theological Seminary, 23
Roderick, Stella, *Nettie Fowler McCormick*, 168, 199, 201
Rohold, Sabeti, 241n21
Roosevelt, President Theodore, 110
Rotterham New Testament, 243
Rounds, Tryphena, 75, 157, 233
Royal Opera House in London, 112
Ruelas, Abraham, *Women and the Landscape of American Higher Education*, 14

Salvation Army support from the McCormick family, 83n76, 172, 232
Sande, Ken, *Peace Maker*, 186, 222
Sandom, Carie, *Difference by Design*, 90n115
Sankey, Ira
    1873 England campaign, 93
    background of, 55n18
    Chicago Fire, 58, 112
    Dwight Moody associate, 14, 95, 146
    Hippodrome campaign, 92
    hymn royalties of, 61, 132, 146
    Simply Trusting Every Day, 107
    singer and song writer, 55
Schaff, Phillip, 259–60
Scofield, C. I., 133, 234
Scott, Hugh, 141, 165, 206, 233
Scott, R. D., 237, 240
Sergeant, John, 2–4, 10, 140
Sheldon, E. A., *Oswego Training Method*, 40
Shipman, George, 53n10, 148
Shulls, E. A., 247, 249–50
Shute, Mrs. William B., 69, 147–50, 163, 211, 218
Simpson, A. B., 177, 234
Skogsbergh, E. A., 64
Smith, Hannah Whitall, 82, 83n76, 87, 151, 160
Smith, Merton
    Chicago Avenue Church, concerns of, 225, 228
    Chicago Evangelization Society participation, 215, 225

Smith, Merton *(continued)*
    Dwight Moody convert, 224
    tent evangelist, 197
    Tyng Mission, 224
Spafford, Anna, 148, 152–53
Spafford, Horatio, 98, 151–54
Spears, Larry, *Character and Servant Leadership*, 103–4
Spurgeon, Charles, 55, 73, 136, 175
Staunton, Phineas, 26
Sterling, Reverend, 250, 252
Stetson, Albert, 35, 37
Stockbridge, Massachusetts, history of, 4
Stoecker, Adolf, 79
Stowe, Harriet Beecher, 45, 60
Strange, Reverend Arnold, 250
Strong, Augustus, 23
Strong, Miss, 237
Student Volunteer Movement, 182
Sunday school. *See also under* Dryer, Emma
    Bible worker participation in, 138–39
    Chicago Bible Society training in, 236
    Dwight Moody, 30, 96, 97, 124
    Emma Moody, teacher of, 93
    Lucy Meyer, teacher of, 82
    Merton Smith progress reports of, 224
    Sarah Clarke's mission classes, 66
    Women's Bible Institute training for, 207
Sunday, Billy, 67, 68
Swift, John, 16

Taylor, Hudson
    China Inland Mission, 151, 181
    inspiration to Emma Dryer, 181–83, 238
    Keswick Convention, 172, 177
    marriage of son, 141
    Mildmay Conference speaker 1872, 182
    support from George Müller, 181
Torrey, Reuben
    associate of Dwight Moody, 96, 97, 98, 109, 173
    Chicago Bible Institute president, 229–30
    Chicago World's Fair evangelist, 230
    description of Dwight Moody, 98, 99, 132
    teaching on the Holy Spirit, 97n33, 129, 131, 173, 230
    Why God Used D. L. Moody, 173
Troy Conference Academy, 82
Troy Female Seminary, 71

Varley, Henry, 62
Victor Herald, The, 3n7, 8–9, 60, 246
Victor Presbyterian Church pastors, 10–13, 16, 21

Victor, NY. *See also under* Dryer, Emma: early years of
    burial plot of Emma Dryer, 248n10
    cobblestone pump house, 8
    history of, 5–6
    missionary soil, 5–6
    Proprietors' Church, 5, 10, 11, 14, 226
    Victor Hotel, 7
    village operations, 7
Vogel, Ellis, 170, 240, 250

Waite, Caroline, 244
War of 1812, 5, 20
WCTU (Woman's Christian Temperance Union), 76, 82–85, 197
Wellesley College, 102
Wells, Amos, 256
Wesley, Charles, 262n18
Wesley, John, 87, 159, 172
Wheaton Cemetery, xviii, 157, 246, 248n9
Wheaton College, 21
    Chicago area school, xviii, 10
    fundamentalism, framework of, 155
    presidents of, xviii, 10, 30, 153, 165
    support from the McCormick family, 232
Whitefield, George, 2
Whiting, Sarah Frances, 27
Whittle, Daniel
    as Andrew Bonar's escort to Northampton, 178
    Bible Work, supporter of, 143, 151
    Chicago Evangelistic Committee member, 160
    Chicago Evangelization Society participation, 203, 204, 205
    co-evangelist of Merton Smith, 224
    Elgin Watch Company, 60n36
    Emma Dryer association, 69, 246
    endorser of the *Bible Reading and Prayer Alliance*, 137
    friend and co-evangelist of Dwight Moody, 188, 194
    as George Müller's escort to England, 179
    hymn writer and Bible teacher, 179
    May Institute, supporter of, 164, 227
    Spafford, Horatio, supporter of, 151
    Sunday School Teachers' Convention speaker, 179
    Temperance Gospel League, director of 197
    Wonders of Prayer, The, 173, 175, 179
Wiles, Lemuel, 26
Willard, Frances, 71, 76, 82–83, 83n76, 84n85, 87, 123
Williams College, 12

Index

Williams, A. W., *Life and Work of Dwight L. Moody,* 57–58
Wright, John, 34

YMCA
- Bible Work, location and support of, 135–36, 142, 143, 146, 147, 149
- Chicago Bible Society, affiliation with, 234
- Chicago Fire, 59
- Dryer, Emma, ministry at, 53
- Dwight Moody involvement in, 16–17, 27, 30, 50, 63, 120
- Farwell Hall, 160
- Illinois State Normal University, 46–47
- London, branch of, 86, 158
- May Institute, location of, 162
- Railroad Mission, program of, 169
- rebuilding of Chicago facility, 78, 190
- revival at, 111
- superintendent of, 166
- supporters of, 51, 55–56, 77, 85, 151
- Swedish branch of, 65

YWCA, 59, 61, 62, 63–64, 146, 149

www.ingramcontent.com/pod-product-compliance
Lightning Source LLC
Chambersburg PA
CBHW080544230426
43663CB00015B/2703